CITIZENSHIP IN THE WESTERN TRADITION

PETER RIESENBERG

卍卍卍卍卍

CITIZENSHIP

IN THE WESTERN

TRADITION

卍卍卍卍卍

PLATO TO ROUSSEAU

The University of North Carolina Press

Chapel Hill and London

The paper in this book meets the guidelines for permanence and
durability of the Committee on Production Guidelines for Book
Longevity of the Council on Library Resources.

96 95 94 93 92   5 4 3 2 1

Library of Congress Cataloging-in-Publication Data

Riesenberg, Peter N., 1925–
Citizenship in the western tradition : Plato to Rousseau / by
Peter Riesenberg.
p. cm.
Includes bibliographical references and index.
ISBN 0-8078-2037-7 (alk. paper)
1. Citizenship—History. I. Title.
JF801.R54 1992
323.6'09—dc20 91-45807
CIP

FOR TRUDI

CONTENTS

Preface   ix

Introduction   xv

PART I

Ancient Citizenship: Virtue in
the Service of Community

1. Greece   3

2. Rome   56

PART II

Citizenship in the
Medieval Italian City

3. Medieval Christian Citizenship:
Some Generalities   87

4. The Bonds, Language,
and Emotion   118

5. The Law and Language
of Citizenship   140

6. Citizenship in
the Renaissance   187

PART III

The Subject and the Citizen

7. Ambiguities of Citizenship
under Monarchy   203

8. Citizenship under the
Impact of Revolution   235

9. The Final Citizenship
of the Old Regime   253
Conclusion   267

Notes   275
Bibliography   293
Index   315

PREFACE

◨◨◨

This book has been in process a long time; indeed, it goes back to the fifties when, while examining late-medieval *consilia*, I began to notice the frequency with which citizenship appeared in this enormous record of private and public litigation. Property, perquisites, privileges, protection, military and tax obligations could all depend upon possession, nonpossession, or loss of citizenship.

Over the medieval centuries a law of citizenship came into being throughout Western Europe. Every city and country eventually established or recognized some form of citizen status and developed its own naturalization requirements and procedures. Citizens necessarily became very aware of the importance of citizenship powers in their lives. Since this happened at the very time of the discovery of the ancient civil law and its establishment in the curriculum of Bologna and other universities, and since citizenship was prominent in the classical texts, the legal profession gave great attention to citizenship issues. When Aristotle's *Politics* and other ancient moral and political works were translated and read, they stimulated new thinking on citizenship, all of which eventually influenced the legislation of governments, mostly city governments, attempting to create citizenship policies.

Medieval citizenship was the subject of the first book I wrote. It was substantially completed by the end of 1965, after a year at Harvard's Center for Renaissance Studies, I Tatti. However, I decided not to publish that monograph on citizenship in communal Italy. The subject seemed to demand something more, and about that time events on my campus precipitated by the Vietnam War drew me into campus politics.

Eventually I conceived of the book presented here, one that would carry citizenship from its Greek origins in our tradition to the French Revolution. It appeared that nothing of this ambitious nature existed in English, or, indeed, in any other familiar language, and that such a venture was worth the effort. What follows is my attempt, perhaps a foolhardy one, to write a book that would be scholarly, yet at the same time suggestive to a wider audience in some programmatic way. Over the years many have helped me; their names are gratefully recorded below. They have, I hope, saved me from error in my interpretation of the long period covered in this book.

In choosing to write about citizenship, I did not set out with a moral or political agenda. Certainly this study is not to be taken as a debunking book because it acknowledges the complexity and mixed nature of citizenship. If I have interpreted citizenship in terms of self-interest and reciprocal benefit, I have also tried to reiterate the persistent idealism of the philosophical tradition as well as disinterested virtuous behavior in line with the high values of political philosophers. Indeed, one might stress as a central theme of the tradition, and therefore of this book, the constant advocacy across the centuries of selfless service on behalf of society. It is hard to find in Western political literature an advocate of what might be called the dark side of citizenship, self-interest. There have always been in great number practitioners of self-interest, and always lawyers to negotiate the terms of agreement between the individual and the community, but no age has produced a thinker who consciously attaches virtue to self-seeking at the expense of the community—although one may think of Machiavelli in these terms.

Our problems today perhaps are greater than those faced by ancient Greeks and Romans and medieval Christians. They are certainly different, because the institutions that ancient and medieval citizens depended on, and which their descendants depended on until quite recently, do not work too well for us. Our churches no longer help shape a common morality as a basis for politics; often they provide the issues for a violent politics. Our schools are too confused in their mission and methodology to do anything but attempt to teach basic skills and retail the most traditional and ineffectual civics. With about fourteen million Americans working for some government, public service has become a job and hardly serves as the education for, or means to, virtue. And while ethnicity attacks community largely from the lower levels of the social hierarchy, at the upper levels the affluent and the well educated move into their private world of clubs, schools, and self-policed neighborhoods.

Where, then, can the ordinary citizen find the path to virtue today? Perhaps in voluntarism, using that word in the broadest possible sense to include all forms of altruistic service in the private sector, and perhaps in occasional office holding at the level of local government as well. This would include work on school, church, and hospital boards, in professional and service organizations, in the numerous small-town offices where so much work gets done at little or no pay, even work for all of those charity events that fill the society pages. Participation in these efforts reflects contemporary values such as friendship, professional collegiality, common religious belief, and gender bonding and allows for the distribution of office, honor, and distinction that even our democracy must allow and depend on. Also, such participation channels and amplifies the usefulness of the special training and skills that identify each of us in the specialized modern world. Perhaps because all these conditions arise from the very nature of modern life, and indeed define it, this kind of participation offers an effective way to lead the active moral life.

It is in these small, private, and immediate associations, whose members are linked by common interests, that the citizen can fulfill Aristotle's demand that he rule and be ruled. Since the Renaissance, Bodin's kind of citizenship, which is a form of subjectship that places the individual in direct subordinate relationship to the prince, has prevailed. Stripped of the institution of monarchy, it survives as the basis of the relationship between the individual and the government in every modern country.

If any message can be drawn from this book, it is of the power of the citizen ideal. Citizenship, here conceived as moral choice and action, has been extolled by so many different societies, pagan and Christian, because it has been viewed not only as an instrument useful in controlling the passions and attenuating private concerns, but also as a means well suited to draw out the best in people. In citizenship the passions normally dedicated to self and kin are directed to a higher purpose, the public good. Citizenship has survived so long and served in so many political environments because of its great inspirational challenge to individuals to make their neighbor's, their fellow citizen's, life better and, by so doing, make their own nobler. Such an aspiration made sense to Greeks and Romans in their cities just as it makes sense to us today in our vastly different environment. Community is an attractive ideal in pagan or Christian terms. Citizenship has been one of the basic forces our civilization has mustered to achieve it.

In her recent book, *The Medieval Woman*, the distinguished German medievalist, Edith Ennen, notes that generally women "took little interest in the burghers' struggles for freedom" and were "allowed no political role in the medieval town." I would subscribe to this generalization and, all things being equal, extend it to the situation of the woman in antiquity as well. Of course, such a statement can not be all inclusive and accurate; here and there, now and then, women did exercise certain citizenship rights, especially those relating to property, and sometimes they were included in general statements concerning citizens. I note these facts in this preface as an explanation for the near constant and exclusive use of masculine language throughout the book. Such usage is dictated by the sources.

Occasionally women will appear in the *consilia* when the property they may own or inherit attracts the interest of a counterclaimant or the tax collector. In such cases women frequently were treated as citizens when the obligations owed by their property touched the public welfare and therefore forced them into one of the citizen's roles. But, if this is so, it is true too that neither the statutes nor the theorists consider women qua women when they examine the formal obligations of citizenship, whether these be fiscal or military or political. The lawyers' disinterest in women was casual; but Machiavelli's neglect had to be intentional, given his plea for passionate personal military commitment as an essential basis for citizen identity. Nor could women serve in the various legislative and executive councils that constituted the scene for city politics.

If, in some of the most advanced countries of the West, women still do not possess full rights of citizenship, one should not expect to find the situation otherwise long ago. When it seemed appropriate, I have confronted this issue and attempted to explain, or at least express my awareness of, the limitations placed upon women.

Given the long gestation of this book and its range, I have gone to many friends and colleagues for advice: Roberto Abbondanza, Gene Brucker, Gregory Claeys, Richard Davis, Jack Hexter, James Jones, James Kettner, George Pepe, Herbert Rowen, Gordon Schochet, Quentin Skinner, Robert Williams, and Kristin Zapalac have read all or some part of the manuscript or have helped me in some way. Elizabeth Case, Joseph Losos, William Matheson, Anne Trinsey, Burton Wheeler, and, above all, Paul Rahe, have been especially supportive by being especially critical. I owe thanks also to many institutions. The Social Science Research Council, the John Simon Guggenheim Memorial Foundation, the American Philosophical Society, and the Rockefeller Foundation have, at various times, supported my research, as have successive deans of the Graduate School of Washington University, the directors and staffs of Villa I Tatti, Villa Serbelloni, and the National Humanities Center. I appreciate the confidence in my work all these have expressed. Appreciation must be acknowledged also to the principal libraries in which I have done my work: the Biblioteca Nazionale in Rome and in Florence, the Biblioteca Vaticana, the British Library, the Bibliothèque Nationale, and the law libraries of Columbia University and Harvard University. Here at Washington University the staff of Olin Library has always been helpful, which may be said too of the staff of the Department of History, especially Dora Arky and Sheryl Peltz, who typed parts of the manuscript. My principal typist was Nancy Galofre, to whom I owe a special debt of thanks; Richard Kottmeyer checked the notes and bibliographical references, thereby saving me from many slips. Finally, I delight in acknowledging my debt to my editors at the University of North Carolina Press, Lewis Bateman, Ron Maner, and Mary Reid, for the intelligent and understanding way they worked with me.

As the dedication of this book shows, my deepest thanks is to my wife, Trudi, whose patience, enthusiasm, and trust guaranteed its completion.

INTRODUCTION

𝕫𝕫𝕫

High above the highway between what are now Madrid and Saragossa is the town of Medinaceli. It dominates the high landscape today as it did in Roman times and the days of the Cid. In the center of the little place is a late Renaissance square bordered by superb palaces, buildings that would be admired in Florence or Rome. Why, one wonders, would some of the great families of the Spanish imperial world choose to build their family seats on this lonely, windswept eminence? The answer must be that this was their hometown, and that it was, like most hometowns in that period, small, self-absorbed, certain that, as Shakespeare put it, "there is no world without Verona's walls."

There were, of course, a few exceptions: great commercial cities like Florence, Milan, and Venice, a few northern industrial towns like Ghent and Bruges, even governmental cities like Paris and London were coming to be. But overwhelmingly, the relatively few Europeans who lived in towns and cities lived in places of between one thousand and twenty thousand people, that is, in what might be called small-scale societies.

This book is about that intimate world and the forces that held it together. From the time of Solon and Lycurgus to that of Rousseau and Franklin, most historically and morally conscious people lived in such communities and had remarkably similar ideas about what the good person's conduct should be and how to develop it, generation after generation. Even during the long ascendance of a body of Christian spiritual values that denigrated worldly existence and success, such a code continued to exist; it had to if organized society itself was to continue. I call this body of values and its attendant institutions citizenship, or, more precisely, the first citizenship, for since the French Revolution, more or less coeval with the growth of the large territorial and, to some degree, popular state, a related, but somewhat different, code of moral conduct, or second citizenship, has developed. An emphasis on ideal conduct, the performance of civic duties, the tension between private and public needs, the transmission of values, and the nature of the appropriate educational means to inculcate a desire for virtue are the principal subjects of this book. It will not be about, although it will necessarily mention, technical matters of immigration law and naturalization procedure. Its proper focus lies across the modern fields of history, moral thought, history of education, and political theory.

It is very difficult to define citizenship in a few words. Although it is one of the oldest institutions in Western political thought and practice, it is not one of the easiest to grasp in a single comprehensive thought. Compare it with monarchy, which also has existed a long while, surely longer than citizenship, which we conventionally tag with a Greek origin. Monarchy is unambiguous. Instinctively, from all the sources of our awareness, we know it as the rule of one person, whose legitimacy may come from God, the people, military power, family, or some combination of these recognized as authenticating by the subjects, a few of them or all of them. Moreover, the functions of monarchy are reasonably clear. The king is an executive; leadership is his essential function. Whether an abusing tyrant or a benign deliverer, he stands at the pinnacle of power. His subjects depend on him for victory and survival.

Citizenship is not as clear. There is no single office in which its essence is defined. It has no central mission, nor is it clearly an office, a theory, or a legal contract. We know where a monarch sits: on a throne in a palace. But we can not place citizenship that easily. It functions on the battlefield, in the law court, in an assembly, at the tax collector's office. Nor is citizenship complete in any single or simple person, place, or, more abstractly, situation, for history has witnessed a great variety of citizenships, each with its defining goals and powers. And if it resides in no definite place, it comes out of no single book, fully. It may derive from books of religion, political and legal theory, moral training, even inspirational heroic poetry and song, but it is not produced by any one of these.

There is another impediment to our understanding of citizenship, the result of our conditioning in the modern world. When we hear "democracy" or "justice" we smile in some way, much as we frown at the words "tyranny" and "dictatorship." In an instant review of its values, our twentieth-century Western mind finds "justice" and "democracy" good and their polar opposites bad. The same instant acceptance is true of "citizenship," which is a circumstance we and others are born into. It is part of our birthright and, moreover, is something others seek—and may possess only after time has passed and conditions have been met.

When that same Western mind reviews citizenship and designates it as good, it makes a mistake. It identifies citizenship with democracy, which is approximately correct for the last two centuries, but it ignores the long history of the first citizenship. If, over the first several thousand years of Western history, citizenship has been linked to the progenitive institutions and theories of Western democracy, and to a moral education we appreciate today, it also has been associated with nondemocratic forms of regime. Sophisticated thinkers realized this before the French Revolution. When they looked for authoritative models in antiquity, they were selective. Democratic Athens was admired for its cultural achievements, while it was oligarchic Sparta that served as the citizenship model. Here patriotism, military service, personal character, and the control of government by the few were closely linked.

Indeed, just a bit of reflection will lead to the conclusion that citizenship has been an ambiguous institution throughout history and that it has been compatible with many forms of political organization. From the beginning it has meant privilege and exclusion; it is no exaggeration to say that one of its principal functions has been as an agent or principle of discrimination. It has been undemocratic in basic ways until and after 1789. It has encompassed and defined privilege and constituted the means to discriminate against noncitizens. In this way it has favored the few against the many and restricted the full benefits of membership in a community to a minority. And, if Aristotle and other moral philosophers are right, then citizenship has made it difficult for all men and, eventually, women to fulfill their ultimate reason for existence, that is, to play the role of a political being, to act in the ennobling sphere of ethical politics.

Apart from this service to the history of discrimination, of inequality, there is another troublesome side to citizenship. It has been deeply involved in the perpetual contest between public and private interest. Throughout its long history citizenship has always depended upon society's ability to promise and give what has been needed by individuals and their families. Small as the ancient or medieval city was, there always existed this smaller unit of support and conveyer of identity. The history of citizenship is not the story of the steady victory of the unopposed forces of community interest. Rather, it is of the constant struggle in which the public good has always had to bargain and compromise with the private.

State and society have always needed money, manpower, loyalty, cooperation, and commitment in a variety of forms; the individual has always needed security, justice, leadership, food, and often trade protection. From this viewpoint, there is nothing generous or disinterested about citizenship. It has always been a form of exchange as well as an effort at personal ennoblement in accordance with high moral thinking. Yet, since it has survived despite the great pull of the private self, its history may be seen as part of the long-range development of Western altruism, compassion, and that higher moral consciousness which today thinks not only in terms of the welfare of one's native political society, but also in terms of the well-being of nature and of the human race.

All of these considerations frustrate a neat definition of citizenship. Yet we need such a definition if the ensuing discussion is to be clear. Perhaps, following Aristotle, we should approach a working definition in a human and functional way. After confronting a variety of ambiguities, Aristotle asserts a definition in Book 3 of the *Politics*: "The good citizen should know and have the capacity both to rule and be ruled, and this very thing is the virtue of a citizen." Citizenship may vary according to the constitution of a particular city, but at its heart is the notion of self-government within the law. And although Aristotle allows the possibility of "vulgar persons" becoming citizens, these would not be "genuine citizens." His true citizen would be free and propertied to a degree that would allow time for participation in public affairs. Throughout the following pages this conception of the active citizen is always close to what I have in mind as I attempt to follow the institution and its language across centuries and oceans.

One premise of this book is that there have been two citizenships, forms of the institution different enough from each other to justify such a classification and interpretation. The first lasted from the time of the Greek city-state until the French Revolution; the second has been in existence since then. The first was small-scaled, culturally monolithic, hierarchical, and discriminatory— and also moral, idealistic, spiritual, active, participatory, communitarian, and even heroic in that it commanded personal military service from its citizens. Sometimes the term "organic" is used to describe such a polity in which an Aristotelian true citizen might function. However, in defining the first citizenship we must always remember citizenship's other aspect, which I have called troublesome, and which may also be termed materialistic, attenuated, and passive. These are all words to emphasize the relationship that service in exchange for benefit constituted, an exchange that has been compatible with all sizes of community. It can be seen in the relatively intimate polis and even more in the *civitas* of the Roman Empire, when citizenship had become a body of legal expectations and powers, as opposed to a predominantly ethical relationship between an individual and the community.

Today the men and women of at least the West live under the second citizenship, the result of some of the great forces of modern history. For centuries civic virtue had been draining out of the first citizenship—an ideal from the beginning—given the increasing availability of property in the world, the progressive legitimation of that property by such theorists as Aquinas and Locke, and the simultaneous growth in size, needs, and power of the state. Not that this new age has completely destroyed the tone and accomplishments of the earlier one; in expectable ways citizenship past influences citizenship present, but there are important differences.

The first citizenship was practiced in a limited, face-to-face environment. Citizens were usually a minority of the total population, and they lived within a limited geographical area; they knew and knew of each other. The first citizenship was always partial; the second is almost invariably universal, or at least potentially so. It is based upon birth or specified residence in a large territorial state whose size makes face-to-face politics impossible. The government of this large state is based upon a constitution acceptable to its people, which establishes the principles and mechanisms for the distribution of civil, political, and, increasingly, social justice.

In the first citizenship, politics was frequently intense, and one was not really considered a citizen until he was seen to participate in it. There was, ideally, no place for the uninvolved, since the community's success and survival depended upon the personal contribution of each of the relatively few citizens. Frequently that contribution took the form of military action and battlefield death. Under the second citizenship, personal heroism is not expected or needed from all; now the financial support of the hardworking, prosperous merchant or laborer is accepted as adequate evidence of commitment. The fierce devotion of the few has been replaced with the slack association of the many.

This means that most citizens have lost the real possibility for gaining virtue as defined in Aristotelian terms, that is, through active participation in governing. Once granted the civil and political rights of citizen status, individuals found themselves as never before open to the demands of the new, more powerful state. In France and other countries where basic changes of regime were accomplished, individuals lost many privileges that may have protected them during the previous centuries of local life and princely institu-

tions, such as charters, traditions of seigneurial protection, moderating clerical influence, the force of coronation oaths in an era of intense religious
belief. Now, driven by political need, enhanced by majority support, governments could call upon popular mandates for the legitimacy of their actions.
Citizens were now submerged into the general will and lost that individuality which Aristotle, Augustine, and Machiavelli valued so highly, each in his
own way.

The ordinary citizen continued to be educated in traditional ways. Local
schools, public and private, secular and religious, taught an identical code of
civic values. Every country rested upon an accepted history based upon realities and myths. New citizens were forced to pledge their support of the
common set of goals that defined the nation. But, now free and equal,
individuals found themselves in the limited grid of choices offered by bourgeois society whose values were those of Locke and Franklin. Virtue was
industry, not victory. Artisans, merchants, printers, and manufacturers in the
small, but growing, cities of the Western world replaced the citizen-soldier as
the nation's best.

This did not happen overnight. From the late Middle Ages on, there took
place a progressive and meaningful assimilation of the "citizen" into the
"subject," the transformation of the active political person into the passive
political person. Although the great revolutions at the end of the eighteenth
century accomplished a change in terminology in that citizen, in a reverse
action, now drove out subject, they did not alter reality. The subject became a
citizen again, but of the second citizenship.

In a Europe and America finally fallen to merchant values, a change that
had been developing since the late Middle Ages, entrepreneurial success and
personality enhancement prevailed over community values. Technology has
favored developments in this direction, for if it has provided the means to tie
a country together with a single set of political symbols and commercial
logos, it simultaneously has made possible a private and comfortable distracting leisure. Television has helped in the creation of a passive citizenry that
views its politics at a distance, beer in hand, less and less interested in attending the political rally with its crush, dust, and occasional physical danger.

Meanwhile, the needs of the industrial nation-state helped turn the citizen-
soldier into the organization man or woman. Work, it has recently been
observed, became part of modern citizenship, in America without question,
and in many other countries as well: work as opportunity to work, in the
sense of opportunity to contribute to national strength.[1] By the twentieth

century the good (second) citizen had become a gray figure in a gray flannel suit or the blue coverall of the Continental worker.

Subjectively, the difference between the first and the second citizenships may be perceived as one of stance. Under the first, in its most challenging and uplifting formulations, man always leaned into the action summoned by notions of virtue. The good citizen recognized the importance of his personal contribution to the public good and gave it. Under the second, man, now mass man and woman, leans backwards, away. He or she, now enticed by private distractions, often fails to grasp the potentiality for moral growth in the activities prescribed for citizenship.

Citizenship's survival derives from its usefulness to every kind of government and society. One of its functions is to identify members of the community who are to be protected and rewarded. Also, it contributes to the effectiveness of the individual and the family and thus has the potential for promoting distinction, or, in a more potent word, honor. While the ancient world was comfortable with personal honor, the Middle Ages was less so, but even during this long and extraordinary period, individuality often was grounded upon a legally defined condition of citizenship. Citizenship was one of the few institutions then that contributed to the survival and growth of individual identity in an age in which persons tended to be subsumed under and within some corporate membership.

To put this survival during the Middle Ages in other terms, it might be said that in an era which recognized the validity of lordship, indeed, its necessity, in a period of endemic uncertainty of life, and violence, citizenship served as an analogue to vassalage, for the citizen was vassal to the suzerainty of his city. And, much as vassalage conveyed a freedom under the protection of the lord, citizenship implied, if not guaranteed, the auspices of the city in, for example, overseas as well as local trade. Also, in an age in which rank and privilege were the norm, citizenship institutionalized these in an urban setting. It created between a man and his community what the tie of vassalage created between two fighting men, what the philosopher and critic William Gass has called an "anatomical connection."[2]

As it served these functions, citizenship passed through periods of visibility and obscurity. In antiquity, even under the Empire, it flourished as a key concept in political and legal thought and functioned as a meaningful institution influencing the lives and fortunes of many—eventually all freemen after 212 A.D. Although theory and government did not allow for much participation at the level of Empire, traditional practice and moral education did foster it at the level of the *civitas*, of which there were so many throughout the Empire. It can not be denied, however, that the very notion of a passive—as opposed to an active—citizen came to be the new norm of political reality. From the end of the Empire until the late eighteenth century its role was less significant, although, as we shall see, the intensification of local life during the early Middle Ages and into the twelfth and thirteenth centuries encouraged the survival, if not the development, of an active local political scene.

Citizenship survived, therefore, although the subject and vassal replaced the citizen in both general political usage and actual government. The vocabulary of the institution was embedded in the Roman law, which was always studied somewhere; therefore, even during the early Middle Ages, it retained a place in legal usage. This meant that throughout the Mediterranean city-state world, from Italy across the French coast to northern Spain, not only were the legal aspects of the institution known, but, with the eventual revival of ancient, especially Roman, history from the twelfth century on, the full flavor of ancient activist citizenship as well.

Perhaps this history of citizenship should start before the Greeks, with the Hebrews, the Egyptians, or another ancient people. Indeed, it could go back to the earliest people we know about through written or other records. Every human group has developed institutions by which it recognized and characterized its members and made new members. Language, literature, military service, history, religious belief and practice, cooperative farming and husbandry have always served to bind people to each other.

Yet we begin with the Greeks because theirs was the first extended attempt at self-government based on the actual participation of citizens, and because theirs was the first legislation and theory about social and political organization we have. The Hebrews and others demonstrated ways of life in their histories and produced laws to govern themselves and their subjects in peace and war, but they did not produce a Plato or an Aristotle to reflect upon the nature of man alone and in groups, on the nature of the possible forms of government, and on the relationships of those groups and forms to law and justice considered abstractly—in short, to create the first works of Western political thought. The Greeks did all this and translated their theories into functioning polities as well. Even better, they lived under several forms of government, the histories of which served as data for their political philosophers. In the final analysis, the justification for beginning with the Greeks may be conventional, but that convention is based upon the considerations advanced here. The Greeks were not the first to lead an organized civil existence, but they were the first to stand away from their own politics, examine it critically, and establish institutions to perpetuate their ideas.

Economic conditions have not been central to this interpretation of the long first age of citizenship, although I have emphasized the individual's need for government, legal and military aid, and protection. Perhaps one fundamental fact needs explicit statement and integration into the argument here: that over the more than two thousand years to be traveled, conditions of life were, for most men and women, citizens or not, mean, brutish, and short, at the very margin of existence. For such people a connection with, and participation in, government might mean the advantage that led to survival, if not success. This is not to suggest that since the late-eighteenth-century French and American, as well as Industrial and agricultural, revolutions a new kind of national citizenship has solved the universal problem of want, and that there is no longer such a force driving political activity. Rather, it is to imply the massive need for personal involvement in politics during the first age of citizenship before modern science and technology began to better the lives of most human beings. All politics was the politics of survival in the period of marginal existence, pre–creature comfort. Not fear or greed, but need, was, perhaps, the ultimate cause of political involvement—need that was given inspiring statement by the moralists to be examined.

Perhaps this short book covering a long period is a study in the persistence of a delusion or myth: powerful, given its ability to provoke and command money, energy, and talent, and constant, given the everlasting mutual needs of cities and citizens. Perhaps there has been one long decline from Solon or Pericles until today. Perhaps one should look for an early Toynbeean moment after which all is decline, or, more precisely, for a succession of such perfect moments: the age of Solon, the early Roman Republic, the first days of the medieval commune, perhaps even the birth years of the American Republic. In such moments citizenship may really have worked, in that individuals believed and heeded the inspirational calls of their priests and secular leaders and for a while were unselfish in their willingness to give to and die for their country.

Each of these ages eventually was followed by a period of decline during which the original spirit faded as it was theorized and turned into an educational device. Yet decline was never extinction, and so powerful and useful were the ideal and practice of citizenship that they survived at some minimum level of function from one Toynbeean moment to the next. The active citizenship of early Greece and republican Rome turned into the passive citizenship of the Empire; the true exercise of citizenship during the Italian communal period was followed by that of the princely despotisms of the Renaissance, which maintained the fiction and rhetoric of the earlier age; and the exciting days of revolutionary America eventually matured into the slack nonparticipatory democracy of a later time.

PART I

ANCIENT CITIZENSHIP: VIRTUE IN

THE SERVICE OF COMMUNITY

1

GREECE

BEGINNINGS

It is clear why the Greek city-state world created the peculiar Western institution of citizenship.[1] It was a world composed of many little fortified places, each with its surrounding countryside, each with some tutelary deity, ruling families, traditions, and, perhaps, linguistic peculiarities. Land and sea warfare was endemic, and so was, eventually, an aggressive commerce. In a basic sense, some principle or institution of individuation was needed to define and reward membership in the community. The little states needed service from their people in times of crisis and attack; their people needed military and legal protection. In this competition of many little communities, each seeking both survival and political and economic expansion, some quality or edge had to be given to those who belonged to the city, served its gods, and fought for it. These individuals had to be distinguished by the grant of some special status based on certain rights and privileges from those whose relationship to the community was not so intense. Some people, for example, wished merely to reside in the place seeking economic opportunity and were unwilling to surrender previous political and religious attachments; others had made a commitment to the community, which they still were proving; and others were excluded by their servile status from the essential mark of belonging: participation in politics and war.

Citizenship became important as Greek society developed, when resources and powers were significant enough to be contested. Later in history it would become important again, when Rome, for example, found itself a proto-imperial power, and in the Middle Ages when, from the late eleventh century on, cities had to take stock and decide which of their inhabitants were to benefit from the new commercial and political circumstances, and why. In ancient Greece, citizenship became the device used to apportion land and privilege as new people claimed political experience now that they too possessed wealth derived from trade or primitive manufacture.

However, at this early time, the sixth century B.C., the presence of a new source of wealth did not mean that the basic problem of subsistence had been solved. For centuries Greek society remained precarious, as the continued emigrations demonstrate. If citizenship developed against this background of scarcity, it functioned as a means of discrimination and distribution. This is proved by the constant juggling with the requirements for citizenship. There was never a moment when the local leaders did not face the problems of hardship, which forced them to consider who would and who would not be rewarded and saved. Everyone needed the community, and quite early a reward system developed. In return for the services it needed in military and naval formations, on the walls, and eventually at religious and athletic events, the community gave the special benefits individuals needed.

All this occurred in the post-Homeric period, an era in which documentation and specificity are hard to come by. By the sixth century much of classical Greece was in place, including many of the issues that would constitute the substance of Greek politics for several hundred years: differences between town and country, rich and poor, this tribe or deme and that. In this situation it is clear how citizenship became a central political issue. Who had which privilege became critical. Thus, we might say, from the very beginnings of Greek political life—politics in the sense of leaders, factions, votes, conflicts, goals, rewards—citizenship became important. Leaders were, it appears, aware of the implications of every change in citizenship law. They saw the grant of citizenship not only in military terms, in making available new sources of manpower, but also in social and political terms, in determining whether city policy would reflect the interests of a specific class or interest group. And they acted accordingly. It is no exaggeration to say that the constitution of a polis changed with every modification of the law determining the citizen body. The laws, embodying as they did the values and interests of poor and rich, townsman and villager, determined what the citizen of a given city was to be like. They shaped his entire person, made him one of a kind and different from, if not hostile to, all other kinds. As Demosthenes put it, "A city's laws are its character," by which he meant the character of all the individual human beings raised to maturity in its specific moral, cultural, and legal environment.[2]

To say this is to claim that citizenship is the theory within which the Greek city-state developed. For hundreds of years citizenship was a functioning institution; then, in the era of Plato and Aristotle, it was theorized. There were fights over it and laws about it before the theorists caught up. Indeed, by the middle of the fifth century, citizenship had become one of that basic group of institutions that together constitute the framework of ancient life.

Each Greek city-state had its special history—its duties, rites, constitutions, important aristocratic families, and good and bad relations among its founding tribes; yet there were similarities, processes and institutions that enable us to think of a single political culture much the way we see central and northern Italy during the Middle Ages as in many ways homogeneous. Towns were small, more like villages than towns for hundreds of years; they were deeply established in and related to the agricultural environment—again, much as all medieval towns were to be; and in all, full citizens, so characterized by their at least initial possession of land and birth-defined rights and responsibilities, constituted a minority of the entire polis's population. The rest were slaves, women, aliens, or some specifically designated inferior group like the Helots in Sparta, who were not part of the political community.

One must not, however, see too many similarities between ancient and medieval cities. Not the least of their differences was the noneconomic nature of the ancient polis. As Max Weber long ago pointed out, ancient cities were not centers of production for distant markets. Moreover, much more than medieval cities, which were centers for both production and commerce, they were open to the presence and influence of those whose residence and way of life were rural.[3]

Perhaps it is necessary to emphasize here the intrinsically rural nature of the polis, usually translated as "city-state," for we are conditioned to think of a city as an urban, that is, built-up, area. The polis did have its downtown core—there were citizens who lived near the agora, say, in Athens, and under the acropolis—but most Athenians lived scattered over the countryside and came to town only to do political, religious, or other business. And what is true of Athens is even truer of lesser places, those with fewer people engaged in merchant, artisan, intellectual, and similar activities. The surprise in all this must be that Greek citizenship, in both its Athenian and Spartan forms, in large measure inheres in the countryside, and some of its characteristics and the issues it created in local politics reflect considerations of geography and organizations of human beings that antedate the political organization of the polis.

Eventually a hierarchy developed within the citizenry, distinctions being based on landownership, proper tribal membership, or regional residence, that is, birth and/or registration. Each category carried with it specific rights and obligations. System though it was, this ladder of citizenship changed in relation to circumstance. It varied with the need of the city for more citizens, or more of a certain rank; the results of war or the demands of production might force such a shift. The development of new military tactics gave more importance to a middle range of citizens who fought on foot with less equipment than the mounted citizen aristocracy. Changes were possible, too, because of shifts within the landowning population as some increased their holdings and influence at the expense of others. Finally, war shaped the citizenry in yet another, if obvious, way. It, and exile, which invariably accompanied war, removed from the population men whose replacement at a certain level of trust was necessary if the city was to be run and defended.

Everywhere, as tribes and clans perpetuated themselves in some mountain valley or fertile indentation on a rocky coast, communities were formed. Originally led by some military hero, his family, and their associates, these little societies faced problems of definition as questions of status, right, privilege, and power arose. Leaders had to know who was and who was not to receive the full benefits of membership in the state. Although "state" did not mean much in those days, "privilege" did, for people added up privileges to constitute for themselves the economic, legal, and political basis for survival. Privilege meant the capacity to receive spoils in terms of things, land, and slaves; it meant protection of the laws and gods; and it meant the right to bear arms, to perform like a free man in a society that honored personal heroism in the frequent wars of the time.

Citizenship came into being as the earliest leaders sought to distinguish the loyal and worthy from the casual members of the community, and it became an issue as new forms of wealth came into being. When this happened, when there were men whose claim to political voice and power was based on commerce, as opposed to agriculture, and on personal accomplishments, as opposed to family status, citizenship became a permanent issue in the internal politics of every community.[4]

SPARTA

Here Athenian citizenship should come up for discussion, for the mind turns instinctively to Athens as the least implausible Greek source and inspiration for our liberal constitutionalist tradition. But to do that would be to ignore the other Greek citizenship, that of Sparta, the dark one, which antedates the Athenian. As there are two Romes in history, the Republic and the Empire, so are there two Greeces, Athens and Sparta. Each has stood for a battery of values in later history; each has had its enthusiastic devotees. Today citizenship so much suggests participation in the political process that we balk at accepting the fact that Sparta contributed at all, let alone significantly, to the citizenship tradition familiar to us. Nevertheless, it must be acknowledged that the Spartan model was more influential than that of Athens throughout the *longue durée* of the first citizenship, that is, into the era of the democratic revolutions of the late eighteenth century.

Sparta's citizenship is dark and neglected because it cannot easily be placed in the tradition of Western democratic government. Our inclination, rather, is to see it as a historic ancestor of the detestable militaristic and authoritarian governments of our century. Athenian citizenship seems at first glance compatible with our own. As citizens, Athenians acted the way we do: they served on juries and in the army and paid taxes. What is more, they left records of deliberations and votes and lived in a world that, if it was still largely agricultural, tolerated commerce and the materialism that accompanies it. Athenians did many things and found a place for them in the theory of their society; to us there does not seem to have been one single overriding and controlling aspect of public and private life. We are comfortable with Athens because its essentially Periclean image somewhat deceptively reminds us of much of what we enjoy as our best self-image.

These are some of the reasons the powerful and distinctive contribution of Sparta to the history of citizenship has been neglected. Over the past two hundred years, especially in the Western democracies or liberal monarchies, historians have not extolled the militaristic states of the past or seen much to learn from, in this case, Sparta. Moreover, Sparta never produced a Thucydides to put self-serving words in the mouth of a Pericles, nor a class of articulate and disputatious men whose interest in ideas and institutions makes them look like prototypes of English parliamentarians or American founders. Further, it appeared that Sparta was hardly a city in any meaningful sense, but rather an agricultural community with peculiar institutions that could not possibly have contributed anything to the roots we search for in our past. Putting aside these and other misconceptions, we can see that the war society of Sparta gave a great deal to the foundation of Western citizenship. Its contribution came out of the very nature of its constant war or preparation for war, in which performance on the battlefield in the service of the community conveyed the highest honor. Spartan citizenship is an intensification of the Athenian notion of public service in that commitment is seen exclusively in life-and-death battlefield terms. Public service is more than the payment of taxes or occasional service in the law court or in the trireme. It is, rather, the full-time dedication of most of the citizen's best years to a steady, vigilant, and dangerous military career. The enemy is always present: the enslaved Helots, the defeated Messenians. In Athens, citizen activity could be casual, occasional, not always tied to the very existence of the public weal. Athenian life had room for humanistic education and commercial and artistic activity. Sparta had to focus entirely on war and did so, training its young to fight in the war for survival that always threatened. Out of Sparta, especially as depicted by Plutarch, comes the model of the citizen as warrior fit for fine and glorious sacrifice of life for his country.

What is more, other values sharpen the focus. There is no place in the Spartan's life for any distracting attachment, not to a wife, a child, or property. The good life is strenuous because it demands the citizen's full attention to maximum service in the specie of his own body. The purity of the Spartiate's ideal of service is comparable to the monk's commitment to his version of a spiritual ideal. And it might also be noted that Spartan asceticism well served a society living on the margin of existence. A man could more easily give his body in return for honor, a reputation for virtue, than the property he did not have, especially when his poets encouraged him to do so.

If Sparta did not have Thucydides, she did have Tyrtaeus, the poet of her mid-seventh-century wars. Plato and others made him a transplanted Athenian, but what immigrant into that suspicious Spartan society would have had the temerity to compose a poem on citizen duties for his new people, not to mention five books of war songs and an exhortation to old and young in battle? His origins are of less importance than his historic accomplishment. Tyrtaeus's is the literary formulation of the warrior-citizen ideal that figures so strongly in Roman history and that of every medieval commune and is taken up again with passion by Machiavelli. One might say that if Tyrtaeus did not discover the military element in the doctrine of citizenship, he elaborated and refined it.

Like Machiavelli, Tyrtaeus understands the history of his country and his times, and it is this history that determines his moral message. Given the threat of slave uprising and other war, the poet defines the good man in terms of military performance. This is not ordinary performance, however. Citizen-soldiers must be more than armed and trained; they must be driven by a love of city to prefer death to capture or defeat. "Here is courage, mankind's finest possession, here is the noblest prize that a young man can endeavor to win." Excellence is achieved on the battlefield, not in the agora or the academy. In another vocabulary, civic virtue is defined in terms of absolute military efficiency. Moreover, the individual achieves greatness not in acts of virtuoso soldiering, but in the act of dying for the community. That final act of membership, of social solidarity, the final act of sacrifice in battle, confers excellence as he "falls among the champions . . . so blessing with honor his city, his father, and all his people." In this ideal of dying for the common good Tyrtaeus, it has been observed, modified Homer's stress on the heroic individual, and one might add that he approaches Pericles' vision of the reciprocal relationship between citizen and community. Like the Athenian leader two centuries later, Tyrtaeus promises rewards to the fallen hero and to his family. His proper death will bring honor not only to his city but to "his children, and his children's children, and afterward all the race that is his . . . he becomes an immortal though he lives under the ground." All men will "give place to him . . . the youth, and the men his age, and even those older than he." Battlefield glory is powerful enough to alter society's basic hierarchies. To this total commitment the alternative is more than removal from the community, greater than oblivion. It is disgrace, shame remembered and celebrated generation upon generation. This moral and constitutional program of "good order" Tyrtaeus sums up in the word *eunomia*.[5]

This special citizenship developed because of the particular conditions that shaped the Spartan polity. Her citizenship developed against the backdrop of war and fear of rebellion. Whatever actuality and authenticity we accord the figure of the law-giver, Lycurgus, it is probable that quite early in its history Sparta was organized as a community of privileged landowners, a quasi-feudal society in which each warrior received a portion of land to maintain himself and his equipment.

Eventually, military events forced modification of the original system. First, military tactics changed. The mounted warrior was replaced by the trained infantryman; the hoplite now fought as a member of the phalanx. Then, as Sparta needed new hoplites, she expanded the citizenry, in effect creating a hierarchy of citizenries. Eventually, the very success of the hoplite armies in bringing new territories and peoples under her rule changed the nature of Spartan life. The citizen became an awesome, apprehensive warrior ruling a large population, which was excluded from public life and which included not only the servile Helots but also the Perioikoi, who lived in dependent villages. Their political and military concerns being constant, Spartan citizens were, therefore, denied any career other than the military, any success other than victory.

To preserve Sparta as they saw it and enjoyed it, the Spartan leadership constructed a set of quasi-military institutions supported, as we have seen, by a passionate desire for glory. At about the time Tyrtaeus was writing his inspirational poetry, the problematic Lycurgus initiated the "reform" upon which rested the following five hundred years of Spartan history. He distributed land to all who were to be full citizens and enrolled them in one of the common meals that was to be a central institution throughout Sparta's history. These were the *syssitia* or *pheiditia* that one entered at the age of twenty or twenty-four. Throughout his adult life the Spartan dined with his comrades, fought next to them in battle, and contributed to their common table from his *kleros*, his land. Life within this group was a key phase in the total education of the Spartan.

Taken from their mothers in their seventh year, boys moved from class to class, herd to herd over the next twenty-four years, living in barracks, strengthening themselves in many ways. Only in his thirties was a citizen allowed to marry, produce a family, and lead a somewhat less rigorous existence. But even then his patriotic education never let up as he participated in the rituals and celebrations of public life when he was not in the field. These, incidentally, included much dancing and marching and exposure to the stimulating lyrics of Tyrtaeus and other martial poets.

The Spartan system was successful for hundreds of years, defining success as political survival and victory over the Athenian empire. But eventually, by the third century, the élan of the citizen class began to deteriorate. Only at the very beginning had the citizens been equal. Some soon became wealthier and politically more influential. Factors other than military reputation entered the system. Over time, as some landowners increased their holdings, others lost theirs, the basis of their membership in the military mess and citizenship. Meanwhile, as this shrinkage of the citizenry was taking place, the numbers of Helots and Perioikoi grew, as did the city's commitments overseas. The result was an inadequate and beleaguered citizen population defensively lording it over an angry majority now swollen with former members of the ruling class.

Modern distaste for Sparta's military regime also dismisses her contribution to the history of Western constitutionalism. Solon flourished about 600 B.C.; Lycurgus initiated his reforms, which shaped so much of Sparta's history, almost a century earlier. These were noted and analyzed, and in some ways praised, by Plato, Aristotle, Xenophon, and Plutarch and were influential throughout antiquity; yet in recent popular and even scholarly thinking they have been largely ignored except by the few professorial admirers of Sparta. Sparta could not have successfully maintained internal security while waging foreign wars had not her political institutions served the interests of her leading men and, through a unique educational system which relied upon the community, as opposed to the family, guaranteed loyalty to the regime.

According to a tradition preserved and perhaps confused by Plutarch, the oracle at Delphi gave Lycurgus a "Good Order," the basis of his political reforms; later he effected a land distribution which gave nine thousand Spartiates the economic base of their political and military standing. This new regime constituted citizen-soldiers, who alone participated in political and military life, and eventually included two kings, principally military leaders, five ephors, who presided over justice and foreign policy, and a council of thirty citizen-elders, the *gerousia*, and a popular assembly. The details of historical development and constitutional function remain uncertain, but the fact of a distribution of power is clear. Aristocratic families retained a traditional leadership role in military and political affairs. Their discussions led to proposals placed before the hoplites, who constituted a kind of popular assembly. The exact relationship of the assembly to what was in fact a ruling oligarchy remains unclear; at a minimum this assembly played a formal constitutional role in the making of public policy. It heard debate, though whether it could in some matters block action proposed by the *gerousia* as well as voice its approval is open to question. Aristotle did not think it could, but even in his day outsiders had difficulty in getting and understanding precise details of the Spartan system.

In sum, despite all those aspects of its distinctive civic culture that strike us today as unsavory and illiberal, Sparta must be seen in the mainstream of Greek politics. That is, although it limited the vote, office holding, and policy-making to a few, it involved the many in processes of debate and consultation and in procedures that assured public acceptance. In a community of a few thousand in which traditions play a significant role, no element was strong enough or, most likely, willing enough to destroy a good order identified with a semideified lawgiver. Like the army, the common table, and probouleutic procedures, the assembly was an institution of civic education and citizenship and must be recognized as an element in Sparta's total impact upon both ancient and later imaginations.[6]

Changes in the nature of Spartan citizenship so closely accompanied changes in the political position of Sparta in the Mediterranean world that one is tempted to establish a connection. In any event, under Rome Sparta became insignificant except as an intellectual and moral influence upon the military ethos of her conqueror. Like Athens and Alexandria, if without their books and scholars, Sparta was an education to the Roman world.

ATHENS

It is against this background that we consider Athens's history—unique, yet similar to that of its neighbors and available to us thanks to the surviving efforts of its own historians, orators, and philosophers as well as the more recent work of archaeologists, epigraphers, and other scholars. Given the preponderance of Athenian "data" that survives, it is understandable why Athens has in a sense been a code-word for Greece. But there is a substantive reason for this as well. It was largely in Athenian analyses and speeches that the theory of the city-state reached Rome and its successor civilizations. Ancient political thought until well into the Roman period never got beyond the city-state as presented by Plato and Aristotle, and as studied in Athens by Cicero and others of Rome's ruling class.

The first significant attempt to change the nature of Athens by modifying its citizen body is ascribed to Solon, and it can be said with a rough truth that the history of Greek citizenship begins with him. Little hard evidence exists for the period before Solon, although the tradition in which King Theseus unified the villages of Attica may be accurate. Even if it is accurate in affirming a unification, exactly what that unification was in terms of the social and political units that were affected and when it took place are unknown. Households, tribes, and variously designated kinship corporations all appear in the records.[7] In contrast to the order presented by Aristotle in the *Constitution of Athens*, pre-Solonic Athenian society seems to have been a complete confusion of overlapping memberships and loyalties. Every political individual was enmeshed in a web of relationships, each of which provided some identity and benefits while demanding something in return. The privilege of office holding was early dependent on "birth and wealth." One's ability to float successfully in this world conferred security; before Solon it probably constituted the best dynamic or functional definition of citizenship possible. As yet a clear sense of the "shared purpose or spirit" demanded by Aristotle did not exist.[8] Only slowly during the seventh century did a ruling class and institutions of government and justice develop, supported by a population that believed in and relied on them. The failure of Kylon's coup d'état reveals a population determined in adequate number to defend their polis, which by then was a perceived constitution with a body of customary law that obtained over a territory with known limits.[9] A territory frequently at war was therefore in a situation which generated an intense patriotism.

Before Solon (fl. 590) no clear concept of citizenship existed. As yet there were few political decisions to be made, and political issues hardly existed. But with the development of activities such as commerce and commercial farming, which resulted in a more differentiated social structure, and with the growth too of intercity rivalries manifested in petty, intermittent, but destructive war, who was and who was not a full political person with arms-bearing responsibilities as well as a voice in determining community policies became a matter of constant concern.

If Aristotle was right in his report that Solon was of aristocratic birth but "by wealth and position belonged to the middle class," then the act of establishing a constitution was more than an event in political history. It was also a significant moral event, the exercise of political power by a social idealist who represented modest wealth and who stood against domination of the community by "proud" landowners "plunged in a surfeit of abundant goods."[10] Now others besides the great landed aristocrats determined policy in a world narrowed by the existence of a formal document. Codification, in this interpretation, was forced by Solon upon the traditional leaders who, even if they had, until that moment, ruled not exactly capriciously, had not exactly ruled in accordance with recognized custom. It is his activity in these two historical terrains that gave Solon his significance, both to those in the generations following him and to us in our attempt to reconstruct ancient Athenian history. He saw the changing nature of Athenian society and its implications for internal politics and the military life, which continued to be so important, and attempted to reorganize Athens for a peaceful future.

To this time the leaders of the community had been the greater landowners, military chieftains who determined strategy and did the fighting. Because they fought, they enjoyed the fullest political rights—one hesitates to say citizenship, which in a strict legal sense did not yet exist. In these early days no man devoted his attention to politics alone. He had other obligations, most of which were at least as immediate to his personal welfare as the political: to the family, clan, religious association, and to the geographic base of his status and identity. From its very beginning the moral history of citizenship is a record of the conflicting demands upon the individual for his loyalty, effort, time, and money.

And there were problems. In the generations preceding Solon's leadership, hostilities had erupted between rich and poor and among great noble families, each with its constituency at every social level. Athens faced attempted coup d'état and mob action by landless and oppressed peasants who, if not legally unfree, found themselves deeply in debt. So burdened, the peasant and his family lost full control of their property. Many were headed for slavery and were already in a kind of personal servitude. This situation in other city-states led to tyranny; in Athens it produced Solon as the mediator acceptable to all for his patriotism and wisdom. It is important to understand that Solon did not make landownership a prerequisite for citizenship. Before his time, and for long afterwards, citizenship was a condition for landownership, not the reverse. One must be very careful in describing what he did in relation to contemporary conditions of landholding. It is very likely that these varied from region to region within Attica, that public and private property were interspersed, and that several forms of tenure coexisted. All these conditions suggest an intricate set of relationships between the rich and poor with regard to a variety of obligations public and private.

What Solon appears to have done is cancel some of those debts, perhaps those arising from the inability of small free farmers to till their private plots without financial assistance from the rich. Such marginal peasants were not able to handle both these debts and the obligation of a sixth they owed to some corporate holder of land they tilled. Close analysis of Solon's own poetry suggests that if he did redistribute property throughout Attica, it was not in an effort to achieve perfect equality. Rather he was attempting to allow the survival of differences between rich and poor while preventing the further growth of land-hungry speculators and predatory landlords eager to amass larger and larger farms. It is just this kind of activity that would have won for Solon the sort of moral greatness almost immediately associated with his name.[11]

By canceling all debts of the debtor-citizens, by forbidding the pledge of one's person, and by reorganizing the citizen military forces on the basis of economic condition, Solon made citizenship an important issue in Athenian politics. Thereafter Athens had no citizen whose independence was limited by any kind of personal servitude. The number of men eligible for participation in public life was now permanently enlarged. At the same time, Solon inaugurated agricultural reforms, which helped the large farmers who had lost their canceled debts. And he maintained their dominance in society by dividing the citizenry into four classes on the basis of wealth. Such differentiation may not have been original with Solon, but already in antiquity he was credited with its establishment.

Authorship is not important; what is important is the fact that citizens in the three top categories were given military responsibility in proportion to their wealth. The wealthiest constituted the cavalry and thus retained their de facto leadership, at least for awhile. Since military service was of vital importance to the community, and combat was likely to be part of a citizen's actual experience at some moment in his life, the life of the individual and the life of the state were conjoined. Solon also used wealth as a basis for assigning political rights and responsibilities. If he granted the poorest citizens, the *thetes*, entrance to the *ecclesia*, Athen's primary legislative assembly, he retained for the wealthier classes real political control. They alone were granted incumbency of the more important executive offices and membership in the Council of Four Hundred, which, while it excluded the *thetes*, nevertheless did include the hoplites; thus composed, it established the agenda of the assembly and supervised the magistrates. Solon then was no social revolutionary. He accepted the assumptions of timocracy, that honors, privileges, and responsibilities be in relation to wealth, as did most ancient social theorists, and utilized the preexisting divisions within society as a basis for tinkering with the constitution. Everything he did in his aristocratic concern for the community's welfare was directed toward a single goal: the establishment of a society of harmonious social classes.

We may say that Solon had a vision: he wanted a lawful society whose members were agreed on their common goals and mutual responsibility. The goal is *eunomia*, which, borrowed from Tyrtaeus, suggests "idea of 'good order' . . . together with that of an appropriate distribution of wealth, power, and resources within society." To achieve this, he proposed his economic and constitutional reforms. He attempted to liberate the miserable debt-ridden citizens from any animosity to the polis, to bring them back in, while allowing the powerful to retain what they considered to be their rightful role as leaders. He sought to put the interest of community above interest of class or clan. The usual act of a successful politician was to banish his opponents and identify the polis's interests with and as his own. Solon, however, having righted affairs, went into exile for a decade to give his programs a chance to succeed.

Solon's accomplishment may be viewed as moral progress along the route that leads from personal and familial self-centeredness toward an ethic of civic cooperation. He persuaded the rich, whose wealth now might be of an extent hitherto unknown, to devote considerable resources to the public welfare. And he elevated the poor into some exercise of public spirit by admitting them to the *ecclesia*, where they might at least devote time and thought to consideration of public issues. Already governance itself acted, in its command to citizens to participate, as an educational force. Yet Solon remains a conservative reformer. As one scholar carefully observes, "*Arete*, the goal of life, is evaluated in terms of prosperity and good reputation; and for him [Solon] too the primary loyalty is to a group smaller than the city."

True, but Solon's view does encompass the city as a whole, which is remarkable, as is his deftness in managing to institutionalize that view. He surely realized that too sudden and heavy a pressure upon his fellows might have been counterproductive, hence his concern with the proper pace as well as vision. He knew that he had little with which to convert his fellow citizens to cooperation, hence the careful planning of the institutions of involvement as the institutions of moral education, and the broad scope of his reforms. Like other universal legislators in history, like Charlemagne, for example, he recognized, or at least may have intuited, the interrelationship of social, economic, and political change and the relationship of these three broad areas to the ethical improvement of the individual. What Solon wanted was a better citizen, one who would find it impossible not to participate in public affairs. Hence the tradition, recorded by Aristotle, that "Solon passed the following law specifically aimed at apathy: 'When there is a civil war in the city, anyone who does not take up arms on one side or the other shall be deprived of civil rights and of all share in the affairs of government.'" Solon may never have promulgated such a law. What matters is the association of this memory with him and its currency with Aristotle some 250 years after his death. Here is encouragement of an Athenian patriotism, perhaps, but certainly not the massive encouragement of sacrifice in battle of Tyrtaeus. Moreover, Solon differentiated between the conditions of slavery and freedom and clearly linked the active citizenship he advocated to freedom. His restrictions upon immigration also contributed to the process of differentiation between those who were and those who were not citizens. As certain activities were prohibited to newcomers, at the same moment others were restricted to citizens, and the nature and desirability of citizenship became clearer, being now established in law.[12]

During the century or so following his death, for all its moral insight and grandeur, Solon's reform came apart. Athenian society remained troubled. The landed magnates continued in authority and built coalitions around one family or another. Solon had sought to construct a state, a central government whose interests all citizens were to serve at the expense of traditionally more parochial commitments. That aim was frustrated as a new, intermediate form of allegiance developed, groupings of social and political interests based upon three geographic regions, those parts of Attica conventionally known as the plain, shore, and hill. These were not the bases for regional parties in the modern sense; they were not even homogeneous in terms of social class and occupation, but rather, they were combinations of "special-interests" led by some outstanding leader and his family. The presence in these factions of very wealthy members of the merchant class, new men with ambitions to be realized and needs to be met, gave them added strength and push and contributed to the unsettled state of the community.

These new political alignments reflected economic and social problems. Solon's reforms had not solved every problem; some rich men had been hurt, many farmers continued to be poor, weak, and angry, and land continued in short supply in relation to those in a growing population who wanted it. It was out of this sort of need, in which both existence and social status were involved, that the old patterns of dependent loyalties developed and new leaders arose.

One of these great factional leaders, Peisistratus, eventually proclaimed himself the leader of the people, put together a coalition of Athenians and foreigners, and after several failures, became tyrant of Athens. Peisistratus made no new laws on citizenship but did add shape to certain institutions that in turn helped mold the Athenian state. The urban area of the polis was by now becoming more visible as it added population and the homes, shops, wharfs, and warehouses that its diversified population needed, and as it built new political and religious institutions and housed them in monumental and beautiful buildings that enhanced and engaged the citizens' lives. In his activity we see a "peculiar mixture of religion, patriotism, and self-aggrandizement." For example, he promoted the cult of Athena in the Panathenea. This traditional festival continued yearly, but now a grander Greater Panathenea, to be celebrated every four years, was inaugurated. The tyrant himself interfered to reorganize the recitation of the Homeric poems, and by introducing chariot racing he attempted to make Athena's festival a rival to those at Delphi and Olympia. In this way he added to the image and identity of Athens in the world, that is, to the sense and presumably the pride of being an Athenian in each citizen.[13]

This centralizing cultural activity had its political and legal analogue. Like a medieval monarch intent on spreading a common justice, Peisistratus sent out a legal official to travel over Attica, bearing a common city law, and he was also responsible for one of the earliest taxes collected throughout the entire state. Although a tyrant, he maintained Solon's constitution in force, thus giving it continuity and providing the people a sense of living in a stable community whose system of laws, its *politeia*, survived. Finally, Peisistratus inaugurated an aggressive foreign policy. To "bread and circuses" he added "service for the fatherland" and through successful foreign war continued the integration of individual citizens into a common purpose, accomplishments, and memory. In effect, the Athenian empire began its history under the Peisistratids.

Not all the elements of the fully constructed polis were yet in place. Social division continued to be a problem and remained so right through the period of the independent city-state. Yet it is clear that at Peisistratus's death the polis was more coherent and visible. It had much more common history, complete with legendary figures, heroes who had given the laws and joined and protected the fold; it had its tutelary goddess now properly celebrated and soon to be housed in a marvelous building fit for her worship; and it had its law courts, assembly buildings, and meeting-commercial place, the agora, all definitively located, properly housed, and attended now over several more generations. By the end of the sixth century Athens had become more of a city, as we would use the term. Its urban center had ceased to look like a village, like all the other little settlements scattered over Attica. It was becoming a true capital city whose buildings and institutions had functioned for one or more generations—time enough for the populace to use and come to appreciate them, and for poets and politicians to exploit their worth. In every generation the polis was what it was; it was also, obviously, the product of its own past, a memory created by intellectuals and passed on to the people.

English history of the nineteenth century often is presented in terms of reform bills, with Parliament responding to basic changes in an industrializing, urbanizing society, granting new classes the vote. The result was, in effect, a new constitution for the country as a changed Parliament legislated in response to a more popular will. In Athens, something of the same kind of fundamental shift took place in the fifth century after the reorganization of the citizenry by Cleisthenes (d. ca. 500). Although his actions were essentially political in motivation, they naturally reflected social and economic changes in Athenian society. Athens was becoming a center of trade and some manufacture and mining in addition to its traditional functions as government center and agricultural marketplace. It was also an attraction to immigrants from the entire Mediterranean Greek community.

Cleisthenes was another ambitious aristocrat. Unlike Solon, he came to power violently, an adventurer whose success was assured by his Spartan allies. But like Solon, he fundamentally altered the Athenian state and the way men thought about it. His structure saw Athens through the following two fantastically creative centuries, which provided so many of the goals and means of Western civilization. In a narrow legal way he redefined Athenian citizenship in relation to new territorial units, but in the broadest sense he gave every free male Athenian a new identity that depended upon involvement with the community—or, better, involvements with the several communities upon whose smooth and integrated function Athens's entire performance now depended.

Cleisthenes' reform must be understood in terms of the *diapsephesmos*, or scrutiny, that followed the violent end of the Peisistratids' control of the city. In the "reign of terror" occasioned by the attempt of a new aristocratic faction to control politics, an attack was made upon the supporters of the defeated and exiled tyrants through the depoliticization of some of their followers, those vulnerable given some ambiguity of citizen status.[14] (This was the first but not the last time such a device was made an instrument of Athenian politics.) Exactly where this examination of credentials took place, in the *phratriae* or, perhaps, the *phylai*, is still open to question. That being so, it is likely that there was no uniform interrogation procedure or set of citizenship demands throughout all the varied communities of Attica. The city-state now held more than a native and homogeneous agricultural population. Many foreign artisans, mercenaries, and probably even farmers were now living in the city and scattered settlements. It seems likely, too, that, as later was the case in Italian medieval and Renaissance cities, there were many foreigners who tried to live quietly, out of the eyes of the state, while earning a living in various ways.

If we have no certainty of procedure and citizenship demands, there does survive some indication of the results of the scrutiny, which on close inspection seems to have been more a savage retribution than an orderly examination of persons and documents. A near-contemporary speaker suggests that followers of the defeated tyrants were "put to death . . . exiled . . . [or]

deprived of their rights." No citizenship lists as yet existed. In such a climate of violence no formal defense was available that at least might be presented to some aggressive officer of a new regime. In effect, Cleisthenes' reforms provided this new measure of identity, if not personal security.

Solon had freed the debtors, brought them into civic affairs, and made them all equal under law. But he had not tampered with the complex religious, tribal, and family qualifications for citizenship that had existed from the earliest times. Cleisthenes did. And he sharpened the institution in terms of obligations and benefits. Now an Athenian had a regularized way to prove his membership in that community which now could be seen as not only the grantor of privileges but also the guarantor of life.

Before his reforms, to be a citizen required membership in a *gene*—or clan or phratry—and certainly in one of the four original tribes. Members of a clan looked back to a common cult practice or to the memory of a military comradeship that had united the members' ancestors. There might be several phratries associated with one clan. Now Cleisthenes struck down the old Athenian organization and made local residence the basis for citizenship. His unit was the deme, roughly village, of which he designated about 140. Apparently the demes already existed as minor centers of public life and organized religious and economic activity. Cleisthenes made them the basis for personal identification, even in the city, where, very possibly, he transformed preexisting neighborhoods into demes. Also, he linked this local registration with the institutions of government in downtown Athens. The importance of this reorganization was recognized by Aristotle, who noted that thenceforth, "the Athenians speak of one another by the names of their demes."15

Aristotle also described Cleisthenes' division of the population into ten new tribes, each of which included population from all three areas of the polis: the plain, the shore, and the hill. Cleisthenes' aim, he said, was the "mixing up of the population so that a greater number would share in citizenship."16 Perhaps this was Cleisthenes' way of integrating, and thus rewarding, those new immigrants who had contributed to Athens's economic growth, or who had followed his leadership in the struggle with his rival, Isagoras. It is most likely that Athenians with any legitimate claim to citizenship were included in the arrangements that made the new polis. We know too that the tribes served on the basis of a new military organization much as the demes came to constitute the basis of political activity. After Cleisthenes, in Athenian history, the eighteen-year-old male was presented to the deme by his father. If accepted and recorded on the lists of the deme, he then became a citizen with full political and legal rights. In effect, by making deme registration the sine qua non of Athenian citizenship, Cleisthenes submerged all other affiliations, family or religious, and left the territorial-political paramount. Nor did the distinction between ancient or new citizen matter in a formal way. Family names, hence family influence, of course continued to play a role in politics, but apparently not to the extent before the reform. Eventually there was but one kind of citizen in the formal pattern of the Athenian constitution, subject to one kind of law. This is Cleisthenes' contribution to Athenian democracy. Inequalities persisted in Athens— they were always accepted within the ancient and medieval definition of citizenship—but now there existed for all citizens of every place and every rank in the social hierarchy one form of entrance into the political community and one set of legal restraints and privileges.[17]

In establishing a procedure that legitimated the young new citizen and brought Athenians from many different regional and occupational backgrounds, Cleisthenes continued the improvement of Athenian democracy. That is, he acted to reduce tensions, to give more men a share in the political community, and to draw urban and rural populations into a tighter mix.

Another effort of his brought into citizenship "many foreigners and slave *metics*." One scholar has argues that these were "alien craftsmen who had settled in Athens during the tyranny," as well as poor farmers. They may also have been the people whose existence Aristotle hints at, new citizens enfranchised by the tyrants in the mid-sixth century, or noncitizens resident in Attica, doing business there across the Mediterranean. If this is so, Cleisthenes must be seen too as a social thinker intent on assuring civil peace by including in the community successful new men.[18]

However, he also has been viewed as a careful politician intent on rewarding his followers; analysis of geographical relationships suggests that in his reforms Cleisthenes aimed to increase the political power of the city area, from which many of his supporters, including a significant number of the generals, came. Cleisthenes clearly appreciated citizenship as an institution to be manipulated for maximum political return. He was aware of the consequences that changes in representation would bring, and he was willing to take the risks of constitutional reform to benefit from those consequences. One does not know whether civic high-mindedness or partisan meanness was behind his renovations. What is significant, however, is not whether Cleisthenes was an idealistic statesman or a crafty politician. To be emphasized, rather, is his willingness to confront the problems of immigration and naturalization with all their political implications and his daring reordering of the entire community in response.

Tied to the new organization of Athenian citizens into ten tribes was the creation of the Council of Five Hundred. This institution, which replaced an earlier Council of Four Hundred, became the principal political institution in the reorganized city. Although its decrees could be overruled by the mass meeting of the citizens, the *ecclesia*, it functioned to make policy for Athens in every field but justice. Each of the ten tribes contributed fifty men to its membership, and these were chosen with some regard for the size and importance of each deme within the tribe. Actually, since five hundred was too large a body to give effective government, the council was broken down into representative units of fifty. Citizen participation and turnover was facilitated by service in these units, the *prytany*; they served to give political education to generations of Athenians who there learned skills of administration, procedure, and judgment.

Some scholars believe too much is associated with Cleisthenes, too many reforms assumed to have been completely accepted by a population essentially unfamiliar with rapid change. That is probably so, although the Athenians were well aware of Cleisthenes' purposes since his reforms passed through both the council and the assembly. Again, what is significant is not a verdict on whether Cleisthenes accomplished what tradition declares, but rather one on function. Cleisthenes' structure was in place and working well by the time the Persians attacked, first in 490 and again a decade later. It saw Athens through those two successful wars and into the benign period of the early empire and then enabled her to survive bad times and ultimately defeat in the Peloponnesian War. Throughout much of this period democracy flourished. One man had one vote. He participated in the law courts, the assembly, and the council and bore administrative, military, and naval obligations. These activities were solemnized when, in 501–500 each citizen was required henceforth to swear allegiance to the common welfare and purpose of the Athenian people and polis. At about the same time, it has been observed, Athens arrived at clearer definitions of those not citizens, yet members of the greater Attic society—first *metics* and then Athens's *proxenoi* abroad. The latter were those granted quasi-citizen status in return for quasi-ambassadorial services to Athens in their native cities. In sum, citizenship was now established as *a*, if not *the*, central institution of the Athenian constitution. It had a significant history and conveyed significant value. Athenians knew this and others too, as is evidenced by the development, by about 475, of the practice of granting citizenship as a reward to foreigners in some way congenial to the Athenian people.[19]

In this long period only Pericles (495–429), the great democratic leader, orator, and statesman, modified the Cleisthenean constitution on citizenship. In 451–450 he passed a law making citizenship depend upon the Athenian origin of both parents. Aristotle's explanation, that the decree was "in consequence of the increasing number of citizens," is rejected by most modern authorities.[20] These, however, cannot agree. We are told Pericles acted on behalf of the Athenian young women seeking husbands, out of concern for racial purity, to reduce the cost of paying citizens on state service, or, by making it rarer, to magnify the prestige of Athenian citizenship. He may even have seen the decree as a timely political device in his relations with his rival Kimon. Any one of these hypotheses gives us a Pericles sensitive to the meaning and use of citizenship and alive to its legal definition and its usefulness as an instrument of social or political control. He knew the benefits the institution conferred, saw their impact upon status and allegiance, and was certainly aware, as the great funeral oration demonstrates, of what we call today symbolic meaning.

It is this sense of history and political self-consciousness that should be emphasized—Pericles' completeness of view. He saw the centrality and complexity of the institution and skillfully integrated it into his leadership of the city. Citizenship was on his mind, so to speak. He used it again, about 450, as an instrument of discrimination when he instituted pay for citizens who sat in the courts. Perhaps he was trying to preserve this benefit for the most Athenian Athenians in the most Athenian of institutions, the vast juries. Aristotle says that Pericles was prompted to "offer the people what was their own," given his own inability to pay for popular support. By reporting negative comments, Aristotle appears to blame Pericles for this tampering with fundamental institutions, since from his time on, he says, "it was always the common men rather than the better men who were eager to participate in drawing the lot for duty in the law courts."[21]

This political, if not calculating, side of Pericles must be understood along with the nobler image he projected in the funeral oration. Aristotle and Socrates both see the Peloponnesian War as a crisis in the history of citizenship. By the end of the war many Athenians were no longer asking what they could do for the polis but rather what it could do for them. The empire no longer existed to provide revenues to maintain the poorer citizens who had come to expect public support. Now citizens squabbled for spots on the juries and places in the fleet, which might provide a minimum income.

This is what Pericles tells us in his great speech, which is Athenian democracy's most successful advertisement. Pericles lauds forthright, fearless, and adaptable behavior. He explicitly claims that those who died at Marathon did not shrink from danger, did not act "upon a calculation of interest." They fought, he insists, "in the confidence of freedom and in a frank and fearless spirit." He points with pride to the excellence of Athenian political democracy and to the sufficiency for peace and war he and his generation have achieved. Excellence, he claims, is recognized in all; individualism is tolerated for its contribution to the city's strength. And, indeed, commitment to politics in a democracy constitutes the good life.

Such is Pericles' flattering picture of Athenian life and values. But can it be trusted when in this very speech Thucydides himself supplies evidence for another view? Pericles seems aware at all times of a tension between public and private interests. Those praised have put public service before private advantage; they have not been "enervated by wealth" or hesitant about "resigning the pleasures of life." The implied enemy throughout his talk is a personal, self-indulgent, material existence.

It is because he knew his Athenians so well and had to assume their materialist and calculating natures that Pericles carefully responds to their private needs. The oration itself is in the nature of an exchange, an attempt by the leader of Athenian society to repay a family for its human loss. He gives value to the praise lavished upon the dead, noting that it "grows not old" and confers upon the hero "the noblest of sepulchres," that is, "the memory of the Athenian people." To this he adds tangible rewards in his final paragraph: the heroes' children will have state support until their majority. He may actually conceptualize a commercial approach to civic virtue in his final words: "For where the rewards of virtue are greatest, there the noblest citizens are enlisted in the service of the state." Does this tell us that supporting the Athenian ethic of service we instinctively admire was a schedule of rewards and benefits of which each citizen was aware and on which he counted as he marched or sailed off to war?

In his speech Pericles seems aware of the complicated appeal for commitment he must make. Citizenship both rewards and excludes in his talk. Reward is associated with the public honor the city confers on its heroes, plus the promise of aid to those who may heroically defend the public weal and to their families. He mentions the noncitizens in his audience and offers them a vision of a superior moral life through which to get bread and wine. Always in this society, which understands exchange, Pericles asks his listeners to calculate wisely and make their choice to serve. Perhaps he could approach his listeners this way because there were so few distractions to the citizenship of the polis, that is, no immediate, aggressive subinstitutions of society competing for the commitment of the individual, offering him important alternative rewards. No guild, religious association, or political party as yet offered benefits that could match those granted by the state. Life and identity were offered and defined by the polis almost exclusively: even the family was hardly competitive in the totality of its demands and gifts.

However, Pericles' importance in the history of Greek citizenship and for the moral history of the West does not rest upon his political reforms and the underside of his funeral oration. It was, rather, through the high-minded words of that speech, as reported by Thucydides, that he has had the greatest influence throughout history. His speech reveals citizenship as a moral tradition and presents to us the unity, completeness, and interrelatedness of the life of the polis, not just of Athens. In it he extols the community texture and ideal that from time to time over the following two thousand years has made Athens a model in the democratic tradition. He also, in effect, sums up the history of citizenship to his day, showing us how complex an institution it had become by the fifth century. As past, present, and future are represented, we see citizenship as part of an educational program and of an inspiring moral tradition in which each generation acknowledges a connection to all others and a responsibility to them all for maintenance of the community and the traditions. Religion, territory, the peculiar politics of a polis are all part of a tradition. They make the individual what he is; he, in turn, sacrifices for the community, putting its interests above his own.

In his oration Pericles means to transcend any technical, legal sense of citizenship. He handles it as he would a moral principle, a dogma. At a time of crisis he believes it necessary to remind members of the community who they are, what they have accomplished, and why they must fight. There is pride here, but not boasting. Considering the funerary nature of the occasion and the pressure of immediate events, Pericles' words are remarkably matter-of-fact. Perhaps they can be cool because so much of what he says is known by his fellow Athenians, having been part of their civic education.

Pericles' words went out to an audience divided into many social and legal categories; he refers to "this numerous assembly of citizens and strangers." His speech surely was meant to inspire all segments of the population to sacrifice for the imperiled city. However, the distinctions within Athenian society, which made it less than the wonderful model his words describe, have been lost in history, and perhaps, given his persuasiveness, could be forgotten at times even then. What survived to act as a historical force was Pericles' positive vision, that of the conscious, willing, active citizen devoting himself and his goods to the welfare of the community.[22]

Citizenship suffered no significant changes until another period of crisis, the struggle between the oligarchs and the democratic leaders during the final stages of the Peloponnesian War. Thucydides tells us how Peisander, one of the oligarchs, in the name of fiscal retrenchment managed to reduce the number of paid offices in the state. Only those on military or naval service were to be paid. In effect, this reform changed the Athenian constitution. It restricted office to the wealthy, those whose property status made them hoplites, those who could afford to assume public responsibility without pay. The oligarchs estimated that the citizenry would be reduced to some five thousand solid, dependable citizens. They also intended to create a new Council of Four Hundred, which would actually rule for the five thousand.

The controversy over the scope and rewards of citizenship provoked a civil war as Athens struggled against her enemies, for the oligarchs used their position to rout out popular democracy, especially in the fleet where so many of the poorer, landless citizens, the *thetes*, served. After nearly a year of civic discord the Periclean system was restored. The *thetes* were restored to the political community and to their stipends for service in the fleet.

The final years of the Peloponnesian War brought crisis after crisis to Athens. A succession of oligarchic and democratic leaders attempted to solve social issues while bringing victory and failed. Each change of regime brought some change in the constitution as the political part of the community was either enlarged or reduced in size. Citizenship became materialized and politicized. It also became legalized, that is, over time more and more laws were passed to affect citizenship. Mixed marriages between Athenians and aliens were forbidden; severe penalties were threatened against those posing as citizens or attempting to infiltrate an Athenian phratry. Simultaneously, new laws progressively defined and limited new classes of outsiders.[23]

On one occasion the oligarchs proposed restricting the fully active citizenry to three thousand. On another, the grant of citizenship "to all who had fought for this democracy" was proposed. In effect, citizenship became the instrument of penalty and reward—and therefore of political power. Since those who led and legislated represented social interests as well as family factions, the eventual solution to, or statement of, the problem of citizenship must in part be seen as a matter of class.

The war ended in 404. A commission established in 410 was already at work revising the constitution. By 400–399 its work was inscribed on the walls of Athens—to remain there until Macedon imposed a new kind of government in 322. This final version of Athenian democracy restored the Council of Five Hundred and the extended suffrage according to Pericles' revision. A later law of the 390s allowed pay to ordinary citizens for attending the assembly. This provision irritated conservative moralists down to the end of the regime, but no doubt it contributed to the social stability of Athens during its final democratic years. One reason for the long and relative success of popular government in Athens was the city's considerable wealth, which was spread around. With her imperial and commercial receipts Athens was able to satisfy its population, an accomplishment no other democratic polis ever managed for long. The evolution of a distinct moral and political personality had its base in the wealth of political and economic imperialism. Even in Periclean Athens, with its image of disinterested, if not enthusiastic, citizenship, most Athenian citizens were, and had to be, concerned with the pay for citizen service their status promised. Oligarchs and aristocrats forever questioned where these benefits ranked in the average citizen's scale of values.

Over two centuries, then, not just the exercise of citizenship entered Greek life, but also an awareness of what it meant to be an Athenian citizen in terms of legal and monetary benefits and political privileges. No man could come of age and enter into the world of property, politics, and war without becoming conscious of who he was, what he must do, and what was coming to him. One must imagine the citizens of Athens like modern soldiers: each of them learned "the system" to survive. And if some were more knowledgeable than others, barracks lawyers, all had some competence in the exercise of personal privilege. Every Athenian citizen could look about and see how different he was from all the other kinds of persons in society: aliens, citizens of other Greek cities, *metics*, slaves, freedmen, each with his specific bag of burdens and privileges, each a bit different from his neighbor for some reason of birth or special treaty—in effect, personal history, which might, for example, include emancipation.[24]

The citizen may be seen more clearly if contrasted with others who made up the population of the polis, and here one thinks most specifically of Athens. *Metics*, slaves, and, of course, women each had a special place in society and possessed certain rights which empowered and limited them vis-à-vis the citizen. They all lacked what Aristotle called *timai*, or political status: the ability to vote, to serve on the juries, to serve in the most prestigious military formation, the cavalry, and to participate fully in the religious life of the community, linked as it was to the polis's political identity and its soil.

The *metic*, who might continue to be a citizen of his native city, in Athens was viewed as an immigrant who, after a relatively short period of residence, was subject to a special tax, the *metoikion*, which, like the medieval head tax, designated a special inferior legal and political status. Indeed, theoretically, in Aristotelian terms the *metic* may be seen as an anticitizen and not completely human, given the fact that he could not realize the potential in every man to exercise his rationality in political circumstances. However, *metics* could be and were highly educated and influential, like Aristotle, and they in fact owned property and were rich, like Cephalus to whose mansion Socrates is diverted at the beginning of the *Republic*. And if they could not help make the laws by which they were ruled, they could win honor fighting in hoplite formations to preserve those laws, in rare cases winning citizenship by special recognition.

In addition to their political incapacity, *metics* generally suffered a social one. Since they could not own land, which was the basis for a citizen respectability based upon agriculture cum military service, they were forced into banausic occupations. These mostly artisan and commercial activities, although recognized by some as of enormous importance for Athens's general prosperity and political success, were commonly regarded as spiritually demeaning, the work of slaves as well as *metics*, and as such unfit for free and fighting citizens. Yet, as the case of Cephalus suggests, rich and educated *metics* conversed and caroused with the best Athenians, thus contributing to a common civic culture and friendship.

To a limited degree this may also be said of slaves, for some were highly refined and educated and mingled socially with their free masters. Most slaves, however, did harsh and low-prestige labor such as farming, mining, and productive work in shops. Such slavery coexisted with the beginnings of Greek society, and if one is unsure precisely when the *metic* came into history, it can be stated with some certainty that slavery was part of Greek life from the beginning. It is there in Homer; it is one of the most fundamental assumptions of Greek thought about the inequalities and hierarchies in both nature and society. By the fifth century, and certainly by the time Aristotle wrote the *Politics*, slavery had become not only a "natural" institution in theory, but also an absolutely essential one in actuality.

Athens, Sparta, and all the other cities depended, each in its own way, upon slave labor acquired by conquest, purchase, or birth for much of the human power that produced food and goods. Given the origin of slaves, therefore, and the banausic nature of their daily work in the mines and fields, the question of their participation in politics did not arise. It was their work that allowed others to be free for the leisure and politics that constituted the best life of the citizen.

No easy characterization of Greek slavery is possible. Many performed the same tasks as free men. In Athens, most were privately owned, but even there some were the property of the polis, as were the Helots of Sparta, who were privileged to live in families and communities and, in times of war, were formed into special units and allowed to fight for what in effect was their fatherland. Although slavery may be qualified in so many ways, one fact may be asserted without qualification: no Greek slave participated in the organized politics of a polis. This limitation, or defect, was their basic defining characteristic.

The same may be said of women. They could not inherit or hold landed property in their own right and therefore were prevented from entering public life. For all the influence they might in fact exercise, they were excluded from the fundamental arena of Greek life, politics. If Plato, with an unusual generosity, allowed women to participate in the most exalted curricula specified in the *Republic*, and Sparta allowed them to train with the young men, Aristotle was more traditional. In his definition, the citizen had to be "a man who shares in the administration of justice and the holding of office." Moreover, the work of a woman resembled that of a slave, and, as Herodotus observed, women preceded slaves in doing the hard work of the household.

Also among those excluded from the acts of citizenship were male prostitutes. Pederasty was accepted in Greek life; indeed, it was seen as one of the bonds that knit a city together as it contributed to the spirit that fortified hoplite armies engaging each other in fierce hand-to-hand combat. Nevertheless, in Athens and other cities, prostitution was seen as incompatible with citizen status, for it made impossible the full exercise of individuality in the political, religious, and legal processes of the community. The person of the citizen was to be free of obligations that might force him to serve the interests, indeed, the passions, of another individual, not those of the polis.

A citizen who, therefore, surrendered his body, which in some way belonged to, was part of, the community, did such harm to the body politic that he could no longer be trusted as a full fellow citizen. The community was put at risk by the use of his body as a woman or a slave might use their bodies: as a source of pleasure for another human being, presumably wealthier, stronger, and more influential, whose demands had to be satisfied before those of the polis. He no longer possessed a free-standing individuality in political activities: voting in the assemblies, say, not to mention participation in the juries, which determined matters of justice, or the religious ceremonies, which might determine the success and survival of the polis itself. Also, dependence upon another weakened the oath that bound citizens to each other as citizens and to the community and their duties in it. Significantly, that oath had a military aspect. If pederasty was accepted as a rite of passage that made comrades of fighters in the line of battle, prostitution weakened, womanized, and degraded a man and bound him into commitments that might transcend those owed the public welfare and his comrades in the phalanx.[25]

Self-consciousness extended to qualities nonlegal and nonpolitical, but rather, cultural. Athens and many other Greek cities were port towns, residences for many foreigners who lived long periods away from home. Attic literature is filed with references, often disparaging, to these people, their speech, business habits, dress, religion—all aspects of their differentness. Although citizen, alien, and *metic* lived side by side and trafficked with each other daily, they rarely joined in fundamental acts of worship and politics. Eventually such group distinctiveness was institutionalized in the *politeuma* of Hellenistic cities; in the period of Athenian democracy, however, self-organization for group survival and success had not yet taken place.

The culture of citizenship status was also supposed to be for the citizen juror the basis for his decision, which is to suggest how complete and complicated the civic education of an Athenian was. It began in the home, military service, the temple, and on the playing field, and continued through life at the theater and on jury duty. In the course of time he grew familiar not only with the basic expectations and values of his society but also with those of his special class or group within the community. Apparently, in theory and fact, citizenship everywhere played a role in daily affairs.

We have just seen that in the course of the sixth and fifth centuries citizenship, conceived now in a legal and political sense, became an issue in Athenian

politics, the subject of legal and political manipulation and legislative reenact-
ment. Over those two hundred years the Athenian citizenry lost its simplicity
and homogeneity. No longer exclusively an agricultural community, Athens,
along with other Greek cities, was drawn into a mesh of unsettling international relationships—economic, political, and cultural. She found the expansionist Persian Empire at her doorstep, and not much farther away, also
extraordinarily different, Egypt and the other regions of the millennial Eastern civilizations. These contacts must be acknowledged as we examine
changes in values that accompanied the rise of Athens.

During those same years a moral transformation began that has not
yet been fully accomplished. Early Greece had its values set by warriors
whose priorities were clear: strength, aggressiveness, acquisitiveness, self-
centeredness, and self-enhancement. As society became more domesticated,
more civil, and as its basic structures and needs changed, it faced a big
problem: how to create a new man fit for the less violent, less rural life. As in
a similar social setting much later, the Italian city-state world, the problem
was never solved.

In Greece, as in medieval Italy, the tempestuous aristocratic personality was
needed by the new, changing state. Such a man had oratorical and military
skills that had not been mastered by the new bourgeois or democratic rulers;
in a word, he had authority and leadership. Given constant war or threat of
war, the Alcibiades type was too necessary to be destroyed. Middle-class or
less aristocratic government had some success in quelling violence, but ultimately it failed because it could not do without the aristocrats in time of
danger. It had to allow cultivation of their individualistic personalities and
those very habits of life based on arms that made them so useful. That it did
so down to the end of Greek freedom is attested by the pleas of fourth-
century orators. The reputation of the Greeks for moderation and the very
settled look of their marbled cities obscure the presence of illegal day-to-day
violence, or the threat of it, in their lives. Eventually in Greece, as later in
Italy, after a couple of hundred years of compromise in the form of mixed
government, into which the aristocrats with their individuality of values and
aggressive skills were never completely integrated, the military prince took
over again. In antiquity, he is named Philip, Alexander; in the Renaissance,
Lorenzo, Ludovico.[26]

As the center of life moved down from the fortified hills to the plain and
the coast, new definitions of the good man became possible, indeed, necessary. The new society was more complex. Besides flocks and arms, it knew

land, movable goods, and coined money as property. Settled life was accompanied by the growth of new social classes—husbandman, landowner, merchant, manufacturer—and by civil and social conflicts. This necessitated politicians to dissipate conflict, and also educators, playwrights, poets, and philosophers to create and disseminate a new ethic. *Agathos* (good) came to have a new constellation of meanings.

The quieter virtues are already apparent in the great dramatists of the early fifth century. If the new moral emphasis is not altogether clear in Aeschylus and Sophocles, it is in Euripides. For him the husbandman is the "true agathos," "for such men administer well both their cities and their own households." Their activity brings prosperity and demonstrates self-control and a concern for justice. One scholar calls this new usage "democratic" in that it gives value to lives engaged not in fighting, but in productive effort to the benefit of the family and the city. Athens's security is seen to depend not only upon the personal heroics of the few, but upon the group effort of the many citizens in the fleet. The tragedians saw with the clear vision granted their genius that new social realities demanded a new ethical balance.

Soundness of judgment and participation in politics are hallmarks of the new *arete*. By the sixth century, the good citizen (*agathos polites*) can be defined in terms of his contribution to the "advancement of the city" as well as in terms of his personal achievements. Civic performance now competes with lineage as the basis for honor. And tied to performance is a notion of moderation, since cooperative effort depends upon self-control, the limitation of one's personal desires and ambitions. In competitive sports, naval engagements, debates in the law courts and the *ecclesia* and other assemblies, one must serve harmoniously with his fellows. If he does, the polis will succeed; it fails if he does not. Civic success in this way has become the touchstone of excellence, that is, *arete*.

This is not to say that the old egocentric ethic disappeared suddenly and completely. It did not; indeed, it survived right through the ancient world. But after the sixth century, given the interdependency necessary in a more complicated society, an alternative ethic was possible and found its advocates. Since Plato and Aristotle were among those advocates (albeit as men of their time exhibiting the tensions in their own society), the new values were profoundly considered and taught. The period from the tragedians to Aristotle is roughly 150 years. During that time Athenians were called upon to stop the Persians, create an offshore empire, achieve commercial success over a large region, and wage war on land and sea throughout the central Mediterranean.

That they performed this variety of activities with relative success attests to the efficiency of the new ethic, its integration into the pattern of life choices available to Athenian citizens. The demands of Athenian experience necessitated service. At the same time, all the military and administrative jobs were obligations the fulfillment of which brought *arete*. Excellence was now defined in terms of successful public service, itself seen as the dynamic aspect of a life of justice and cooperation on the part of the citizen.

Citizenship, in other words, necessitated not just a new civil being, as created by Solon and his successor reformers, but a new moral man as well, one whose personality had to be changed if he was to fit into the new order. Hence the importance of education in this period of Greek history. Theater, athletics, family instruction, and patriotic rites all taught the harnessing of the passions of primitive self-interest. They aimed to bring the individual's interests into harmony with those of the community. Taken together, all these forms of education—and one must not forget the reading of Homer and other acknowledged literary-moral classics—constitute both an introduction into the community's view of successful civilized existence and a rite of passage. They made the youths aware of proper behavior, not only the formal commands of authority, but also the informal symbolic acts and formulas by which the community conducts its business.[27]

Thus education in a common moral tradition became the basis for successful citizenship. Since the community is small and dependent upon the willing, knowledgeable performance of an even smaller number of persons, it must allow only one pattern of behavior, which must be accepted by all members of the community. Conflict within is unthinkable in circumstances of near constant conflict without. Death or exile are the only responses to nonconformity, which equals treason, in a moral society in which harmony is the only possible condition—and in which, as Plato and Aristotle both agreed, the virtues are inseparable.

Throughout history citizenship has proved compatible with many forms of government and even with a variety of ethical systems. In ancient Greece, Athens was at the center of a spectrum, given its balance of idealistic values and self-interested rationalism praised by Pericles and revealed by Thucydides. If the rigid moral certitude of Sparta was at one end of the spectrum, the self-seeking individualism of Alcibiades was at the other. In his career we see citizenship out of control, disrespectful toward the laws and gods that established the norms of respectable behavior.

Having served Athens, Sparta, the Persians, and now again seeking Spartan acceptance and leadership, Alcibiades extols the true patriots' freedom from legal restraint. He acknowledges his love for Athens, "insofar as I once enjoyed the privileges of a citizen." Now, in attacking Athens, he attempts to regain her, to bring her back to proper ways. The true patriot, he claims, is one who "when unjustly exiled . . . in the warmth of his affection seeks to recover her without regard to the means."[28] Alcibiades' citizenship, then, is flexible, personal, immediate, self-centered, almost a contradiction in terms since it advances the self at the expense of any formally defined and functioning concept of the public weal. He has mocked his gods, traduced his fellows in birth, and yet calls himself true citizen out of some kind of arrogant, self-serving pride.

Although, in later history, Sparta and Athens have stood for different systems, their dissimilarity should not be overemphasized. Both were traditional communitarian states with constitutions and political institutions in which, to be sure, varying percentages of the population participated. Both had limited citizenship and allowed for actual political inequality on the basis of wealth, family prestige, experience, and so forth. Below the few citizens were majority populations composed of variously defined aliens, slaves, and women. Both states based their systems upon a quasi-mythical historical foundation, something of a sacred history. They involved religion in patriotic education and defined their culture as an ideal way of life, which created an ideal human being, the fully participating citizen aware of his traditions and current obligations. Both saw society as transcending the individual, imparting to the individual those human qualities and special characteristics that made him an Athenian or a Spartan. Although both cities (and every Greek city) paid attention to Panhellenic oracles and fames, overwhelmingly their focus and sense of obligation looked inward and backward.

Finally, in both communities citizenship was of central concern to the leadership class, which guarded the dignity of the privileges it conferred and the benefit those privileges brought to its own members. The ruling elites recognized that, to paraphrase Shakespeare in *Coriolanus*, citizenship was the city. Aristotle had a distinct idea of class. If earlier thinkers and reformers did not, they nevertheless acted on the assumption that the quality of a community depended on the qualities of its leaders and always attempted to control access to the leadership. In this way the history of the Greek city-state world reflects the politics of citizenship within each city-state.

Whether in Sparta, Athens, or another polis, citizenship was a privileged status. A citizen was surrounded by persons less fortunate in civil society than himself, foreigners and slaves, for example. To be a full citizen was, it has been said, to be a member of the right club. Athens's citizenry was a rather large club—there were perhaps 40,000–45,000 members in the late fifth century—but it was a club nevertheless, with membership lists, officers, rituals, rights, and responsibilities. It also had rules and early developed the means to teach them, not only schools for those of a certain class, and the family for all, but also the temple, law courts, theaters, and the streets with their calendar of politico-religious festivals. The entire cultural experience was political education. And politics was itself central to the daily social life of the polis, functioning as its play, its ceremony, and, in a word, its amusement. Through the social aspects of politics the individual was linked to his neighborhood, and through it to the larger community. Every civic institution taught a pattern of values that was viewed as ancient, immutable, and of divine origin. No distinction can be made between ethical, political, and religious values. One must think of Greek political education in terms of civic morality or civic religion. The individual, the family, and the community were closely related, and if there was one of these which gave meaning to the others, it was the community. That, however, was at some level of abstraction. The family was always so near and helpful, so obvious a support to the individual. Hence the need for, and power of, civic religion, which served to counterbalance those pressures on the individual to place the needs of family first.

Every aspect of a young man's life reinforced an identification with the community. Military service according to wealth in the cavalry or hoplites, or naval service in the triremes for the poorer citizens, constituted instruction in valor and brotherhood. The development of athletic skills was also viewed as enhancing the individual's ability to serve the community. At the level of excellence, the athlete would bring honor to his city at the Panhellenic games; competent, he would fight well on the battlefield.

This reminds us that in the education of an Athenian citizen youth, pederasty also played a role; it possessed none of the opprobrium it has had through so much of later history. It brought a boy into association with older youths, and, as we have seen, for many it was a rite of passage into the military world of the young hoplites, whose lives depended upon each other's concern and love. Also, while initiating the young man into homosexual experience, the practice warned him off softness (*kinaidoi*), that decline into a life of ease, luxury, self-indulgence, and sexual exploitation that would imperil his career both as a citizen soldier and political activist. Entrance into adult civic life required an Athenian to pass a scrutiny which examined not only his physical condition, but also his potential manliness, steadiness, and prudence—his moral qualities—for these were all required in the performance of a citizen's role. One could not be sent into battle or allowed to do verbal battle in the assemblies and law courts if he could not be trusted, if he was not seen to be educated into the basic value system of a martial and political society.[29]

Religious festivals took up many weeks of the year. Not only did they include prayers for the welfare of the Athenian people, but they were also occasions for the material betterment of the masses. On the great feast days the meat of the animals sacrificed was distributed among the poor in something of a celebration that united all citizens. Piety and civic pride were closely linked, which meant reinforced effect from one's participation in the more important rites. As today in confessional societies, religious acts initiated and sometimes accompanied important matters of state.

The theater, too, constituted part of a civic education. Aristophanes, especially, used his plays to clarify public issues, criticize public officials, and present his view on current matters such as citizenship. In *The Frogs* he pleas for the rights of slaves who have fought in the fleet for Athens, and his chorus demands "equal rights for all citizens." Earlier, Euripides had questioned the meaning of Athenian identity in his *Ion*.

Apparently the law courts and assemblies also provided theater and instruction in public life. Citizens came here as jurors and participants in public debates. By the end of the fifth century a body of semiprofessional politicians and speech writers had appeared whose speechmaking skill brought political influence as well as, in the case of the rhetorically skilled writers, fame and large fees. The average Athenian citizen learned his politics not only in attendance upon these orators and in voting, but also from the substance of the cases and issues argued. As a juror, one heard appeals based on the citizenly conduct of the defendant, his military career, his record of administrative service. What kind of man he was, as demonstrated by his public life, could count more than the facts of the case or the law itself. Finally, citizenship law touched such matters as landownership and inheritance, matters of general interest. In the courts and assemblies citizens were developed through the very act of sitting and listening to clever men advance arguments. Being in such an assemblage, they learned procedures and came to appreciate their role and value in the system.

Even an illiterate person might come to know the laws by heart, and certainly the majority of Athenians were not illiterate. A relatively high level of literary sophistication prevailed, at least among the urban citizens. There was also a popular fascination with ideas, competing theories, meanings of difficult concepts. This interest in, quite literally, the marketplace of ideas increased along with the growing importance of the agora in Athenian life. It was not only the principal market place but also a center for the exchange of gossip, tips, and political advice, as well as abstract philosophical thought. Socrates and other teachers congregated there to pick up students or to pick on an opponent's ideas. His activity and that of the Sophists in the second half of the fifth century must be seen against the backdrop of great and unprecedented events that demanded the creation of new skills and the maintenance of old attitudes in the Athenian population.[30]

This was the time of Athens's hegemony over the islands, of her deepening involvement in trade, and therefore confrontation with wealth, and the time, too, of a sequence of political and military crises that led eventually to defeat in the Peloponnesian War. Increasingly, the concern of the Sophists was to make the citizen something of a statesman. Their purpose was to take men whose education had hitherto been fundamentally political and give them more analytical and practical skills with which to face the severe demands of governmental service and the creation of public policy.

The old education had been focused on moral discipline and development of character. It was unscientific, even antirational; essentially it was a gentleman's education with emphasis on civility, deportment, and the body, the kind of training given to the sons of an aristocratic ruling class into the twentieth century. To call it political is to think in terms of campus government, student or faculty, or a job in the courthouse of a small southern or New England town, as constituting a political education. One learns who is who, how to maneuver programs to completion, what constituencies exist and how they must be handled, how to get things done. A sense of history is part of such an education and is never without moral judgment on heroes and villains in the past.

To this conservative, practical education the Sophists opposed new programs, new attitudes, and a sense of mission that one frequently finds in educators who are sure they have found the right way. They did not espouse a program of education linked to doctrinaire sympathy for Athens's masses or for the democracy Athens had become by that time. Sophist techniques were available to anyone clever enough to perceive their value and wealthy enough to afford them. This means that most students of the Sophists continued to come from the blood and commercial elites. Such youths and their fathers saw the value in being up-to-date, especially when that currency might ensure the conservation of a family's social status and political power.

A great scholar has defined the great "social problem" of Greek education as "how to repress individualism and develop the character of every citizen on one communal model."[31] The Sophists' solution to this problem was to cultivate and emphasize the personal achievements of the individual as he sought to advance himself and his family in wealth and power. The Sophists, themselves mostly of middle-class origin, taught attitudes and skills some-what incompatible with the old self-sacrificing ethic. Their skills were rational analysis and effective oratory, which they offered at a time when there was little or no sophisticated, advanced teaching. They taught to win in politics and law without the traditional aristocratic concern for morality and truth. However, and this qualification is real and important, their principal arena continued to be the public interest. If they won, it was to be a victory over issues and personalities in the public sphere. A commitment to the com-munity continued, if attenuated, and if diluted by concern with personal performance, display, victory, esteem in the eyes of an audience. The public man produced by the new education continued in public service, even as that service became professionalized. Pressure for professionalization arose in part out of the needs of the polis, in part out of the inner histories of the academic disciplines themselves. By the fourth century Plato, Aristotle, Demosthenes, and Isocrates had all lived and written. To be effective, one had to master their works, especially in the field of politics and law, in which a variety of linguistic skills was needed.

As a result of these developments, citizenship now became more fractured and complex, in the sense of the body of citizens practicing a common virtue. Earlier there had been rich citizens and poor citizens, but apart from military or naval responsibility, which was based on a capacity to serve, rich and poor were interchangeable in the positions the polis had to fill. More, rather than fewer, careers were open to persons of little education and talent. By the fourth century things had changed. Political leadership demanded oratorical skills that could only be bought. The public recognized the existence of a governing elite, which, although dependent certainly upon a democratic base, had become skilled in creating and manipulating its popular support. It is not surprising to see that a romantic rhetorization of the democratic ideal took place simultaneously with the split within the citizen body, now on the basis of literacy and leadership as well as class. The speech makers of the fourth century, even as Macedon was growing to the north, rhapsodized a democracy that was now in reality split socially and was increasingly susceptible to demagoguery by effective members of a political elite.

Perhaps this idealization of citizenship is of a piece with the new restrictive Periclean definition of citizenship and other legislation that attempted to fight immigration and arrogation of citizen status by outsiders. It has been suggested that by the end, if not the middle, of the fifth century Athenians had such a high opinion of their society and its manifold accomplishments that they grew increasingly antagonistic toward those who would share such glory. With an empire, honors and material rewards abounded; were these to be too liberally granted away to those who had not participated in Athens's rise, and who might not know the full range of obligations assumed by an Athenian citizen? If citizenship was a form of contract, could newcomers be counted upon to commit themselves to the polis as would the native-born?[32] And would they understand the complexity of Athens with its intricate civic texture of interwoven political institutions, religious festivals, theatrical offerings, and military responsibilities? Aristotle and Plato were to worry about the proper size of the perfect polis; no doubt such worries circulated much earlier. Hippodamus and other town planners were active long before the social philosophers of the fourth century. What one finds, then, is a certain closing of ranks, especially among those classes who had everything to fear from a growth of public power.

THE PHILOSOPHERS

Such is the setting for the two great ancient political philosophers, Plato and Aristotle. They came from different backgrounds: Plato from the landed aristocracy, Aristotle from the newly important professional and middle class. But both subscribed to the code of traditional values, which they saw as being threatened and weakened in their day, the period of Athens's suffering and failure during and after the Peloponnesian War and the accompanying rise of popular power. Their views of citizenship in part reflect a desire to preserve the best qualities of traditional life, that is, institutions and social attitudes based upon a political consciousness that was aware of the conflicting demands of private and public life and recognized a call to serve the public good. Theirs is a rhetoric of concern for the preservation of the sense of community, which was always in danger, and was especially so during the wartime crisis in which many sought to protect themselves and gain personally during the failures leading to Athens's defeat.

Under such circumstances, Plato's complicated attitude toward Sparta is understandable. He may have established the Academy out of a desire to educate the best man for city service. He had envisioned a public career, which vulgar elements now frustrated in his native Athens. Sparta offered the attractiveness of order and stability achieved through carefully controlled education. Plato did not accept the full brutalizing program that produced the citizen fit only for war, but he did appreciate the completeness and effectiveness of the limited curriculum. The Spartan's willingness to die for his country, revere and support its laws, and subordinate himself to its history were acceptable to Plato. What he rejected was the indifference to peace as well as the dedication to violence that constituted the definition of political virtue in the Lacedaemonian community.[33]

In the *Laws*, Plato designs his ideal community for a minimum of social friction. This means that land, which he assumes will be the economic base for a citizen's support, must be distributed fairly. A moderate life for each man will not provoke disruptive enmities. He wants no more than 5,040 citizen households to provide self-sufficiency for the new community. Under these conditions, each man must befriend his fellow citizens and trust them. If a rough equality of landed wealth will help to produce social harmony, so will cultural uniformity. He would prefer Cretans and, from elsewhere, Peloponnesians, for these meet his cultural requirement for a "community of race and language and laws, and in common temples and rites of worship." A stake in property and a stake in culture will underlie the citizens' commitment. Thus the legislator may easily persuade them to virtue. A culturally homogeneous, agrarian citizenry of moderate comfort clearly is his ideal.

In this society membership in a hearth, not actual possession of land, confers citizenship. Plato apparently was more interested in social origins than in economic conditions. Proper "descent from citizen parents," probably from both parents, is all important. In this demand he reflected not only recent Athenian experience, but also common practice throughout the city-state world. Aristotle's general theory on political development, based upon his analysis of hundreds of constitutions, confirms this.

Birth formally conferred citizenship, a potentiality. Proper education and activity made a Platonic citizen, and it is in his educational theory that Plato makes his Cretan city an innovative state. Conventionally, education was a family affair. Plato took it out of the family's hands and made it, as in Sparta, a public activity. Its function is "that training in virtue from childhood which makes a man eager to become the perfect citizen, knowing both how to rule justly and how to obey." No subject escaped his evaluation: music, dance, athletics were all examined with an eye to moral benefit. He feared overexcitement of the passions and the exacerbation of individualism. Group effort in the chorus and athletics was good, for it involved the youth in communal activities, which constitute a training of the will. The self-discipline learned on the playing field or stage was to be useful in public life, as the citizen learned to restrain his ego and regulate his life to harmonize with the needs and desire of his fellow citizens.

Presiding over the community's educational system was a mature citizen, preferably the father of both boys and girls. Plato describes him as the "greatest" officer of the state, since it is he who will produce the adult males upon whose wisdom and character the continuation of civilization depends. This minister of education ranks with the philosopher king as one of Plato's great creations. Unfortunately, he has not received the attention he deserves, perhaps because only Sparta, so ill-regarded by many intellectuals, had such a system of public education, and perhaps also because he was to preside over a curriculum that was distinctly old-fashioned in its emphasis on athletics and literature for all but the wisest few.

In training the virtuous citizen Plato recognized and theorized the value of public life itself: games, spectacles, religion, and theater. Basically religious, these institutions serve to bring man close to his gods and to teach him their ways—for example, in principles of rhythm and harmony. He saw the relationship between the nature of childrens' games and their eventual political attitudes. Only if games are allowed to remain traditional will the children develop a proper conservative response to change. To maintain the dignity of games as a bulwark of the past, he encouraged the "consecration of every sort of dance or melody." Public festivals are to be carefully ordered for maximum effect. Only the positive is to be emphasized, and the poets shall be constrained to speak only of the lawful, just, beautiful, or good. Plato sees every occasion as an opportunity for moral education. Even, or especially, the funeral service is to be used for this purpose. Also striking is his conscious subordination of private sentiment to the community's needs and purposes. An individual becomes less and less an individual, in Plato's social and educational theory, as more and more of him is tuned to respond to society's calls. Even after his death the good man serves the polis: his praises are to be sung in a publicly financed eulogy whose obvious intent is the inspiration of the next generation.[34]

In all this there is nothing radical about Plato's view of citizenship; only his sharp ideas on education break with the past. Indeed, what is noteworthy about Plato's continued emphasis on community and a small scale to life is that it came after the Athenian polis had passed through its imperial phase, during which old ties began to fail and commitments weaken, bonds among men and to the historic community. Perhaps it was because he perceived these developments as pernicious that Plato wrote as he did.

Although Aristotle was not of Plato's high aristocratic background, he too came from among the leading men of Greek society. His father was a court physician, and Aristotle received the best possible provincial education before studying in Athens with Plato. He stayed in the Academy for almost twenty years; this is the period (367–347) when Athens flourished as the cultural as well as commercial center of the Greek world, and when Plato in his old age was inscribing his negative comments on the disordered democracy Athens then was. On Plato's death Aristotle moved to Assus in Asia Minor, where, with other disgruntled pupils of Plato, and with the help of the local tyrant, he established a school. In a certain sense, as an exile from the cultural capital, Aristotle may be seen as one more victim of the unstable Greek city-state world. In his case a combination of civil and academic politics affected his life. However, if the affairs of one political entity, Athens, made him move, the existence of another, Macedonia, made possible his new scholarly career, which is to say that Aristotle never extricated himself from the complexity of Greek political arrangements. Indeed, Aristotle may have been an active and willing participant in the high-level politics of the eastern Mediterranean involving Macedonia, Athens, the states of Asia Minor, and Persia. His closeness to Philip and Alexander may have made him something of an adviser, if not agent, of the Macedonian royal house, and he may have seen its growing control over foreign affairs, war, and peace, as necessary if the internal violence now evermore characteristic of Greek civic life was to be controlled.[35]

Like Plato, Aristotle was a moralist who placed proper education at the center of his political system. We think of him as a cool empiricist; he was, but in many ways he wrote like a conservative social theorist, wary of any innovations. In his concern to preserve right morals, there is no aspect of life he does not examine and prescribe for; in Book 7 of the *Politics*, he theorizes on both the nature of physical exercise and the childbearing period in a woman's life, in which she "should render service to the city by bringing children into the world." Private life was not to be immune from scrutiny and regulation, so closely intermixed were the personal and the public, the religious and the secular. The woman caught in adultery merits the "stigma of infamy," the strongest moral condemnation, for she has transgressed law based upon deep religious beliefs.

Education is all important for Aristotle because it creates good citizens. Citizens of a democracy must be especially good, since they all share in governing and implement and continue to shape the constitution, which is the formal cause of their felicity. They must be trained to perform public acts, to learn both to obey and to govern. Aristotle is first concerned with proper physical education, but even before the age of five, moral education is to begin. He cares about the tales children will hear and their effect upon future values. Moral trainers must also monitor leisure time lest the child learn vulgar language and habits.

Censorship is a fundamental part of Aristotle's system, which may turn out a democratic citizen or an oligarchic citizen depending on the total impact of the constitution. What he cares about in either case is giving the young citizen a sense of "belonging to the community," of "being a part of the community." Hence Sparta wins high praise for the careful attention it gives the young. He clearly approves a constitution in which the community, and not the family or some other private agency, organizes education. Since a community has a common end or purpose, some public, rather than private, institution must assume responsibility for directing all citizens to recognizing and serving that purpose. Within this framework, Aristotle discusses music, athletics, social skills. In every case his primary interest is the moral dimension of the curriculum and pedagogic technique: will these add to the student's usefulness to the polity?

Yet Aristotle has some doubts about Spartan education. For the philosopher who regards the contemplative life as the highest form of human existence, Spartan education could hardly be acceptable in its entirety. It turned out "children resembling beasts," not educated citizens who would have used their privileged status to become wise and virtuous in the service of the polis.[36] For Aristotle, to be virtuous is to be engaged in intellectual, humane, and socially beneficent pursuits, not war. He favors careful civic control of education, but in the final analysis it is to the magnanimous gentlemen trained in the private as well as the public world that Aristotle looks for service and leadership.[37]

Reading Aristotle this way, and remembering Plato's similar approach, one wonders about the Greek reputation for individualism. What is striking in the two greatest thinkers of Greek civilization is a massive commitment to conformity. Two major educational traditions flourished, the philosophical education of Plato and Aristotle and the oratory of Isocrates. Their curricula may have differed, but both had a common goal: the creation of the citizen who would receive, reflect, and transmit the moral and political values of past generations. Book 8 of the *Politics* is Aristotle's contribution to the theory of civic education. It follows and is meant to be related to his discussion of citizenship in Book 7.

So important is citizenship in his analysis of Greek constitutionalism that Aristotle devotes an entire book of the *Politics* to its theory, noting that "the nature of citizenship, like that of the state, is a question which is often disputed." He rejects definitions based on residence, legal capacity, or age, but rather emphasizes functions: the citizen is one who governs, "a man who shares in the administration of justice and the holding of office." What governing may entail will vary from city to city according to the demands of specific constitutions, but the citizen par excellence is the citizen of a democracy, since that form of government depends upon the political activity of many. Not origin but action is what makes a man a citizen, at least in a philosophical, analytical sense.

This is not to say that democracy alone produces citizens. Oligarchies produce citizens whose activities will be suitable for life in an oligarchic polis. Thus Aristotle allows for variety within his basic definition and for change— generation and corruption—and keeps his politics in harmony with his entire system. What counts everywhere in politics is activity; the specific nature of this activity gives each polis its peculiar defining constitution. Aristotle makes purpose or end a synonym for constitution in that an activity is maintained for a formal purpose or cause. Aristotle's approach here is consistent with his usual functional analysis of all phenomena. This emphasis by Aristotle (and Plato) on action has given "citizen" its distinctiveness in the Western political vocabulary. Active participation in the political process, action that is assumed to have effect upon conditions or policies, distinguishes the citizen's life from that of the subject.

One question forced upon Aristotle by the complexity of his ethics concerns the relationship of the good man to the good citizen. His concern for function and his usual sensitivity to empirical reality—in this case, the great variety in the political world—leads to a flexible definition of the good citizen. Indeed, in Book 3 he never even attempts to define the good man, as if to emphasize the social nature of the individual human being. His focus rather is on the good citizen, whose activities only serve the needs of his city, as dictated by its constitution to be good. And his emphasis is upon prudence as the virtue, "the only form of goodness," that the ruler, that is, the citizen in action in the ideal state, must have.

To this point in his argument, Aristotle has presupposed a society of homogeneous free men who have been educated in a set of specific values as well as skills, and who, as a result of that training, acknowledge an obligation to serve the community in juries and as members of the assemblies. But then the realities of Athenian class distinction intervene to pose the question: "Must mechanics be also included in the ranks of citizens?" Again the perceived realities must be classified in his biological approach, and again he must make a distinction that will "save the phenomena," as ancient and medieval natural philosophers would say. He looks around, sees that in effect a citizenship tier exists in the Greek world, and develops a theory of hierarchy. In some final sense only the wise and prudent may serve in the policy-making office of the state. But in the judicial offices, and presumably lesser administrative positions, even the free mechanics may participate. They are citizens in those states, whose constitutions allow for their participation, recognizing that in return for their material contributions to the polis, they must be allowed some role in government. After all, a mechanic is not a laborer, he is an artisan, a craftsman, who may have a large material stake in society. Presumably, his sagacity, effective in amassing property, will be put to good use for the community.

In general, however, if Aristotle's sentiment is distinguished from his analysis, the mechanic is to be excluded from the ranks of citizens. His constant handling of material things deliberalizes him, makes him a slave to property and self-interest. Also, it keeps him constantly in the world of commercial affairs, allowing no time for the pursuit of that leisure which, in Aristotle, is positively viewed as time to be spent thinking about higher matters: ideals, improvement, abstractions.

Because mechanics, to say nothing of laborers and slaves, will rarely have the interest or time to cultivate their minds, Aristotle prefers to exclude them from citizenship, although they are productive, because his citizens must be presumed to have, and indeed, must have, a trained intelligence. Unlike modern citizens, whose principal activity is casual participation in an election or on an occasional jury, Aristotle's citizen is a constant actual performer of civic duties. He votes on laws and judicial decisions and serves in executive capacities on a rotating or elective basis. For Aristotle, for all his commitment to a biological model, society (class) is static; one is what one is: mechanic, slave, landowner, merchant. He does not conceive of citizenship as itself an educational device, a training ground for responsible men and women who may move from one occupation and social status to another. Citizenship is exercise of status after one has passed certain obstacles: proof of birth as a constitution might demand, registration and recognition, and an education emphasizing traditional behavior.

Finally, Aristotle conceived of citizenship as a dynamic institution enmeshed in the complete system of interrelationships that constituted public life. He recognized that states varied in their citizenship requirements in relation to their real needs, extending the privilege when in need of manpower, for example, or restricting it when the population proved adequate to meet its needs. As he studied many city constitutions, he saw differences everywhere, which he accepted and subsumed under the distinctions his mind so easily devised. Moreover, his knowledge of history, of what this or that Greek city had done under different circumstances, added to the data provided by the formal constitutions. He knew and categorized not only what might legally be done, but also what had been done by Thebes, Sparta, Athens. His description, for example, of how the requirements for citizenship can expand or contract roughly follows Athenian practice in the fifth century.

Aristotle's interest in the citizen and citizenship is complex. To the institution his approach is analytical; it is there, part of Greek life, enough to classify, demonstrate function, and indicate its ethical implications. This Aristotle is no radical like Rousseau proclaiming the rights of man and citizen. But in his consideration of the individual, there is another Aristotle who is interested in more than the status and function of that constitutional element termed citizen. This Aristotle is the moralist in search of the best being, who wonders what education and actions will bring the human being to his highest accomplishments and dignity. The polis exists for the sake of "worthy and beautiful actions." Within it the citizen who governs well when called and submits to law when obliged reaches his full human potential.[38]

This is not to say that Aristotle disagreed with Plato on the issue of the best life. Although he concludes in the *Politics* that the active life is best, there he writes with an eye to practicality. In the *Ethics*, writing unambiguously, absolutely, he extols "the activity of the intellect . . . as the perfect happiness for man." Man should strive for the utmost, and "so far as in us lies, to put on immortality, and to do all that we can to live in conformity with the highest that is in us . . . the best and most pleasant life is the life of the intellect, since the intellect is in the fullest sense the man."[39]

Part of what makes citizenship a historic Western phenomenon is its literary formulation and critical examination by Plato and Aristotle, the two founders of political theory. Together they gave the institution a core meaning and an aura or network of associations which have lasted through the centuries, or which, at least, have meant the same thing to thinkers in those generations, who have looked to one or another of these two authorities for guidance. Cicero, St. Thomas, Montesquieu, and Rousseau all found in the original Greek analyses something ideal and valuable for their own time. Although Plato and Aristotle disagreed on some matters, on citizenship their views basically coincide. They see the community as primary, as in many ways the creator of the individual human personality, and hence the legitimate object of the individual's care. Because, in Plato's thought, society is at heart religious, the citizen is to be educated in traditional religion, and to an almost holy obligation to protect its values. For Aristotle, however, who, strikingly, ignores religion, the obligation to work at political life for the benefit of the individual and his neighbors derives also from the very definition of the human being as a social animal. Man works out the meaning of his existence by functioning in the community as his legal condition permits. In this sense the citizen is the highest form of political being—at least in a democracy.[10]

Much of this classic Greek view was received by the Romans, especially by Cicero, and accepted and modified by them. They could do this easily because, if unique in its imperial success and generous citizenship policy, in most other ways Rome was like every other little community which traced its history back to hazy mythical origins through the heroic sacrifices of many generations. That the first Romans who came into contact with Greek reality and the Greek theoretical analysis of politics were citizens, not subjects, is important. They soon saw the usefulness of Greek political philosophy, the applicability of its concepts and vocabulary, to their own experience. Citizenship as a legal and political institution was already under full development in Rome. The Romans perpetuated the discussion of duties and privileges, now in the Latin language, through which the institution came to play its major role in the West.

In defining and meeting political and constitutional problems that have proved to be perennial, and in providing many of the usable answers for them, Greece, especially Athens, greatly influenced Western politics. More precisely, it provided the model for working, participatory democracy in

Athens, and in Aristotle and others, the vocabulary and conceptual expectations of citizenship. In terms of historical influence, what matters is not the incompleteness and shabbiness of Greek democracy and citizenship, but rather the image that went down the centuries, the image of an organic society reasonably successful in distributing power and property to its people, while allowing some means of glory to its more able and adventurous citizens. To at least some later peoples, including the Romans, Greece also left the vision of the good religious community based on active participation by the best men. The Greeks theorized society as manmade, if God-protected, and open to change produced by men thinking and politicking under law. That they left this dream in persuasive literary form, in books that entered the ancient literary canon, is significant. Thucydides, Plato, Aristotle, Zeno, Demosthenes, Xenophon, Isocrates entered the schools. A century before Cicero and Caesar, Romans began to attend those schools, in Athens and Rhodes, for example, and to bring their teachers home. Rome, then, took the Greek vision from books and from living apologists and integrated it with her own history and morality to that moment—the turn of the third and second centuries B.C.

What do we emphasize in evaluating this Greek civic experience? The narrowness of the system, its restrictions on citizenship, the inequality implicit in a hierarchy of citizenships, the fact that the numerical majority in any polis were excluded from "the right to rule and be ruled," as Aristotle put it? Or shall we accentuate the positive, noting how unusual many Greek cities in the contemporary Mediterranean world were in allowing a significant and ever growing number of persons citizenship privileges, and in developing an education and a politics that saw responsible participation as a good thing, and noting too that the principal philosophers of the period approvingly developed theories of citizenship that were to be influential through history—if not always in the service of a modern, liberal position. As a recent, most distinguished historian of the period puts it, "Binding decisions reached by discussion and argument and ultimately by voting was a Greek invention."[41] I agree with this basically positive evaluation of the Greek political experience, which emphasizes the incorporation of all social classes into the political class, at least in Athens, and, along with that of other authorities, credits the average Athenian with political awareness, if not savvy. He is aware naturally of all the abuses of the system, sees the importance of the "aristocratic" community in preserving identity, indeed civic life, yet argues for the validity of the total citizenship experience both in the lives of the ancients and in the tradition leading to our present democracy.

HELLENISTIC CITIZENSHIP

In the age after Macedonia's brief ascendancy Alexandria, Antioch, and Corinth became large international cities, many of whose residents were foreign merchants who lived for years away from home. Nor were they the only kinds of centers to attract aliens and travelers. Intellectual capitals like Athens and Rhodes and cult centers like Ephesus drew students, scholars, devotees. A new kind of large-scale international life developed alongside traditional local life. Political institutions, religious beliefs, and philosophical systems now extended their range, competed with and affected each other as never before. First a serviceable Greek commercial language and then a common Mediterranean civilization based on a classical literary curriculum in the ancient Greek tongue held this world together. Whatever cultural unity there was in the ancient world before the triumph of Rome and Christianity came from this cultural ideal, *Humanitas*. What became a formal curriculum in Alexandria in the third century B.C. was eventually still taught in Cologne and London in the third century A.D.

Part of that education, what has been called "the Religion of Culture" of the Hellenistic age, extolled traditional virtues and values as it taught them in a long and technical course of studies, as well as in homey learning situations on the family estate. Typically, part of the curriculum was some kind of civic and military training, the *ephebia*, which came in a youth's mid-to-late teens. During this training, which might be compared with that of the "class" of a modern European conscript army, youths lived and worked together, creating a brotherly camaraderie as well as muscle. We know most about the Athenian *ephebia*, but the institution existed everywhere, even in the eastern areas controlled by the Seleucids. There, perhaps, it was especially valuable in a region new to Greek civic love, for it functioned "as a kind of civic novitiate, a system of moral training in preparation for the full exercise of the rights and duties of citizenship."

The Athenian *ephebia* was, in fact, something of a religious experience. It began with a "pilgrimage to the principal sanctuaries of the city"[42] and demanded of the young warrior-citizen an oath of obedience and total commitment that a Jesuit would find familiar. With the decline of Athens, the integrity of the institution as a common school for citizenship that embraced men of all classes eventually weakened. The *ephebia* became an aristocratic sporting club in which young men played a constructive civic role, for when they were men, the young aristocrats were those who served as ambassadors, curials, generals, and administrators.

It must have satisfied some set of useful purposes, for the institution survives into the records of Constantine's generation. For all the clubby qualities it developed, the *ephebia* perpetuated a way of life which has always included a notion—to some, a repellent notion—of noblesse oblige, of responsibility, care, and commitment. Taken together with the gymnasium, where the same young man simultaneously studied the combination of athletic and academic subjects that made him a Greek, it functioned as the central inspirational device of the late polis.

Hellenistic curricula also conserved and perpetuated the past. The cutting edge of contemporary science was not taught, but rather the great recognized masters of the humanistic tradition: Homer, Hesiod, Pindar, Sophocles and Aeschylus, Aristophanes and Menander, Herodotus, Thucydides, and other historians. Once the stories and other rudimentary aspects of these works were mastered, higher teaching emphasized their morality. Stoic and other teacher-critics were interested in the lessons to be drawn from great literature: who were the heroes of old and what were their great qualities? Such were the questions the grammarians put to the great authors. To be sure, the writers of letters and speeches so constantly decked out their products with the right literary references that we are conscious of a decorative, as opposed to moral, intention. Nevertheless, they chose their allusions with care, understood what they cited, and, therefore, must be credited by us with some real interest in seeing literature influence life.

Reinforcing intellectual commitments were certain classic Greek institutions, especially urban life itself, which early was conceptualized. Its theoreticians saw the relationship between the physical environment and the essential functions of a city, claiming that no place could be named a city without an agora, a gymnasium, a theater, a temple, a government building, and "water flowing down to a fountain." So wrote Pausanius, the geographer, in the second century A.D.[43] But much earlier social philosophers had seen the interconnection between, say, a fountain and the development of warm neighborly relations that flourished in the sight and sound of its flowing waters, or between the agora surrounded by municipal offices and participatory public life.

This is to emphasize that the imposition of monarchical government during the Hellenistic period did not wipe out the local political life, which for hundreds of years had been seen by Greeks as the defining characteristic of their civilization, making them such different beings from Persians and other Orientals. Alexander and his successors used the city as an instrument both of colonization and of local administration. Where they founded cities they either created institutions of local government familiar to them from Greece or tolerated such institutions where they found them in place. Like Renaissance princes, Hellenistic rulers manipulated local assemblies and ruling elites and even allowed local administrations to continue in their hands—all within the limits provided by their captains. They did this because they had to. They were without the technology of effective control, and, hoping for cooperation and civil peace, they recognized the emotional basis to social order, one dependent on traditional religion, athletics, theater, ceremony of every kind. They also saw value in local political traditions which, throughout the Greek world especially, looked back to some history of self-rule. So under the Hellenistic monarchies local political life largely survived, attentive to immediate issues and dominated by local families, based on inherited values, and perpetuated through familiar institutions. Despite the new overarching monarchical institution, the actuality of polis life may be seen as a common feature of Hellenistic civilization and a live inheritance from the earlier period of the independent city-states.

Even before Rome came to dominate this world, again leaving basic structures of society and government intact in order to maximize their return, two large-scale historical developments began that were to change traditional community life. Each man had been, in the days of classic Greece, inextricably bound to the polis. Now the individual—citizen, noncitizen, and slave—was pulled in new directions: up toward membership in a great society, a large state or city, a league, an international trading or intellectual community; and in the other direction, down toward membership in some tiny cult or club, religious, ethnic, or both, in which his identity was known and appreciated by a few associates or brethren. Both developments had implications for citizenship, as they affected the bonds of allegiance that held the polis together.

Monarchy was one institution through which an attempt was made during the Hellenistic period to integrate city-states and their citizens into some larger purpose and service; it eventually became the successful model for the organization of the West for more than two thousand years. The other model tried in this period, the one that failed, was that of the league or confederation. These were formed for defense or offense; one was created under pressure from Philip of Macedon to reach a wide-ranging peace. They never caught on because the individual city-states were never willing to surrender any significant portion of their self-rule to a central organ of the leagues. Yet several things must be said of Hellenistic federalism: if the leagues failed to produce any lasting, effective, institutional model, they nevertheless provided the independent polis with several generations of continued existence; they also contributed to the weakening of the citizen's commitment to his native place.

For example, in Greece the growth of city leagues allowed the dilution of the merchant's allegiance to his native city, since it was the league that guaranteed his status. Then, in the course of the fourth and later centuries, *isopolity* developed as a practice whereby the citizen rights of one community were given in bloc to those of another. Cities exchanged *isopoliteia* and included it in treaties of alliance. Such rights in another city were in potential until one moved there but were important to one who did in fact migrate. They included the right to own land, marry, and to trade without payment of duties, just the sort of advantages that helped in a competitive economic world and that might compel the transfer of affection from one's own city to another. Similar was the institution of *proxeny*, which was both a title and honor, and a body of privileges. *Proxenoi* were citizens who represented another city in their own hometown. In return for this service they were regarded as diplomatic representatives at home and were granted immunity from seizure as well as the right to own land in the city they served. If this was a way for cities to make alliances surer through the creation of networks of personal and legal relationships, it was also a way for individuals to benefit as they sought their own best interests. Finally, cities granted honorary citizenship, which the recipient might easily translate into legal or economic advantage. By the first century B.C., throughout the Mediterranean, it was not unusual for a man to have collected several citizenships, a practice continued into the Roman imperial period. We know this dramatically from the story of St. Paul.

In this international world of commercial cities, however, it was not only the businessman who sought success moving from place to place, putting old allegiances behind him. There is something very modern in the picture of intellectuals, poets, teachers, orators, and others whose skills were widely in demand leaving home to seek financial reward and the dignity of honorary citizenship abroad. The fact that Attic Greek was the common language of culture and government facilitated their pursuit of career. In this widespread society of travelers, resident agents, exiles, professors, soldiers, and missionaries, the bonds of society could easily become less spiritual, and the material the more persuasive, as men sought the means to survive and prosper, always with the best possible immediate protection.

In all of this, the tutelary gods seem to have been interchangeable, especially for those of the educated upper classes, who guided their lives by one of the new ethical philosophies. Of these Stoicism eventually became the most popular, especially in Rome. But even before Panaetius may have made his great impact upon Roman aristocratic circles, Stoicism appealed to those for some reason alienated from native god and community. It offered a physical explanation of the universe, a philosophy of conduct that emphasized rationality in accord with nature, while justifying traditional virtues of public responsibility. And it spoke of a cosmopolitanism, a cultural and moral unity, that embraced all men. Now some notion of world brotherhood existed to compete with parochial, exclusivistic definitions of man in terms of Athens or Sparta or Thebes.

Often this notion of world brotherhood has been seen as one of world citizenship, but this was not the case in the Hellenistic world. It is one thing to believe that each man possesses some tiny portion of a world spark or soul, and in some fundamental human sense is brother to everyone under the sun, and another to call that equality citizenship when by definition and function citizenship was a discriminatory institution in a hierarchical and compartmentalized society. The Stoics were not political or social revolutionaries advocating renovation in the real world. What they asserted was the ultimate moral equality of all human beings, a concept which was to have its day in the future, under Rome and Christianity.

In searching for new antipolis forces in the world we must mention this kind of an idea, but we must be careful not to ascribe to it at this time the importance it eventually had. *Isopolity*, honorary citizenships, *proxeny*, and the development of the Attic tongue as the common language of all Mediterranean urban society—all these probably had more to do with breaking down localism than the osmotic diffusion of almost mystical notions in social and political thought. Thus, we can say that the forces holding the polis together were being loosened as alternative theories such as Stoicism and alternative realities such as the new international life made new choices of activity possible.

All this is to suggest that the old Greek polis was breaking down into, to use the modern phrase, ethnic components. If originally citizenship had conferred identity and its benefits, now new, more intimate "corporations" were beginning to perform the same function in a much more complicated world. Moreover, in the Hellenistic period, no melting pot concept existed as a model for the integration of new peoples. Identity was too marked: everywhere people were recognized for what they were culturally; culture was perceived in much smaller units then. Only such vague Stoic notions as cosmopolitanism indicated any higher, total, acceptable binding forms.

We are trying to explain why men broke out of the pattern of centuries and gave up the total commitment to their native city that was expected in ancient society. Both material advantage and abstract idealism in the form of the concept of the brotherhood of man surely played a role. Quite different, a spectrum away from the *proxeny* of ambassadors and the ethical theory of gentlemen scholars, was the private world of cell and cult. The same international society in which, far from home, some outsiders identified with the official icons of their new kingdom or city, saw other strangers choosing to remain close to their kindred and familiar gods. These turned away from the new political and religious life in an effort to maintain an old life, or establish contact with one of the universalist, salvationist religions sweeping out of Asia across the Mediterranean: Cybele, Isis and Osiris, Orphism, Judaism. Bound together by common beliefs and memories, by a life-style different from that of their host community (which usually included religious ritual), such people constituted a distinct subculture. Large commercial towns like Piraeus and Alexandria eventually played host to many such communities and gave them some constitutional status within the city at large. They became *politeuma* and worked out a schedule of reciprocal obligations—and sometimes terms of citizenship. Usually these enclave communities were composed of working-class populations, but not always. In Alexandria, the large Jewish community constituted perhaps a quarter of the city and included members of every social class and occupation.

What is important about such communities is that they demanded allegiance and created a new dimension to citizenship. After family allegiance, a constant, the individual's next loyalty was to his little group, which gave him comfort and support. His political activities, if any, did not contribute to the success of his city but rather to that of his ethnic community. His connections with the official polis were nominal, heartless, for he got little out of it in areas that mattered, matters of the spirit. Ultimately, out of this milieu, and at great social and intellectual distance from the cosmopolitanism some Stoic philosophers offered, came an intense concern for personal moral growth. And from this came both the moral genius of Christianity and other new religions and the artistic genius of great poets and other creative individuals.

The modern state allows only one citizenship, which it defines in terms of birth, service, commitment, swearing of loyalty, and several other categories, both subjective and objective. Before 1789 and the rise of the nation-state, things were different. Governments not only tolerated the existence of internal communities based on activity or provenance, or, in the case of Jews, religion, they actually used them, encouraging their officers in internal, that is, self-government. As we have seen, this situation began with the Greeks. It persisted throughout the Roman period and was revived with the general revival of urban life in the eleventh century, to remain part of European life for as long as the Old Regime lasted. The *longue durée* in urban constitutional history is defined in part by the tension between or among multiple calls for allegiance, that of the city and those of the other organized and recognized communities to which the individual also belongs.

From the third century on, it became easier for the good man not to be the good citizen. In earlier Hellenic days, the distinction would have been difficult. Now, however, privatism was possible within the total community. Cult promises and philosophic analyses offered certainty and escape. Stoicism provided some theoretical counterbalance to the moderate emphasis on personality and self that lasted for centuries, until Christianity contributed its own ideas in this vein. The conditions determining the basic relationship between citizenship and Christianity were established long before the conversion of Constantine in the fourth century A.D., indeed, long before the time of Christ.

2

ROME

BEGINNINGS TO THE GRACCHI

The history of Roman citizenship is much more complex than that of Greece and, if less intellectual, in its historical impact, grander. But because Rome became a monarchy and an empire, the actual meaning and function of its citizenship is ambiguous. The meaning of citizenship under an empire needs clarification; Rome itself always needs clarification since its history embraces two quite distinct political periods. Indeed, of the two, the Empire probably dominates in our minds; we know it left us Christianity, Roman law, and Mediterranean civilization north of the Alps. But what the Republic left us, we are not so sure, its demise associated as it is with those vivid but confusing characters of Shakespeare's plays. And Cicero, whose persona should be un-ambiguous, given his republican values, somehow loses personal and doctrin-al clarity because of the ad hominem nature of his orations and the variety of his work. Cicero never became the Pericles of Roman republicanism and citizenship.

It is unfortunate that no single large, clear concept survives for the popular appreciation of Rome. The fact is that if Greece left for future generations the model of a participatory citizen democracy, what Rome left was equally im-portant: not an embellished model, but the institutional reality of a society that worked for many centuries on the basis of a law of citizenship. Rome built an empire on citizenship, using it to reward allegiance and service. Her theories and regulations were written into the *Corpus Iuris Civilis*, which eventually shaped the statutes of medieval city-states and, much later, the laws and values of northern European monarchies. Eventually, too, if Rome never had a Thucydides, she had a Plutarch, whose personification of Roman values added an accessible dimension to the tradition of Cicero. And, more than anything else, Rome eventually managed an empire on the basis of a universal citizenship of free men and a Stoic notion of the universal brotherhood of mankind. In creating the Empire and a theory of universalism, Rome provides the background for the great transformation of citizenship values that occurs with the advent of Christianity.[1]

The date 509 B.C. is the traditional date for the end of the monarchy, the beginning of the Republic. By that time less than a tenth of the population governed the rest. These were the patricians; the free men they governed, also citizens but of an inferior status, constituted the plebs. For about a century the patricians maintained their control, until the invasion of the Gauls. In the course of that intervening century, as Rome's commercial and artisan population increased, and as the number of free peasants throughout the surrounding territory grew, the size of the plebs in relation to the patricians also grew. In the successful Sabine and Etruscan wars, a few of the plebs fought with and for the patricians. When the Gauls struck and conquered Rome (about 387 B.C.), it became clear that a few was not enough and that Rome had to reorganize its army.

Servius Tullius much earlier had built Rome's first circuit of stone walls and included the plebs in the army. Now, in return for their service, they were no longer to be treated as inferior citizens, but rather on a par with the patricians. Later, political institutions such as the popular assembly and the tribunate of the people gave form to the new, more representative cast of the state. By extending citizenship, using it as a device to pull large numbers of substantial men into the political and moral community, the patricians showed great political skill and an awareness of the usefulness of citizenship in strengthening Rome: in 381 they offered Roman citizenship to the citizens of one of the Latin towns, Tusculum, which had helped them against the Gauls. Earlier a kind of partial citizenship had been granted to the Caeritans, who also had been steady allies.

What Rome had discovered was an effective way of enlarging the human and fiscal potentialities of the state, one that satisfied its own needs and political requirements as well as those of the citizens of the city-states it was attracting. No Greek city had ever dared to be so generous on as grand and meaningful a scale. After the Peloponnesian War, some Greek city-states had established a federation in an effort to preserve their independence in an age of monarchical domination. The Aetolian and Achaean leagues granted citizens of member cities a citizenship in the league itself, but this was as far as the Greeks ever went in surrendering municipal individuality. Moreover, they never created any institution whereby individual citizens might have a voice in the making of league policies, nor did they ever develop a theory of federalism. Essentially, for all their political experience and wisdom, the Greeks never got beyond the concept of domination in international relations.[2]

Whether Roman citizenship was originally and essentially Roman is an open question, for Rome's earliest rulers were the Etruscans, whose political institutions may themselves have been influenced by the Greeks. Livy tells us of a Greek presence in Etruria; archaeological evidence confirms him. Chronology would also support such a hypothesis.[3] Yet, fascinating as such an approach may be, one wonders whether it is necessary to document the origins of Roman citizenship. Surely what is significant is the similarity of need and response in the earliest days of both the polis and the *civitas*. Both had to know their permanent residents and most enthusiastic supporters. To court them and their resources the embryonic polities had to name and reward them. Thus they recognized a class of property-owning warriors on whom to depend. Such an interpretation can be indifferent to the geography of origins since what counts is the identity of function in similar, if not identical, circumstances.

Later, in the fourth century, Rome again showed the wisdom of conciliation when, after a bitter Samnite war, which ended with the breakup of the Latin League (338), she offered the rights of full citizenship to several towns, recently her enemies. Arica and a few other places were so treated, while the citizens of many Latin cities were granted a new kind of second-class or limited citizenship: legal and economic rights without political rights (*civitas sine suffragio*). The men of the Latin towns might do business in Rome and marry a Roman, but they were not to participate in actual politics. Here we see that a policy of hierarchy was introduced almost at the very moment Rome began the creative use of citizenship as an instrument of state building. She started with a careful policy of discrimination and maintained that approach until the ultimate universal grant in 212 A.D.—more than five hundred years later. In maintaining the political superiority of her own people, she was doing what came naturally to Mediterranean powers in antiquity. Yet she maintained and spread long-existing political conventions while innovating in ways no Greek city had ever attempted.[4]

By these treaties a balance was struck—in Rome's favor. While the citizens of the Latin cities enjoyed only those privileges granted them by Rome, Rome's citizens enjoyed full rights in all the cities it had privileged. Moreover, the Latin cities were expected to supply soldiers for Rome's wars. So were the Latin colonies, which Rome founded in increasing number, some composed of Latin allies, some of purely Roman inhabitants. Essentially these colonies were defensive military-administrative settlements, placed at strategic frontier places past which an attacker would have to come, either by land or sea. They were peopled by Roman citizens.

This story may also be told in terms of the "Conflict of the Orders," the struggle between patricians and plebeians that conventionally begins with the first secession of the plebs in 494 and ends with the Hortensian law of 287, "which made the decrees of the plebeian assembly binding for the whole community."[5] However, the struggle of the plebeians for political voice and power did not end in a given year with the passage of a single law; rather, it continued as long as economic and social conditions forced men to resort to political and sometimes violent means to get what they needed. Such an interpretation would carry the "Conflict" through the era of the Gracchi and into the civil wars of the first century.

At occasional moments in this long history citizenship became an issue, not necessarily the question of its extension, but of its substance. Both patricians and plebeians were free; the critical question is what did each *ordo* expect in terms of legal rights and other functional benefits? As men were beginning to conceptualize citizenship and struggle for it, how did they envision citizenship bettering their lives?

To the patrician, citizenship meant possession of vast tracts of grazing and farm land, a legal situation in which his power in court could not be withstood, and control of the magistracies that guaranteed maximum opportunity to gain virtue, honor, and state contracts. It meant too a multitude of clients and near unopposed power over his agricultural workers, free and servile. Adding to his status was a monopoly of the religious offices, control of which hallowed patrician causes, and even a special purple border to his toga that advertised his status and commanded deference.

Expectations of the plebeians varied with respect to short-term conditions, such as the need for manpower during or after a war, and with respect to their wealth. What they all always wanted, however, was some standing in the human community, recognition by their patrician betters that they too merited the law's protection of their persons, property, honor, and prospects, and therefore their entrance into Rome's structure of magistracies and assemblies. Many of the plebs were substantial citizens, having prospered as Rome had grown as both city and state. They had been educated into the moral code stressing responsibility and service that already guided the conduct of the best men. Citizenship offered them virtue and wealth, while to their poorer comrades it promised the minimum legal benefits of freedom and therefore some prospect of material improvement.

After a century and a half of conflict between the two orders a compromise was worked out, variations upon which continued to be made into the first century. The wealthy plebeians, the landowners, merchants, and successful artisans, were granted political voice and now the possibility through marriage of upward social mobility. Like many revolutionaries, they wanted entrance into the full benefits of the system, not its destruction.

One way they achieved this was through military service. A fundamental change in tactics, the replacement of the mounted aristocrat by the plebeian hoplite, gave the wealthy plebeian his chance. Service in successful armies with the expensive equipment he himself furnished gave him an undeniable stake in the commonwealth; a new self-importance gave strength to his demand for plebeian political institutions. These, once established, grew in their activities as they developed in their structures; the *concilium plebis*, the *tribuni plebis*, and the *plebiscita* all are manifestations of this new politics.

As they supported these institutions, even the poor plebeians profited. They too gained a place in the army according to their wealth, at times a grant of land, and, in 450, in the Twelve Tables, a written law. Although this codification formalized distinctions between classes, it did offer protection to the mass of Roman citizens against the potency of the aristocrats and the top reaches of the plebeian order. The lowliest plebeians even won the opportunity to fight. Plebeian citizen-soldiers in the legions were divided into five classes on the basis of wealth. The lowest two classes were equipped with only a spear and a javelin or a sling. Beneath these were the propertyless, but they served as well. Thus, opportunity for booty and honor was given to all within this timocratic hierarchy. The result was an exchange of service for status and privilege that held for several centuries of successful conquest.

By the beginning of the second century, then, Rome had achieved a complex and successful policy for maintaining a large and growing territorial state peopled by a relatively content population. Within several broad contract forms, she negotiated with other cities, always sensitive to matters of size, distance, strength, and an estimate of a city's sentiment toward Rome. Since the citizens of the variously allied cities were in large measure left alone to manage local municipal affairs and, indeed, were exempted from the basic military tax paid by full Roman citizens in the capital, they were for a while apparently well satisfied with their side of the bargain. And, since Rome made no attempt to disturb the social balance in any of the allied towns, she retained the loyalty of the local aristocracy, however it might be organized. Through the success of her leadership, Rome had become the great power of the Western world, ruling over Italy from the Rubicon to the Straits of Messina. She had managed to expand her original tribal organization from four to thirty-five tribes, thereby maintaining the fiction of political participation.

The mechanism by which this was accomplished was a body of political institutions, assemblies, which proved flexible enough to encompass an expanding and increasingly extensive citizenry. As Rome's political population grew through treaties, conquests, inclusion of the poor, and as a result too of a species of civil war, several assemblies came into existence and progressively changed to accommodate the new political players. By the middle of the first century B.C., two assemblies were meeting, each with a recognized sphere of activity. It might be said that the relative success of these institutions over many centuries made possible Rome's military victories, for they allowed new political classes to vote and play a role in determining state policies and to serve in the legions—in effect, to feel part of and benefit from membership in the political community. Rome's leaders managed to accomplish all this by channeling the activity of new citizens within existing forms, which depended both upon a hierarchy of distinctions based upon property and on the traditional organization of Roman society on a tribal basis.

Originally the *comitia centuriata* included all Romans assigned military responsibilities according to their wealth. The centuries organized by King Servius Tullius in Rome's early days were divided into *equites*, *pedites*, and unarmed service personnel. Throughout its long history the *comitia centuriata* was dominated by the richer and more influential citizens who, therefore, controlled the selection of consuls and praetors, an essential function of the *comitia*. Over time the original military function of this assembly changed into something broader: it became the political structure into which all new citizens were assimilated on the basis of their potential performance.

How the 193 centuries voted and counted votes was complicated and today is not perfectly clear. What matters for citizenship is that the assembly worked as an instrument of integration, allowing new Romans to identify with Rome's early history and with current government. Yet, while new citizens participated in voting and other civic rituals that mattered, they were in fact deprived of a voice that really counted. Real control remained in the hands of the traditional wealthy voters who remained in town close to the forum, and whose votes counted more than did those of lesser citizens. The role of the censor in this distribution of political power is obvious: it was he who, in determining the worth, and therefore responsibility, of each man, assigned to him a specific measure of opportunity for service to the community. The potentiality for accomplishment, fame, and, consequently, virtue in the eyes of the political class depended upon the censor's judgment.

The other assembly that constantly played a significant role in republican politics, like the *centuriata*, elected magistrates and approved laws. Its terminology varies. Under a tribune, the tribes constituted the *concilium plebis*, while under a consul or praetor the same citizens constituted the *comitia tributa*. The activities of these two bodies differed according to the presiding officer, but by the end of the third century the activities of the people appear to predominate. Eventually there were thirty-five tribes whose members could attend these assemblies, the number having grown in response to the need for new possibilities for enrollment. When organized into tribes and participating in these tribal assemblies, the citizens voted as individuals with equal votes. It was out of these more democratic assemblies that most legislation binding on all Roman citizens came. And it was in these assemblies that the ordinary Roman exercised his political rights and, in theory, functioned as a true Roman should, realizing his Aristotelian and Stoic definition and perfection.[6]

Over time and under stress, this system became less manageable, less responsive to the variety of class and political interests developing within Rome. Although the patricians eventually allowed plebeians into the consulate and other high secular and religious offices, and although decisions of the plebs, the plebiscites, were recognized as binding upon patricians too, such concessions did not really change the oligarchic structure of authority, since the Senate, in various ways, managed to awe and control the tribunes of the people. In effect, a new aristocracy eventually came into being, in which patricians and wealthy plebeians joined to control political office and patronage. Yet the constitution held; Rome survived the Punic Wars because her allies throughout Italy stayed loyal. She defeated the mercenaries of Hannibal with her citizen-soldiers and those of the Italian communities. Even after Hannibal's victory at Lake Trasimene, most of Rome's allies held fast and continued loyal during the following century while Rome extended her military range and civil administration.

By the end of the second century, Rome had beaten Carthage and had decisively and irrevocably intervened in Greek and Near Eastern affairs. She had managed her success in part by mobilizing her own resources and in part by constructing a supportive coalition of beaten and threatened tribes and city-states throughout central Italy. For a while intelligent policies worked to Rome's benefit: she continued to allow each city's ruling elite internal control of its affairs, while retaining for Rome overall management of foreign and military policy. Victorious, Rome had no tax disputes with her clients.

Eventually, however, many distinguished local leaders began to feel left out of Rome's success, as did newly important social elements within Rome, the knights. The old senatorial class had begun to feel these pressures and the need to confront the problem of empire, which was related. How were they to regularize relations between Rome and the many new Asian and African territories now Roman in some sense? And were they to share, with their allies and clients in Italy, if at all, the benefits of citizenship, which now were expanding as Rome's wealth was growing?

Not only did citizenship mean the possibility of political participation, it also meant an enhanced legal and civil status in the commercial world then falling under Roman control, the financial magnitude of which was enormous. The career of St. Paul demonstrates the protection citizenship could deliver against the physical violence of the Roman justice system; local officials backed off from brutal punishment when made aware of his birthright status.[7]

Gaius Gracchus may have seen all this when he proposed a law in 123 or 122 to give citizenship to the Latins. Exactly why he did so is uncertain. Did he hope to gain more votes for his popular causes in an expanded and now appreciative Roman political arena? Or did he act out of an acute sense of history, being aware that Rome now needed large numbers of new men in her military forces and administrative cadres, and that past policy dictated present generosity? Or was he aware of the anger rising among the Latins and Italians against Roman arrogance and abuse? His plan to give full citizenship rights to the Latins while advancing the Italians to their status might have handled this problem effectively and peaceably without the violent war it eventually took several generations later. We will never know, for the law was not passed, and Gaius was murdered. We can say only that this extraordinarily gifted politician saw the importance of citizenship in the solution of many of his country's most pressing problems.[8]

Under the Gracchi more than ever, citizenship functioned as an issue of politics as well as a political institution.[9] In the final generations of the Republic after Gaius's murder, the same may be said of patronage. Like the mobs in the streets and soldiers in the camps, it played a role in the acquisition of offices and determination of policies. And there are other similarities and relationships: Like citizenship, patronage was an institution the Romans used to serve the state. Like the family, it constituted a distracting alternative to abstract public allegiance and indiscriminate civic friendship. Yet it also functioned as a mechanism by which new men were brought into the political community.[10]

Citizenship recognized the interdependence of Romans and the citizens of lesser communities. Its employment as public policy gained military and financial, not to say moral, support from those it protected, gave an opportunity, and endowed with legal and political rights. Patronage recognized the interdependence of the less powerful and the greater families. The former needed advocacy in their search for office and status, while the latter needed loyal supporters, clients, in their attempt to last, that is, to maintain their political and social dominance. Patronage enabled the pushy plebeian or knight, the enfranchised slave, the resident alien to gain access into public life, perhaps to win a magistrate's office. The number of the great political lineages was not very large, perhaps fifty. Estimates of the size of the probable clientele of such a clan range from about thirty to several hundred, which means that at most a few thousand of the most politically ambitious and able were involved in the network of patron-client relationships. But these were, of course, among the most capable people in the Republic.

Patronage was something more than a political and moral custom and practice. If oligarchy was the reality that "lurked behind the facade" of republican government, patronage was the instrument of oligarchy, the means by which the great families retained real control of Roman offices, and through them the honor and image that constituted success for a great clan in the Roman political system. Money, prestige, military assistance, and political advantage came from foreign clients, as the careers of the elder Tiberius Gracchus and Pompey show, while from clients closer to the capital derived all manner of support: besides the timely loan for legal or military assistance, a patron could count on the appropriate vote, visible show of solidarity, and marriage alliance. The function of this kind of proto-feudal relationship, confined to the benefit of a tiny fraction of those eligible for public office, explains how in every generation the few managed to perpetuate themselves in office and control the many. Over centuries, in the many treaties and arrangements Rome made with conquered peoples and disgruntled allies, she did grant some or all the rights of citizenship. However, through the institution of patronage the traditional ruling elite retained control of the political side of citizenship while allowing many thousands the commercial and personal privileges and benefits that grew in importance as the Republic's overseas possessions grew, and that apparently satisfied the material desires of the new citizens.[11]

In this way patronage presented the political class with yet another demand for loyalty and thus helped to stimulate the moral literature to which Cicero (106–43 B.C.) was a contributor. His *On Friendship* and *On Moral Obligations* may be read as answers to questions about priorities of obligations. His calculatedness and matter-of-fact approach may put us off today; to his contemporaries his codification and analysis gave guidance to those who, like his son, were preparing to enter the turmoil of complicated human relations that helped define politics in those dangerous days. What such men were after, those three hundred or so members of the great political families who sat in the Senate, was honor. They also sought to live out, visibly, the obligations of a moral code, worked out over several centuries, that prescribed responsibility, loyalty, and service to family and community. Honor met service on the battlefield and in the magistracies, which is why the latter were so coveted.[12]

With his agricultural reforms, which were to take the form of land grants to individuals scattered across Italy, probably Italians as well as Romans, Tiberius Gracchus was challenging this system. He meant to have thousands of clients in his debt scattered throughout the tribes and over the countryside, but which on occasion he could concentrate in a strategic place as he did on the Capitoline the day of his assassination. Tiberius had recognized the changing and deteriorating condition of rural life; he saw an already impoverished peasantry threatened by competition from cheap slave labor flooding in from Rome's conquests east and west, and by the success of an enclosure movement which created large estates dedicated to both commercial farming and grazing. "Thus the wretched became a constituency."[13] And thus Tiberius Gracchus showed the way to a succession of effective and ruthless political chieftains over the last century of the Republic.

By 287, the Samnite Wars over the control of central Italy were over, and the *plebiscita*, the acts of the plebeian assembly, were recognized as law. It is generally agreed that at this time a republican constitution came into being that lasted until Augustus and the final days. Part of that constitution was the articulation of the *cursus honorum*, the sequence of senior magistracies that came to constitute the ultimate demonstration of citizen behavior. The number of consuls and censors remained stable; the number of praetors and quaestors expanded and contracted according to need and in response to political pressure. What persisted was the idea that if one was a member of the special group of senatorial citizens, or aspired to its membership, he had to serve his time at each level of increasingly demanding and important state service. In a succession of performances that was open to public scrutiny he learned to handle men, money, administrative responsibilities, and the religious venerations that necessarily were integrated with political and military decisions. That, inevitably, office holding was accompanied by graft, speculation, and other governmental sins is true. But truer, that is, more effective in history, is the survival of the ideal of sacrifice and purity in the service of the public good. Formalized in moral literature and the curricula of classical schools and taught to all who received education in the thousand cities of the Roman world, this model or vision of the right public life was strong enough still in 590 A.D. to persuade a Roman citizen, Gregory, to accept the papal throne.

This climb to power through a succession of public trusts brought fame and dignity to the political Roman and his family. It enhanced prospects for marital and political alliance and bettered prospects for future office holding, which in late-republican times almost guaranteed wealth from some proconsular position. Also, it stimulated a rush of clients, as men pledged their loyalty in hope of advancement and protection. In every way, an upward march through the magistracies brought a noble Roman to the forefront of his fellow citizens' consciousness; this meant, of course, greater influence in the Senate. For the most notable it meant entrance into history and the law, and for new men, membership in a superior social as well as legal class. Privately, magistracy surely brought a sense of accomplishment, a higher self-regard for having lived a life of demonstrated virtue.

By proposing his agrarian law Tiberius may also have been thinking of his progress toward the consulship, his standing in the *cursus honorum*. He came of a great political clan, indeed, of two. His father had succeeded as both general and civil official; his widowed mother had trained him for high office. The city watched for signs of another brilliant political career. Then, posted to Spain as quaestor, he signed a treaty which disgraced Rome and which was eventually rejected by the Senate. Mancinus, his commander, was convicted; Tiberius was protected by family and friends, his career somewhat bruised. His next responsibility, as he struggled to get back on track, was as tribune—something of an eccentric office not directly on the path to consul and censor. In allowing himself to become the active agent of the circle of aware and concerned leaders that drafted the *Lex Sempronia Agraria*, Tiberius may have been trying to impress both these mature politicians who were bringing him along and his popular constituency. The length to which he was willing to go—he threatened or was seen as threatening the very constitutional structure of Roman politics—reveals the pressures upon those who would scramble up the ladder of the *cursus*. A career might thrust one into the evils of Asia or the barbarisms of Spain, but it would all be worth it to have the funeral of a Roman hero and to bring eternal glory to the family name.[14]

POLYBIUS

Polybius, the Greek historian, came to Rome during the course of these developments and attempted to describe the institutional and moral structure which had brought Rome to world power. He came from the land of the polis into Italy, which for several hundred years had been the scene of a new creation: a large-scale territorial state built out of small, individual historic units of land and people. His analysis reveals how alive the old Hellenic civic code remained in his own set of expectations and how Rome, in effect, independently had developed and maintained an analogous set of values as she expanded over the peninsula.

Polybius was born about 200 B.C. and was active in the following half-century. His career was spent in war and government in a Greece divided into highly politicized confederations and recently come under Roman influence. The major event in his life was a seventeen-year internment in Rome, as one of a thousand Achaeans whose presence in Italy was to guarantee the good conduct of their people back in Greece.[15]

It is as true of Greek cities under the Macedonians as well as of Italian cities under Rome that, despite their political subordination to a greater power, they retained much of their cultural and political identity and life, which is to say that the polis was very much alive, despite the existence of monarchy and the growth of city leagues. It continued to be, along with the family, the individual's principal source of identity. When Polybius discusses the Athenian constitution, he assumes without surprise or adverse criticism that "customs and laws" are the fundament in every state that "makes men's private lives righteous and well ordered and the general character of the state gentle and just." Speaking generally in the famous analysis of the Roman constitution, he demands that a true democracy be understood as a place "where it is traditional and customary to reverence the gods, to honour parents, to respect our elders, and to obey the will of the laws."[16] For him, still, the constitution is the city; it makes the man, so much so that the thought of erasing a city from the map, of "depriving its unhappy inhabitants of all hope for the future was evidently conduct unworthy of any Greek state, and especially unworthy of Athens."

He had earlier told the sad story of the Lyttians who, while fighting an enemy, had had their city destroyed behind their backs. Polybius's anguish is clear as he describes how, suddenly, they became "aliens without a city instead of citizens." Again, a polis's sense of its integrity is revealed in the story of Thearcis, a notorious traitor, whose claim to citizenship was denied by the Clitorians, lest the good name of the entire citizen body suffer. The city had a reputation for its "noble love of freedom," which the notoriety of the traitor, whom they now claimed to be "the son of a foreign soldier," was not to disparage.

Corporate identity was especially strong when it came to rights, and Polybius is always aware of the material side of citizenship and concerned enough to report details; he knew this was the sort of a technical legal detail his audience of citizen merchants and statesmen would want to know. So we learn, as did they, that in addition to a crown awarded for conspicuous valor, Rhodian citizens received from the Athenians "equal political rights at Athens with her own citizens as a reward."[17] Whereas in this alliance political rights are specified, Polybius's account of the treaty between Rome and Carthage carefully notes that a Roman "in the Carthaginian province of Sicily and at Carthage may do and sell anything that is permitted a citizen. A Carthaginian in Rome may do likewise." Individual, specific advantage is again his concern when he mentions the "many private advantages that resulted to their citizens" that the leaders of Arcadia and Messene obtained from Sparta.[18]

That Romans were also alive to the possibility of advantage is seen by Polybius as important in explaining Rome's success. In the famous Book 6, his analysis of the Roman constitution, having spoken of the "very important part" the people play in creating the "bonds by which . . . human society in general is held together," he notes the economic role of government. Rome has to let a "vast number of contracts . . . for repair of public buildings . . . farming of rivers, harbours, gardens, mines. . . . Everyone is interested in contracts and the work they involve." Some contract for the actual work, and others handle finance behind the scenes; what counts in Polybius's view is the widespread popular interest in this aspect of Roman government, the broad distribution of material benefit to the citizenry. He sees a connection between private and public benefit and is aware too, throughout his history, of his audience's interest in all matters of civil and political status. His readers, men of affairs, had to be knowledgeable not just about the pedigrees of men they might find themselves confronting in the world, but about anything pertaining to legal-civil conditions that might make a difference in trade or legal or diplomatic relations.[19]

Polybius is also interested in the formation of what today we would call "national character." He knows it is constructed by birth and institutional design, and, like Plato, he is sensitive to the creative use of music. Arcadian youths "study it constantly . . . singing . . . the hymns and paeans in which by traditional usage they celebrate the heroes and the gods of each particular place." In addition, "the young men practice military parades to the music of the flute."[20] Also, he notes how the Romans have codified military rewards, reserving a golden crown for "the first man to mount the wall at the assault on a city" and honorary gifts for lesser services—to those who save fellow citizens or allies, for example. Public reward meant to "excite to emulation and rivalry" is a conscious educational device of the community.[21]

The community knows what it wants, in civic Rome as well as in civic Greece. The good Roman is to be brave; he is to husband his resources, not flaunt them before his fellow citizens in need, as did Hasdrubal the Carthaginian, who gave drinking parties during a famine. He is to be honest as Scipio was honest, "taking absolutely nothing" from Carthage, "although he was not particularly well off." And he is to be responsible and active; during the Punic War, Rome, like Athens hundreds of years earlier, depended upon one or more citizens for the maintenance of a warship. She won in part because of the "patriotic and generous spirit of the leading citizens . . . according to their means."[22]

The good public-spirited Roman could learn to be active, as we see from Polybius's account of his friendship with Scipio's older brother, Fabius, to whom Polybius habitually spoke and addressed his questions. On one occasion, blushing, the eighteen-year-old Scipio asked Polybius why he ignored him. Was it because he, Scipio, was "a quiet, indolent man, with none of the character of a Roman, because I don't choose to speak in the law courts"? Polybius denies this hypothesis, assures the youth of his admiration, and then describes the steps Scipio thereafter took to make himself the model Roman.[23]

Within five years Scipio had established a reputation for temperance and self-discipline, rejecting the temptations for one of his age and class. Then he distinguished himself in "magnanimity and clean-handedness in money matters." His responsibility toward the property inherited from the mother of his adoptive father, as well as his generosity toward his brother, won him a reputation for "nobility of character." Probity, generosity, responsibility, and eventually courage—all came to him in the eyes of the Roman people who, apparently, were constantly evaluating the merits of their leading citizens.[24]

The mob in Shakespeare's *Julius Caesar* and *Coriolanus* becomes more comprehensible as we perceive through Polybius how closely watched were Rome's chief men, how their every action or inaction became stimulus to gossip and evaluation. Instinctively, the little people, then and throughout the long period of personal local politics that lasted well beyond the Renaissance, acknowledged the dependence of their welfare upon the personal qualities of their few leaders. *Coriolanus*—Plutarch's as well as Shakespeare's—tells us something else: that, as citizenship became less indigenously Roman and its privileges more socially diffused, members of Rome's ancient ruling elite grew more restless and angry within the constraints now imposed upon them by the developing republican constitution.

Polybius, then, reveals a lot about the unity of Mediterranean civilization in this period. Hellenic civic and personal values persist under Rome, while in Italy the ruling class had flourished over centuries under a similar moral code. It is no wonder that Rome's upper classes took to Greek culture so quickly; they found so much there that supported and gave intellectual underpinning to their own values. The Romans most admired by Polybius think, restrain their passions, worship their gods, honor their ancestors, and valorously serve their family and country. By the second century Rome had developed its counterparts to Greek institutions of moral training and, what is more, had come under the influence of Greek Stoicism with its emphasis on personal virtue and the unity of mankind. By being virtuous the good man served the narrow interests of family and city as well as his responsibility to the human race.

Also, as Polybius allows us to see quite clearly, the high ideals of the day did not deny the legitimacy of self-interest. Those Romans who served in office impeccably and financed the triremes might maintain their public virtue while farming the mines and maintaining city gardens. Polybius recognized the essential honesty and usefulness of the quid pro quo. He makes no negative judgment when he describes the many state contracts available to Roman citizens who were not of the senatorial class. That he mentions these contracts in what amounts to a constitutional analysis is significant, for it reveals his perception of the complex set of mutual demands and expectations made upon each other by citizens and the government. If the consuls depend upon the Senate, both depend upon the people for material support and moral approbation, the people in this case being those citizens of substance who could afford to bid for state contracts.

THE SOCIAL WAR

Polybius died about 120 B.C. By then the senatorial order, which had achieved great success, was changing. Seduced by the wealth and power to be derived from imperial service in the East, many senators began to put self and family before the Republic. Their quest for the private rewards of public service quickly provoked opposition. The Gracchi may be seen in this light as they died to restore probity to Roman public life. They understood that Rome had long been an oligarchy in which the plebs counted little; aristo-cratic families passed offices around in a routine which not only excluded the lesser orders in Rome itself, but also worked against the position of the Italian allies. By the beginning of the first century, two issues had become linked in opposition to senatorial dominance: the political and social interests of the mass of Roman citizens and those of the badly treated allies whose strength, added to Rome's, had guaranteed centuries of military success.

The resolution of the conflict history knows as the Social War, the war of the allies (socii). It was fought over the distribution of power within the Roman state, in an attempt to force Rome to grant equality and a common citizenship. Not all the subordinate peoples rose up against Rome; the more privileged Latin allies had remained loyal. But the Italians north and south of Rome did field an army of one hundred thousand men in an attempt first to gain more protection from rapacious Roman magistrates and then, once organized, to establish "an independent nation."[25]

After a nasty, three-year war (91–88) a negotiated peace returned Rome to that initial policy of openness which had characterized her expansion up and down the boot. Rome granted citizenship, defined now as membership in one of the eight existing tribes, to all Latin colonies and all faithful allies, to Umbrians and Etruscans who might be rewarded in the field, to members of Italian communities who might claim it within sixty days, and finally, to all communities in designated areas in the area of the Po. This proved a satisfactory compromise because it allowed the ruling oligarchy to remain in control while giving the new citizens both formal membership in the political community and the civil benefits of a citizenship. Since the political benefits of citizenship were so few, one suspects that it was the legal and material, as opposed to the political, side of citizenship that most Italians really desired. In any event, when, several years later, Sulla brutally restored senatorial power, the new citizens kept what they had won and did not attempt to block his way.

Finally, if the Social War brought political integration and legal uniformity, relatively speaking, it also advanced cultural standardization. Movement in this direction was centuries old, beginning with the earliest Roman moves to conquer. Over the centuries Etruscan and Samnite individuality had gradually diminished. Now, almost willingly, the Italian allies cooperated in their own cultural self-eradication. Regional culture flickered as Roman language, education, religion, art, law, and values were offered and received. Long before the Empire, a process of cultural imperialism began.

As citizenship was granted to more and more people over an area that extended hundreds of miles around the capital city, small-scale politics—the politics of the Latin polis, which Rome once had been—inevitably came to an end. The first century witnessed the devolution of political power into the grasp of factions composed of great families, each rallying behind the personality of a soldier hero, someone whose talents and accomplishments as well as money could win him popularity along with oligarchic support. In effect, because of this new political situation, the first century must be viewed as a critical period during which Roman citizenship was changed in its basic meaning. To this time it had emphasized the potential for political participation, direct personal involvement in the city's affairs. It had also demanded military service. The virtuous Roman left his plow when called to defend the *patria* against Gauls or Carthaginians. Allowing for obvious differences, early Roman citizenship approximated original Greek citizenship: both emphasized a variety of personal obligations as well as privileges, and obedience to law as well as the exercise of authority. Both may be seen as pure examples of the first citizenship.

Now, with Rome a maritime empire, with many of its most influential men involved in trade and the perquisites and rewards of overseas governance, with real decision making no longer in the hands of legislative bodies amenable at least to some popular influence and control, what citizenship conveyed was legal status, advantages. Also, as Roman proconsuls found themselves in Palestine, Bythinia, Egypt, Gaul, and Spain, among peoples whose society and culture differed so radically from their own, Roman citizenship came to stand for a certain kind of civilization, that of the dominant people, whose successful conquest implied cultural superiority: not only were Roman armies better, also Roman language, law, and style of life. Earlier, Greek life forms had prevailed under and after Alexander and his generals. Now Roman campaigners carried the supremacy of Latin civilization over most of Western Europe as well as the ancient East.

CITIZENSHIP LAW AND POLICY

City life and Roman law were principal parts of the transported Latin civilization. In the imperial centuries the city everywhere served Rome as its basic unit of organized political life. At the same time the Roman law specified those powers a citizen had that defined his political and legal capacities. Roman citizenship conferred special rights, made one man more than another. Between the early centuries of the Republic's expansion, when the grant of citizenship was used to create social and political bonds, and the late Empire, when it was used again as a means to hold the state together, citizenship essentially was a status, which conveyed certain legal powers or benefits. It was also a moral demand in that, out of historical and contemporary ethical belief and practice, it placed before a man a schedule of his responsibilities toward the *patria*. Finally, citizenship came to represent a certain class culture, the end result of a formal "class" education based upon a curriculum common to the schools throughout the city-state world. A citizen knew who he was: his rights and values were supposed to be very clear. All of this foreshadows the medieval world.

What the allies fought for was a collection of practical benefits that would put them on a level of legal and sociopolitical equality with the Romans. Citizenship assumed recognition of personal freedom, but beyond that it was a bundle of privileges of a private- and public-law nature. The *ius connubii* was the right to marry under civil law; it brought to the husband powers over his children, his wife, and their property that constituted a familial sovereignty. The *ius commercium* gave the citizen a position in the business world enhanced by his ability to litigate in the courts and convey property in a variety of ways. In an era of conflict and overlapping of law and jurisdiction, such capabilities were significant. In addition to these important benefits, the citizen had certain defenses against a sentence of death and, as we know from St. Paul's successful protest in Acts 16, immunity from bodily punishment.

Finally, citizenship granted the *ius suffragium*, a collection of political and military rights that incurred responsibilities. If one could vote for magistrates, one had to serve in public office. And if a citizen was eligible to share in a legion's booty, he was also expected to fight. The ability of any individual citizen to avail himself of political privileges depended, of course, upon his personal abilities and qualifications, and his proximity to Rome when political decisions were made.

It depended too upon such great changes within the Roman world as the transition from Republic to Principate and to Empire. However, even that great event must not be overemphasized, for although the political side of citizenship was eventually attenuated, the civil side largely survived. Under the Empire, citizenship remained what Cicero called it, a legal society (*iuris societas*).[26] The Empire, now with a philosophic rationale, became an enormous legal unit in which, theoretically, principles of Roman morality were translated into daily activity. Already by the end of the Republic the pattern of citizen life had been set, not just in Rome, the capital city, but also in the many semi-independent *municipia*, civic entities allowed by Rome to maintain a constitutional and cultural local existence. This is the formal picture largely derived from legal and historical literature.

From this account it is clear that Rome grew from polis to empire without a grand design and that her leaders pieced together a successful political system from practices readily available throughout the Mediterranean. It is also evident that this achievement was accomplished first on the ground and only then in the minds of its managers. No formal political theory ever completely justified Rome's greatest single successful art, conquest; Greek ideas only rationalized the sequel to conquest, government. Such was the historic role of Stoicism, which, by the mid-first century, had become something of the accredited philosophical system of the Roman upper class, as we have already noted.

STOICISM AND CICERO

Founded by Zeno (335–263 B.C.), modified especially by Panaetius (185–109 B.C.) and Posidonius (135–50 B.C.), who popularized it among the Roman aristocracy, Stoicism was a complete philosophical system. Its physics, logic, and ethics were all related in a world view that a member of the Mediterranean ruling class might almost naturally absorb any time during the five hundred years between Panaetius and, say, the late Roman extoller of pagan virtues, Symmachus (340–402 A.D.). Cicero was influenced by it, as was the emperor Marcus Aurelius (161–80 A.D.). As technical moral philosophy and personal ethic, Stoicism survived Rome's passage from polis to empire, republic to monarchy.

Stoicism's ethics comes out of its physics. Because God in a sense is everything, man possesses some part, a spark, of the divine fire; that spark is his rationality, which in adolescence becomes aware of its place and function in an organic universe. Being a rational, political animal—modern commentators emphasize Zeno's reliance upon Aristotle—man must define his proper conduct. The perpetual Stoic concern with right doing derives from the very nature of the beast; Stoic speculation itself fulfills the human condition. To "live harmoniously" in Zeno's phrase means to live in accord with the structure of righteousness God has positioned in the universe, following wisdom, temperance, fortitude, and justice. It means being virtuous in action, choosing and doing in accordance with the rational perception of what is right.

Since society exists, the Stoic must participate in it. Since it manifests the divine, he must be concerned for its welfare. Hence the wise man, as Diogenes Laertius, the ancient historian of philosophy, tells us, is "pious and God-fearing." He will "take part in politics if nothing hinders him . . . marry and have children." He will mature in human society, rejecting "solitude . . . for he is naturally sociable and active," and he will "undergo training and discipline in order to increase his power of physical endurance," no doubt to increase his effectiveness in the army and other forms of public service. Finally, Diogenes Laertius reports that "it is also one of their tenets that the exercise of virtue is a continuous activity . . . the good man is always occupied in the exercise of the power of a soul which is always perfect."[27]

Such is the background to Cicero, who attempted to spell out for the Roman ruling class what it meant to be a good citizen. His model, revealed in some of the finest moral literature ever written, survived the simultaneous death of Cicero himself and republicanism and had a long career in both pagan and Christian times. Cicero grew up in an equestrian family during that war which ended, as we have seen, with the extension of Roman citizenship, and he died during the war that made the Republic an empire. When he was born most men of his class still were simply country gentlemen; when he died surely many, if not most, had been educated into wealth and power somewhere in Rome's Mediterranean empire. Cicero wrote for them and their senatorial betters, who had been exposed longer to such temptation, out of a concern for the preservation of traditional Roman political virtues. He saw his colleagues facing fundamental choices in ethics and education and determined to rationalize a way of life being threatened.

Trained in Greece as he was in oratory and humanistic studies, and in Rome in the realities of legal and political life, he sought also to present to educated Romans a vision of the good man's role in the preservation of a world community. He provided this not in a single book but in a flow of volumes composed both while actively serving the *patria* and in retreat from the dangers of an active political life. His *On the Commonwealth*, *On Moral Obligations*, *On the Orator*, and *Dream of Scipio* along with other works spelled out the good Roman's obligations to his community. Cicero's elegance as well as his comprehensiveness added to his contemporary impact and assured his effect upon later generations. So did his relative conservatism, for, in stating how the good man ought to behave, Cicero made no new demands, nor, indeed, did he go beyond the Greek assumption that theory should inform action. Rather, in his elegant prose he summed up the virtues of his class and gave them an accessible philosophical discussion—and, in the *Dream of Scipio*, a religious compulsion.

For Cicero, man is a moral and rational animal, and, given the fact that the divine spark burns in him as well as in every other human being, a social animal as well. Since he has reason he is compelled to use it, preferably to the benefit of his fellow men. Cicero's exhortation to public service derives, then, from more than awareness of how Rome's system of public and private rewards works; it comes grounded in the psychology, physics, and cosmology of the Stoic schools. Yet he is careful to differentiate himself from the more purely philosophical Greek tradition; the Greeks were always too wordy and discursive for Cicero, who wrote for the use, as opposed to the mere edification, of his fellow Romans. Later Roman writers were influenced by Cicero's vocabulary of civic love and friendship and by the heroic example he set in his final days—that of the patriot willing to die for his country and its constitutional values. Not just pagans, but early Christian thinkers and medieval

Christian civic leaders read his *On Moral Obligations*, *On the Republic*, and other moral and educational works.

Since he possesses reason and speech, which Cicero regards as the effective mechanism by which to stir men to political and moral action, man must use it to get at truth, which exists in the moral as well as the physical universe. Ideally, he should put his life and accomplishments at the service of his fellows, for all men are "born for each other" and "to exchange acts of kindness." Only man has a sense for the right kind of existence, a feeling for "order, propriety, and moderation." Given their powers, which constitute a form of responsibility, men who choose to be private are "traitors to social life." Cicero knows that a life of retirement is easier and safer, but he asserts the moral superiority of the active life, which "is more profitable to mankind." He wants able men "to enter the race for public office and take a hand in directing the government." Statesmen are "no less important" than generals, especially those who act "for the benefit of those entrusted to their care, not of those to whom it [their care] is entrusted."[28]

Yet, for all this public-spiritedness, Cicero remains alive to the race for honor among the great political families, the established as well as those pushing their way into office. He writes of activities as contributing "more to their own greatness and renown" and that "the noblest heritage is a reputation for virtue and worthy deeds." Cicero is, of course, aware of the various ties that hold a community together—citizenship, kinship, religion, patronage, friendship and of the questions about priority of obligation that had been raised. His choice is the same as the Greeks': "Country would come first, and parents."[29]

He is also aware that, for all his natural potential for reasonable choice, man must be properly educated, so, in *On Moral Obligations* and especially in *On the Orator*, he is educational as well as social theorist. For Cicero such a distinction would be unreasonable, since for him, as for all ancient social thinkers, one cannot analyze society without considering the way citizens of each individual community are formed.

Cicero does believe that it is possible for man to learn how to behave. In one passage he says philosophy should be education's central subject; in another he gives enormous value to oratory, for which he specifies a broad humanistic curriculum.[30] Upon the trained orator the well-being of the community depends; he must be more than skillful in words. Cicero realizes that the city, if a great human creation, is nevertheless a fragile one and requires leaders who have a knowledge of virtue and the skills of language needed "to win over the hearts of man and attach them to one's own cause"—presumably benefit to the public good. Virtue is attained by reason; the application of virtue, by study of the past.[31]

Conscious of the distinctiveness of Roman culture, Cicero proposes that the orator be trained in the law, history, literature, and religious tradition of his people. Such study will make him more effective, persuasive; it will also provide him with a right feeling for the values he must live to preserve. New men are to share the rule of the world, but they must be taught what it is to be a Roman if they are to bring the best of Roman civilization to benefit those they rule. He is aware that questionable new values and practices have penetrated Rome from Greece and the East, and he worries lest traditional Roman virtue crumble before the temptations of great wealth and power; he is concerned not only for the integrity of officials, but also for those Romans who had learned law and business east of the Adriatic.

Cicero was a firm believer in private property and acknowledged that the wise man is "justified in caring for his private interests."[32] Yet he stands in the civic communitarian tradition as well when he demands that this search for private gain be consonant with the "morality, law and established institutions" of his society. He is concerned also with intention; the goal of wealth-seeking should not be personal enjoyment alone, but in the interests of "our children, relatives, friends, and, above all, our country." And those national interests "ought to be dearer . . . than anything else in the world."[33]

Cicero was aware of citizenship throughout his life and works, in terms of his service both to Rome and to literature. At another level, that of the practicing lawyer, he was also involved with the institution, as we know from his oration *Pro Archia*, which shows us the courtroom Cicero, the lawyer whose job is to retain Archias's citizenship. Poet, humanist, philosopher, longtime resident in Italy, Archias now found his citizenship questioned by his patrons' enemies. These note the absence of any written record of his naturalization. Cicero bases his defense on more than the appropriate technical argument. He attempts to defend Archias by grounding his worthiness in literature, or rather, the literary man's contribution to society. Citizenship may be exercised on the battlefield and in the forum, but also in the teacher's skill in creating the moral man who will want to serve his country. Noting that several cities have honored Archias with civic rights, Cicero argues that Rome should do likewise—since Archias has honored Rome in his immortal histories and poetry.

Cicero died in the middle of the century in which, politically and territorially, the Roman Empire was being put together. He wrote, however, for the class that had ruled Rome for centuries and now was finding itself pushed by men like himself, although Cicero, like newcomers and converts so frequently, was more a defender than destroyer of the old order. Indeed, he may be viewed as codifying the civic ethic of the class which, deriving from a small-scale political community, still thought in pre-imperial terms, never dreaming that a vast new world was soon to supply Rome's new men, not just a few more families, a few more towns in central and southern Italy.

Cicero wrote as a long-lived political culture, to say nothing of system, was coming to an end. His values were those of a small group of oligarchs, whose families had passed the leadership of Rome from one to the other. Therefore, his values are a part of Roman citizenship, as is their acting out by the tiny part of the entire citizenry constituted by the oligarchy. What, the question arises, was citizenship to the hundreds of thousands of citizens who were part of the legal-political community of Roman citizens that stretched across Italy, who had, some of them, actually fought for the status of citizen? Aristocratic ideals filtered down and were translated into activities that benefited both the individual and the community.

Over hundreds of years Rome had constructed a "coherent structure" for citizenship. Every citizen knew what was expected of him given his place in the hierarchical ordering of Roman society. Although based primarily upon wealth, the place of a citizen was also affected by his merit as determined by the censors. Once established in a given rank he knew his military and financial obligations and benefits and what his political powers were as well. Both the citizen and the city were aware of how integrally they were involved, how dependent each was upon the other for the performance of essential services. Translated into activity, this meant, until the end of the second century or thereabouts, that ordinary Roman citizens served in the army, paid taxes when necessary, and participated in numerous elections. Apparently they recognized their dependence upon the quality of individual leaders who offered themselves for public office and carefully scrutinized candidates for the various magistracies. After 150 B.C., more and more of their would-be leaders held positions on political and social issues that ordinary people saw as critical to their lives. Witness the passion the Gracchi inspired thanks to their espousal of "the new idea that a citizen had a right to be economically assisted by the state."[34] If the oligarchs were concerned to exploit citizenship for their own continuation in office and their families' continuation in power, the less wealthy citizens were more interested in the material benefits citizenship brought.

By the end of the second century these benefits were so considerable they were acting perniciously upon the traditional ethos of citizenship. Historically, citizenship had called for a payment of taxes; now Rome was so rich those taxes were no longer required. Moreover, that same wealth did away with the military service every Roman owed his *patria*. Citizen mercenaries, recruited from the lower classes, now filled the ranks and gave their allegiance to Marius, Sulla, or some other general or politician who promised them good pay and retirement benefits. Other members of the same class now looked to the state for free bread and to self-advancing politicians for free circuses.

The original and ideal republican citizenship, if it ever existed, had emphasized duties as the basis for the receipt of legal and civil privileges. Now, long before the Principate and Empire, a process began in which these privileges were separated from what had been the defining functions of citizenship, political and, especially, military service. In effect, a new kind of politics came into existence during the first century in which the private advantage of the powerful and that of the poor came to reinforce each other at the expense of the traditional constitution.

However, if there was a demoralization of values, there was a heightening of political life. The struggle for power among the oligarchs and generals—Caesar, Crassus, Pompey—led to the further development of a set of what has been called "alternative" institutions: public funerals, triumphs, greetings and gatherings, games festivals, even trials—all of which became part of the new politics, which focused upon an individual. These could be devices for civic education in traditional morality (the public funeral) or contemporary issues (the satirical theater). In sum, they served to make the citizen aware of his history, self-interest, and choices. Before Augustus and his successors put an end to the substance, if not the rituals, of all this engaging political life, hundreds of thousands of relatively literate and sophisticated, urban and rural citizens were part of the political process.

This is the current judgment of ancient historians. Roman citizenship not only produced a traditional, active political class that made and administered policy, it also attracted to issues and participation a large and active citizenry. There were more restrictions in Rome, as opposed to Greece, on what these people could do, but within those limits of constitution and influence, they assumed some financial obligations, served in the military, and voted in the assemblies and on the issues open to them. They also made mob violence an operative part of the Roman constitution. If crowds rampaged through Rome's streets for pay, they apparently did so out of interest in issues as well—the programs of the Gracchi, for example. If nothing else, this street politics demonstrates a level of awareness and concern. If Roman politics was not as truly democratic in a modern sense as was the earlier Athenian, nevertheless there did exist a real Roman politics, albeit in terms, forms, and issues that may clash with our perception of what constitutes vital politics.

This must be emphasized: that the politics of the Republic made real demands upon citizenship just as citizenship helped establish the course of politics. Citizenship meant service in the various magistracies, but that was for the few. For the many it meant participation in the great number of elections that, in a variety of assemblies and courts and in preliminary sessions, constituted the political scene. No Roman citizen *had* to attend, listen, discuss, and vote, but thousands did, perhaps seventy thousand, out of the more than million and a half citizens scattered across Italy with the right to vote. They poured into the Campus Martius and other designated places not only from the city wards, but from all Italy, from wherever they lived and were inscribed on some tribal list.

This activity has been described as a "major occupation" for the Roman who took his citizenship seriously. It was also a major influence upon Roman town planning and the design of at least one of its largest buildings. It is both ironic and understandable that after the death of Caesar, with Rome clearly headed toward some form of princely regime, first Lepidus and then Augustus's friend Agrippa, who left us the Pantheon, contributed to the construction of an enormous voting pavilion, the Saepta, which was almost one thousand feet long and wide enough to accommodate thirty-five lines of voters.

The importance of all this voting was already seen in the ancient world by Polybius, and then a century later by Dionysius of Halicarnassus (fl. first century B.C.) and Cicero. According to Dionysius, the Roman people "choose magistrates, ratify laws, and declare war." And, indeed, for more than a century before he wrote, their role in these activities central to government actually had increased. A fully active citizen would have had to participate more than twenty times a year in various voting actions. In addition to his appearance at the voting site, which could take the better part of a day, and to which he was called at dawn by the trumpet, he attended an informational session, the *contio*. This, it must be emphasized, was an integral part of the political process; on some occasions, when bills and judicial decisions were involved, attendance was compulsory. Here the citizens observed candidates and heard arguments for and against proposed laws and policies. Reputations, careers, and future policies were determined at these assemblies.

Rome was never a democracy. Of the millions who lived within the limits of the Republic only thousands voted, for reasons of legal status and proximity to the city and its polling places. Yet those thousands included rich and poor, artisan and agriculturalist, urban Roman and country Roman, old families and new men. Citizenship lists were in constant flux as new towns, peoples, or families were granted citizen status on the basis of a treaty or the sponsorship of a patron. Enough people cared about this citizenship activity, even at the end of the Republic, that it became part of the code of prescribed gentlemanly behavior as well as the stimulus to public benefaction on the part of Rome's wealthiest and most distinguished citizens.[35]

CITIZENSHIP UNDER THE EMPIRE

Cicero's public morality elevated the *patria*, but exactly what that *patria* was lost its clarity under the emperors. While imperial publicists tried to extend the concept to a universal Rome, most residents of the Empire continued to think of their native town or city as their true fatherland. To be sure, in their elegant and self-conscious circle, pagan rhetoricians such as Symmachus and Libanius (314–93 A.D.) extolled Rome as the culmination of one thousand years of civilization, but this was hardly a message to create loyalty and patriotism among the masses in distant cities. Indeed, Rome never managed to create a model for citizen activity that transcended class and local place. It created the cultural programs that guaranteed admission to Rome's ruling class, but never an emotional intensity to undergird and match. Reaction to the demands of the fisc and the army cumulatively overpowered any impulses to serve Rome, conceived as the inheritor and preserver of civilization. Virgil, Horace, and the other poets proclaimed this message as did emperors, on coins and in the inscriptions carved on triumphal arches, but without the intended effect.

Nor did Caracalla's edict of universal citizenship help. Issued in 212 A.D., the *Constitutio Antoniniana* made all free men citizens but by so doing exposed more provincials to the growing tax demands of Rome. The greatest long-range accomplishment of this edict was not to stimulate greater affection for the emperor; rather, it was to accelerate a process of Romanization in the area of law and administration that had been going on for centuries. The ubiquitousness of individuals with the legal status of Roman citizens, and their demand that they be tried in accordance with their privileged status, had long promoted local adoption of, or at least familiarity with, Roman-law procedures and principles. Now, as many more men were to be judged under Roman law, legal activity became more homogeneous all over the Empire. The Empire may also have been strengthened by the entrance into its service of able provincials to whom the civil service was now open as a possible career.[36]

However, this development may not have been completely beneficial. If the Empire's well-being is conceived of as something of a balance between the vitality of the center and that of a thousand localities, the movement of local talent into the great imperial world may well have weakened local civil and commercial life. The success of ancient civilizations had always depended upon the energy of countless little places, their accomplishments in religion, art, politics, and literature. Now here was another possible drain upon the local vigor, upon the quality of local culture.

Eventually Rome developed a theory that identified its civilization with the universe, but too late to command universal allegiance. In Epictetus (55–135 A.D.) Rome becomes the world, a union of rational creatures. "You are a citizen of the universe and a part thereof," he wrote. "This universe is one city (*polis*)." In this community of rational citizens, the good man is to "take no thought for his own private interest . . . but to act as a hand or foot would act if they had reason, and never to think and plan as an isolated unit." And, echoing the great long classical emphasis on the need of mankind for social activity within an organic community, giving full value still to the excitement of creative community life, he asks: "What is a man? A part of a civic community (*polis*); indeed, of two communities, first the community of Gods and men, and then the [civic] community, which we describe as the nearest possible approach to it—the community which is a small copy of the community of the Universe."[37]

Such notions, however, were not enough to make men place obligations to mankind above those to neighbor and especially to family. The rewards were not great enough, except for the relatively few who, coming from Spain, the Balkans, or the East, rose high in the bureaucracy or army. But in actuality these had already cut the ties binding them to a local world as the prerequisite to their success on the imperial level. It took the church fathers to create a new system of loyalties and obligations, one based on a new definition of man and a new system of rewards.

During the Empire men were, in effect, citizens of two cities, Rome and their native place. But that was not enough. Many needs could not be satisfied by either the grand legal promises of imperial Rome or the emotional rewards of local status and success. Increasingly, citizens wanted something more, some promise of greater rewards than those to be won on earth. In a world become less sure, they sought consolation for a variety of reasons; many sought it in fellowship associations that prescribed a total living here as well as a certain saving there. Nor was this new to Rome. As we have seen, the vastness and strangeness of the Hellenistic city—one thinks of Alexandria, Piraeus, Ostia, Rome, Corinth—was mitigated by the ethnic or religious community, which granted an individual his identity of tightest fit. These primary corporations, called *politeuma* or *katoika*, were recognized in law. Indeed, the state caused their existence by a public act which recognized the preexisting social and, especially, religious realities. The thousands of Jews of Alexandria constituted a *katoika*, as we have seen, but so did the few in any other city throughout the Empire. Members of such a community affected the same style of life, spoke the same language or dialect, and believed in the same promise of a better hereafter.

By the third and fourth centuries A.D., a new wave of such cult groups had swept over the Empire from the East. Mithraism and Christianity were the most successful of these, promising eternal rewards for the right ethical conduct, right belief, and worshipful activities. Christianity finally triumphed and, within a few generations of its promulgation by the emperor Theodosius I as the official religion of the Empire (391), had created a new theory of citizenship and several new models for living. Together these constituted an effective refutation of a thousand years of classical life.

PART II

CITIZENSHIP IN THE
MEDIEVAL ITALIAN CITY

3

𐐜𐐜𐐜

MEDIEVAL CHRISTIAN

CITIZENSHIP: SOME

GENERALITIES

THE CITIZENSHIP OF THE FATHERS

Christianity not only rejected that model to which Aristotle and Cicero contributed, and which Symmachus and Libanius, two spokesmen for the philosophical paganism of the late fourth century, in their orations still defended, it offered a complete and satisfying alternative system that was hard to deny. Beginning with new beliefs, Christianity quickly shaped a culture which gave meaning and excitement to this life with its new rituals that "dramatized social and moral imperatives" and promised even more in the hereafter. Up to this time Rome's secular ceremonies had demonstrated the values and myths of classical civilization, which had assumed, though secular, a sacred quality. Now a new Christian order was celebrated in truly religious rites, which transformed individuals as it dramatized the new goals and values it placed before them.[1] The church fathers elaborated new theories and models for life; those who created a Christian ritual system also helped by providing a reiterated institutional framework in which values might be expressed and confronted again and again.

Even before this happened, Christian and Jewish voices had proclaimed the unworthiness of Rome and its materialist civilization. While nationalist movements disturbed the peace of the provinces, agitating for changes in the conditions of this world, Jews and Christians created their own kind of disturbances by prophesying terrible events; common to both groups were visions of vast calamity and destruction, to be followed by the creation of a new order. The law of Moses was to rule for the Jews; later, for the Christians, the Gospels and new allegiances were to prevail. Before, one looked to Rome for leadership; in the new era one looked first to Jerusalem and then either within or above to discover the city of the spirit. This is no union of mankind based on reason and universal natural law, but rather a community of the faithful, those bound to each other by ties of love, mutual dependence, and belief in a transcendent truth as preached by a transcendent leader. Passion, as opposed to analysis, prevails in this mode of life, and two related movements or directions predominate in it and reinforce each other, one toward the ideal or spiritual, away from the material and real, and one toward the heavenly.

By the fourth century, certainly by the time of Augustine, who died in 430, Christianity had composed a complete program which challenged and offered to replace the pagan moral and social pattern of life that had developed over a millennium. Instead of the emphasis on loyalty to the community, or service to the state, Christianity now recommended a narrower loyalty to the self and to the brotherhood one had entered through baptism and communion. Analogously, the active life of responsible citizens was rejected in favor of the solitary existence of the anchorite, the isolated monk who became the ideal Christian man, alone, contemplative, his body immune to physical discomfort, his mind enraptured. To the classical division of loyalty among family, local government, and civilization as presented by Rome, Christianity opposed its narrower Christian corporatism and its unlimited commitment to the Kingdom of God. Eventually, of course, Christianity was to enter the world, conquer it, and change it. But that was not its plan in the beginning. Even as victory came in the fourth century, it took time for the Church's leaders to accept responsibility in the world and develop theories to justify worldly activity. Some of them never accepted this new role, as the history of the vital, ever-reviving monastic movement shows.

Before we examine the new Christian theory of citizenship that Augustine and others produced, we must acknowledge and examine pre-Christian antecedents to Christianity's aversion to the conventional public morality of the ancient city-state world. The idealized pagan picture is that of a society homogeneous in culture and political status, all of whose entitled members contribute loyally and responsibly to the public welfare. The reality is a society highly differentiated, composed of many classes, groups, and associations, each marked by linguistic, legal, cultural, racial, and, most frequently, religious identity. Beneath the formal, respectable institutions of the city were the frequently disreputable family or clan or ethnic organizations whose members were new in town, still on the fringes of decent society, not yet in the political class. Such associations offered comradeship and help in unfamiliar urban surroundings and also served as institutions of socialization through which one passed from some local ethnic background into conventional civic life. They comforted an immigrant through his years of assimilation, or, as in the case of many Jews, they strengthened identity and slowed or prevented assimilation.

For the history of citizenship, the importance of such institutions is that they embody and carry forward a morality that was not only authoritative but also opposed to that of the establishment. In sociological terms, they constitute the institutional base for the religious counterculture, frequently lower-class, based on emotion and idealism that coexisted with the emotionally cooler and more materialist official culture of the Roman state. For all those who could not participate in the worship of Rome or have hope of gaining Roman citizenship—slaves and foreigners, for example—membership in such cult organizations brought comradeship on earth, the protection of some spiritual power, and the promise of heavenly life. Separated from the material rewards of ancient life, members of such groups denied the value of earthly goods and pleasures and exalted the less tangible rewards of paradise. Parallel to current philosophical notions about pure ideals and forms, they added their frustration, anger, and desire, so producing a new battery of values.

By the time Christianity rose from such an environment to eminence and power within Roman society, it had, of course, modulated its message and was prepared to compromise. Yet the precise, if not technical, language of Paul was always there to be confronted: "Now therefore ye are no more strangers and foreigners, but fellow citizens with the saints, and of the household of God."[2] Hard-liners were, and have always been, on hand to emphasize the idealist side of Christ's message.

The confrontation between two value systems, those of paganism and Christianity, may be seen in the debate in the mid-fourth century between two citizens of Antioch, Libanius and St. John Chrysostom. Libanius was a rhetorician, historian, friend of the pagan emperor, Julian. A learned Hellenist, he sums up a classical pagan literary education. For Libanius, paganism was civilization, the polis, the best environment for living the good life. He writes vividly of stoas and the agora, seeing clearly how the physical structure of the city shaped social and intellectual life. He saw his activity in the education of his fellow citizens as his proper conduct in the service of his community. His values and his kind of career had a long history, one which antedated Christ. Chrysostom was a student of Libanius, who at the age of eighteen experienced *conversio* and became a Christian ascetic. For Chrysostom, proper conduct meant furthering the conversion of Rome. He saw paganism still hanging on, in defiance of imperial law. His job was to fight both pertinacious paganism and heresy, another threat to his generation of orthodox believers.

It was in his "Sermons on the Statues" that Chrysostom developed a theory of Christian citizenship. To punish Antioch for the destruction of statues raised in his honor, the emperor had ordered the city razed—or so thought the citizenry, panicked by rumors, whom John now lectured. He would not be at all sorry to see the hippodrome, the theater, and the public baths destroyed. In contrast to Libanius, he sees such places as the embodiment of evil, "fountains of iniquity." The "dignity of a city" is not in its "large and beautiful buildings" nor in "that it has spacious porticos and walks . . . but in the virtue and piety of its citizens." Antioch's place in history was determined by one single event as recorded in the book of Acts: "It came to pass that the disciples were first called Christians at Antioch." Its love of Christ gave it its first dignity. The charity of the Antiochenes toward their Christian brothers in Jerusalem gave the city its second dignity. "If thou art a Christian," Chrysostom writes, "no earthly city is thine. . . . Though we may gain possession of the whole world, we are withall but strangers and sojourners in it all. We are enrolled in heaven: our citizenship is there."[3]

Chrysostom's good citizen was also a faithful subject, owing and giving proper obedience to constituted authority. Good Christian living meant rendering Caesar his due and bearing witness to Christian truth through Christian love. A city was more than a collection of people, much as for Augustine a state was more than a robber band. There had to be some animating, informing principle. For Chrysostom this was *agape*, that intense loving-kindness, which is more than the cool distribution of right that motivated good pagan government.

Chrysostom was not the only Christian thinker of this period interested in the problem of Christian citizenship. At about the time Libanius and Chrysostom wrote and lectured against each other at Antioch, St. Jerome in Palestine and St. Ambrose in Italy had come in another tradition to accept an important set of assumptions. They recognized the existence of Rome as a universal state, a theory propounded by pagan panegyrists for hundreds of years and ultimately based upon the Stoic concept of universal brotherhood. In theoretical pagan terms, Rome was a world-city of cocitizens made such by the emperor Caracalla. The Fathers accepted this concept of the Empire and equated it with the final age of man. Roman political universalism and Christian spiritualism thus were merged. The good Christian was to act the good subject, serving in the world as best he could.

This theory established the basis for civil conduct in this world but did not make clear the full nature and range of that conduct in relation to Christian theology and metaphysics. Another group of theorists, the most important of whom was Augustine, worked that problem out, relying upon a tradition to which both Platonic and Christian thinkers had supplied elements. For hundreds of years Neoplatonists had discussed the relationship of this world to some higher, purer one and had created metaphors and a vocabulary to deal with the issue. For example, the Hebrew scholar, Philo of Alexandria, wrote of Jerusalem as a holy city, which is in the world "only in one sense." "In another sense," he wrote, "it is in the wise man's soul." Even earlier, St. Paul had warned, "For we have not here a lasting city, but we seek one that is to come." Augustine may have been also inspired by the Psalms: "Glorious things are spoken of thee, O city of God," and "There is a river whose streams make glad the city of God, the holy dwelling places of the Most High."[4]

Augustine's inspiration may have come from these specific words; certainly he was influenced by the diffused tradition of Neoplatonism, which stressed the spiritual and identified the ideal as the real. But by the time he wrote the *City of God* as a response to those pagans, who, still influential, could now point with recrimination to the sack of Rome now Christian, the vocabulary and the concepts of Christian supernaturalism were familiar to the age. It remained for Augustine to formulate the problem in terms of several antagonisms—between body and soul, natural and supernatural, matter and spirit—which were to go down the centuries. That in this he was not altogether original does not detract from his importance; what is significant was his statement of individual issues and problems in the context of his total system, which, like Aristotle's, was all the more authoritative for its completeness, and which, like Aristotle's, became the basis for a complete outlook— what we call the medieval world view. Augustine wrote on every subject important for a faith still organizing itself for popular appeal and institutional survival: on worship, organization, authority, history, and great theological questions. His notion of the proper Christian life must therefore be seen as drawing power from its place in his entire system. Cicero is important to us for his summation of the values of many Greco-Roman centuries. But Augustine did more; he took the terminology of pagan civil-moral life, filled it with a new emotional strength, and quite literally gave it a new direction.

For Augustine, the City of God was a metaphor for goodness and spirituality throughout history, for that side of man which is forever turned toward God. The City of Man stands for man's evil tendencies and for his material concerns. Roughly, the former was identified with Jerusalem; the latter, with Babylon. The City of God may be thought of as heaven; the City of Man, as this world. The one is ideal, goal, aspiration, exhortation; the other is reality, immediacy, wary existence. Approached philosophically, his concept of the two cities serves Augustine as a principle of discrimination and ordering in ethics, ontology, and even epistemology. As such, it helps the Christian believer to sort out his world. Its history helps too: Cain established the City of Man, and although Abel did not establish the City of God, he was of it, as are all who strive to follow God's commandments.

There are good citizens of this world, as Augustine, the bishop and activist polemicist, knows, those who try to make the best of a bad situation. In Augustine's view, they are *peregrini*, resident aliens far from their true homeland, aching for their return. As we have been told, "peregrinus" is not "pilgrim" in any sense of movement toward a physical place. The weight of the word is in its anguish, its despair at separation. *Peregrini* are citizens of the City of God passing through the City of Man. In their sojourn here they are to accept the conventions of society—the state, laws, and other institutions ruled by a concern for justice—and are to do good within the institutional structures these create. Like pagan social theorists, Augustine was aware of the complexities of life in the world and saw the need to define right conduct in terms of social reality. In his theory, as in his episcopal office, Augustine dealt with real people whom he recognized as striving in their earthly pilgrimage (*peregrinatio*) to be decent, loving Christians. He was aware that people need each other, if nothing else, as the objects of acts of goodness in this life.[5]

True Christian citizens are those who in spiritual development, as well as in fact, model their lives on Christ and the Apostles. The City of God is the sum of their human acts as well as their residence in the afterlife. Activity in the hippodrome or theater no longer counts. What counts is membership in this elect group, which, although no longer congregated within the walls of one place, but dispersed throughout the world, still is defined by baptism, a common faith, and conventional good conduct. By making ordinary human acts take their meaning and value from their place in a hierarchy that reached to heaven, Augustine created a new model for life. This retained many good pagan habits, such as obedience, filial piety, law abidingness, and modesty, but gave these a higher purpose. Such acts take their justification now from the Decalogue and the Gospels and lead not to worldly success but rather to eternal rewards. They are based upon such Christian concepts as *caritas*, *agape*, *fraternitas*, and *justitia*.

The good Christian subject of the new Christian empire aspires to become the good citizen of the City of God.[6] The old pagan reward system, which delivered offices, honors, and exalted family status, was replaced by a Christian counterpart promising eternal life. This world pales in significance, and the good man and woman live it best within a framework that prepares them for the City of God. One earthly version of that structure is civil society, as manifested in the Roman Empire, which Augustine accepts and justifies as God's coercive instrument for the reform and education of sinful man. The good Christian accepts it too, obeys the laws, creates no unrest; he works, suffers, and prays. Another version is the monastery, which in Augustine's day was flourishing, fashionable, and promising. Although he was concerned with the quality of monastic life and wrote one of the earliest monastic rules, Augustine did not conceive of the monastery, or, for that matter, the Christian Church, as the City of God. No earthly institution could be equated to it; indeed, it was not the kind of institution that could be bounded by time or place. It was one plane or dimension of being that defined each person and mankind simultaneously.

What made Augustine's conceptualization of a new Christian citizenship so influential was both its timeliness, coming as it did when the old Roman code of values could serve fewer and fewer people each generation, and also its usefulness to a new society, which needed a new practical definition of the good life. Augustine's thinking could serve both the decaying cities of the Empire and the resurgent countryside. By the end of the fourth century the old classical world of the polis and *civitas* was dying; the categories in which Aristotle and Cicero wrote made little sense now that the physical base and social environment they assumed no longer existed, that is, the city with its organized public life, competitive senior families, adequate finances, and supportive, dependent countryside. The political ambience had changed too; the republican institutions of Greece and Rome, which had depended so much on individual participation, had been replaced by imperial authority manifested in many specific forms. A large, relatively well-educated citizenry was also gone.

However, if men participated less in government, we know they participated more in private life. Economic and social exigencies compelled reliance on members of the family, neighbors, and religious leaders within the local community. This arena was fit for the cultivation of private (Christian), as opposed to civic or public (pagan), virtue. Loyalty and service were now expressed toward members of an intimate society, who were bound together in brotherly love and dependent upon each other for food and protection in an era of increasing violence and simplicity of life. Christian morality made sense in a small-scale life constructed around restricted relationships such as those between parents and children, neighbors, lords, masters and servants. Moreover, instruction in such a morality moved out of the theater, law courts, and gymnasium into the church. Fewer senators and curiales survived to provide games and festivals to inspire citizen commitment and document their own. Now it was the bishop from the pulpit who exhorted his parishioners to save their souls through self-discipline, prayer, and the exercise of communal affection.

ABBOTS AND BISHOPS

While bishops worked in their fashion, abbots worked in theirs. A great new institution had come into existence to play a significant role in Western history. By the sixth century monasticism was well established throughout the western Mediterranean, principally under the Benedictine rule. Thousands of men and women chose to move out of civil society in an attempt to pursue a solitary, spiritual, frequently contemplative life. Some were successful; many others failed and found it necessary to organize new kinds of communities if they were to achieve any part of their goals. Viewed in this light, the monastery is a new kind of polity.

But if the goals of this community were new, being so specifically religious, its social mechanisms could not be. Like any institution born into a complex existing world, it produced as it needed them a variety of familiar subinstitutions with which to meet worldly challenges: laws, buildings, symbols, and educational devices. Monastic citizenship differed significantly from that of the ancient city yet was in some ways congruent in that it gave new answers to the same set of defining questions.

To the question of what is the community, ancient political thought had given several answers. In republics, active free citizens who paid taxes, did some form of personal service, and participated in the law-making process, were members of the community; frequently membership in a clan or tribe and/or residence in a specific region or place was a prerequisite. In monarchical states, those who obeyed administrative pronouncements received support and protection. Membership in the monastery, however, rested on a formal, if not quasi-sacramental, commitment to a life defined by the four Benedictine vows or another set of demands. Monastic citizenship, then, had a sacred basis and produced a special life-style visible and meaningful to all. And, like classical citizenship, it constituted an exchange. In return, usually, for entrance into the group life with obligations of service and prayer, the *opus Dei*, it promised respect, care, and eternal salvation. In the Roman legal world there was no one higher than a citizen. In the Christian hierarchy, straight through the Middle Ages, the monk was the best man, the most honored and venerated. He enjoyed this merit because more than any other he served his fellow Christians through prayer, intercession on behalf of those not strong enough to renounce, as much as he, the City of Man.

The community in which the monk performed this virtuous service was a distinctive society organized within physical and ecclesiastical boundaries and subject to its own laws. In it authority lay not with some popularly elected officials or board, or with a divinely chosen leader, but rather with a father-teacher chosen by the monks for his virtue, which translated into spiritual power. Theoretically, the choice of a master was inspired; prompted by some divine agency, the monks chose the right man. Within this little territorial state, subject to the will and wisdom of the abbot, the good citizen obeyed the rules, thus preparing for his real eternal life. Good conduct was valued in the monastery, and punishments were available to insure it; but in an ultimate sense, no matter how good a monk's life was, it was not perfect or real. On a scale of being and values, it was incomplete and impure, but it was better than anything else in human experience, the best promise there was on earth of eternal life.

This is the peculiar reward of monasticism: not a ceremonial arch to commemorate a victory, or advancement to higher public office, but a promise. Observance of the rules for privation leads to etherealization and to God. Much the reverse of the pagan scheme, the ideal Christian life aims at nonliving. Indeed, the monastery was viewed as a necessary if unfortunate compromise, for it enabled the continued participation of an individual in a corporate activity. In Western Europe, although every century produced its hermit saints, most monks lived in organized communities. Ideally, the monk would have lived alone on his column top or in his cave making a solitary effort to follow a spiritual life.

This emphasis on the individual and solitary reveals to us that the basic impulse in monasticism is personal and anarchic. Yet each monastery eventually had its dormitory, brewhouse, school, and church, along with other specialized buildings. One may visit today some of these enormous apparatuses that still function as they did one thousand years ago, integrating many different kinds of activities in an attempt to follow hard rules. These, however, point to monasticism's great paradox, if not weakness: that any attempt to achieve personal perfection demanded more than the individual acting alone, in fact demanded corporate acts of prayer and mutual regulation. Once within his monastery, the monk prayed incessantly and in between his acts of devotion performed all those works—copying, teaching, gardening, cooking—that had to be done if the new and usually primitive community was to survive.

Clearly, to some degree, the monastery was the more intense Christian formulation of the classical idea of community; the parish and diocese were less intense formulations, less spiritual because more bureaucratic. The monastery is the Christian polis, being both a physical place and a spiritual ideal, and imposing upon its members a special tradition, set of beliefs, and ritual practices. Athena is replaced by St. Radegunde, athletic performance by saintly accomplishment, and law court and theater by complex ritual.

The invention of monastic citizenship helped to destroy the ancient civic world. There already existed a perception of society as divided not between citizens and noncitizens, but between rich and poor. The monks, especially those in the Eastern Empire, now made a point of comparing themselves to the poor, in this way making themselves doubly special. By the end of the fourth century imperial legislation recognized civic distinctions based upon economic status. In effect, theologians were helping to create a new definition of society, ignoring the traditional categories established by the jurists.[7]

Viewed as social organism, the monastery is a special kind of small community, a sort of *politeuma* of the saints. Its members are closely bound to each other and to it; there are mutual responsibilities. A special society, it functions as the scene for the highest activities possible in Christian citizenship, contemplation and prayer. It was also the place where an individual might exercise his virtue publicly, thus influencing others to do good, and where his success and celebrity might win for him leadership of the community and possibly sainthood itself. What the polis and the civitas were to paganism, the monastery became for Christianity long before there were distinctive Christian cities—the place to exercise virtue where the good man might approach the City of God on earth.

However, one should not emphasize the active side of the monastic life. In all the dichotomies of the age, monasticism was always on the side of contemplation. The monk was viewed as the epitome of the contemplative, as opposed to the active, life. In the long medieval debate over the best Christian life, monasticism was the most effective institutional statement of the superiority of contemplation. The fact that monasteries eventually were numbered in the thousands all over Europe added to the statement. Viewed in these terms, monasticism must be seen as a rejection of citizenship in the full classical sense of the term.

During the early Middle Ages, centuries of violence and danger, the success of monasticism was important. It represented survival on a basis other than force. There exist no contemporary analyses of the politics or sociology of the monastery, of its role in society. But we can see that if it did not offer a new theory of human cooperation, it nonetheless functioned as an alternative model. Here were men—not citizens but brothers—working together in a well-disciplined way to achieve a common goal. That goal was personal in that each was to claim his own salvation, but it was attainable only through acts of cooperation to which the strength and spirit of each contributed.

Although citizenship survived only as a diminished and relatively unimportant institution during the early Middle Ages, yet, in the small number of places in the West that persevered as cities, it helped pull and keep the world together by making Christian citizens out of pagan Romans and Germans. As the world became rural and as political power moved out of the city and onto the great estate, it was one of the few political institutions that continued to function as in the ancient past, not out of theory, for churchmen were devising new theories now, but out of the mutual great needs of individuals and organized society. Much as the chieftain gave protection on his villa or in his warrior band, the city gave protection within its walls and through the activity of its bishop, its saint, and its relics. Neither trade, nor government, nor intellectual activity supported urban life any longer.

Religion now supported the little cities that held on to existence as bishop's seats or the sites of shrines. The bishop's court became the focus of all political and economic life, and local activities again became exclusive in determining the nature of urban life. During the Empire many cities had taken on a veneer of cosmopolitanism, defined in terms of international trade, education, tourism, governmental administration. Now that thin crust of homogeneity superimposed upon the indigenous life of preexisting Semitic, Celtic, Greek, Latin, and other communities disappeared, whereupon the basic localism of premodern Europe became attached to a new institution, the local church headed by a bishop. Urban, or rather civic, identity now largely derived from episcopal leadership, which itself fused religious and political authority.

From this time on in European history, religion and politics are tied together, not only at the level of pope and emperor, but also at that of local leadership. Loyalty is to the city through its bishop and saint, and parish loyalties culminate in the cathedral. During the hundreds of years that end with the revival of more purely secular political institutions in the eleventh century, popular political activity on crisis occasions takes place in the square before the bishop's church and is directed by him. There is no public life that is not in some basic aspect religious. In the past, Athens and Rome had depended upon their tutelary deities, so in a sense there was nothing new in this arrangement. But now the relationship between man and God was intensified, and there were few secular distractions or alternatives. What in Italian culture is called *campanalismo*, that intense and all-encompassing focus upon city affairs as symbolized by and directed from the bell tower of the city's mother church, enters European history.

The primary agent of this new Christian cultural-political development was the bishop. If the monastery preserved the models of Christian spiritual life, the episcopacy became the means of beneficent change in what was left of the world. By the late fourth century the bishops were increasing in importance as their flocks grew and as Roman civil authority came to rest in their hands. Progressively, the latent civic individualism of imperial urban life came to focus on the bishop as the savior-leader of local society. Later, throughout the Middle Ages, in every town, the bishop was to be associated with the fundamental identity of the community. In late antiquity, what the emperors did not give the bishops, the bishops eventually took. They were competent, and, what is more, they had the means to rule since frequently they were members of landed local dynasties, which regarded the local bishopric almost as inheritable private property.

Meanwhile, another kind of localism developed in those areas eventually ruled by Germanic tribes. In northern Europe and Germany, where the episcopal office did not become the possession of an established local dynasty, it fell into the hands of a local tribal leader. There, where no preexisting urban framework existed for the Church to adopt as a territorial base, religion was organized on a tribal basis. Since tribal government generally followed the movements of the leader, at first no single place achieved regional importance. But slowly certain places became favorite residences, and there, eventually, a tribal capital came into existence in a de facto way. In such a place the bishop would be related to the leading elements of the tribe. This, then, is another basis for a restricted but existent urbanism. Here in the north, as in the citified regions of Roman Gaul, local political power provided protection for the city and its few inhabitants.

The saint too provided protection in this age. Every place had its own, which is to emphasize that, in the creation of a new urban identity, religion was all important. To the auspices of the local political power was added the power of the saint. Each little place survived and was known through this confluence of powers. The localism of Mediterranean antiquity thus was replaced by the Christian localism of the early Middle Ages. In other terms, the town and its people received a new identity as dependents of a complex new religious authority in which the saint, not the bishop, was the predominant figure. Since it was under the saint's auspices that the community flourished or decayed, it was to the saint that prayers were directed.

Also contributing to both the isolation and cultural individuality of each little place that survived was the agricultural economy of the early Middle Ages. And the intensity of local history, in the form of such memorable events as sieges, famines, and miraculous demonstrations, played a role in creating a sense of place. Rome has never forgotten the dramatic confrontation between Pope Leo I and Attila the Hun. Every town began to construct its heroic history in this period, as its bishops and saints cooperated to preserve it. To some degree the classical slate was wiped clean. The European landscape bore less and less the physical and social imprint of Greece and Rome; new local civilizations came into being everywhere.

Thus was constructed, or reconstructed, the basis for early medieval citizenship, a new localism basically dependent upon religion. The new Christian city was created by the same process that made Athens, only now the scene of creation includes Europe north of the Alps, the religious foundation is some idiosyncratic version of a rough common Christianity, and the human basis is, progressively, the progeny of Latins married to Germans.

Within the city that was at the same time religious capital, shrine, and military fortress, the bishop assumed leadership. In late imperial days the state had burdened him with civil responsibilities. Now, in Germanic times, administrative competence was exclusively in the bishop's hands. If authority and tradition in each monastery were embodied in the abbot, in the city they were in the bishop. His ties to the patron saint above as well as to his predecessors were important. They gave him confidence in the continuity of his see and gave his flock a sense of security and identity. Toward the end of the sixth century Gregory of Tours could write, "The wretch did not know that with the exception of five bishops all the other bishops of Tours are connected with my family stock."[8] If he knew this, so did his people, to whom the choice of their bishop was always a matter of central importance.

Early in the Middle Ages then, the structuring of new civic identities began, largely around the bishop. He came to be viewed as the civil and spiritual leader of the area for the populations both within and outside the walls. In later centuries this development was to prove important when secular governments used an original relationship to a bishop to justify expansion into their neighbor's territory. For the moment it meant that the large majority of the population in an area, the peasants, also looked to the bishop for their identity. His activities as judge, general, and priest gave them everything they needed for survival, and if they tilled the bishop's fields, his *oeconomicus* gave them economic direction as well. Identity flowed down from the bishop's person/office; his powers conferred life and personality to all those dependent upon them. His success in keeping the enterprise going provided his subjects with an awareness of their ancestors, laws, and civic institutions.

Whereas in Gaul the Church, especially the bishops, dominated each city and constituted the basic educational institution, which affected the Germans, in Italy that institution was the city itself. There, especially in the plain of the Po and the coastal regions, which retained Byzantine influences, if not political ties, civic institutions frequently survived. Urban assemblies, administrative hierarchies, and courts, for example, functioned under Gothic officials known as *Comes Gothorum*. They decided suits between Germans and Romans within their unified jurisdiction and supervised locally elected officials of Roman background who were responsible for taxation, guarding and maintaining the city walls, and the provisioning of Gothic armies. In effect, the Germanic conquerors came to learn something about using a city. If they did not understand its cultural significance, they realized its financial, military, and political possibilities. They saw it as a place to be mobilized—

through the activities of its important people. In late Rome, the senators bound the peasant to the soil; in Germanic Italy, from the fifth century on, the new rulers bound the magistrate to his bench and the resident to his quarter so that essential functions, especially justice and defense, were maintained.

But if the surviving city and its population are exploited by the new authorities of the community, they act reciprocally upon the Germans, forcing upon their consciousness an awareness of the constituent working parts of a more complex society, for to maximize benefit from the city, the barbarians had first to learn how it worked. For many Germans, walls and bureaucrats must first have been viewed without much differentiation—as two things possessed and to be exploited. One must not exaggerate either the size of the city or the effect it had upon the Germans. All cities were very small, with populations of a few thousand, if that. But they were cities: their populations did not farm, and they possessed vestiges of greater size and function.

By this time the Church was already part of the urban mechanism, which meant that the Germans in Italy as in southern France had to recognize the importance of the bishop and learn to handle him. Their appreciation of his activities was the closest they came to understanding the intellectual and spiritual qualities of city life. As Arian Christians, the Goths were never fully integrated with the surviving Roman orthodox population of the cities. Then came the Lombards, who conquered the Po valley and much of inland Italy in the late sixth century, establishing a kingdom and several dukedoms which lasted about two hundred years. They converted to the orthodox Roman faith; with this event the organic involvement of Germans and Latins began on a significant scale. Most Lombards lived in the country along with most of the indigenous Latin population. But some did live in such cities as Perugia, Bologna, and Pavia, and they show us a special case of the fusion of two peoples and the creation, eventually, of new civic institutions, including citizenship.

It was a case both like and unlike that of the earlier Goths. Like, in that the Lombards continued the Gothic practice of allowing Latin institutions to survive, while converting them to their own service and profit. Unlike, in that once orthodox Catholics, the Lombards were accepted by the bishops, who urged cooperation upon their parishioners. For their part the Lombards conveyed powers of government to the bishops. They recognized that the city was a special juridical entity and that it survived under the bishop's administrative and spiritual powers. Churches and public spaces in front of churches were protected by the threat of enormous fines, and public meetings in places other than the bishop's sacred space were forbidden.

NEW POLITICAL INSTITUTIONS
AND PHYSICAL REALITIES

The critical place/event was the *conventus ante ecclesiam*, which was, in effect, a new public institution. It came into being during the period of invasions and folk migrations when the narrowly constituted upper-class Roman curia could no longer direct or mobilize the community. The *conventus* replaced the curia and opened participation to the entire free male population, Lombard and Latin. Participants are referred to by the old Roman terminology: the documents speak of *cives*. While this word was retained, with its ancient suggestion of purposeful activity for the community's welfare, the other traditional word which designated leadership, *curiales*, was dropped. In Lombard pronouncements, the leaders of the new community are called *notabiles, optimates*. Whether the bishops presided over the new assembly is not known, but the competence of the *conventus* over public matters is certain. It elected the bishop, maintained the fabric of the city's public works, including the cathedral, and supervised market matters and public health. Discussion of these public issues was recorded by an official of the community, a public notary, whose acts were deposited in the bishop's church, which also served as town archive.

We see here the fusion of public and religious life in and around the bishop and his physical establishment. His wisdom, administrative skills, and resources are essential to the community, while the economic needs of his court contribute to the growth of an even larger population of merchants, who move constantly from city to city, from Italy to the eastern Mediterranean. The citizenship of these *cives* is demonstrated by their service in the Lombard army, which prescribed armament scaled to wealth and thus reinforced the *conventus* as an instrument of unification. Under the pressure of events that called for major decisions and major sacrifices, distinctions between German and Latin tended to fade.

By the end of the Lombard period in Italy (754), the Merovingian period in Gaul (ca. 700), by the time, that is, of Charlemagne (768–814) and the

Carolingians, some new social and political institutions have appeared in the cities of southern Europe. Europe is still overwhelmingly tribal and rural, but in the cities new identities are being created. In Germanic society, identity came from the kindred or tribe, from some grouping of persons bound by blood ties, or it came from some form of proto-vassalage formalized by an oath of mutual engagement between two military comrades. To his family, tribe, or lord, the individual owed loyalty, honor, and usually some military and justice-keeping service. Now, if a city man, he retained those personal obligations and added a civic identity conferred by residence in a place.

Residence, however, is not a static concept. It means participation in the critical life of the community: decision making, fighting, and praying. Birth within the place and service to it convey membership in the group and identity deriving from that membership in the eyes of others. Eventually, the more fully developed city was to confer distinctive cultural attributes, but in the eighth century these were still minimal. For the moment, it is enough to say that two different styles of authenticating political life had met, and that for some purposes, increasingly political, Latins and Germans functioned as citizens in the classical sense of that word. In the German world, no Aristotle had ever expressed a formal theory of citizenship, but, more important, the exigencies of life in a wandering tribal society had created an analogy: there too men and women came of age instructed in the benefits and obligations that came to them in their station in life. New cooperative activities were serving as mechanisms by which German and Roman social hierarchies were being integrated. The full sense of ancient citizenship was missing, but men of different backgrounds were, in fact, acting as citizens.

Although personality of law might be retained in court, and although Lombards and Romans each had a class hierarchy based on wealth, nevertheless, a single urban population was well under construction, held together by its daily economic, military, and political activities. Most of all, as Germans and Latins worshiped side by side in churches built for a single orthodox population, ties to the bishop functioned constructively. Indeed, a new identity took shape based on the history of a given territory over centuries, the new political institutions such as the *conventus*, and the special Christianity of the place as embodied in its relic, its saint, and its bishop. The Germans' need for a religious link among people thus was retained, which surely facilitated their acceptance of the Roman concept of citizenship based on birth or residence within a given precinct.

In an age which liked to touch what it talked about, the physical components of a city also contributed to its identity. Walls, other fortifications, rudimentary public buildings, along with the bishop's cathedral, all gave a sense of corporeality as well as continuity to life. The men who supported the material fabric of city life, although they might be ranked hierarchically according to wealth and civic expectations of their level of service, were all citizens if they were free.

Flexible in such a way as to allow some individuality to two populations, Roman and German, yet structured enough to shape the cooperative efforts of men of many laws, the early medieval town remained relatively stable in these circumstances for centuries. The form it achieved by Charlemagne's day lasted into the age of Gregory VII (d. 1085), that is, through the second period of invasions. As Europe suffered from the Vikings, Magyars, and Saracens, bishops organized tiny municipal armies while they continued to pray. In France, and more so in Italy, where there always had survived a measure of "public self-consciousness," the bishop persevered as the central urban figure.

Eventually a rudimentary canon law played a role in forcing together the bishop and the city. Under Charlemagne the tithe became a formal obligation, so that there was now a religious tax as well as an occasional secular one. The importance of the Church to the laity was now clearly stated in money terms. A single unit—dependent on secular and ecclesiastical cooperation, and embracing the populations of an interdependent urban center and a surrounding rural region—had come into existence.

If there was one significant Carolingian institution which developed through the ninth and tenth centuries, it was the *parlasium*. Its functions are not completely clear, although they are very similar to those of the *conventus*, but we do know that it was not held in the square before the bishop's palace. Frequently it met in a place with secular traditions or atmosphere, a Roman theater or amphitheater, and handled matters of a public, secular nature. It functioned as something of a mass public assembly; manumissions were made in it, and legal disputes were sometimes settled and publicized there. Also, Byzantine analogies suggest that military decisions were taken in the *parlasium*. Here, then, is another public institution in which Germans and Romans engage, under conditions of constant local warfare and the impact of the invaders. History was created by adversity: pressure from the outside generated new institutions and loyalty to them. We are talking of much of Western Europe from the ninth into the eleventh centuries.

However, that same period witnessed the first medieval urban conflicts, those between the traditional leaders, especially the bishops, and their subjects, especially the merchants. Guilds, as organizations of artisans, functionaries, and merchants, had existed in northern Europe from the eighth century; in the south, some form of corporate organization had never ceased to exist. Now, from the tenth century on, townsmen grew in self-appreciation and came to desire rights of self-government. The result was the novelty of urban politics as the traditional authorities such as bishops and counts faced new interest groups in the petty nobility, merchants, and a new urban professional class composed of lawyers, notaries, and other administrators. As these groups struggled with each other over taxes and fines, the unity of the body politic was further established through this very conflict over control of city government and its spoils. Over large areas of Italy, the nearby rural nobility was also drawn into urban politics as, in the course of the eleventh century, each city intensified its control over a countryside that both protected and fed its population. The leadership skills of the nobles, especially their military competence, were invaluable.

The process of political unification was marked not only by the addition of new political assemblies but also by new buildings. Marketplaces and town palaces appeared to perform activities essential to urban life. Since towns all over Europe became centers of administration, the number of such governmental buildings grew. In many cities, in addition to these secular buildings, fortified stone churches served a public need at moments of siege and defense. In sum, a physical mass grew along with a population mass as urban life flourished. Every one of these constructions, it must be emphasized, had important social, political, and economic effects. To build walls and large edifices the population had to pool its resources and work together. But if investment of large sums provided employment for a variety of artisans and suppliers, it also raised problems of fiscal responsibility: how were obligations to be distributed throughout the community? In what proportion were ecclesiastical and lay groups to contribute? How were the various secular groups to divide their responsibility? The solution of such questions made politics a function of growth, as the needs of the physical enterprise forced some unity upon a population becoming ever more complex in the number and variety of its interest groups. The search for the basis of civic identity must take cognizance of the physical aspect of that identity—the degree to which even at an early date, spiritual affinity or patriotism was linked to a place or a monument overlaid with associations.

THE REVIVAL OF COMMERCE,
LAW, AND ORDER

For the three centuries between Charlemagne and Henry IV (d. 1105), the records are quite dark on legal matters connected with citizenship. We have few town constitutions or commentaries on likely texts in the civil law and no way to get at the specificities of relationships and status. Yet the documents occasionally refer to *cives*, which suggests that some sense of ancient history and law was preserved. And we meet this word in connection with those public assemblies in which often the entire free male population turned out to confer and vote. Clearly the Roman associations of the term survived. It was enough during those years to think of simple burdens and simple acts of assent. But then, toward the middle of the eleventh century, many things began to happen, all of which had their impact upon citizenship. As we have seen, much of the long-term medieval city was in place. It had by then achieved a primitive social, political, religious, and constitutional shape, to say nothing of a physical cast. Earlier centuries had provided history and memories most of which were tied to the bishop, whose leadership, and the saint, whose powers, had protected the city and guaranteed its survival. Physically the town was now a unity within walls; earlier distinctions between burg and *wik*, for example, had been effaced. The wall, which had taken community effort and money to erect, surrounded a distinctive urban geography, and within that wall most men were part of the political community. Whether merchants, notaries, comital or episcopal administrators, or artisans, they regarded themselves as members of a civic whole. They looked to the city for the identity which birth in a given location, as opposed to tribal ancestry, had come to confer. They knew that the legal powers they needed to function successfully as townsmen were derived from that birth: essential urban needs such as personal freedom, mobility, and the exercise of a congenial law, usually incorporated in a charter of liberties.

This was a merchant society, and as it developed it became more competitive: individual against individual within each city, to say nothing of the rivalry between cities everywhere in Europe, especially among the city-states of Italy. Each merchant sought some marginal benefit by which to beat a competitor; each civil servant sought some principle by which to discriminate for or against some friend or enemy. In the scramble for resources, then, possession of a certain status of full competence, that is, of the full rights of citizenship, gave one access to the full potentialities of the new economy and the new government. Both were growing at an unprecedented rate in this age; opportunities were everywhere as Europe entered its first boom period in a thousand years. Some sixty-five years ago, in a book which formed this century's basic view of the medieval revival of town life, Henri Pirenne made the merchant the key figure.[9] It was the merchant who, first as a wanderer and then a settler, provided the intelligence, capital, daring, dynamic imagination, and greed that created medieval city life. Pirenne's strong views provoked the scholarship that has modified this picture. The merchant retains significant importance, but now we know that artisans, notaries, teachers, rural nobles, ecclesiastical administrators, physicians, and others also contributed significantly to the intensity and variety of city life.

Many of these were citizens, and whatever they did for a living, the political side of their lives must be recognized. Pirenne argued that the merchant was distinctive because of his new career, which was fueled by what we now call the profit motive as well as by his desire for salvation. The same might be said of the citizen who also acted out of a complex motivation, if not ideology, in which the material and the moral were linked. The activism that had always been part of the citizen tradition necessarily became part of the merchant's life. Soon it became clear that the city and its business succeeded only when the businessman played the role of civic activist. This perception came when a revived classical scholarship provided the model, history, law, and vocabulary of republican Rome.

There is no point in debating, as medieval students would have done, which was the more influential, the merchant or the citizen, for in most cases they were the same man. What has to be emphasized, however, is the mutual reinforcement of the two conditions or activities. Both identities contributed to a single impact upon Europe's development. The merchant provided the drive and material basis for the new urban civilization. The status of citizen conferred value upon the merchant's materialism and eventually the theoretical justification for the politics of popular participation and representation that came out of communal history. Under such circumstances the citizen merchant became a figure of great power, real and potential, in medieval society.

As competition grew, so did the need for a basis of discrimination. As higher education became more readily available, its possession became one basis for social differentiation. Literacy became desirable as a mark of social class since it was restricted to those of the feudal and merchant aristocracy who could afford it. Titles became more significant in this same period, as the

European nobility organized itself for the first time in ways that have lasted until today. Consciousness of citizenship may be seen as part of this same movement and process. Like rural nobles, urban men sorted themselves out as the search for privileges became intense.

This process of classification and organization is one of the great events of European history because it took place in every significant field. In law, it produced first Gratian's *Decretum* (ca. 1140), which organized the canon law, and about a century later Accursius's *Glossa ordinaria* on the books of Justinian. In theology, it produced Abelard's *Sic et Non* and eventually the more sedate *Sentences* of Peter Lombard. In the social world, women, Jews, homosexuals, and heretics now were given more fixed places in a more ordered and self-conscious society. No wonder the period that witnessed the organization of townsmen into guilds should also have made an attempt to decide, more rigorously than had been done since antiquity, who was a member of the political community, and with what consequences for the performance of his career.

The effort to define citizenship was made disciplined and rational by the availability of Roman history and legal science. The same cultural movement that advanced literacy among the European laity provided the basis for thinking on citizenship. No medieval historian or theologian ever wrote a treatise on citizenship, but chroniclers and legists became aware of the term and its many variations, especially in Italy, and soon every legist glossed or commented upon certain classic laws in the *Corpus Iuris Civilis*.

By this time a general revival of ancient culture was under way. Knowledge of ancient Rome as revealed in its historians gave a model and vocabulary for political organization. It is no accident that the executives of the early communes were called consuls or that the legislative body was often called the senate. If the Republic was inspiration here, the vocabulary was provided by the Empire, specifically the works of Justinian. The *Corpus Iuris Civilis* became central to the curriculum of Bologna before 1100; it provided a complicated, yet serviceable terminology of citizenship. The Code and Digest made careful distinctions among various kinds of citizenship or other local and imperial status. They also specified a variety of possible forms of relationships between the individual and the community, spelling out city-citizen expectations in each case, as these had been developed over a thousand years of ancient urban civilization. Western society came into possession of this substantial body of citizenship law at the moment it needed new sets of words and the theories behind those words with which to distinguish between those who were and were not competent members of the new community.

Moreover, at the beginning of a new period of thinking about political and social relations, the Roman law provided, in a working context, ideals and goals as well as terms. For example, since medieval Christians had necessarily to be concerned with justice, the new legal science was at the basis of the new politics of power, or was supposed to be. Justice, in one simple Ciceronian formula known to the Middle Ages, was giving each man his due. In the legally aware communities of medieval Europe, that meant first defining a man in legal terms. Was he a native or alien, Christian or Jew, orthodox or heretic, full political citizen, or one with modified legal and political competence? How these questions were answered determined so much in the world: what political offices were open, what trading possibilities, what guild memberships, what property-holding legitimacy. Careers in the Middle Ages were not ordinarily open to talent. They were based on birth, and also on power deriving from citizenship status. Status meant legal capability.

This new concern with citizenship represents more than fascination with the prestigious ancient world. It is intricately connected to every aspect of Europe's social, economic, and political revival and constitutes a return to patterns of order and reflection unknown since Rome, as well as to a level of material civilization based on unprecedented wealth and a relatively wide distribution of property. Citizenship becomes important because wealth is now to be won as never before in Christian history. (It is no accident that the twelfth century, like the nineteenth, saw a remarkable growth in speculation about the purposes, nature, responsibilities, and justice of property. The scale of its availability had to be considered by those whose role it was to think about realities in relation to authorities and values.) In these new circumstances in which so much wealth was to be acquired, the benefits conferred by citizenship were critical. They provided the power to enter the arena and win, or at least compete with some advantages.

In part, the new wealth of Europe resulted from the work of peasants, from the new agriculture and the widespread rural prosperity assured by a growing market for farm products. It derived also from the activities of itinerants whose various new or increased activities took them out of one environment and put them in another. Crusaders traveled across Europe to the Holy Land and Byzantium. Merchants and pilgrims traveled everywhere. Peasant sons, no longer needed on the land, moved to the growing towns. Exiles sought refuge in new homelands. Students and professors traveled from university to university seeking knowledge and career opportunities. Every one of these movements, which reflect the great changes of the age, touches upon citizenship. Every community found it necessary to think about the place of the newcomer in society. Every entrant into an existing community faced problems of reception and assimilation—but saw that he was not alone. Europe was in full movement as never before.

Nor was this movement only physical, geographical. This is the era of great social mobility. It is when the poor boy Godric becomes an entrepreneur before he becomes a saint, when Lusignans and Hautvilles create feudal empires within a few generations, and when countless landed families disappear from the records, destroyed by an aggressive neighbor. All this activity is related to citizenship in that in every area citizenship is a prerequisite for the legal and political competence essential for social eminence, for acceptance by preexisting and forming local elites.

These developments between, say, 1050 and 1150 mark the end of one urban age and the beginning of another. They began in Italy and were certainly in place over most of its central and northern regions by the beginning of the thirteenth century. Their penetration and establishment north of the Alps and into Eastern Europe extended over the entire late Middle Ages.

Basic to this process was the fact that city and citizen desperately needed each other now, and both appreciated the articulation of responsibilities and benefits the subtle vocabulary of the Roman law provided. The city needed services and taxes and a moral outlook that promoted active participation in its affairs; the individual needed clarification of his benefits in a new situation of economic competition and the protection of a place whose political and economic power were recognized outside its walls.

Perhaps the interdependency would never have been so clear had it not been for the economic revival Europe experienced from the late eleventh century. One is almost tempted to say that citizenship became possible as an institution in the Middle Ages only when a certain level of economic activity had been reached. That level presupposes the existence of a physical city of some size, the regular use of money in trade and eventually banking, specialization of labor, and at least some craft or industrial activity. Only when medieval society was this highly developed was there something to tax and defend as well as some authority to grant the privileges that made citizenship valuable.

The medieval city, certainly the more important Mediterranean ones during their periods of glory, was probably more complex socially and, especially, legally than is usually assumed. People of many backgrounds and legal conditions lived there: native-born merchants and artisans with the full legal and political capacity of citizenship; persons from the nearby countryside, in Italy the *contado*, with some legal and political capacity as specified in a treaty or peace agreement; immigrants at some stage in the naturalization process; aliens, perhaps merchants from another city, or pilgrims under the protection of the canon law with no intention at all of becoming citizens, with every intention of returning to their native place, even after years of life abroad; Jews living by their own laws in their own community; and perhaps in some Mediterranean region even a community of Moslems living according to their law as they flourished in a specialized occupation. Every one of these persons had some distinctive combination of legal and political powers, and these distinctions do not even touch questions of social class, de facto political importance, and the like.

To draw this picture is to assert the similarity between a rich medieval port like Venice and a great cosmopolis of the ancient world like Alexandria, and to document the continuity of certain basic forms of social organization from the ancient into the medieval centuries (or, if not actual continuity except in a few rare Italian cases, the existence of certain structures in societies of a similar nature). Again the larger town functioned as an entity composed of several subentities or corporations, each with its special life, identity, and needs that did not entirely coincide with those of the city as a whole. The city tolerated the existence of alien and Jewish communities because it could not possibly homogenize them into a single city life. Once more it expected general cooperation in return for the freedoms and protections it gave. It empowered guilds to monitor the activities of their members because it could not efficiently govern large numbers of individuals. Seen this way, the medieval city—if we think now only of the large, complex ones with differentiated populations—tolerated several citizenships as had the big ancient towns: its own citizenship, which gave an identity for the world, and the de facto citizenship of the group or quarter, which identified and empowered an individual within the community. The common elements of both citizenships were, first, the fact that they both conferred identity and status, which conferred legal and political rights, powers, and responsibilities, and, second, that both were based upon some ethical or moral foundation—ultimately a commitment of service to the group which itself represented a high ideal.

That both the city and the group possessed educational institutions to educate their members suggests a high consciousness of purpose.

CITIZENSHIP IN THE NORTH

Finally, we must apply limits to these generalizations. Geographically, the events described were largely restricted to Italy and the northern shore of the western Mediterranean and, with some differences, to the Lowland and Rhineland regions of northern Europe. Their development depended upon the size and social complexity of the city involved, and also upon the extent of its independent political life. In the feudal and monarchical regions of Europe, neither the social, political, nor literary-moral basis for citizenship was as yet, to the twelfth century, significantly developed. When they were developed, however, we may recognize enough similarity to the institutions of antiquity to allow mention of "the first age of citizenship."

This extended discussion of the Italian city may appear a distortion to English-speaking readers. The question must arise for those whose automatic assumptions are of the primacy and exclusiveness of Anglo-Saxon institutions: what of English citizenship during the Middle Ages? And what of the Flemish cities, Bruges and Ghent?

The emphasis on Italy is justified by the precocious institutional development of the Italian cities, and above all by their actual function as independent political units, each with its own internal and external history over many generations. In the north, in Flanders, France, England, and the Rhineland, there were eventually great cities—great in size and economic, political, and architectural accomplishment. But they were not independent; they were parts of the feudal world.

Italy, on the other hand, possessed what might be called the essential requirements for "genuine" or "true" citizenship in Aristotelian usage. It had in its cities independent, working political institutions in which citizen activity was absolutely necessary if the functions of government were to be performed; it had a public language with which to discuss and conduct a public life; and it had a historical consciousness of the moral history of antiquity, which increasingly served as a model for its own. In all this there is a certain vividness in Italian civic history; it is clear and unambiguous in its nature, meaning, and influence upon events. Italy had citizenship in theory and citizenship in fact.

In the history of northern Europe, citizenship is not vivid. It existed, but not as one of the principal institutions by which a political way of life—civic republicanism—was defined and run. It functioned within a political framework, monarchy cum feudalism, that largely derived not from the urbanized ancient Mediterranean, but from the forests and valleys of northern and central Europe. What held feudal society together was the bond of vassalage, a formal contract between two men of the ruling class. Personal relationships, not birth within a given territory, determined not only one's ability but also one's political role. The important men were kings, dukes, counts, and barons. The important political entities were kingdoms, duchies, counties, and smaller fiefs. Cities and towns existed in this world, to be sure, but as special constitutional and social units which were allowed certain governmental functions by their legitimate lords.

Here is the essential distinction: in the north, although the economic basis for urbanism—trade and, eventually, some occasional manufacture—was the same as in the south, the cities were not free. They were not in any sense sovereign. They did not manage their own political policies, and frequently their economic life was determined by the politics of the monarchy. (One thinks of the English embargo on raw wool going to Flanders during the English-French war around 1300; Flanders was a fief of France.) Basically, northern cities, however important they became, were abnormal political and social entities embraced in a feudal world. A king or count governed such a city and took it to war if necessary; only under some compulsion did the ruler consult with important local oligarchs on matters of politics and taxation. His policies did not have to coincide with the interests of his cities, although, of course, often they did. To be popular and economically secure, rulers frequently did what their merchants and bankers wanted them to do—but they did so as a matter of grace, not constitutional necessity. In Italy, as we have seen, the merchants were in fact the legitimate executives of the community and made policy accordingly.

Against this background citizenship, defined as some form of participation in the political process and/or performance in some administrative capacity out of a perceived sense of duty, did not really exist in the north at the level of the kingdom or feudal state. It did exist, however, within the city, although probably not with the full resonance of the institution as found in Italy and elsewhere in the Mediterranean, where the legacy of Rome was strong. Part of that legacy was ancient history with its models in the pages of Livy and

Plutarch; part was the extended study of Roman law with its complicated discussions of citizenship, residency, alien status, and the like. Only slowly did this Roman inheritance penetrate into northern Europe.

The citizenship of the north was then a localized, limited institution, practiced within town walls by those people of a special law, the burghers, who lived there, and limited largely to their concerns. To be sure, the larger and more complex the city—the larger industrial towns of Ghent and Bruges might be taken as examples of the limits of northern European development—the more complex the social and political life and the greater its influence on feudal politics. As in the south, urban politics reflected class, political, and factional differences. Many aspects of local justice and administration were handled by locally elected officials in addition to bureaucrats appointed by the king or count. Professional jurists and notaries were formally educated as in Italy and often used Roman law concepts and formulas.

But all this politics and administration were carried on within the political constraints of the feudal world, in which urban life, even at its oligarchic level, constituted a sort of second-class existence. In the typology of this study, northern citizenship is a debased or imperfect first citizenship, akin to that of the Roman Empire, as opposed to that of the Republic, or of the ideal democratic Greek polis. What flourished was a measure of restricted self-government dependent on princely policy. Merchant statesmen exerted only a limited autonomy, the range of which was determined by a ruler's view of his kingdom's or principality's interests. In such a situation the individual's activities might be active and purposeful, but his scope of action, his potential political impact, was always controlled.

City life in the north eventually produced civic traditions, architecture, and pageantry, religious and secular, which reflected the entrepreneurial success that paid for it—in sum, a richness of local civic statements that compares with the Italian. But as active politically and economically as they were within the walls, northern merchant-citizens lacked some kind of total competence to make their citizenship complete—if, that is, to be complete citizenship needs both contact with the Greco-Roman tradition that launched the institution and true, meaningful, and purposeful freedom of action. Within these limits of our analysis and their medieval realities, northern urbanism developed familiar civic attitudes and institutions because within the feudal framework cities and city people had conventional needs. Each city needed the support of its citizens, if not to pursue its own policies, to fulfill its obligations to its local lords. Residents had to build and guard walls, pay taxes, and perform personal military and administrative services. In their interest, since they did business locally, regionally, and internationally, townsmen sought from the city what they needed in the commercial arena: legal as well as political status and powers, true weights, measures, and coinage, political protection, overall direction of economic affairs (especially in times of crisis), and, always important, various forms of discrimination against the ability of noncitizens to do business as successfully as themselves.

Thus we may say that the same basic pattern of reciprocal need and advantage that existed in the south developed in the north, but without the very self-consciously held Roman resonances of the south. Subjectively speaking, the feel of northern urbanism is different. In the north, to change the focus somewhat, cities and their institutions constitute an epiphenomenon, a disturbance in an overwhelmingly rural scene. In the south, especially Italy, the cities are everything; for all its greater geographic extent, they dominate the surrounding rural world.

Generally speaking, the history of English citizenship in the Middle Ages bears out these generalizations. It played its role primarily within town walls, but not before a significant relationship with the king was first established. Before there could be citizens of London or York, there first had to exist the legal framework within which men might organize as citizens. From the twelfth century on the English monarchs provided those charters which were in fact negotiated contracts by which each party gained. The king assured himself of loyalty, money, and men on a regular basis. The townsmen won many rights of self-organization and government, all of which were based on royal comprehension of the special nature of their way of life and willingness to allow it legal recognition. Specifically, the town received privileges or freedom in return for a fixed fee, the *firma burgis*.

What the city fathers wanted is obvious. To pursue their economic goals they needed a congenial merchant law, the right to organize their members in a municipal corporation with the prospect of perpetual succession, the right to sue and be sued, the rights to hold land and make by-laws. Also, their town needed a seal by which to regularize and authenticate its legal acts. Together these "five points," which developed into a customary package of urban liberties between the twelfth and fourteenth centuries, made the town a legally competent corporate entity.

By providing this armory of legal power the king or lord made it possible for the town to meet its obligations. Since it was his grant, the town corporation acknowledged its dependency upon his person and, eventually, office and thus accepted a place in the hierarchical order of feudal politics. Moreover, this dependency was manipulated by the king, who conferred dignities and titles upon municipal officials and drew them closer to his person on ceremonial occasions. During the late Middle Ages London's lord mayor grew in dignity as the king came to depend upon the city's resources as delivered by its leader.

In London and other English cities control of the town corporation came under the control of the guilds. Guild membership soon became a prerequisite for citizenship, and by the middle of the thirteenth century citizenship became a political issue. What made it so was the constant preoccupation of townsmen with privileges. In England as well as Italy, merchants and artisans cared more for the enjoyment of the legal and economic benefits of citizenship than for the exercise of political rights. Indeed, political activity grew more and more burdensome—because expensive—as the number of political assemblies grew in response to the multiplication of issues on both the national and local levels. Participation in town assemblies, to say nothing of parliament, meant time away from money-making and a public commitment to a person or cause that might bring economic disadvantages.

Because citizenship meant benefit, it was to be protected and restricted; this is why it was politicized. We see this happening in London, where from 1274–75 an official register of apprentices was kept, and more or less simultaneously a law of citizenship was spelled out. One might enjoy the "freedom of the city" by patrimony, or lawful birth within the city, by apprenticeship, and by redemption, that is, by purchase.[10] What happened in London happened elsewhere; across England an articulation of the law of citizenship took place in the last quarter of the thirteenth century. In general, the rules were restrictive, and the lower ranks of artisans were excluded. Given the economic uncertainty of the period—one thinks, for example, of the economic warfare waged by England and France against each other at the beginning of the fourteenth century—it is not surprising that guild members were concerned to protect the privileges of citizenship against dilution through any extension of citizenship.

This was why citizenship became so live an issue. Those who struggled for it wanted more than a voice in the political process; they wanted a desperately needed equality in the competitive business world, for only citizens could displace foreign merchants by pricing their goods in certain special ways, and only they could open retail shops to deal with the many noncitizens in the London market. Those clamoring for citizenship saw it as a means to wealth and higher social status. They saw all this at a time when those already possessing citizenship were finding themselves pressed economically, and in an era when legally trained bureaucrats were finding ways to enforce the laws. As we have seen, Europe over two centuries had become more ordered, regulated. Officials were in greater number now, demanding proof of status, examining documentation, writing things down. Italy, the first scene of modern business and government practice, was a thousand miles away, but by the end of the thirteenth century parts of England and a few other regions in northern Europe were beginning to approximate its ways. The push for citizenship in London is analogous to that in Florence: for members of the lesser guilds it seemed to be the prerequisite for political and economic power.

We can say, then, that in a certain sense citizenship existed in northern Europe in ways of action, even if not fully in the classical tradition as that was sensed in so many ways in the south, or in full awareness of the history and meaning of certain key Latin words. Nobles and elevated townsmen progressively saw their obligations in terms of Roman law concepts such as *Quod omnes tangit* as well as feudal obligations; burgesses acted on the local scene as did their southern counterparts; and even peasants must be credited with a form of practical citizenship. On the manor, the actuality of cooperation reflected religious theory and prevailing need. So, without the specific Roman law background, without the volume of intercity rivalries which made citizenship so important in war and litigation, without, until the Renaissance, consciousness of the full ancient moral heritage which so positively presented a civic ethic, without, too, a public language that constantly changed in meaning to reflect political as well as social realities, without this almost classical Mediterranean civic environment and inheritance, a kind of citizenship is perceivable, nevertheless, in northern Europe.

Citizenship in the north was not as independent as the Mediterranean model, being more closely tied to royal or feudal command. And it never functioned within an inherited tradition of service elevated to a moral ideal. But, nevertheless, northern feudal politics provided possibilities for urban men to gain experience in public affairs, realize the various benefits of participation, and to identify their personal and family interests with those of their city. This is not the full world of traditional Mediterranean civic morality, but a significant part of it, enough to pull northern Europe eventually into the main course of citizenship history.

4

⛩⛩⛩

THE BONDS, LANGUAGE,

AND EMOTION

For about one thousand years after Constantine, Christians preserved an allegiance to the Heavenly City that progressively replaced the one owed by citizens to the Roman state. Then, in the course of the twelfth and thirteenth centuries, a new civic consciousness developed in Italy, its progress facilitated by the simultaneous activity of new and important institutional and legal structures: governments, universities, large banking and trading firms. Both the new civic spirit and the new structures influenced each other and flourished in a revived urbanism that came to approximate the social situation of antiquity. The new spirit was in fact a new public morality, a largely secular patriotism, which constituted a spiritual counterforce in theory as well as in practice to the religious emphases that had prevailed for so long. Over time it produced a new body of symbols, a new architecture, ultimately a whole new civilization that we call secular. The key figure in these developments was the merchant, whose activities led him slowly, but never completely, away from the values of otherworldly society, and whose wealth paid for the things that made his life more comfortable and more beautiful. Politically the new man is the citizen—a more embracing type than the merchant—who responded with some enthusiasm when called upon to expend not only his time and property in the service of the community, but also quite possibly his life. This willingness was based upon an uneasy but growing acceptance of the ancient commitment to the purposeful active life.

THE CREATION OF CIVIC LOYALTY

That this great transvaluation took place is quite remarkable, for much of previous history stood against it. The strength of the new civic spirit is indicated by its very ability to overcome the variety of opposing forces it faced. First among these was religion, whose best ethic and most effective preachers continued to prefer contemplative spiritual to active secular concerns.[1] Religious feeling was always intensified through local devotion to a relic or saint, as we have seen. Immediate countervailing interests were also embodied in a guild or political association and, above all, a family.[2] The notebooks and letter books of Florentine merchant patriarchs reveal not only economic activities, but also a concern for family reputation and political achievements, and continuous solicitude for the cousin in exile or back in the little village, the original homeland of a now powerful urban clan.

All these centrifugal forces in Italian urban society made for instability. Every city faced the problem of creating positive ties strong enough to counter these many pulls away from public issues and business toward private concerns, what has been called "amoral familialism."[3] They had not only to counter these private attractions but to reorder priorities and make public concerns primary. Perhaps what enabled the city to draw as much love as it did in this competition was its promise of material benefit through legal and merchant privileges and of power and prestige through political and administrative service.

In other terms, a compromise of theory and performance was reached. The *vita activa* gained in value as mendicant preachers, Roman lawyers, and eventually civic humanists rehabilitated it, and as rewards and honors came to men who actually gave something of themselves to the community. This compromise is revealed in a variety of ways: for example, the attempts to distribute the responsibilities of short-term office holding among many were certainly a response to citizens' disinclination to serve as well as a device meant to prevent control of an office by a single individual or group.[4]

The citizen knew he was supposed to pay taxes, yet so normal was evasion that in its recipe for legal action against a citizen, the standard notarial manual of the thirteenth century chooses as its example the case of "one unwilling to assume his proper taxes and responsibilities."[5] Nor were resident aliens eager to gain full citizen status if that increased their tax load. Two Florentine petitions for citizenship list residencies in the city of eighteen and forty years. Obviously, to become or not to become a citizen was a decision carefully weighed in terms of political benefits and monetary costs. Perhaps this explains why these two men, one of them a physician, lived in a restricted political and legal condition for so long. Or perhaps the tense politics of the time—it was a period of suspicion, conspiracies, exiles, and purges—made it expedient for these two men both to wait, and to make a commitment only when the consequences of their citizenship oath became clear.[6] The citizen also knew that he was supposed to bear arms and was ambivalent about that, too. Money, war, personal antagonism, commercial rivalries, and class conflict all weakened a city as it attempted to create effective governing institutions.

Countering these considerations was a concatenation of positive forces, all operating under great strain. As it attempted to survive through its citizens' support, each city played out its history against a backdrop of war, famine, plague, economic uncertainty, and social instability.[7] The history of any town, stripped of the beautiful buildings, sculpture, and paintings that suggest calm and prosperity, is a chronicle of hard times. Good times, those days when government worked smoothly and honestly to give justice and security, some food, and the promise of work, are sometimes difficult to discover.

If all this is true, precarious public life itself must be seen as a first cause for survival. It forced men to constructive community activity: to build walls, cathedrals, and chapels, to rationalize corporations for more effective business and banking operations, to organize military formations on a parochial and citywide basis, and to create the cultural and moral underpinnings of such ventures. The city mobilized in response to danger and developed an ethic of civic cooperation, and with it the elaborate law of citizenship that everywhere defined a citizen's obligations to his commune. In the twelfth century theologians and canonists developed a theory and law of crusade, which included schedules of spiritual benefits proportional to the crusader's sacrifice. In the thirteenth and later centuries theologians and civil lawyers elaborated a law of patriotism with its pattern of reciprocal obligations and returns. In each case such a law was necessary to codify needs on both sides and, on purely idealistic grounds, to guarantee some material benefit to all those in society. Let us now examine the binding theories and institutions.

Religion continued to play a unifying role. Each city had saints in every parish church, and an overarching saintly protector as well. It was in his or her name that communal armies fought when they attempted to extend their dominion to the limits of the historic diocese. Religious and political ceremonial fused, as in Florence on the feast of San Giovanni. Then the political symbols of the city were exhibited, and not only urban Florentines, but also representatives of the rural nobility, offered candles in honor of the *comune imperante*. Three days before the feast day public heralds called the citizenry to mass at the baptistery and to work on the flooring of the piazza between the baptistery and San Pietro Maggiore at the expense of the city and the guild of the *Lana*. In the middle of the piazza was placed the *giglio*, the red fleur de lis, symbol of the commune, alongside the red cross of the *popolo*, banners, and other civic symbols. On the day of celebration, a procession of the higher clergy and officialdom passed throughout the city, a public homage to secular authority that was hardly an expression of purely religious feeling. In the early fourteenth century the leaders of the commune took over from religious authorities the offering to the Virgin of the holy banner called the *palio* for which the city and not the bishop paid.[8] Patriotism was literally carved out of the Church: in the mid-thirteenth century a Florentine abbot laid a cornerstone bearing an inscription that placed Florence first among the "Latin cities," ahead of Rome and Paris.[9] In education the Church left its mark upon the curriculum and its goals, especially that of civic harmony and concord.

In the thirteenth century the elaboration of civic pageantry was just beginning in most of the Italian cities. In each city the process began when several developments matured to the point at which some or all clicked together. Population growth, military crisis, unusual local cultural events—these would produce a poem, a celebration, a religious commemoration. When civic consciousness becomes visible in Bologna, the university is achieving a Continental reputation. In Milan, the moment comes a century later, toward the end of the thirteenth century at a time when the Visconti are establishing their legitimacy by various means. In Venice, the process had begun centuries earlier when that city declared her independence from Byzantium and started on her imperial policy. Of course, before, during, and after a vivid ritualized honoring of an event or individual, the normal processes of history went on: victories, defeats, exiles, returns, embassies, miracles, and crusades.

We are examining here the complex teaching process by which the medieval city attempted to inspire its young and the newcomers within its walls to service. It did this by a use of ritual, folk history, literature, and symbols that was extremely sophisticated and that by the thirteenth century was a skill already centuries in the making. The earliest *laudes*, praises sung in honor of a city, date to the mid-eighth century, and already the basic elements of the genre were in place: emphasis upon the city's age, its beauty and that of the surrounding country, the valorous activities of its chief citizens, and the power of the bishops, saints, relics, and religious images lodged in the many churches and monasteries of the city. A little later a local poet linked Verona to the surviving Roman ruins, again signs of antiquity and greatness—any link to Rome, whether real or created, was always exploited—and to the glorious accomplishments of the first bishop of the city.[10]

By about 1000 many of the elements of Venice's arsenal of images and events had been built into a program of civic education. The documents already speak proudly of the *patria Venetia* and the *populus Veneciae* whose *dux* leads them to victory. Banners derived from Byzantium excite the people when they throng to the lagoons to see the marriage of Venice and the sea. Sometime in this period San Marco was institutionalized as the city's hero-saint and the birth date of the city's foundation precisely set at 25 March 421. By the twelfth century the myth of Venice was in full creation; historians found antecedents for the city's contemporary wealth and success, while at the same moment creating the villain in its past, Byzantium. Eventually, by the sixteenth century, eighty-six days of the year were consumed in holidays which in some way celebrated the polity and the socioreligious system which made it work. Of these, perhaps fourteen were devoted to the relationship of the city to San Marco and the sea, focused on Ascension Day. Then as now these rituals "provided a medium for discourse among the constituent classes and between the literate elite and the masses."[11]

In Florence, too, we see the city fathers, merchants, lawyers, and notaries acutely aware of what it took to create the kind of civic identity they wanted. Toward the end of the thirteenth century members of the new guild government began to view the old cathedral, Santa Reparata, as tied to the past, to that feudal aristocracy which had ruled Florence. They wanted a new church that would reflect their success in politics, war, and commerce and that would also reflect a new social policy, the harmony across class lines, which would bring further prosperity to the commune. The vast nave of the new church was to bring together in worship men and women from every quarter and occupation.[12]

While the new cathedral was rising, the Dominicans and Franciscans were building their new-style urban churches. Moreover, in theirs, the Dominicans especially were proclaiming the virtues of urban life. If the sermons of Albertus Magnus are any indication of what was actually preached from the pulpit of Santa Maria Novella, we know that now, in the tradition of Aristotle, churchmen praised cities for the security they provided in dangerous times and for their liberty, unity, and beauty, as well as the civic friendship that bound a people together. Cities in general, and Florence in particular, were so well praised as places in which good might be accomplished that they became in the popular imagination proper scenes for saintly activity. Indeed, by the end of the century St. Francis was viewed as a merchant saint, and apparently no problem was seen in his rejection of his father's merchant life. By then, after all, theorists were claiming that merchants and the wealth they created were necessary for the social and political success of the community.[13] By the early fourteenth century the Dominicans had established schools in Florence in which they taught Aristotle's definition of man as a social, political, and rational animal, and his view of the city as essential to human functions.[14] In the church and school and in the streets, ordinary Florentines could now feel more comfortable in their daily pursuits than ever before, knowing that for many generations their city had been the scene of meritorious activity.

In this new physical and moral scene the young Florentine man grew up surrounded by the signs of a great past. He came to know the significance of each church and palace, every feast day, every nuance of costume and symbol that marked a person off in terms of class and allegiance. He learned that there was a right way and a wrong way in everything, and that it behooved him to learn the right way. Every choice was or could be interpreted as a commitment to some faction, saint, or commercial house that might lead to success in business and politics or to failure and, as we know from the history of the greatest Florentine, exile. In this dangerous, close, and intense urban world, one was educated for survival and sought as many auspices as possible.[15]

This meant veneration of the religious images and relics as well as the cultivation of powerful friends and family members. And, in the great instability of city life, it meant involvement in the most powerful symbolic acts available to one in his social status. The wise individual reached out for those involvements the city itself offered him—in competition with the support offered by guild, family, tower association, or other potential forms of allegiance. The city offered positions of leadership in its bureaucracy, army, legations, and its ever growing number of public ceremonies. This competition was not exactly inexplicit and subterranean: in the early fifteenth century, the city ruled that only its arms and insignia might be placed on the ceiling of San Marco.[16]

The purpose of this education was multifold. First, it was to make the man a city man, to civilize him in some basic way so that his habits were not those of dangerous rural boors. The ceremonies in which he was to participate were, in the words of a later observer, to "show us to be civil men, different from peasants." City life depended on peaceful cooperation and thoughtful, discursive behavior; its goal, social harmony, was the same as that of religion. Yet the civic years marked more than saints' days. Again and again the city celebrated its victories over enemies internal as well as external, which conveyed to the young the importance both of careful and correct choice and of valorous achievement in the management of a successful career.

Next, its purpose was to educate the individual in the history of the city as conceived by the current regime and to involve him in mass celebratory acts of fellowship in which, at least for a while, the divisions of the past were papered over. During the two hundred years or so between 1281 and 1496, each of the governments that ruled Florence used the streets as well as the churches to publicize and advance its specific program. What must amaze us, apart from the scale of investment and integrated preparation—of art, music, sculpture, military training, drama—that went into them, is the political sophistication with which they were orchestrated by the ruling elite. Guelf merchants and Medici princes seem to have had a natural flair for popular political education. But perhaps it was not sophisticated at all. Perhaps it was just normal in a civilization in which everything was taken as a sign, and in which learning the vocabulary of signs constituted a large part of one's preparation for significant social relations in a highly structured world.

Over several centuries the central authority pulled more and more events and specific constituencies within the civic imagery and pageantry of the commune. To celebrate the feast of St. Julian, which marked the victory of the conservative oligarchs over the rebellious cloth workers, the *ciompi*, in 1378, even the Jews were invited to participate. On other occasions contingents of peasants were drawn into the city, where their presence on imperial occasions was testimony to urban power. There they were awed by the magnificent spectacles or, in other terms, educated to reverence and performance. It was no accident that St. Julian's Day was magnified at the end of the fourteenth century after suppression of the *ciompi*. Merchant oligarchs learned quickly from the former feudal masters of the city the importance of the majestic image.

What did the citizen learn from this curriculum of processions, *entrées*, festivals, religious celebrations, mass feasts? He learned "to come to terms with [his place or position] within the solemn setting" provided by the public ceremony. He saw his identity enhanced by the messages of self-approbation.

And he saw and presumably approved one use to which his taxes and loans were put: this enhancement of his citizenship through public display.[17]

Eventually, prepared by centuries of such political narcissism, Florentines saw themselves not only as a historic people, but as a chosen people. In the late fifteenth century Savonarola spoke of the "divine destiny" of Florence, of the Florentines as an "elect nation." Earlier Florentine history had prepared the citizens for great work in Savonarola's time: was not Florence the daughter of Rome and the spiritual center, over recent years, of a Christian renewal? Rome and Jerusalem now had produced a successor. The poets, who wrote in inspired words, had spoken earlier in millenarian terms. Now the dour Dominican was fulfilling a tradition which called upon the Florentine people, especially the poor citizens among them, to produce the civic harmony Christ demanded. Florence was the new Jerusalem, whose glory would be achieved by the humble, not the proud. Ancient history, Rome, and religious history, Jerusalem, together produced one ethic that stressed "good government and piety, social justice and power, temporal and religious leadership."[18]

In sum, the elaborate open-air public life of the city, representing as it did the mutually reinforcing institutions and symbols of church and state, was empowered to pull together into a common enterprise as many of the constituent elements of the population as possible, as individuals or as members of corporations. That common enterprise was political survival, *Libertas*, the foundation for which was economic survival and success. This festival life was also a route to personal distinction, for through it a citizen might demonstrate his love of his fellow citizens, as he rode in resplendent armor or advertised his contribution to the enormous expense of constant celebration. In this, of course, not only the citizen, but his family and dependents might rise in public esteem.[19] Thus citizenship, as it was manifested and enhanced in public spectacles, became an aspect of the social language, broadly conceived, that knit the city together.

THE LANGUAGE AND ETHICS OF PATRIOTISM

Out of this complex educational program, and in the context of the many urban crises that constitute Florence's history—and that of every town— there developed a supportive body of values and a special civic rhetorical vocabulary. This vocabulary became standardized throughout the common urban culture through the works of legists, theologians, historians, and poets. Its key words are *patria*, *amor*, and *animus*, which flow into various formulas for the love and service of country. An examination of these words will reveal the feeling behind them and the way this emotion manifested itself even in the careful, restrained language of the lawyers. The terms conceptualize the movements in the streets and show what kinds of thoughts and commitments civic educators hoped to arouse.

By the fourteenth century *patria* had for a long time been identified as one's native city.[20] The civilians and theologians of the first age of European self-discovery had already examined the term; Accursius (d. ca. 1260), the great Roman lawyer, described his own birthplace as *dulcissima*, the sweetest place of all, and designated as treason any action against it.[21] He found authority for this view in ancient history in general and specifically referred to the view of Cato, Cicero, and others that love of country precedes love of family.[22] The Neapolitan scholar and statesman, Lucas da Penna, identified one's city with one's father: like a father's authority over his children, the authority of a city over its citizens has a religious quality about it. To the jurists such considerations were not mere figures of speech; they were meant to shape conduct in the world. Lucas constructed a hierarchy of obligations in which duty to country follows immediately after duty to God. In doing this, Lucas was quite conventional; as feudal lawyer as well as civilian, he was quite aware of the necessity to establish priorities. For him one's *patria* was his true *pater*—hence the need to save the fatherland first. In one passage his extremism on this issue calls to mind totalitarian pressure upon children in our own century: if a son should discover his father failing in any way in his obligations to his city, he says, the son should reveal his father's bad ways. Generally, the good citizen "should put the good of the fatherland before that of his parent."[23]

These norms found their way into the *consilia*, that enormous body of late-medieval case law, which shows us how jurisconsults judged specific cases on the basis of city statutes, Roman and canon law, and similar cases previously decided by other jurisconsults. Because most of these questions arose out of the day-to-day experience of city life all over Italy, they constitute an excellent source for the history of citizenship. They give specific judgments with regard to actual people, issues, places, and sums, not just juristic animadversions. The *consilia* honestly reveal the place of citizenship in the active lives of men and women, and in their scale of priorities.[24]

On one occasion the Venetian jurist Marianus Socinus (d. 1467) was asked to consider whether a Venetian statute prohibiting the marriage of Venetians outside the city applies in the case of a Venetian girl, Margaret, in Avignon who marries someone of questionable Venetian parentage. At stake is the woman's inheritance. Eventually he decides that Margaret's husband can be considered to be a Venetian, given his heritage and the fact that one "is always assumed to have an intention to return or revert to his own country, especially one who is a citizen by birth, because the love of country is so very sweet." He goes on to analyze love of country as a natural and spiritual condition. With a mind to return, residence abroad of even a thousand years would not change the husband's essential Venetian being. Marianus makes his judgment with full knowledge of the social philosophy behind the Venetian law. Venice wants its women home to bear sons who will contribute to its welfare. She wants them to be native Venetians. Marianus reassures us that the lady lives in Avignon to become wealthy, that her goods will be used in Venice's interest, because "it is important to the Venetian state to have rich subjects." For this jurist, citizenship bestows a special quality upon one's character. Sons, he says, are born more of their country than of their fathers, and if need be, one should fight for his country against his father. What Marianus has done is interject another parentage between natural child and natural parent, that of the city herself.[25]

The Church as well as the family suffered as the civil state successfully intruded itself into traditional relationships. An extreme, but revealing, statement of the new priority, if not morality, is the judgment of the humanist and legist Aretinus on the Pazzi conspiracy. Florentine authorities had caught, tried, and executed the murderers of Giuliano de' Medici, among whom were high churchmen. As punishment, Sixtus IV had placed the city under interdict. In defending the policies of the Signoria, Florence's executive commission, Aretinus argues that Florentine citizens had every right to defend their city. Indeed, citizens should lose their citizenship were they not to act so, even against priests, friends, and members of their own families.

This *consilium* represents the position of those in secular public life who were trying to make allegiance to the community transcend allegiance to the Church, as institution, and, indeed, to make a supportive corporate citizen of the local church. The story of the struggle between the papacy and the empire is part of the popular history of medieval Europe. Not so the struggle between the multitude of urban governments and their local ecclesiastics. If the bishop continued to be an important spiritual and ceremonial figure in the life of every city, by the late Middle Ages he had also come to be, frequently, an antagonist. As the city-state grew to self-government, it had to confront its bishops and many religious corporations, monasteries, chapters, and mendicant houses with its needs.[26]

It has been said that the French Revolution resulted from the clash of a rising nobility and a rising bourgeoisie. The unseemly and bitter struggle between city and Church resulted from the clash of a rising Church and a rising communal movement. Its intensity is somewhat masked at the municipal level by the ordinariness and technicality of the issues. Mostly money and jurisdiction were at stake; only rarely does a vivid figure appear, an Arnold of Brescia, a Cola da Rienzo, with a vision to proclaim, or some platform of reform on which to erect a new and pure society.

Squabbles over money and jurisdiction drew in the lawyers; soon they were debating when a city might tax ecclesiastical corporations. The Sienese and Florentine constitutions allowed for taxations of individual clerics. Such provisions provoked litigation, as did formal contracts which forced religious institutions to perform distasteful obligations. Twice in the thirteenth century, for example, Padua forced bishops of nearby cities to act the citizen, that is, to build a palace and pay taxes as would any newcomer into the community. In matters of service and finance these bishops, important as they were in the religious and symbolic life of the city, were assimilated to the lay citizen.[27] At least one jurist allowed the cleric to make his contribution in spiritual coin. Bartolus (1314–57) expects a new abbot in town to help the city through prayer as would a new soldier-citizen through feats of arms. As long as he stays and prays, the abbot is to merit the privileges of citizenship. If he moves away, he loses them. There is no indelible cultural mark here, but rather formal legal recognition of a quid pro quo.[28]

The works of many jurists are filled with careful discussion of such contractual expectations. Eventually every contingency was examined: the Church's responsibility in times of flood, garrison demands, broken dikes, or wall construction, for example. In general, the jurists allowed the principle of necessity to prevail: religious establishments were to support the general good not only by prayer but with property in times of emergency—emergency always to be defined. Property had its obligations, and medieval jurists would perhaps have been surprised at the great freedom from tax responsibility the modern secular state allows the Church. Such were the policies of communal leaders who, usually the town's richest citizens, were themselves the largest taxpayers. Besides, in an age of endemic anticlericalism, it was good politics to strike against rich priests and failing religious establishments.[29]

These cases document the very material needs and demands of the city at a time when it sought to gain maximum strength through a process of political homogenization. They suggest that more was at stake than an animosity born of a conflict of ideology over the place of profit and interest in society, or as a response to the threat of an aggressive papal foreign policy. At issue were matters of day-to-day hurt and need. The community as a whole needed ecclesiastical resources, and individual taxpaying inhabitants, many if not most of whom held office at one time or another, could expect to find their tax burden lessened were the clergy only to do their share.

Needs of state backed up by theories of civic cooperation and responsibility prevailed, not in any absolute way, but imperfectly, partially, slowly, litigiously, with grief to all involved. Litigation arose not only from the cloudy wording of statutes and from the very skill of the lawyers, but also from the overwhelming needs of secular governments. These needs forced civil authorities into positions of aggressiveness; they saw the wealth of the Church with eyes less and less clouded by sentimentality.

These changes and demands manifest a changing set of values and a clear emphasis on willing and doing, as opposed to merely contemplating. New civic values were translated into demands for conduct that could easily clash with traditional notions of right and wrong. Allegiance to the city could mean obedience to a new ethical code. No wonder the widely respected jurist of the fourteenth century, Baldus (1327–1400), compared citizenship to slavery.[30] The will of the individual was now subject to that of his city. A civic master might do more than compel a citizen to move, build a house, pay taxes, do all the conventional things a citizen was to do. It might ask the traveling merchant to spy upon the military forces of a neighbor. Such activity was legitimated as a special form of ambassadorial service and was expected not only of laymen, but from friendly friars as well.[31]

Not even an oath was to frustrate a citizen's service to his city. Considering the importance of the oath generally throughout society, and the great number of merchants, lawyers, teachers, and notaries who worked abroad, this constituted an attack upon one of the bonds that was meant to hold society together. For example, a Sienese bound by his oath to serve another city was expected to break that oath to avoid injuring Siena. Sienese were permitted foreign employment by statute but were expected to break any commitment by which the honor and welfare of Siena might be hurt. And, of course, in the service of Siena itself, failure to give priority to her well-being was, under certain specified conditions, to bring heavy fine and banishment.[32]

Students and teachers, as well as the professional civil-servant, were subject to pressure. Presumably committed to a search for the highest truth, no matter where that might be, the Florentine student was urged to find it at the new and weak university of his native city—under threat of a one-thousand-lire fine. Nor was the brotherhood of learning advanced by the series of oaths sworn by the professors at Bologna, in which these jurists promised not to teach elsewhere or to aid students outside of Bologna. Quite explicitly the intent of the action is to prevent weakening of the Bolognese *studium*, a realistic objective given the competition for outstanding teachers, and the economic importance of the presence of a large group of scholars to any commune.[33]

In all these actions prescribed by local government, the individual is drawn away from some standardized value or model of Christian behavior and asked to consider obligations to his city superior to all others, while in fulfilling normal citizen obligations, such as an advisory and administrative service and tax paying, he is expected to place the material public good before his own and that of his family.[34] What city fathers dreamed about could actually happen, as in Venice in the mid-fourteenth century, for example, after the Genoese captured Chiogga, just a few miles down the coast. According to a contemporary account, the people rushed into the piazza wailing that "the city is lost . . . its liberty and wealth, public and private . . . Venice itself." If some "ran to hide their money and jewels," others proclaimed "that the patria was not lost while a man still survived to bear arms." A popular leader chosen, people ran to enroll in the militia and offered the *patria* gold, silver, jewels— whatever they possessed of value, even the clasps and brooches worn by the Venetian women. A forced loan of 5 percent was quickly subscribed. Families distinguished themselves with offers of service without pay to the commune, and, during the protracted amphibious operations in the lagoons, not a day went by without "some gentleman or citizen offering his services in this or that enterprise."[35]

Expectations of such commitment were based upon a fundamental as-sumption that there existed in the breast of every loyal citizen a willingness to sacrifice for the good of his community. Government had to assume good will, and the word government here means precisely those persons raised in that physical and rhetorical world filled with festivals, legends, and examples of personal and family sacrifice, all to the greater glory of the commune. The concern of legislators and theorists was for the proper animus and/or *amor* of citizens, both old and prospective.

Years ago Marc Bloch used the term "bonds of society" to designate the ties and pressures that held together the feudal world. At the basis of those bonds was the willingness of two men to serve each other in specified and mutually beneficial ways. Will, some form of consent, and expectation of material reward were also at the foundation of civic relationships, indeed, of productive urban life. Feudal relationships were codified only after centuries of function. Civic responsibilities, on the other hand, were almost instantly theorized and inscribed, for the period of urban growth and need coincided with the rise of the university-trained class of jurists and administrators. In a variety of specific ways, these worked out a law of love or civic affection specifying governmental demands upon every kind of urban resident and reciprocal benefits as well.[36]

The basic principles of this law or rule of civic love were first established in the twelfth century when, at this early stage in the revived study of the Roman law, scholars were still defining words. Confronted with the many related, but different, terms the Romans had devised over centuries to denote various kinds of legal and political capacities, medieval jurists had to discriminate among them. One text they analyzed was a title in the Code, *de incolis* (on residents or inhabitants), especially the law *Est verum*, which became one of the principal texts upon which a medieval law of citizenship was developed.[37] On this law, which holds that those who do not live in a city shall not be forced to fulfill municipal obligations there, an anonymous scholar observed that a resident's status depends on his will alone. In other words, he assumed that residence reflected intention and that intention represented a knowing commitment to assume responsibilities within a given place. In the middle of the next century Accursius, whose gloss became the basic authority and teaching device for the rest of the Middle Ages, made the commitment precise. He defined intention as a period of ten years; only over that length of time would an individual demonstrate his involvement in the city's affairs and come to be regarded as loyal by, presumably, the full-fledged members of the community, the citizens.

In another comment Accursius stresses the power of the will, noting that a son, although he may never efface the memory and the influence of the birthplace given him by his father, may "by his own will take himself where he wishes." He then goes on to consider the tax obligations of a son who leaves his father's city, which, taken together with office holding, is also the subject of his gloss to the law *Libertus* (D. 50.1.17). Here he uses the following example to emphasize the concept of individual choice in determining where a citizen's obligations are to be fulfilled: "Likewise, if my father has his residence in A., I do not become a citizen there unless I want to be one." In all these simple expositions, then, Accursius asserts the ultimate moral and legal ability of the individual to create his own life independent of his father's. There were pressures keeping him close to his family—social, moral, often financial—but these did not have to bind the son to his father's life.[38]

As we might expect, the lawyers began to examine the concept of animus and qualify it. In discussing the ability of a son to establish himself away from his parents, Bartolus, the greatest of the medieval jurists, rejects an argument based on the idea that the son's will and mind are not fully developed. He takes what almost might be called a quantitative approach: it is enough for the young man to have the greater part of his resources (*maiorem partem facultarum*) for him to establish *domicilium*. The very fact of his move and reestablishment is considered adequate proof of his animus, even if he may not have the fullest intellectual awareness. Baldus, the other leading jurist of the fourteenth century, agrees that the father cannot make slaves of his children, nor may he swear any *fidelitas* for them. A son must want to be a citizen and must make his own profession to any corporate group as well as city. Baldus also compares the citizen both to the slave and the vassal in terms of the strength of the bond. Given the law and mystique of feudalism, and the purity of the affection that was to exist between lord and vassal, it is clear when Baldus links citizen and vassalage that he wants the son to be very certain in any change of citizenship. His demand for constancy is clear too in what he writes of the resident who would become a citizen. His intent had to be *firmus, non vagus*, and if he withdraws from the city and then returns, he is to be considered a wanderer in the interim; presumably, although Baldus does not say so, time spent out of the city as *vagabandus* does not count toward meeting the time requirement specified by statute in each city as prerequisite for citizenship.[39]

A very formal attempt to establish a basis for determination of intent is that of Marianus Socinus, Jr., (1482–1556), although what he writes is no more than schematic statement of long-existing practice. He develops his solution in a *consilium* that examines the fitness of two brothers to receive an inheritance; by the terms of the Mantuan statute, landed property cannot pass to those "not paying taxes and bearing obligations with and for the commune and citizens of Mantua." The men may inherit, first, because their will is demonstrated by their very living and trading in the city; second, because the greater part of their property is in the city; and third, because they have resided in town over a significant length of time. Since the principal purpose of the statute was to ensure benefit to the city, and since the brothers do in fact bear civic responsibilities, they may receive the disputed property.[40]

What we see in this variety of sources is a widespread sensitivity to the importance of desire and will in the making and functioning of a citizen. To be a good man, it is not enough to reside and pay taxes in a city; the person must show much faith and much love, to twist the words of an early commentator on Dante.[41] He must, under certain circumstances, be prepared to reject his parents and, perhaps, deeply held ethical principles. And he might have to forgo the pleasures of his native countryside and live in the city, at least some months each year. Finally, what may have been even more difficult for some to follow were demands that swords be sheathed and that citizens cease the street brawling that apparently pleased them so much.

The existence of such a person, who acts in ways that at times may conform neither to traditional moral codes, rational self-interest, or social conditioning, especially within the family group, confirms what has been written about republicanism in the Italian Renaissance: "It did not identify the essence of man with his intellect. It tended rather . . . to find man's essence in his will."[42] It was the will of man in the role of citizen that enabled him to break out of conventional channels to act in support of a new spiritual entity, his city, and that ultimately guided his choice as he made political, economic, and moral decisions. Linked to this will of the individual was another, the will of the people, considered as a whole, which could create a new law and approve a whole range of sovereign acts, such as waging wars and levying taxes. Augustine and the Fathers were not often cited by the civil lawyers, but perhaps this broad emphasis on will goes back to his view that a consensus on values is prerequisite for the existence of a community.[43]

This medieval emphasis on the will of the individual is striking. It represents something of a modification of the view of the citizen and citizenship held in the ancient world. Then, as we have seen, citizenship was a category of existence; only with the greatest difficulty could a person shuck it off or assume a new one alongside the original one. Greek civic culture was more enveloping and formative than the medieval analogue; the city's god or goddess was closer, more immediate, less tolerant of rejection. Easy statements about individualism in antiquity ignore the common fate of Socrates, Alcibiades, and Caesar. In the Middle Ages community continued to shape and dominate the individual, but perhaps not to the same degree. New ideas, values, and objective realities made switching allegiance more possible, or, in other terms, the power and scope of action of the individual's will could be greater.

The Christian concept of freedom of the will granted the individual the possibility of choice, not only between good and evil, but also between Perugia and Siena. Local culture, including religion, still determined identity and loyalty, but within Europe one could move knowing that although the saint might change, he would still be under the protection of Jesus and the Virgin Mary. Medieval Europe was an international civilization in ways the ancient world never was. Moreover, conceptually, the will was never as central to the systems of pagan philosophers as it was to St. Augustine and his successors.

This freedom to choose was exercised as well in a society that was quite different in the thirteenth century, say, from what it had been in the ancient past. In the Italian city-state world, commerce was much more important than it had been in Greek or Roman days. This meant that many men thought now in legal and quantitative terms about matters, such as allegiance, that earlier had been matters of quality, not quantity. Because the new legal culture, combined with a heightened impulse toward rational calculation, permitted and facilitated such an approach, the will was translated into specifics of territorial and capital investment. Budgets of some kind had been part of the European experience in politics and business since the twelfth century, and theologians wrote in terms of increments of goodness, so it is not surprising that now legists and constitution drafters approached patriotism in similar terms.

EXPECTATIONS OF CITY AND CITIZEN

A declaration of intent on the part of a citizen or would-be citizen is a formal act, as is a vote to accept him taken by some communal legislature in accord with the theory of the Roman law. The question arises: what made a man decide to transfer his person and allegiance, or an assembly to vote a given way on taxes or war or, more immediately, on an application for citizenship? The answer to these questions of motivation is the same: a kind of rational calculation of the real consequences of the act. There was *amor patriae* unquestionably, but also sensitivity to the immediate self-interest of the individual and his family, or, perhaps, some institution of special significance. No one was more conscious of traditions and theories of morality and legality than Baldus, yet it is he who acknowledges a proecclesiastical bias in the conclusion of one of his *consilia*, a consequence of his residence "in lands in sympathy with the church." Analogously, when the great Florentine families invested in ambassadorial service in the city's public debt, they did so out of public spirit and out of certain knowledge that public service would redound to the eminence of the family and in that sense the investments would pay off.[44]

In return for support that, besides money, military service, conformity to its culture and law, and veneration of its saint, might demand action against both family and church, the city was prepared to help its citizens. Not unsurprisingly, this basic aspect of the relationship was often expressed in concepts that remind us of the reciprocal obligations of lord and vassal. But whether the mutual obligations of city and citizen were immediately influenced in fact and language by the surrounding and long dominant feudal world is open to question, for if the right language was at hand in feudalism to be used in describing the urban situation, it is also the case that the needs of citizen and city were so basic that they could only be expressed in the ultimate vocabulary of aid and protection. This is not to say that the urban resident was left with only the most general promises of assistance, which might be made specific only in proportion to his ability to command attention on the basis of social or political power. Whether citizen or member of one of the several inferior legal categories in town, an individual knew quite well the benefits he might use. Indeed, prospective citizens calculated advantage in financial and legal terms, and in their *statuti* cities tried to make privileges very explicit; what was left in doubt constituted the basis for intervention by the jurists.

Citizenship was a condition of mind and sentiment, an emotional state carefully created and nurtured by city government. It was also a moral condition which carefully established a priority of values at times not quite in accord with the traditional norms of the Church, as earlier developed in a simple, overwhelmingly agrarian society. But if these, it was as well a highly developed legal institution with the specific reciprocal obligations of those involved carefully spelled out.

A definite consistency of outlook and policy may be seen in two communal acts, the earlier of Genoa, the second of Venice about 175 years later. In 1143 a Genoese notary drew up a pair of documents which constitutes a contract of exchange between Opizo of Piacenza, now *iudex* in Genoa, and the city. Opizo swears allegiance to Genoa, save in matters pertaining to his native Piacenza, and promises to serve his new masters, the consuls, well. For its part the city permits him to invest up to one hundred lire yearly "for trading on the sea as a Genoese citizen." They did this, they acknowledge, in their certainty that Opizo "willingly" served Genoa and had confirmed this act of will by his oath.[45] On 10 June 1312, the Great Council of Venice explicitly advised a Paduan merchant that his ability to "commerciare come Veneziano" depended upon his fulfillment of certain communal obligations.[46]

Neither of these merchants seems to have been a full citizen. Clearly, Opizo was a professional civil servant in town in some temporary judicial capacity. The Paduan may have been living in Venice long enough for the authorities to take note of his civic freeloading. In each case the individual found it desirable to establish a formal relationship in meaningful terms. Perhaps each man eventually became a full citizen of the port city to which he owed his fortune. We know only that the agreements here do in fact cover the kind of desiderata mentioned in citizenship petitions and grants.

These exchanges in the maritime cities are only explicit examples of what might be left unsaid in the relationship between city and citizen or resident. The citizen was aware of his town's general concern to defend and aid him. If one "lives in Volterra continuously for ten years . . . , the consuls and *podestà* must defend him as a citizen." A few years later, in the Viterbo statutes of 1251, the oath of the *podestà*, the hired, temporary city executive, obliges him to "maintain each and every citizen in person and property." A century later Baldus, comparing the relationship of vassal to lord with that of citizen to city, wrote that the citizen who leaves his city imperils it and by that act loses "all the laws of the city," by which he meant to include its encompassing protection.[47]

Besides commercial privilege or the right of investment, the city's auspices might take other forms. Florence acknowledged its obligations not only to pay citizens in public service, but also to protect them abroad and pay ransom if necessary. If somewhat special, Venice's promises were similar as the republic searched for its citizens in the sultan's prisons, distinguishing those who were full Venetian citizens from others. As they negotiated alliances or made peace, cities sought tax benefits and commercial privilege for their own. For example, the alliance of 1167 of the Lombard cities called upon the Cremonese to "safeguard and protect the men of Mantua and Milan in our land and water." Florence tried to guarantee free transit for its merchants and their goods for seven years in its agreement of 1256 with Arezzo. Orvieto did likewise.[48]

Given the value of the benefits involved and the possible financial and military consequences for the protecting government, it is not surprising that the lawyers soon began to enunciate general principles. Bartolus might succinctly link the will of the citizen, which created an indissoluble union with the city, with the receipt of privileges, but he needed a whole treatise to discuss, in specific terms, whether reprisals should be granted and to whom. Throughout this treatise one gets a sense of mercantile calculation as well as legal analysis. And again he evidences that medieval philosophical preoccupation with the essence of terms that is reminiscent of analyses of the degeneration of kingship into tyranny. If one did not function as a citizen, he was not to be treated as one.[49]

In general, it is true to say that having assumed a broad responsibility to defend and protect, city governments tried to honor their agreements with private citizens. Such was the advice of the jurisconsults. In a judgment involving a tax exemption, the jurisconsult Ludovicus Bologninus (1449–1508) so cites the view of Bartolus, Baldus, and many other authorities.[50] Baldus himself allowed that cities ought to interpret the benefit of reprisals "broadly." And Albericus de Rosate (d. 1354), considering whether a privilege granted by a town to a poor citizen may be withdrawn now that the man is wealthy, decides it may not—out of general considerations for the sanctity of contract and also for reasons of municipal honor and reputation, which he considered important given the number of agreements entered into by the government.[51]

Such were some of the material gratifications of patriotism. Called upon to produce and to serve, in some instances to act for secular masters against traditional religious teachings, the citizen knew that at least some of his needs would be met by himself if and when he served in some temporary governmental capacity, or by others like him similarly committed to the active life. In modern terms, he knew himself part of a civic culture, and if he traveled at all he knew too that his city was in many respects similar to others whose men and institutions met in commercial and political dealings. One burden of this chapter is the argument that against conventional moral ties, a force developed in the environment of the Italian city that was to act as one of the bonds of old-regime society, until the shattering experiences of the French and Industrial revolutions: a love of native place buttressed by material benefit. It was against this intense, if limited, affection that national figures from Mazzini to Mussolini had to struggle. The remarkable fact is that, partial and ambiguous as we have seen it to be, this love of city was so strong. Moreover, this moral force was developed without the institutions and technology available to the modern state. Surely the involvement and identification of religious objects with the state, taken together with the existence of historic and present enemies, helped to sustain medieval civic patriotism.

This medieval city love was not a class but a mass affair. Unlike the civic humanism of the Renaissance, which was an elitist movement embracing many wealthy merchants, the activist patriotism of the Middle Ages was less intellectual, less consciously literary and cultural, and more social, built into and upon the very nature of life. In other words, it was a more total sociopolitical phenomenon than the classically inspired civic humanism of the fifteenth century. One functioned as a citizen in office, in the field, and as a taxpayer long before he was inspired by Bruni to do so. The means for the diffusion of the everyday functional patriotism of the prehumanist variety were popular and visible, if their message was not so elegant. One function of the civic humanism of the Renaissance was to make elegant and clearer a new model for life. It was in this guise and in the curricula of the humanist academies that this life-style of the Italian city-state world went north to influence the careers and values of leading men.

In Italy the old-style patriotism had served a variety of functions. During the wars, plagues, and hard economic times of the thirteenth and fourteenth centuries it had helped hold each town together; to some degree the success of the few great states that remained at the end of this period depended upon their ability to tap the resources and enthusiasm of their people. Beyond this, patriotism became a critical feature of, one of the demands of, the common law of citizenship that constituted one of the general characteristics of medieval Italy. The jurist of the fifteenth century makes the same demands upon the citizen as the consuls of Genoa in the mid-twelfth. Florence, Venice, and the smallest commune reflected a common civic culture as they educated their children to sort out the services due family, church, and state.

If this chapter has emphasized the nature and intensity of patriotism, it has also tried to keep in the picture all the counterpressures upon the theory and actuality of self-sacrificing public service. Perhaps this is the note on which to close: we must remember that even in Florence, Venice, and other cities during their republican (communal) heyday, men were passive subjects as well as active citizens. It may be dangerous to overemphasize their ability in this period to change things through political action based upon rational analysis. Much of what they did was conditioned by a structure of ideas and institutions that included Christian teaching, family responsibilities, the hierarchic social structure, and the discipline of school and guild. All these defined a passive, receptive role for the individual, not an active, creative one, which is to say that for all we talk about "acts of citizenship," with the creativity that phrase implies, there were definite limits within which even the most innovative and most active citizen acted.

5

〓〓〓

THE LAW AND LANGUAGE

OF CITIZENSHIP

Today's civic textbooks by themselves do not create the perfectly rational or ideal background for acts of citizenship—even in a society with many kinds of reinforcing theories, institutions, media, and freedoms. Much less, one must presume, would the ideas of distant Romans suddenly have created a compelling new institutional and moral world in the Florence of the Renaissance. Behavioral science has demonstrated too much about the determinants of human activity for us to believe in too simplified an explanation of conduct.

We have seen how the town attempted to educate its sons to produce the model citizen through a variety of influences. If that proved to be a difficult task, so was the production of a satisfactory definition of the citizen, one that would flow from Justinianic texts and mesh well with contemporary realities. When they looked into the past, medieval scholars learned that no single imperial act made all free men citizens everywhere with equal rights and obligations. No city's citizenship law was exactly the same as its neighbor's or had passed through an identical history. Some form of citizenship flourished with or without the memory of Rome. Yet it may be said generally that in the cities of both northern and southern Europe a pattern of civic institutions developed. In Mediterranean Europe, this pattern was based on a common experience, which was given expression in medieval Roman law. In the north, the urbanizing experience came somewhat later, and its development for several hundred years was expressed somewhat in the language of Rome, but not in its law. North and south of the Alps, the extent of feudal and royal authority influenced the development of both cities and citizenship.

Christianity was also influential, and citizenship in its fullest theoretical expression was limited by the fact that it could only function in a moral and political world which could tolerate and dignify the active—as opposed to the contemplative—human being. This meant that for a long while, until the fourteenth century, perhaps, citizenship developed as secular theory and institution without a formal place or justification in Christian thinking. Therefore, when medieval jurists and constitutional theorists first approached citizenship, they were forced to understand it as the product of another civilization, pagan antiquity. They were necessarily limited in their approbation of it, although they saw its usefulness to their own urban world, just then approaching the urban complexity of antiquity. Hence the interest in its technical legal side, which we see in their fascination with ancient terms and their attempts to reckon their medieval equivalency. Hence, too, their long puzzlement over many imprecise medieval words—*comitatensis* and *districtualis*, for example—which had no exact ancient predecessors, and which were products of a complicated early medieval history beyond their understanding.

The best approach is to view citizenship as a dynamic institution that changed with respect to time and place and with the developing sophistication of those who had to use and define it. The city-state world of the Mediterranean knew it earliest and, through its university scholars, so many of whom were Italian born or trained, best. Eventually, however, the term gained a northern European currency as city life developed, a legal class matured, and the feudal and monarchical governments of the region began to appropriate some of the concepts associated with citizenship for their own larger territorial use. This presupposes the eventual spread of the technical Roman law vocabulary from the south into the north, a process which was continuous throughout the Middle Ages and the Renaissance.

PROBLEMS OF DEFINITION

The Middle Ages received an institution and a vocabulary from the ancient world but naturally shaped both to its own needs. Generally speaking, medieval citizenship never became the intense political issue it had been in ancient Greece. And, although it was used frequently, as in both Greece and Rome, to honor persons of potential usefulness to the community, and although immigration and naturalization were accepted and institutionalized, it never became the instrument of foreign policy it had been for Rome. Nor did the Middle Ages receive from late antiquity a strong tradition, a widely diffused popular ethic, which valued civic service. Rather, as we have seen, Christianity confronted pagan virtue with its own, which emphatically asserted the supremacy of contemplation over activity, the next life over this one. Ancient activism and its approbation developed out of society's need; so eventually did medieval activism, which had to struggle a long while for any theoretical defense and formal approval. That came only when the medieval city needed the specialized services of its now complex population, and when philosophers and lawyers found ancient arguments with which to modify traditional Christian views.

By that time, however, medieval Europe approximated not the Roman Empire, but rather the conquered parts of Italy and the rest of Europe, Africa, and Asia before their incorporation into a universal state. That is, Europe was divided into many local units, some influenced by the survival of Roman law, some taking their basic characteristics from a Germanic inheritance, and others mixtures. Feudal government everywhere further accentuated localism and particularity. This political situation determined the basic pattern or nature of medieval citizenship as limited and local. It was restricted to cities in northern Europe, Spain, southern France, and, in Italy, to the territories of the larger city-states such as Florence, Milan, and Venice. Throughout the Middle Ages and the Renaissance, the growing national monarchies never knew citizenship at the level of kingdom, only at the municipal level, and, in some cases, only with specific reference to the resident of that part of a town originally ruled by the bishop, the *cité*.

For all these reasons it is impossible and meaningless to say "a citizen was . . . ," for, in fact, there was within each city a hierarchy of citizens of varying capacity as well as persons of other legal and political status. These might be immigrants in the process of naturalization, indigenous population too poor to be inscribed on a roster of taxpaying citizens, or resident aliens whose hearts belonged to their native place and who intended to live with minimal emotional and fiscal ties to their place of actual residence. The social mix of any decent-sized town would also include, outside the visible body of solid merchants, artisans, and professional men, many menial workers, drifters, and criminals who remained largely an invisible class.[1]

Any attempt to find a definition of *civis* must, therefore, begin with the uncertainties of the jurists themselves. As Bartolus wrote in the fourteenth century, after two centuries of increasingly complex analyses, "Today we use this vocabulary broadly and improperly." Only after this warning does he attempt to discriminate among *municeps*, *civis*, and *incola* and to warn his reader of the large body of conflicting juristic opinion. He knew from his familiarity with *consilia* and other components of the so-called common law that statutes were not always precise and that their defects brought cases to his desk. He surely expected disagreement, for although legal education focused on the same common texts, those were read and interpreted by men whose experience and commitments differed and who, therefore, each viewed the common source and authority, antiquity, somewhat differently. Finally, he knew that careful definition of terminology was not mere scholarly exercise. Whether one fell into this or that category determined his, and sometimes her, civil and political powers, potentialities, and tax and military obligations.[2]

Just as we properly speak of medieval liberties and not Liberty, so too should we properly speak of citizenships and not Citizenship, but not in broad terms of first- and second-class citizenships—that is our modern idiom. Rather, we should think of a spectrum or hierarchy of citizenships, with maximum citizens possessing the fullest possible exercise of civil powers, in litigation, and political powers, in the creation of civic policy through voting and candidacy eligibility for the entire range of political office. The power of the saints that men sought during the Middle Ages had its counterpart in the powers of citizenship. These powers were grounded in status, which itself was a function of birth (both locale and parentage) and social class. Status, in medieval eyes, was not a simple, unitary, static abstraction; rather, it represented a congeries of powers to be activated upon need: for legal competence against a foreigner; for economic power in a boycott; for political power through the legitimate acquisition of a political office, occupancy of which meant security for one's self, family, and dependents. Always status determined capacity, which is why the lawyers calibrated definitions with such care, and why certain key words developed traditional, although not uncontested, meanings. If this is so, then one way to define citizenship is to examine its function in relation to the vocabulary of approximations that surrounded it.

Take, for example, the *consilium* of Alexander of Imola which deals with the purchase of land by a *districtualis*, that is, one who lives in the region around the city, as opposed to the urban area. A statute prohibits sale of land to foreigners. The jurisconsult must decide whether the *districtualis* is a foreigner, whether the sale/purchase is legal. Alexander decides that it is and that the statute never meant to view the *districtualis* as a foreigner. The intent of the statute, its "mens," must be observed, and in support of this view he cites an impressive group of jurists.[3]

One kind of citizen was the *municeps*. In Bartolus's view it is a general term for town residents. Like Azo, Bartolus assumes some etymological connection between *municeps* and *munera*, burden or responsibility. Although he complains about its looseness and weakness, nevertheless he reserves the word for the purest or best kind of city dweller. Not every *civis* may live in his hometown bearing responsibilities; the *municeps* does. In this usage a *civis* of Asti may be away at the Champagne fairs, by his absence, so to speak, depriving the city of his involvement in its affairs—while paying taxes and retaining his legal status as *civis*. But the *municeps* lives in Asti and by performing the right political and fiscal duties there achieves a kind of purer state of citizenship.[4]

If citizenship reaches perfection in the activity of the *municeps*, its minimal state is approached by the *incola*. This word, too, has a feel to it conferred by centuries of discussion. According to Jacobus Rebuffi (d. 1428), who succinctly states the common view, the *incolatus* is defined by two things: the free act of the individual who moves to a new town, and the location there not only of his person but of the greater part of his property. In a general sense, the *incola* is considered less committed to the city's fortunes than is the *civis*. He may shrug off his allegiance and move away before receiving citizenship in a formal act. Yet, though his obligations are less than those of the citizen, they do exist, and a substantial literature attempted to establish which personal and property responsibilities the *incola* was to bear in a variety of circumstances. Committed to the city by his voluntary association, not by necessity, the *incola*'s benefits were less than those of the citizen. In more medieval terms, the *incola* was qualitatively inferior to the *civis* in the eyes of the law and of society. Only time and/or service could perfect his condition, assuming his eventual act of overwhelming commitment.[5]

More difficult to define was the word *subditus*, subject, whose use varied over time and in respect to the nature of government and size of territory. By the fourteenth century *civis* and *subditus* were converging, becoming interchangeable. The sovereign city was making subjects of its citizens by all its demands upon them for money and military service, while at the same time, in many cities, the changeover from a republican government to some form of princely regime was making the term *civis* more and more obsolete. All this took place as medieval Europe was coming to have a better understanding of ancient Rome, a clearer sense of the difference between the Roman Republic and the Roman Empire.

To judge from the jurisconsults, the benefits of citizenship and subjectship came to be the same, and both depended upon loyal performance. This blurring of edges is already observable in Baldus, who calculatingly uses *subditus* as something of a catchall with which to encompass all those having the benefit of reprisal—the subject of a particular *consilium*. It served to designate all those under the prince who merited this legal privilege.[6]

The very fact that Baldus occasionally uses the word this way suggests a conscious choice, for he usually uses *civis*. For him, the citizen jurist of Perugia dealing daily with the statutes of many communes, the key word of regular usage and intimate familiarity is *civis*. A century later the shift is very apparent in the vocabulary of Riminaldus, whose instinctive frame of reference is the princely territorial state. In a *consilium* concerning the right to accept an inheritance, he emphasizes the will of the government, the prince, in conferring rights. He argues with Baldus and rejects the mutuality of involvement between a citizen and his city, and the will of the individual who commits himself to a civic identity. A new emphasis is apparent here; the bond between citizen and city is dependent upon the government, which alone may define the relations it wishes to maintain with its people. Surely this shift in emphasis must be explained at least in part by the impact of fifteenth-century politics upon the operative vocabulary of the jurists.[7]

The process whereby juristic language was affected by changes in political reality is also revealed in the legists' employment of *habitator*. Early in the period of urban revival the term referred only to residency, and not necessarily to citizen status. However, since residence demanded assumption of some local responsibility and enjoyment of some citizen privileges, the *habitator* in fact functioned much like a citizen. The confluence took place as recognition of the city's real need, which was not for sheer residence but for the service and money that made residence effectively contribute to the city's strength. In effect, a new unified citizenry emerged. In each generation new qualifications for full membership were set, but at the same time avenues to acceptance and membership were kept open.[8]

This merging of terminology, which reflects a merging of people, is part of the history of equality. Although categories of distinction were to survive in law and politics many centuries, the medieval urban world demonstrated a progress toward functional equality.[9] This development benefited both individual and society. The community benefited because it was to the town's economic advantage for a large number of men to be legally competent and maximally effective in the marketplace. Individuals benefited because as they sought the full citizenship that brought them the fullest possible legal capability, they performed the demands made upon them by municipal statutes; in other words, even if not full-functioning citizens to begin with, out of self-interest they did what citizens did and eventually joined their ranks. By the fourteenth century, it was his actions that made the citizen, the fact that he did the things a citizen, in terms of moral theory and public law, was supposed to do. The widespread common law of citizenship gave value in return for what it needed and prized: civic activity.

Citizenship was one of the ways medieval urban society sorted itself out. In the eyes of the little local world one was known quite literally by the company he kept. Whether he was Guelf or Ghibelline, Montague or Capulet, a member of the wool merchants guild or that of the butchers mattered. His family, of course, mattered most of all; his patronymic told people who he was and what he might do. To use a phrase of the cultural anthropologist, medieval townsmen were "contextualized persons." They "took their definition from relations they are imputed to have with the society that surrounds them."10 Citizenship was one of the grids by which they were delimited or defined. In the Middle Ages one was the sum of units of social and legal definition, the sum of one's group affiliations, rather than a freestanding individual. Only in some ultimate theological and moral sense were people equal. For everyday purposes each man or woman was a unique identity constructed from the catalog of society's constituent parts.

If citizenship was one grid among many, it was an important one. It meant something special in an age which respected rites of ordination, homage, and coronation. Citizenship not only conferred certain economic and political powers, it was a kind of special mark, which not everyone on the street possessed. The status was not exactly a glamorous or rare one; its extension contributed to the creation of a class of men with somewhat equal legal and political powers and potential economic capability.

In a society which constructed many hierarchies in its fear of chaos and search for order, citizenship helped position a man high and strong. By so doing it advertised his competence, thus providing protection to him and others. It asserted a claim to certain deferences while at the same time providing those around him the information they needed to protect themselves. Everyone in the system knew what boundaries to observe. Viewed this way, citizenship may be seen as yet another device with which to reduce tensions by making expectations and reality explicit. The citizen, acting as only a citizen might in law, commerce, politics, war, was doing no more than the noble who wore his sword, the cleric his tonsure, and the merchant his fur hat: he was identifying himself to society in all his powers.

The verbal complexities we have noted exasperated medieval writers as they do us, but they reveal how urban dwellers were distinguished in daily practice. Citizenship status determined what legal, economic, and political shape their lives might take. The city itself must be viewed as the scene of constantly shifting statuses as some men won new rights and others left the community to invest their resources and spirits elsewhere. Changes in citizen rolls and status evidence the loss and gain of power, economic, political, and social, to a community.

MOVEMENT AND ASSIMILATION

A clear appreciation of self-interest suggests why cities gained immigrants, why individuals left familiar circumstances to attach themselves to a new place. They knew what they needed and were willing to sacrifice to get it, whether they came from a nearby town or distant city. What they left and lost was the ease of familiarity—that comfort of easy association with old friends, neighbors, priests, and saints, knowledge of streets and ways, and idiosyncrasies of diet, speech, and law. But they may also have left restrictions on their careers, limitations on social advance, and maybe crushing tax obligations or a dangerously weak position in local factional strife.[11]

What they gained was some material improvement. They spoke as did their new city's rhetoricians about love of liberty and of the good state of the commune. But what a new citizen also sought was some privilege, such as the right to invest in the great trading fleets of Genoa and Venice or the public debt of Florence. In Venice, permission to trade was denied new citizens not assuming municipal obligations. From his petitions that have survived, we know of one Venetian from the *contado* who ran back and forth for a week between San Marco and his hometown nearby, to bring proper proof of his citizenship to the authorities. In Genoa, some of the earliest clear references to citizenship we have are linked to trading privilege.[12]

In the Mediterranean, it must be emphasized, trade was not limited to a new commercial "middle class." From the very beginning of the commercial revival, nobles, lawyers, and notaries saw advantages in trade. Treaties between Genoa and the feudatories up and down her coast recognize the mutual gain to both parties of investment by the wealthy landowners. No social taint ever attached to those members of the aristocracy or professional class who invested their capital in commercial or banking ventures. Indeed, each city was constantly on the lookout for new sources of capital and willingly rewarded new investors.

This explains why investment was emphasized in the contractual arrangements between cities and nobles, and, indeed, in every treaty with those newcomers who sought to benefit from a new fatherland. Whether an immigrant was a cooper, soldier, or distinguished jurist, his identity and capacity were known to his sponsors and to someone in the small, personal city government. His ability to build a house worth one hundred, four hundred, or six hundred lire was known, as well as his degree of commitment to the city's special ideology, if it had one—say, the Guelfism of Florence. This helps to explain the very tailored nature of the bills devised and passed to convey citizenship. In some Florentine legislation, what we might call group citizenship acts, the terms of house construction and residence requirements would vary for different persons listed in the same act.

Besides the right to trade, the other major benefit sought by prospective citizens was some kind of tax relief. This is evident in acts conferring citizenship, town statutes, and in questions about tax responsibility put to the jurisconsults.[13] Verona offered foreign agricultural workers fifteen years' freedom from the usual peasant exactions; in Siena, long debate ensued over the tax exemption finally granted an important family the city wished to attract.[14] Such were some of the benefits men and families sought as they ventured into a new or better, in any event, another, civic culture. That they valued these highly is known from the records they preserved under lock and key and, when necessary, fought for, as an entire little literature of legal controversy shows.[15]

Each man sought what he needed. Students were attracted by low rents and citizen status, which meant legal privilege. Professors, physicians, and other learned professionals were promised not only high salaries or the chance of large income, but also a diminution of tax responsibility.[16] Again, a minor but distinct legal literature exists on the questions of which benefits may be exercised in the face of what civic urgencies. The meaning of "to be treated in all matters as citizens" was asked again and again.[17]

What made transfer to another city possible, as well as desirable, was the basic uniformity of urban life throughout Italy, if not the Mediterranean. Italians and others were able to establish themselves and succeed as well as they did from Barcelona to the Crimea because throughout that region institutions, law, and values were relatively homogeneous. An ethic of work and material success was universal, if not yet espoused by all religious thinkers and preachers. Urban politics and the organization of merchants and artisans were much the same everywhere; one thinks of assemblies and guilds. A generalized Christianity satisfied for a while as one learned local venerations to local saints. Proof of such a common urban life exists in the naturalization procedure each city kept available for its formal acceptance of new people. Somewhat remarkable, however, is the fact that although the lawyers, polemicists, and others constantly refer to new citizens, to the extent that they developed the concept of "new citizens" (*novi cives*), the archives themselves do not suggest a teeming Ellis Island situation in the history of Florence or any other city.

From Perugia, for the period 1369–89, there survives a tax roll compiled by officials designated to account for outsiders. Their little book tells us where the immigrants scattered themselves throughout the five "gates" of the city, and from where they came. Only 170 names appear on the list, and of these the vast majority came from small towns within a radius of thirty-five to fifty miles—Gubbio, Norcia, Narni, for example. Only six were born north of the Alps. The tax list only occasionally gives occupation, but it does note two knights, four *magistri*, one judge, and one physician from Holland.[18] The rest must have been agriculturalists and artisans. Florentine evidence is so scant as to be suspicious. Yet, incomplete as it may be, it suggests that Florence too was the goal of families from the small towns near the big city, places which had always sent people to town, there eventually to greet new greenhorns and ease them into urban life. Arezzo, Volterra, Prato, Pistoia were places of middling size whose most and least successful inhabitants might be attracted by the magnificent advantages of the Tuscan capital. Not completely unfamiliar with urban life, they would not have been kept away by fears of the big city.[19]

If this is so, then by the fourteenth century the pattern of immigration was changing. The typical newcomer is no longer, as he is said to have been, the successful farmer; rather, he is a resident of some minor place who moves to the big bustling town or city. Already he is familiar with the processes and social demands of a nonagricultural society. As one might expect, Florence's range was greater than Perugia's. It pulled more physicians and legists from places more distant; its rolls of new citizens include the Count of Urbino and Jacobus de Belvesio, the noted jurist and counselor to the king of France.

To judge from this Perugian and Florentine evidence, and from the pattern of immigration into Venice, which is similar, the following hypothesis might be drawn: that cities drew their new inhabitants primarily from towns and villages ranking a step or so beneath them in commercial vigor, success, and physical and cultural attractiveness and dignity. In effect, a network of regional relations existed, and one is tempted to draw an analogy with the spread of commercial and legal practices from the sophisticated larger place to the many smaller places with which it dealt. And, of course, politics always reflected in this age a pull to the center: in other conventional terms, we are dealing here with another aspect of the growth of the territorial princely state of the Renaissance.

Why relatively few naturalizations appear in the records is not altogether clear, especially when it is unlikely that large numbers of new citizens were created outside the prescribed procedures. Perhaps by the fourteenth century, fewer people were leaving villages and small towns. Perhaps they expected to survive better in the countryside than in the frequently diseased, economically depressed, and besieged cities.[20]

Today we know about invisible segments of society. Perhaps the medieval town drew many who tried to live within the walls without making a ripple that might be sensed by the tax collector. Statutes are filled with orders to officials to keep the records up to date, but it must have been difficult to keep track of every merchant, artisan, and physician who paid taxes in another place. In every city one can imagine those who found citizenship not worth the trouble and expense, who found it superfluous to career or success, who chose to remain relatively inconspicuous, apparently finding life tolerable as foreigners.[21]

Such a person was one Franciscus, whose son, Cristoforo, petitioned for membership in the Milanese College of Judges. Jason de Mayno (1453–1519) considered the request, the arguments pro and con, and the requirement of the guild that its members be native-born or their sons. Jason argues that Cristoforo be admitted to the guild because his father had been born in Milan and, though he had lived many years in Genoa, had always intended to return to Milan—a fact known to the Genoese who had consistently treated him as a foreigner, that is, as a member of the Milanese community within Genoa. In conclusion, Jason cites two famous jurists whose judgments support his view; he notes that he has seen "many" such cases decided in favor of the child who happened to be born abroad of a father who had never surrendered—in effect, ignored the burdens of—his original citizenship.[22]

Once a person had some evidence of citizenship, either by birth or privilege, he held on to it. "It" might be notice of his birth in a parish register, listing on the tax rolls, or a physical charter which went into the family strongbox. Without such official paper one could lose his privileges, if challenged. And he could lose those benefits of citizenship in other ways too.

"Privari patria grave est" ("to lose one's fatherland is serious indeed"), wrote Philippus Decius (1454–1536/7) in an astringent phrase that suggests the fear men had, and were supposed to have, about possible loss of citizenship rights.[23] If the principal concept behind a grant of citizenship was society's expectation of some service from the newcomer, the principal reason for loss of citizenship was nonperformance of expected civic duty. The jurisconsults and the statutes agree on that point. Baldus's opinion that a citizen who refuses to help his community in moments of crisis should lose his citizenship is stated in the laws of Florence, Arezzo, Perugia, and other cities.[24]

What else was to be gained and not to be lost? What was it that the newcomer sought as he entered the city and experienced its special life? What was it that others enjoyed that attracted him? In other terms, how, then, to describe citizenship itself, in contradistinction to all the approximations and variations we have examined, and with respect to the motives of those who sought a new status? It may be said, perhaps, that without being an absolute condition in any way, true and original citizenship was an intensification of all the conditions and powers available in the community. It was itself a variable, which is to deny any validity to the concept, sometimes used, of "second-class" citizenship, for if there were two classes of citizenship, one with rights of political action and one without, then there were, it is true to say, three, four, five classes—in fact, as we have noted, a whole complicated scale of citizen abilities.[25]

In part, citizenship denoted a state of mind and a spirit more committed than those of other urban dwellers, a potential for sacrifice more unlimited than that of the foreigner, a possession of privilege more complete and less burdensome than that of the countryman. Less abstractly, citizenship was fundamentally a legal institution that sometimes is associated with rights of political action—voting and office holding, for example. It may also be viewed as a kind of contract that demands payment of taxes or performance of service, or both, in return for the benefits it conveys. To this basic condition, political rights may be added by circumstances of birth or the language of a formal act, but they are not essential to the institution. Citizenship was a very complex institution which derived its identity and strength from its relation to something else—taxes, military service, government office. If we accept the dynamic approach of the medieval jurists, we must see it as a series of contracts.

Most simply, it was a contract for reciprocal benefits which ultimately gave their return in money: trading privileges would be a good example, legal benefits in the form of privileges relating to evidence and the severity of punishment another. Finally, citizenship was a moral bond. The city-state pledged its enveloping protection in every aspect of life. For his part the citizen acknowledged that he received his education, values, and place in the world from his place of birth in some association with his natural parents, and for those gifts he acknowledged his loyalty and a responsibility to the moral collectivity. He would pay taxes, perhaps serve in some military organization, and hold public office.

That such a contract could be easily broken, any analysis of the institution must acknowledge. A tension existed, perhaps not for everyone, but certainly for those of some education, wealth, and awareness of realities in the city-state world, between the loyalty of a man to his native place and the attraction another city might exert. A man of Gubbio out in the world would certainly recognize the advantages of Perugian citizenship and be tempted to surrender his native identity for the more powerful auspices of the greater place. Not only is this conflict and movement visible from the social facts, it is also demonstrated from the language of the jurists. They speak of citizenship in terms both of the indelible stain conveyed by birth and of a status conferred by the state's approval of an individual's act of will.

If we understand this, we understand the tortuous discussions over detail: not over the nature of the fundamental exchange of service for the benefits of community membership, but over fringe benefits, so to speak, and over the central privilege of political participation. On balance, although the city dweller might see such activity as a demand for time and money, and surely as a way to make enemies as well as friends, presumably he found good value in public service. It gave him the maximum in juridical status, influence in the *palazzo pubblico*, precedence in public pageantry, lay and ecclesiastical, and greater honor to his family in the marketplaces where political alliances and marriages were made. Just how much influence and honor depended, among other things, on which political office was held.

All this political effect was valuable and had to be bought. Those born in a city paid the greatest price, for political rights came to them through their birth, education, entire natural and psychological development. Much of their lives was given over to the city. Those who came from the outside, however, were most often faced with very specific obligations, which, as we have seen, might demand purchase of a house or so many shares of the public debt. Legislation on this matter was passed everywhere, and it is reasonable to believe that policy changed in response to the realities of local politics.[26]

As they appear in various statutes, these requirements have as their primary goal the defense of local security. This is clear most vividly from the Pistoian demand that the town bell always be in the hands of a native-born citizen and the requirement that excluded new citizens from service in the night watch. Administrative posts were also cautiously filled, especially those of notary and ambassador, whose occupants might badly represent the city's interests.

Such are some of the specific precautions the statutes took. More explicitly and generally stated were regulations concerning service in communal deliberative assemblies, those whose votes would establish policy and govern the lives of fellow citizens. To be sure, not all *statuti* specifically face the question "who serves on the council?" but the vast majority did, and they invariably demanded long continuous residence in lieu of, or in addition to, native birth, some economic standing in the community, and payment of taxes over a designated time. Much the same requirements were made of those who would participate in local political institutions within the city, upon whose function certain governmental activities depended: for example, the Società del Popolo of Bologna and the Campagnia del Popolo of Siena. The *statuti* of the former speak of men of good fame and long residence in accord with municipal law, and that of Siena piles up demands of birth and tax fulfillment. In Florence, each Standardbearer of Justice was to enroll every citizen, but only those foreigners who were in the process of meeting formal citizen requirements.[27]

In some cases the distinction between what might be called minimum and political citizenship is made very clear—in Imola, for example, where one might receive legal benefits after a year of residence, but the right to serve in any office only after ten; or at Bologna, where exactly the same figure was used in the constitution of 1250, only to be raised to twenty years in 1288. In Siena, one who had been a citizen but who had lived abroad a considerable time went through the same probationary period as did a foreign-born citizen, ten years. The obvious generalization from all the data is that city concern, as expressed in tests of loyalty, varied in direct relationship to the sensitivity of the political function involved, and, perhaps, with the city's immediate political situation—whether it was at war or at peace, whether it was well served by its alliances or not.[28]

City constitutions always reflected the realities of social history. In Florence, for example, not only citizenship, but also membership in the Parte Guelfa was required of one who would serve the republic. The constitution of 1321 ordered that a register was to be kept of all *popolares*. These alone were to be regarded as politically sound. No magnates were to be listed, no foreigners, and no one known to take bread and wine with the nobility. Apparently, political men really cared about these provisions, for they were invariably raised in discussions about granting citizenship.[29]

Not surprisingly, the jurisconsults were consulted on such matters. Paul de Castro (d. 1441) delivered a *consilium* that evaluated the petition of men in the *contado* to be notaries in Florence, which, it appears, had three different statutory requirements. The statute of the Captain of the People mentions ten years' residence; the statute of the Guild of Judges and Notaries had called for five, but now demands twenty years. Paul's attempt to decide which should now control the petition leads him to discuss foreigners, men from the *contado* (*comitatenses*), and guild-city relations. Eventually he decides that the recent, revised requirement of twenty years should prevail, but on the way to this judgment he says that in such matters citizens of the city and citizens of the *comitatus* have equal rights as Florentines, provided they have paid their taxes. It is clear that Florence, like ancient Rome with her client cities, has contracted specific treaties with specific clauses on citizenship. The jurist wants these preserved and recognized, and he confirms Florence in what we might call her "legislative sovereignty."[30]

How different is all of this from the Greek scene, so simple in its vision of citizenship in moral and political terms, and even of the Roman world, which in so many ways perpetuated and continued to extol an ethic of participatory citizenship in the many cities, large and small, that dotted it. Ancient theory, albeit not law, is almost completely free of this concern with economic benefit. No vast body of ancient legal cases survives that reflects such an overpowering interest in monetary advantage. To note this is to underline the difference between the relatively uneconomic nature of the ancient world and the heightened commercialism of medieval Italian urban life. The coincidence of a booming economy with a fast developing legal science produced a litigiousness and concern for status in legal and economic affairs that provokes a comparison with our own age. In any event, one cannot imagine the near neglect of moral issues in the citizenship literature of antiquity. Perhaps

Machiavelli had these debased conditions in mind when, again, he forcefully pushed service, indeed, military service, to the forefront of citizen responsibilities and simultaneously downplayed citizen rights.

CITIZENSHIP AND EQUALITY

If, on the one hand, government produced and safeguarded this kind of specificity, on the other, it created and guaranteed, within each city-state and throughout the urban civic culture, a condition of equality. We have observed the lawyers homogenizing a vocabulary, bringing *incola*, *civis*, *habitator*, and *subditus* into rough approximation, basing their view on the notion of reciprocal benefit. Now we can see that in the creation of a functional civic equality, while the jurisconsults created the theories and the terminology, their colleagues in government wrote and imposed the laws. As citizens, men were becoming equal in their giving and receiving from the state. Also, as citizens, they were becoming equal in their common weakness vis-à-vis the state, for in accepting their new equal capability they acknowledged the legislative, executive, and judicial power of government. Legal equality may be a cherished goal of a modern democracy, but its early development was accelerated by the rise of executive authority, which could be republican or princely in nature. What appears very strongly in these matters of granting and depriving of citizenship is the acknowledged power and authority of the "state." In the final analysis, it not only determines the identity of the individual but also precisely defines the status of that individual in terms of social, political, and civil power. Government may be seen as creating broad areas for its convenience, in which everyone is equally dependent upon and subservient to it.[31]

Government established a basis for equality by meeting the merchant-citizen's and artisan-citizen's desire for a condition in which he was the competitive equal to his fellow townsmen and superior to the outsider. It did this without ringing slogans or a great single declaration of rights, but rather by offering justice to all, collecting taxes on an equitable basis, and opening its offices and perquisites to a large part of the community.

Already, medieval city government was doing many of the things modern governments must do to create a social unity. It financed schools to provide the young with skills and a sense of their *patria*'s past. This education was open to the children of immigrants to bring them into the community; festivals, songs, hatreds were all instruments to this end. Government forced an oath to observe laws and treaties upon men of all social classes—one thinks especially of those in which merchant privileges bulked largest and served to benefit both *popolari* and nobles. Functional equality existed also in the government service which drew in so many. Finally, government stood to enforce the contractual obligations of merchants when they were equal in the legal rights they possessed, for contract implies and demands certain legal equalities. So, although medieval Italy was no hotbed of radical egalitarianism, it did provide a social and economic structure favorable to the development of a de facto legal equality that transcended many of the distinctions that of course remained in medieval society, distinctions to blur, to be effaced, and to be forgotten. A generation or so in the field with his serfs would make a free man one of them in local eyes, while a generation of the proper clothes, generous charity, and the right marriage could bring a man and his family into the urban oligarchy.

This tendency is visible in *consilia*, which show that it was to a city's advantage to deal with men as equals. Administration was easier that way, for example, in the matter of reprisals. Johannes de Legnano (d. 1383), in his treatise on that privilege, and Paul de Castro, Bartolus, and Philippus Decius in *consilia* all held that all those living in a given territorial jurisdiction should benefit from the privilege of reprisal. Baldus disagreed on this specific case, but in one in which analogous issues were involved, he turned aside narrow legalistic interpretations and, relying on what he called the *opinio vulgi*, accepted common usage.

In many ways even the Jews were homogenized into the citizenry. It is a fact that from the fourth century through the Renaissance, governments and political theories all changed, yet remained constant in their social and legal oppression of the Jews, but it is also the case that in Italy and at times elsewhere in territories subject to Roman law, Jews were regarded as *cives Romani* and as such were protected. Although they were limited socially in many ways, they retained legal rights that permitted them to engage in commerce, banking, and civil action. Johannes Crottus (fl. ca. 1500) ignores the distinction between citizenship by birth and citizenship by privilege in the case of a Jew. Aretinus (1492–1556) allows a Jew to participate in benefits granted to "everyone" in the various jurisdictions of Florence; and Alexander of Imola (1424–77), in a judgment involving adultery, assigns a lesser penalty to a Jew who is of "the very people and body of the city." He then refers to statutes from cities all over Italy in support of his view, although he is careful to specify that Jews are not to be treated as "true and natural citizens."

Clearly, for many purposes of social and commercial life, Jews received citizen treatment. Jews were not, we must be careful to say, drawn fully into urban life. At any moment they might suffer from activated hatred. When and where they were effectively assimilated, it was because the interests of government and society needed it that way. Governments preferred useful richer subjects to poorer, and the more the richer were drawn into the financial structure of the state, the potentially more supportive of the regime they might be. In an age of constant coups and fear of émigré activity, the firmer the bonds between citizen and state, the better.

This process by which the civil community was shaped into a unity, by which even Jews were made part of a legal whole, is observable in both republican and princely states. It is an aspect of the grand theme of the growth of modern government, which grew and became more complex, if not efficient, as it attempted to bring more and more kinds of individuals into a subordinate relationship. As it succeeded, slowly, and not always uniformly and logically, it politicized greater numbers of people into a subordinate relationship, and into its service. In the Italian city world we see evidence of such developments in another *consilium* of Alexander of Imola, who argued that the intent of the common law was to get people to pay taxes somewhere, to do citizen service for some community. Another jurisconsult went so far as to say that loss of citizenship, absence of committed service in a career, constitutes a "defectum" in a man.[32]

These developments were not total, but progressive. Any analysis only suggests a direction, not a condition fully achieved. Both Florentine republicans and Milanese courtiers satisfied the demand of citizens for functional equality and that of their civil servants for conditions and institutions favoring maximum social and political control over citizen-subjects. If these officials and the legists slurred distinctions between citizens and residents, nobles and commonality, and other groups, they accomplished two things. In removing some distinctions they lessened social unhappiness, and they made all men more vulnerable to the authority of the state. In this long process citizenship was the basic institutional form of equality.

THE INTELLECTUALS VIEW THE CITY

Like the Greeks and Romans, medieval thinkers were very much aware of the city, its distinctiveness, and the special nature of the commitments that made it very different from conventional medieval social institutions. City life was celebrated by poets and historians and theorized by theologians and legists. If the former were more vivid, the latter were more analytical as they tried to find a place for the city within the framework of Christian theory and physical, which is to say, rural, reality. For three hundred years, from the thirteenth into the sixteenth century, intellectuals were intrigued by the city and sought to characterize and explain it.[33] It demanded explanation, for its very existence and function denied the norms. A city did not look like a manor. Its inhabitants lived out their lives doing things other people, peasants or knights, did not do. They made and sold things and money and usually left their weapons at home. City politics, which emphasized the participation and judgment of many in, for example, processes of election based on political and legal equality, differed from that of the hierarchical feudal world. The social scene was different too: contrast the stability of the village with the human variety and flux characteristic of the large Italian or Flemish municipality. Finally, the competitiveness and materialism of urban life clashed with the deepest values—charity, cooperation, and harmony—of Christian life. It is no accident that the theologians reacted to urbanism during the late Middle Ages; in those very centuries an expanding Christian intellectual community had to comment on the inescapable fact of urban spread and growth and also, after the mid-fourteenth century, occasional, if spotty, decline.

The jurists clearly distinguished between urban and rural life. Baldus viewed the city as superior to the countryside. He talks about cities generally in abstract terms—to speak of one is to speak of a nature common to all—and he rejects the notion that rural life confers any of the habits and qualities that derive naturally from city living. Bartolus also saw urban life as something qualitatively special, beyond particular physical signs such as walls and buildings. To him the word "city" suggested a superior quality of existence, a distinctive culture. Bartolus is the fourteenth-century objective social scientist, aware of sociological differentiae, who builds legal theory upon analysis of contemporary thought, institutions, and legislation.[34]

Canon lawyers wrote in similar terms. The thirteenth-century gloss to the Decretals of Pope Gregory IX (d. 1243) viewed the city as more than walls and suburbs. And only in a city, wrote Guido de Baysio one hundred years later, could men study the law and the arts at an advanced level. A city is known for the accomplishments of its sons, not for its stones.[35]

An emphasis on culture was sometimes more than a scholarly observation. It could become the basis of a judicial decision. For example, in an interesting *consilium* regarding the custody of a minor whose parents came from different cities, Jason de Mayno decided that although the widow, and not a municipal official, is to rear the child, he is to be reared in his father's traditions, as the law requires. Educated and nurtured in his father's culture (*mores*), and not his mother's, he will become a Florentine, but otherwise he will not; the intent of the law recognizes the distinctiveness and importance of a specific upbringing. Such an education would create a society of free men whose love of country was the bond that at the same moment held together the community in the present generation and perpetuated it into the next. Later, Marianus Socinus was to put the matter very neatly. In discussing a Venetian statute he explains away the demand of the statute that a woman marry within the area governed by Venice. "Extra," he says, can be interpreted two ways: *localiter* and *intellectualiter*. Since the man in question was *intellectualiter* a Venetian, the statute should not hold in the present instance. Here we see emphasis placed upon a subjective view of an individual as being culturally determined. And although he rejected the thought, another jurist, Marianus Socinus, Jr., could state for the sake of argument that not even outright denial could efface the mark of civic culture that one's special circumstances of birth and education conferred.[36]

In the Middle Ages and Renaissance, as in more recent times, one form self-definition took was suspicion of alien cultures. Throughout the Middle Ages, Roman Christian patriotism shows clearly in suspicion of the wily Greek. Northern chroniclers complain about more than the Italian climate as they describe imperial trips to Rome. Romans were viewed as scheming, treacherous exploiters of the holy places. And local Italian historians simultaneously denigrate their neighbors and extol their own kind. This suspicion of the foreigner could take a specifically cultural form, and did so by the fourteenth century, when each city viewed itself as the peculiar product of a unique and beneficent history. The city was viewed by its protagonists as a social and spiritual entity formed according to a determinant moral and cultural ideal. Thus, in the passage cited, Bartolus suggests that the history, culture, law, and dialect of Rome and Perugia gave their citizens a certain human shape or form. Dante himself is in this tradition, as are the fourteenth-century commentators who began the great tradition of scholarship and criticism that flows from his work.[37]

Dante's fundamentally conservative social and political philosophy is revealed in Cacciaguida's complaints in Canto 16 of the *Paradiso*. The old Florentine stands against many kinds of change. On prudential grounds he wonders whether the fewer citizens of the good old days might not be braver and more loyal than the greater population of the moment. He ascribes a different and inferior life to those who live in communities outside the city, suburbs that today are only minutes from downtown Florence. He is against immigration; he suspects the sharp business eye of those from outside the walls. Their values differ from his, and from their integration into the citizen body has come evil to the community. Indeed, "integration" may hardly be the word, given the resulting shift in values that, in effect, has already changed the city. Dante's criticism cannot be limited by one word, say, "cultural" or "social," for it was aimed at the entire human being produced by an entirely different physical and intellectual environment. Given such a sense of the integrity of one's own way of life and such an idea of the differentiae that set it off from the life of near neighbors, we may imagine the image Florentines had of Venetian or Roman urban life and its products, so intense was medieval *campanalismo*.[38]

The poet's suspicion of newcomers—one is tempted to say his racism— based as it was upon social and moral disdain, was explicated and endorsed by his commentators. Jacobus della Lana, who wrote the first commentary on Dante about 1328, notes the evil and drunken ways of those from Certaldo and Figline, by his day part of the citizenry, and complains that they had corrupted the sober and orderly life of the city. He demands good moral character as prerequisite to citizenship and worries lest the number and influence of new citizens prevail over the old stock and change the very structure of society. The *Ottimo commento*, in a gloss to Dante's verse on the arms-bearing citizenry of the past, claims that the newcomers bring "little faith and love." Its author translates Dante's distaste for blood mixture into a sociopolitical criticism: the presence of immigrant aliens will subvert the simple principles of order the city's life demands, its rule of custom, or *reggimento*. Writing about 1340, Dante's son, Pietro Alighieri, asserts that every male citizen must be ideally suited to, be in harmony with, the good of the city, which itself is based upon the virtues of its citizens. His view, as well as the comments of the other critics, was made apropos Dante's phrase, "confusione delle persone." Later in the century Benvenuto da Imola reiterated these hostilities and fears, all of which suggest how strongly cultural and moral, as well as political and economic, conformity was demanded in the medieval city state.[39]

Medieval theorists of cultural identity left no aspect of personality outside their legislation. Bologna, for example, translated fear of cultural subversion into a statutory requirement for office by declaring, in the 1288 codification of its statutes, that no one could hold the office of Ancient, or, indeed, hold any office or be on any council, who did not speak the Bolognese tongue.[40] And to judge from a Florentine law of the same period, private morality was very much a matter touching the public good. The puritanical ethic of medieval Florence conceived as its ideal undesirable the man without skills, inheritance, or productive or socially cooperative habits. Sots, gamblers, those without a trade were to be expelled not only from the walled center of Florentine life, but, indeed, from the *provincia* as well. The fields as well as the streets needed protection; were these persons to remain, the strength and wealth of the state would be imperiled.[41]

Finally, these social thinkers were aware of Mediterranean urbanism's special political quality. In his *Tractatus de Guelphis et Ghibellinis*, Bartolus carefully and objectively examined the party structure of Todi and the very phenomenon of urban factionalism. He accepts it as part of the political scene, to be discussed as just one more datum of urban life. His knowledge of the political and legal culture of Rome helped him to understand the motivation of those who would wear the Ghibelline badge for reasons of social prestige, or those who would switch allegiance out of personal ambition. For him, factionalism is legitimate, although dangerous, for the factions apparently do struggle out of concern for the public welfare and are committed to the regime, itself constituted under that concept.[42] Brunetto Latini, the Florentine historian, also used this Roman law theory in defending the special nature of Italian city life. He distinguished between the king of France and other monarchs who sold political office to the hurt of their subjects and the rule of the Italian cities in which the citizens chose their own governors. They did this, he wrote, assuming that the best interests of the community and of the citizens, individually considered, would be served.[43]

This positive regard for the functions of a civic culture led to the conventional use of certain symbolic words and concepts in describing the reciprocal relations between a city and its dependent communities and citizens. As early as the twelfth century, as successful towns pushed their authority into the countryside, they imposed a matriarchal relation upon villages and other towns. That is, they claimed the *devotio* and *reverentia* due a mother from the subject places in the *contado*, which stood as *filii* in relation to them. Their sophisticated chanceries, concerned with legitimacy as well as civil order and tranquility, developed the notion that rebellion against (urban) mother ran contrary to natural law and hence was evil and forbidden. This is precisely the tradition reflected later in Dante's powerful and succinct expression of mother-love: "Siena mi fa." Sometimes in the conventional discussions over which authority was first to be served, *pater* or *patria*, the power of the city was compared, as we have seen, with that of the father, which is to say it shared the respect owed both parents.[44]

Eventually this concept, loaded as it is with biblical precepts of respect, legal doctrines of control, and emotional qualities of affection, appeared in the lawyers. Bartolus writes of the city's *tutela*, caretaking responsibility, toward its citizens, and their reciprocal respect for the city. He speaks of the city as both mother and father. The metaphor of the body politic was also used: the citizens form part of the body. That such imagery was commonplace by the fourteenth century should not lessen its significance, for in the theologians this metaphor is joined to that of the *corpus mysticum*. Ptolemy of Lucca defines the city as a "unio in corpore animato" and compares the "amor suorum civium" of a city to the ties of charity and love that bind together Christian society.[45]

Such acceptance of the city by a theologian is worth noting, for during the previous two hundred years of European expansion, cities and city values had given the Church immense trouble. The cities of Italy and France had spawned countless heresies, which some of the most important theologians of the thirteenth century sought to control.

Historians have noted how little medieval political theorists wrote about citizenship, and how little they related it to contemporary conditions when they did. The legists discussed it because, as we have seen, valuable privileges flowed from status, and their comments usually were made in relation to laws in the *Corpus Iuris Civilis* that differentiated among the rights and functions of citizens, residents, foreigners, and others. Their language and concerns were technical and analytical, not moral and hortative; they were interested in freeing men from specific restraints and obligations, or gaining privileges, not in specifying a whole code of responsibilities for each individual based on a revived morality from the pre-Christian past. It is relatively rare to find, as we do in the commentary of the fourteenth-century Sicilian jurist, Lucas da Penna, on the *Code*, a jurist asserting in general terms the obligation of all to serve society: one is to perform military service not as a burden, but as a gift freely given according to law. For reasons that are not altogether clear, the theologians did not investigate citizenship as much as they did other contemporary political phenomena.

Perhaps they ignored citizenship because of their associations with the institutions of monarchy and feudalism and their instinctive predilection for the institutions and society of the Old and New Testaments, which are very similar, or because cities and citizens really mattered only in Italy, which was not where the social and political philosophers were concentrated. Paris, where the great thinkers argued and taught, was a royal city whose people, compared with those in the large Italian cities, had a less active role in the governing of their community. Perhaps, as one scholar has suggested, it was because the significant audience for political thought (which always in the Middle Ages was social and religious thought as well) was still, in the thirteenth century, a royal, noble, and ecclesiastical one. And perhaps because Aristotle's *Politics*, given its vocabulary deriving from a different social and political reality, was not completely comprehensible in the mid-thirteenth century, when it was translated and first studied. Yet, there were some who did try to understand the *Politics*.

Aquinas's commentary was a beginner's attempt to comprehend the ancient scene and vocabulary. Although he touches all the issues considered so important by Aristotle, Thomas makes no reference to the little cities that dotted the Italian landscape he knew well, nor to the lawyers who worked in every one of these towns, nor to discussions of citizenship by others at the university that might have helped elucidate a point. To be sure, his straightforward explication in the commentary on the *Politics* does not differ from that he commonly applied to other Aristotelian texts, but here the distance from reality cries for notice and explanation.

In the years after Thomas's death in 1274, as his and Aristotle's influence spread, discussion of citizenship increased. John of Paris (d. 1306), for example, while writing on church-state issues, discussed the origins of organized society itself. "By a natural instinct, which comes from God," he wrote, "they [men] are inclined to live politically, and in a society, and so, in order to live well together, they choose rulers, and choose different ones according to the difference in communities." He was aware of the need for a division of labor and anticipates Locke with his emphasis upon private property as a fundamental cause of political organization. To preserve his property, the result of his industry, the individual may exercise a natural right to create the proper form of government for himself, preferably some form of monarchy. The rightfulness of this action derives first from his existence as an individual moral personality and only then as a political being obliged to act, to choose.

By choosing, individuals act "out of their own power to shape the destiny of their own State." And this action, which is in fact legislation, reflects their rationality in seeing their own best interest.

Apart from John of Paris and Marsilius of Padua, the scholastics did not, as a group, add much to the theory of citizenship, although they did increase the visibility of citizenship in their expanding body of commentary upon Aristotle. They were bedeviled by the Aristotelian terminology which forced them to render *polis* as *civitas* but which could not force them to conceive of a *civitas* as a *regnum*. That is to say, they never saw a citizen as a member of a small-scale community in which he both made the laws and obeyed them. Even a penetrating thinker like Nicholas Oresme (1323–82) thought of the citizen in terms of his function as *bourgeois*, as economic, rather than as public man. Others, such as Peter of Auvergne (d. 1304), for example, made lawyerlike distinctions among various kinds of citizens, each with powers appropriate to his status, but again did not focus on the essential political function of Aristotle's citizen in a sovereign community. Living under a monarchy as most of them did, and probably knowing that in strict legal and constitutional theory many of the Italian cities were still under some kind of formal subordination to the Holy Roman emperor, it is not surprising that they did not make a radical break with the medieval lack of historical perspective, which, as we know, it took the historical scholarship of the Renaissance to change. One Aristotelian concept they did understand, however, no doubt because it jibed so well with contemporary circumstances, was the basing of citizen status upon property. Peter of Auvergne made such a distinction between those citizens who might be elected to some form of magistracy and those who could not. Oresme, whom we have already seen as emphasizing the economic side of man, also ranked citizenships in a hierarchy based upon property.

As worked out by Peter and accepted as conventional doctrine by later scholastics, theory held that two groups (*multitudo*) existed within each political community: one which is fit to rule, given its wisdom and virtue based on property, and the other, "whose members are given to animal and materialistic activities," which is to have no voice in government at all. For some purposes, however, these too are citizens. They might, under the most extreme conditions portending tyranny, rebel against their lawful ruler. Such, at least, was the view of Godfrey of Fontaines (d. 1306).

What medieval theorists missed, with their emphasis upon property as the prerequisite for political action, was Aristotle's insistence upon personal excellence, some moral superiority, as the basis for citizen status. They also missed the extent of political power which came through the right of participation that Aristotle meant his citizen to have. The result was their equation of the citizen limited in these respects to the free subject of a lawful king, such as in the France in which so many of these social philosophers lived. Moreover, from this time on, the distinction between citizen and subject is almost never clear, unless the writer wants to make it so as an issue, between *civis* in the tradition of the Greco-Roman city-state and *civis* as any free man living in a monarchy in town or on the countryside. But this is only to repeat that during the Middle Ages, just as under the ancient Roman Empire, citizenship was compatible with monarchy, both as a principle, in the city-states of Italy that fell to some "prince," and under a king, as in France. As we shall see, this is a phenomenon which survives to the French Revolution and is not inconsistent with one perennial aspect of citizenship, its role as discriminator in a society in which a plurality of legal and social statuses is assumed, nor is it at odds with that aspect of the citizenship tradition which stresses activism.[46]

Meanwhile, one Aristotelian, who, although he studied at Paris under the monarchy, remained rooted in the city traditions and life of Italy, succeeded in penetrating to the real Aristotle. Marsilius of Padua (d. ca. 1342) gave a sense to the meaning of *civis* that is unusual for the Middle Ages. His ideas were not popular then, nor for several hundred years, yet, apparently, they were preserved and occasionally read.

Marsilius was a social philosopher and political activist who wrote out of an immediate interest in his own time and society. Perhaps that is why he was largely ignored in his own day and was buried in the great corpus of ecclesiastical and secular political writing published during the centuries of the Conciliar Controversy, the Renaissance, and the Reformation. There is a danger in overstating Marsilius's significance. A vast literature exists on his modernity; his principal modern interpreter and translator says: "He has been hailed as the great prophet of modern times and the precursor of nearly every significant modern political theorist, doctrine, and development." In fact, he probably was not such a precursor. And certainly his influence was nothing like that of Thomas, whose views seeped into the sermons of Dominican preachers and the curricula of their schools all over Europe. He had no large inner-city churches to serve as amplifiers for his views to members of the active business and governmental class. Over the long run Marsilius had no institutions behind him. Eventually, however, he was read, and in the seventeenth century his ideas were picked up because of their republican tendencies. They probably influenced the thinking of George Lawson and other republican theorists during the mid-century crisis. Certainly he, more than any other late-medieval thinker, attempted to make an Aristotelian analysis and vocabulary serve to explain and authenticate the limited popular governments that ruled all over Mediterranean Europe in the late Middle Ages.

Unlike Thomas and other scholastics whose interests were largely definitional and focused on problems of formal relationships, Marsilius's concerns were practical as well as analytical. He knew firsthand the factional disputes that bloodied the life of the Italian cities, frustrating ideals of civic harmony and brotherhood as well as commercial success. He sought the mechanisms that might bring these communities to their proper condition of peace, to civic health, it has been suggested, given Marsilius's medical training at Padua.

Medicine, some knowledge of the Roman law, probably some ancient history which included a sense of the meaning of republican, as opposed to imperial, Rome, and an intimate, if flawed, appreciation of Aristotle's system—these were in Marsilius's head as he examined the constituent elements of the city-state and attempted to assign to each its proper function in the making of peace. One of these elements was "the people." The people was composed of citizens; hence the need to examine the concept of citizenship. This was all the more necessary given his belief that a popular regime, if properly constructed, would be the right regime for the reconciliation of civic antagonisms.

Popular governments, it should be noted, were not popular in the modern, full democratic sense. For Marsilius and for all his contemporaries citizenship was not the automatic birthright of every man. A citizen, he writes, "is one who participates in the civil community in the government or the deliberative or judicial function according to his rank. By this definition, children, slaves, aliens and women are distinguished from citizens, although in different ways." Not only do citizens constitute some varying part of the entire free community, each citizen's voice may not carry a weight equal to that of his neighbor. In using the concept of the "weightier part" Marsilius casually accepts standard medieval procedure in which, at every level throughout the secular and ecclesiastical worlds, voting was reckoned on the basis of inequality. It was everywhere assumed that persons of rank, age, learning, and other marks of obvious distinction and authority should be credited with more voice than others. In searching for principles to guide his community, Marsilius was careful to rely on many accepted institutions; his reliance upon Aristotle in his acceptance of the idea that the combined wisdom of many men had value must have been disturbing enough for his day. As he wrote, this recognition of distinctions within the citizen voting body was "in accordance with the honorable custom of polities."

For Marsilius, then, citizenship is active. One may serve in the executive, legislative, or judicial offices of government. By serving one gains in wisdom and becomes one of "those men from whom alone the best laws can emerge." Being based on wide experience, these laws will guarantee the "common utility" since "no one knowingly harms himself." Finally, still keeping close to Aristotle, Marsilius claims that laws made by such an enlightened majority of the citizens, who constitute the most influential part of the community, will be better observed since those who are responsible for lawmaking and law enforcing will be willing to be governed by laws they themselves have helped to make.

All of this is manifestly Aristotelian and fit for small-scale communities, but the presentation lacks a clear statement of assumptions about man, or, failing that, a formal linkage with an ethics and psychology such as that provided by Aristotle. Hence there is no exhortation to the individual to do something to perfect himself. A system of offices, councils, and procedures is assumed and then justified, and the individual's actions within such a system are spelled out and justified. But justification is in terms of the system's success, not in terms of an individual's progress toward the self-realization and virtue that one finds in classical philosophy. It was perhaps this cool Marsilian approach that made him acceptable to George Lawson and others during the English constitutional crisis. If these Protestants initially had been drawn to Marsilius by his violent antipapalism, his reliance on scriptural authority, and other evidence of a proto-Protestant stance, what they found serviceable to their immediate political needs was his passionless analysis of governmental function.[47]

In summation, we may say that a legacy of scholastic speculation on citizenship did not enter into the mainstream of European political theory, first, because it was not extensive; second, because it was both confused and uninspiring; and most importantly, because in the age we call "absolutist" it did not really serve.

The medieval Aristotelian vocabulary was not as dense as that of the legists, but like theirs, it finally failed to win wide currency because it never quite succeeded in translating all the different categories of people known to ancient society into precisely understood medieval equivalents; the blurrings and overlappings were too many. The scholastic's language never or rarely reflected Aristotle's meaning and his moral and metaphysical goals: the eventual realization of the individual through social and political involvement. When better history and more powerful language came along during the progressive recovery of the full body of classical literature, the scholastic writings went into the manuscript cabinets of monastic and university libraries, read by relatively few until they reappeared in the scholarly debates of the wars of religion. Meanwhile, from the fifteenth century on, humanist writers inspired by Cicero, Polybius, and Plato, as well as by Aristotle, entered the tradition with new, powerful, and satisfying theories and aspirations.

Medieval Aristotelianism did much to advance the value of activism in the service of a secular political world. It emphasized the community as the ideal sphere of human activity. It gave some value to the human body in all its worldly involvements—indeed, to the entire natural order. It even provided good reasons for the acceptance of the merchant as a contributing and necessary—hence potentially virtuous—member of society. But it did not provide this struggling world outlook with a new vocabulary, a clearly articulated program that was meaningful to the educated, active citizen troubled about his soul and salvation just because of involvement. Its values were too deeply embedded in the vocabulary of the traditional university, and in the antagonisms among the great religious orders, especially the Franciscans and Dominicans. Both inveighed against the world, but each saw the world somewhat differently, as histories of architecture and philosophy tell us. What was needed was a fresh statement about the human condition and the possibility of its salvation less tied to the old curricula in law, theology, and philosophy. Marsilius with all his willingness to follow Aristotle was unable to provide this foundation; Bruni and other humanists eventually did.

As a group the civil lawyers were more partial toward the city than the theologians; their attitudes approximated those of Latin Aristotelians and anticipated the civic humanists. That is to say, they accepted the city as a social ambience in which the Christian could do good. Lucas da Penna, in a comment concerning those who would falsely use religious office as a means to evade public responsibility, asserts that isolated monasteries are not the only places where man can be good. Lot, he notes, was upright in the city but a sinner on the lonely mountain. Solitude is preferable to life among the wicked, but not to life among decent folk. The good Christian life may be led in town as well as on the farm. Lucas's reference to Lot and Moses in his argument suggests an obvious awareness of the implications of his opinion, and the weight of counteropinion in Christian history. Moses may have ascended the mountain to confront the glory of God, but he came down to provide for the needs of his people.[48]

This view of one of the most important jurists of the fourteenth century, of a man who himself had a successful political career, shows us that long before the civic humanist movement which flourished in Florence in the early fifteenth century, at least some Christian moralists were seeking to justify a new kind of Christian life. Activism in the community was now so common and so rewarding that it demanded legitimation. While successful city men were making money, building fine palaces, ruling their cities, winning the admiration and envy of their fellows, some mendicant preachers were constantly reminding them of the meaninglessness and futility of this life. But other religious, frequently Dominicans, followed Aristotle and Aquinas in seeing man's social accomplishments as natural and, therefore, good. Meanwhile, the jurists, understanding the Roman past and clear-eyed about their present, saw what had to be done if the complicated urban society all about them was to succeed. Hence their analysis of contemporary political life—Bartolus's work on factionalism, for example—and hence passing remarks like Lucas's which in effect create an occasion to range traditional authority, here the Bible, in support of the new, activist way of life. Once the "public welfare" was seen in its full social significance, those who spent their lives tending it had to be seen as good.

Turning from the legists, we see appreciation of the city world in the poetry of Antonio Pucci, a Florentine of the late fourteenth century. Pucci is proud of his people, their city, and their things. He admires the goods, jewels, and productive accomplishments, to say nothing of the very physical beauty of the city. He reveals an almost Gothic naturalism and materialism in his lush description of Florence's market, of the active, profitable business life of the city. His picture of goods and monies changing hands, of loose women and swaggering youths, of strangers from the *contado* and beyond mingling with citizens, of all the bustle under the portico built by the commune to foster commerce is hardly a paean to idleness and an approbation of spirituality. His picture is of what a city ought to be and reflects contemporary Florentine values. As evidence that Pucci was a representative and true Florentine, it may be noted that in the same verses he can extol his countrymen for their sacrifices in war and rejoice that, victory in hand, taxes and other civic responsibilities are now reduced.[49]

That these views on civic wealth and family prosperity are scattered over time and place suggests that increasingly after 1250 social commentators of all kinds came to accept the world, its benefits, and incumbent responsibilities. That they did so is comprehensible only in the light of fundamental changes in European as well as Italian life: the new philosophical movement, strong at the universities and filtered to the literate urban population and beyond through sermons and other forms of talk; the legal movement, not so new any more, with its theories of civic and economic involvement, awareness of the facts of day-to-day experience, acceptance of property as intrinsic to the natural man, and desire for material and political success through manipulation of power of all kinds; and the widening commercial movement, which brought measurable improvement of existence to many all over Europe through a greater exchange, abundance, and enjoyment of things.

THE CITY AND THE CITIZEN

Once the city was established by some theorists as a legitimate institution in Christian society, others provided it with proper leadership and authority adequate for its functions. By the mid-thirteenth century a literature on city management already existed, a genre based on the assumption that efficiency as well as morality was necessary for the success of municipal government. Its authors were men of experience, judges, notaries, and others who drew upon contemporary statutes as well as moral literature. One noted work of this kind is that of John of Viterbo (fl. 1228), in effect a manual for specialists; less technical but better known was Book 9 of Brunetto Latini's *Tesoro*, which was devoted to city government. Whether practical or literary in emphasis, these guides to good government included some law, formularies, speeches, and a leaven of wisdom and morality. Concern for the rights and accomplishments of individual citizens as well as for communal needs and glory is evident in these books: for example, in Guido Fava's interest in the civic status of litigants, and the *Occulus pastoralis*'s praise for the deceased citizen who has, by his service, added to the luster of friends, family, and fatherland.[50]

Legitimate authority was provided to cities by the lawyers, especially after the Peace of Constance of 1189, which gave de facto independence to imperial towns in central and northern Italy. Eventually each city exercised the powers of the emperor within its own borders, that is, enjoyed sovereign authority. Its legal omnipotence created its citizens by endowing them with every civil capacity they possessed. Baldus asserted that a town may make and unmake citizens. In the name of the general welfare it may grant special concessions to a desired immigrant even if these concessions differ from demands normally made of immigrants. A statute, he observed, may give Jews certain benefits, and, indeed, if the text of their privileges explicitly grants it, Jews may be protected against, say, bodily insult, exactly as are other citizens.

Baldus's most interesting comment on the power of statutes reveals the influence of contemporary philosophical training upon the jurist. Citizenship, he writes, is a species possessing several natures, and one may possess one or another of these. He is saying, in other words, that a born Florentine may by statute be turned into a Perugian and may function as such, all the while remaining in some metaphysical sense a Florentine in potential. So great is the statutory power of the city that it could, in effect, create persons. On one occasion Baldus likened an exile to one deceased. One who has been banished cannot be called *civis*; this being the case, he loses all privileges that term bestows. Baldus's sixteenth-century editor restates this position and adds that Bartolus and Alexander de Imola thought likewise, which suggests constant attention to this kind of issue.[51]

If municipal legislation could create and destroy entire legal personalities, it could also control them. Statute and jurisconsult agree on this. The Florentine statute of 1415 gave to the executives of the city many powers to regulate the lives of citizens living everywhere under Florentine rule, in both *contado* and town. And Bartolus, relying on experience, writes that a city may, through the power of its legislation, grant a citizen whatever measure of status and privilege it desires. Action in Florentine councils with respect to new citizens is clearly in accord with this theory; the legislation of the fourteenth century is specific to almost every individual or group of individuals in making demands of residence and financial commitment, as we have seen.[52]

This control was not, it must be noted, limited to individuals; city power extended over subject cities, their latitude of action as cities, and the legal capability of their citizens. So Paul de Castro (d. 1441), analyzing a case involving the possible enjoyment of Venetian privileges by citizens of Padua, concludes that since the Venetian statute in question consciously viewed them as Paduans and not as Venetians, the Paduans are not to benefit as do the latter. Panormitanus's views on Perugia's freedom of action under the papacy are similar. At one time Perugia and Siena had agreed to exchange the financial privileges of citizenship. Now, after many years, Perugia was attempting to deny these advantages to the Sienese. Indeed, both towns had come to treat citizens of the other as foreigners. The case concerns Sienese reluctance to grant privilege to a Perugian who now asks for it; the question is, what is the law? Panormitanus (1386–1445) argues against the grant of reciprocal privileges because more than ten years have passed since the privilege was used; because, privilege or no, the Sienese have in fact been treated by the Perugians as foreigners; and because Perugia, subject to the papacy, has neither the legal competence nor the right to contract with Siena. Such an agreement would subordinate the rights of the proper superior to those of the inferior.[53]

This careful control over citizens and subject places was contained within an even wider framework of authority and powers. By the fourteenth century, if not earlier, the lawyers had developed theories that permitted municipalities to tax, construct public buildings, and take all actions in the name of the public welfare, including the founding of another city. The legal literature of the fourteenth century is heavy with attempts to understand, define, and make relevant to contemporary government late-classical theory and terminology of taxation.[54] These attempts are built upon earlier discussions and actual experience. For example, a century before the great financial crisis of the Trecento, Florentine fiscal experts, aware of both immediate needs and theories of citizen responsibility, attempted to find viable criteria for assessing tax burdens. Limited as they were by tradition, widespread legal privilege, and other manifestations of contemporary social and political power, they and their counterparts in other cities nevertheless sought to establish an equitable basis for citizen taxation, and proper distribution of burden between countryside and town.[55]

Taking this literature of legal and political discussion as a whole, we might say that systematically the lawyers raised every question. No action was to be taken by the public authority unless it found justification in law or political theory and could be harmonized with the grand goals of society. Appeals to the public welfare and common good are everywhere in the literature. And at least in the thought of Bartolus, the most respected and quoted of the late-medieval jurisconsults, such theory was ultimately sanctioned by a doctrine of popular sovereignty, itself based on the right of the peoples' representatives peaceably to assemble and deliberate.[56]

By the mid-thirteenth century when St. Thomas, Johannes de Viterbo, and others were defining the status of urban governments, the rights of towns were well understood. They had been growing in range and significance from the tenth century and included not only the right to possess and take property, but also the right to grant privileges to citizens and other residents. These were obtained from emperors, kings, bishops, and other authorities who granted charters to the towns defining their powers. Compensation to the grantor was in the form of some money or promise of allegiance, usually both. By the twelfth century such a charter was made with the understanding that all free persons resident in the place, without regard for social class, were to be protected or privileged by it.

One may say that something of a balance or tension thus existed between, on the one hand, the rights of individuals, based upon law, charter, and Christian doctrine and practice, and, on the other, the powers of government, based upon longstanding theories justifying executive action as well as real need. Again and again the *consilia* show the jurisconsults' attempt to bring justice to a situation in which each party had some right and good theory to support its cause. For all its historical, cultural, emotional, and legal power, the city could not crush the individual. The same body of law that strengthened the community protected the citizens, and, indeed, in the development of citizenship we see appearing elements of a new view of man and of a society very different from that medieval model of cooperating, static parts.[57]

On behalf of the city, without exception, the jurists demanded a general commitment from a newcomer as precondition of his acceptance into the community. And from the citizen by birth it demanded loyalty in terms of military service and payment of taxes. In both demands the emphasis was upon an act of personal will, and although it was assumed that the individual would exhibit his love of country in the expected ways, nonetheless the path was left open for a refusal. The point is that this emphasis on the citizen's will reinforced the sometimes submerged Christian emphasis on the individual's free will, power of choice. As he is credited by the state with this power, and with the power of rationality by the medieval Aristotelians, the individual gains in stature. It is an individual human being who chooses, serves, votes, and who may sometimes die in the line of public duty, not some abstractly conceived component of a corporation or anthropomorphic metaphor.

The historical path toward the present lies in the extraction of the individual from his corporation, in his acceptance and exercise of rights as a unique human being. The very personal status of citizenship is a form, so to speak, of extraction. This is not to say that a citizen did not continue to bear, in some cases until the French Revolution, many obligations that he performed with his collegiate fellows, in a guild, for example. It is to emphasize the fact that as an individual citizen, he paid his taxes, appeared on the roll of potential officeholders, and of course was open to the call to arms in a very personal way. Two movements may be seen in the centuries following the twelfth: the gradual development of Europe into a corporate society that reached its height only in the early modern period, and a simultaneous countermovement which saw the growth of a personal identity characterized both by individual freedom and by a personal, individual involvement in, and responsibility to, a variety of social and political groups.

In return for willing conformity to its law, cult, and culture, the city offered a range of benefits to its citizens or naturalizing immigrants. The fundamental pattern of responsibilities was quasi-feudal: the city was to guard life and property and keep faith. Guardianship meant, for example, application of the law of reprisals, negotiation and ransom in case of commercial difficulty or capture, while keeping faith implied recognition of the individual citizen's rights in property and at law. At a very material level the city kept faith with the best interests of the citizen by permitting him to participate in the trading ventures of the community through treaties arranged with neighboring cities, empowered and protected by native merchants.

The extent and language of a city's concern may be seen in a *consilium* of the canonist Johannes Calderinus (d. ca. 1350), which focuses on a dispute between the bishop of Genoa and the city over a tax of a twelfth on all grain processed at the bishop's mill. The city claims its own facility is suffering loss at the hands of the bishop; therefore, it imposes the tax. He claims the levy attacks his ecclesiastical liberty and income since people are not coming to his mill anymore. Calderinus supports the commune. He worries lest prices rise if the town loses part of its grain supply. In such circumstances, he says, the action of the city should be out of concern for itself and not the bishop. Also, the city may act because its action does more than hurt the bishop; the tax helps the city meet the variety of obligations on which its citizens depend.[58]

What we have here is the juxtaposition of feudal and Romanic concepts: protection and faith and concern for the public good. Together these constituted a strong commitment by the corporation to preserve the individual well-being of its members. That these values were expressed in a wide variety of documents and over considerable time suggests the depth and universality of the commitment.

To judge from the legal and constitutional literature of Italy in the late Middle Ages, say 1300 to 1500, the issue of citizenship was of first and continuous importance. Collections of *consilia* include many disputes over the existence and rights of citizenship; commentaries upon laws dealing with urban affairs in the imperial period are often short treatises which attempt to clarify ancient social theory and legal concepts and apply them to contemporary affairs; and municipal statutes, either singly or in the series of redactions that survive from a few cities, show a continuing attempt to deal with the issue of citizenship in the light of local need and tradition, and the dynamism of social, economic, and political change.

All the great authors discussed citizenship in some aspect: Baldus and Bartolus, St. Thomas and Marsilius, Dante, Petrarch, and Salutati. The smallest rural commune legislated on the matter, as did Venice and Florence. Why this interest? Because the issues radiating from the concept of citizenship touched every great concern of government and society. They did so in part because so many of the fundamental changes that define medieval Italian life and make it a foreshadowing of what happened elsewhere in Europe in later centuries depended upon the existence of a system that tolerated and facilitated movement from one situation to another: movement of peasants into town, of merchants and artisans from city to city and even from Europe to Asia, of professors, legists, and other learned specialists from one employment to another. Each of these actions depended upon the existence of the human right to move and the willingness of a community to receive a new person.

And what is significantly universal in this legal environment is the kind of citizenship rights that attracted interest. It is all too easy to be misled by deceiving tags like "republican" Florence and "despotic" or "princely" Milan into assuming that in the one city men struggled for political rights in something of a proto-Whig effort, while in the other they were crushed flat by an effective central authority. The fact is, rather, that men in every medieval or Renaissance city were both citizens and subjects—in some places surely more citizen than subject—who faced difficulties which they sought to overcome with privileges. Some men faced competition from foreigners in markets or litigation brought by foreign creditors in their own courts. Others desired exclusive access to government or guild positions or to the work government bureaus threw off. Probably most men were not so much interested in the exercise of political rights as in the benefits that might come to them from charters or privileges granted by some ruler or negotiated with some town, or from above, that is, from the government of their city, republican or, in some form, princely. They did discuss the ethics of citizenship and access to political rights, but they were also concerned, for example, about rights of reprisals.

For its part, every city was necessarily cautious about the loyalty of its immigrants, whether the extent of its probationary period was one, three, or twenty years. All this is to emphasize the common nature of citizenship issues facing governments, and the concern of individual citizens in every kind of polity for specific benefits that might strengthen their legal or business position. To make the point another way, too much has been made of Florentine liberty. Tyranny and citizenship were just as compatible as liberty and citizenship. What counted was function; needs of state and of citizens/subjects were pretty much the same throughout the society of city-states. Indeed, it is the existence of just such common features that enable us to talk about the cities in general terms.

Citizenship is today so freighted with notions of individual participation in self-government that we automatically think of it as an intrinsic part of democratic society. In fact, over most of history, considering it as a mechanism of discrimination and reward, it has been compatible with all forms of government. Throughout history individuals have had needs, and so have governments. Citizenship has served as a kind of contract to regularize arrangements between the two. Whatever the mystiques of local government and history that children were reared upon, the proper activities of adults were mostly the same: the routines of administration and business.

We may also think of a relatively universal political structure, for under prince or commune, institutions of government were similar. In the Italian cities, elected assemblies and officials worked together with appointed committees and hired professional civil servants, local or foreign. Citizens were expected to choose leaders from among themselves and knew that service was expected of them. As participants in a political society they came to know both the responsibilities and rewards of public life. Moreover, and this is quite significant, they came to have expectations of the political structure of which they saw themselves a part, and they realized that political techniques might make that structure more amenable to their interests and those of their family and friends. Also, it is clear that many saw government service as a career and were prompted to it by a desire for money and power as well as by the writings of Cicero or some other ancient moralist. In gaining both office and results, citizenship was crucial, for the benefits of politics were denied to the outsider, defined as one who, reciprocally, offered nothing spiritual or material to his political society.

Within this political system the details of reciprocation were made perfectly clear in the statute book by which every town was governed. Citizen duties were specified, as were procedures for assimilation, and prologues tell us why new men were sought and on what basis they were granted privilege. As a literature the statutes reveal a near universal constitutionalism. Specific obligations will vary from city to city, but not basic principles. The similarity of naturalization processes simultaneously reflects the need of many local societies for such procedures and stands as another of the institutional links that held together all of communal Italy. The statutes reflect an intellectual unity as well, for the draftsmen of the constitutions in which these similarities appear were all trained in the schools of Roman law.

Social institutions likewise were relatively universal: relations between classes were manifested in attitudes, dress, functions, and structure, which is only to say that the migrant seeking livelihood and new status in a city would find people and particulars strange, but not the essential institutions of life. Moreover, his journey was likely to be short and through familiar territory, unlike the frightening transoceanic voyages of millions over the past five centuries. In his new abode he would expect, as a newcomer, a long period of probation and exclusion, and those attitudes of suspicion and gradual acceptance that he and his old neighbors had shown toward newcomers and strangers. Yet the system was flexible enough and the needs of society intense enough to permit his eventual integration into the new community.

This relative ease of absorption reflected the realities of contemporary competition. Cities fought for markets and territory. Men were needed as merchants, or weavers, and both the expansionist city-state and the defensive minor commune needed soldiers. Frequent plague and famine also created the need for new men as husbands. A Perugian register of incipient citizens shows the weaver and mercenary on the same list and in the same parish. And Florentine records give evidence of the town's desire to grant early citizenship to the wealthy who would buy shares in the public debt, by so doing to advance the military cause of the commune. To say all this is merely to point out that Italian municipal policy reflected the same kind of urgencies that gave rise to "public welfare" and "need of state" legislation in contemporary

England and France. The widespread notion that performance of public duties prevailed over quality of birth as a criterion for full citizenship reflects in its realism the hard life and choices of the era.

Everywhere common needs generated a potentiality for citizenship and an acceptance of immigration that prevailed over the xenophobia and suspicion —products of war as well as of local culture—expressed by Dante and lesser men. These same common needs help explain the phenomenon of movement from the other viewpoint, that of emigration. They forced men to reevaluate the ties that held them home and prompted them to leave. The lure of economic improvement and the flight from burdensome taxation were apparently enough to overcome local loyalties. In sum, the situation is quite complex: idealistic patriotism and matter-of-fact realism coexist, and in many cases we may assume that material motives prevailed. And what facilitated movement was the existence of adequate institutions of acculturation whose mechanisms were not too complex. Indeed, any immigrant to Bologna from Florence or Padua had already passed through the school of religious festivals, civic assemblies, and folk history that passed for medieval civics. One migrating from Gubbio to Florence tucked St. Ubaldo away in the corner of his heart and eventually came to an equivalent veneration of St. John the Baptist. Late-medieval Italy was not an open society of easy physical and social mobility, yet movement from class to class, city to city, was both possible and not unusual. The colonization of the city is one of the great facts of Italian, if not of Mediterranean, medieval history.

In sum, citizenship as concept and institution very substantially entered into Italian consciousness at this time. It did so as a distinct subspecialty of law and political thought. All the while, as we have seen, poets, translators, philologists, historians, and others were discovering, publicizing, and valuing everything that survived from classical Greece and Rome.

If classical influences were significant in shaping the relationship between city and citizen, it should be pointed out that the fundamental values of traditional feudal society also contributed. That is to say, in the feudal ambience in which cities developed, demands and rewards for service were not new. Feudal experience was hundreds of years old by the time the Italian and other Mediterranean cities were developing, and Italy was the place where feudal practices earliest received formal codification. What we have in the demand for citizen service is traditional theory in a new social environment. Traditional service was that of the vassal to his lord in return for fief and protection, or service to pope and Christ on crusade, the return for which was spiritual (and legal) benefit, carefully pronounced. Now service was in the cause of the city and to one's self as a member of the commune, its army, government, trading population. Reciprocal action from the superior now takes a form more sophisticated than physical protection. The citizen, in return for his service and in addition to physical protection, benefits from legal privilege and from the superior culture which shapes him into a finer man. In the local community his status is marked by the fullness of the benefits he possesses. And abroad he commands respect—or contempt— given the totality of his city's history, that is, from the totality of past and present elements of culture and strength vis-à-vis all other members of the community of cities. If feudal responsibilities eventually took a great variety of forms over time and place, so did the citizen's relations with the town. And if we can discern a form in all these relations and call it feudalism and speak of this abstraction with a certain justice and precision, we can also discern a pattern in citizen actions and speak of it justly, if not with total clarity, as civism.

The pattern into which citizenship fits, it must be noted, is a complex one. Obligations and justifications for actions vary since social and political circumstances in the city were so much more complex than in the country. Most townsmen lived out their lives in their native place, yet there was a sizable movement of soldiers, craftsmen, and intellectuals of all kinds. Elaborate secular and ecclesiastical institutions were developed to engender local patriotism and commitment to public service, yet transfer of allegiance was so common it necessitated a legal procedure designed specifically to facilitate that purpose. The historical, legal, even poetical literature is filled with formal statements of civic values and duties, yet citizens constantly evidenced reluctance to pay taxes and serve the state as they knew they should. The city's security was a prime concern of its citizens, yet those citizens often were forced into the ranks and were pleased to rely on foreigners for their own security. In sum, although a great emphasis was placed upon the individuality of each urban creation, the end result was a system of linked units fundamentally alike in the structure of their laws and society, all of them organized to receive the outsider whose very existence as foreigner had served to rally the native spirit.

A COMMON LAW OF CITIZENSHIP

The difficulties created by such tensions are best seen in contemporary legal and constitutional literature. In *consilia* and commentaries the legists developed a common citizenship law for upper Italy which took cognizance of ancient theory, contemporary statutes, and immediate need. The frequency with which citizenship cases appear in the *consilia* reveals that litigation was constant, and the range of issues the legists discussed in relation to the theory of citizenship indicates that they thought in theoretical as well as practical terms. Often the specific would lead to the general, as in a *consilium* of the fifteenth-century jurist, R. Cumanus, which begins with an examination of legitimacy and flowers into a discussion of the relation of the prince to the principles of the *ius gentium*. Or the jurisconsult might link related questions to form a legal essay which expressed his political theory as well as his legal judgment.[59] However, to the best of my knowledge, there is not a single formal treatise on citizenship, nor a single great medieval citizenship act comparable to that of Caracalla in 212. What we have, rather, is an infinity of careful comments upon specific ancient laws, an equally confusing body of statute law, and the slow development over time of a resulting web of theories and institutions. These are motivated both by theories that might be broadly called uplifting, moral, and altruistic and by interests which must be viewed as materialistic and self-serving. This should not surprise us.

That both *consilia* and commentary had influence in shaping working practice is suggested by the treatment they received from contemporaries. Judges followed the views of jurisconsults in citizenship cases. Some questions were discussed by many jurists over several centuries, which suggests the continued controversiality and intrinsic difficulty of these issues. These discussions were influential, and jurists frequently cited the arguments of Bartolus, Baldus, Paul de Castro, and others as persuasive. Franciscus Pepus, the sixteenth-century editor of Marianus Socinus, lists other jurisconsults who had opined on a similar case, which argues for the continued usefulness and validity of the old authorities in the sixteenth century.[60]

Nor was this body of citizenship law that was so slowly written used only by Italians. French jurists cite *consilia* and other opinions when Italian experience had something to teach them. Indeed, by the sixteenth century at least one French jurist, Nicolaus Boerius (1469–1539), had taken Italian language and experience and adapted them to his own problems on a new, larger scale. No longer is he discussing whether one born in Bologna, say, succeeds to property in Padua or Florence; now the question is whether the son of a Frenchman born in Spain is French or Spanish, or whether the king of France shall seize the disputed property or not. But if the issues are now at the level of the kingdom, much of the argumentation still derives from the city-state experience of the Italian lawyers. Boerius cites Felinus, Panormitanus, and Baldus among his authorities and, moreover, is aware of Bologna's legislation and its naturalization procedures. Another of his decisions is a textbook treatment of issues discussed in the literature for more than two centuries: creation and taxation of new citizens and old, legal status of foreigners, special status of learned experts and religious. Whether we choose to interpret this as the influence of the Italian Renaissance or continued French reliance upon a common medieval legal culture, we can see the universality of certain legal and social problems and the skill of legists in adapting concepts and institutions to analogous issues of national magnitude.[61]

Legal language spoke effectively for several good reasons. Its abstract vocabulary treated citizens in a conceptual way without regard for class and political interest and so offered the broadest basis for legislation in any city. This generality permitted application to the special problems of republican Florence or princely Milan or royal France. The goals of all types of society, similar as they were in the theoretical norms, could be stated in expressive Latin terms, each with its own history and compelling associations.

The jurists knew the value of such language and the consequences of their words. Baldus read a preamble very carefully since "it gave ultimate authority to new statutes." Indeed, medieval lawyers were always fascinated with words. They had to be, of course, for professional reasons, and their whole education was based on literature, the careful study of texts. By the time they were jurisconsults, Baldus, Bartolus, and others had progressed through several disciplines whose focus had been upon the meaning of a text: grammar, rhetoric, and often some scholastic philosophy. From Pepo in the eleventh century on, scholarship in the law had been concerned with the meaning of ancient words and their proper application to contemporary institutions. Surely this is one reason why, over centuries, the legists picked on certain words and discussed them ceaselessly, never arriving at precision. For example, the specific concern for geographical accuracy that seems to be present from the beginnings of medieval discussion of citizenship surely derives from a very understandable concern with boundaries in an agricultural society in which every piece of land and every right associated with it were always a matter of considerable interest. As late as the sixteenth century, the Renaissance jurist Aretinus found it necessary to remark that he had never seen *districtus* well defined—this after three centuries at least of medieval usage, and long after the development of sophisticated chanceries whose responsibility it was to use precise language.[62]

Yet, for all this vagueness, this society of jurists created a very substantial and useful body of legal concepts, perhaps because the best of them, those cited again and again, Baldus, Bartolus, Oldradus (d. 1335), Paul de Castro, Petrus de Ancharano, Lucas da Penna, and a few others, were what we would call today social and political analysts. They were interested in the totality of their society and how its parts functioned. Like their modern counterparts, they were deeply involved in the active life, called upon to be civil servants to cities, princes, and ecclesiastical lords, and to be constitutional draftsmen. Then, as now, such skeptical, realistic, and involved jurists were among the most sophisticated observers of the contemporary scene. Armed with a knowledge of the theory and structure of society, they saw how things really functioned. The questions they chose to answer as well as their answers show the immediacy of their contact with real life. Indeed, it was just this immediacy that made what they said meaningful—albeit wrapped as it was in the formal language of the law and morality—to succeeding generations. That language was quite familiar to every educated man in the sixteenth century, if not in the two following centuries as well.

The *statuti* also evidence lawyer capabilities and reveal not only contemporary theory, but also the many immediate problems faced by cities. The willingness of each community to confront increasing complexity, and the extent of its reliance upon legislation to solve the problems of life, is also revealed. In this literature, as in the *consilia* and commentaries, certain general principles pervade the individual constitutions, each the product of a long local history. What is interesting is that problems of, and attitudes toward, citizenship remain substantially similar in all towns and cities regardless of size or the form of government. The passage or revision of citizenship statutes might occasion political conflict, as in Florence in the mid-fourteenth century, but once adopted, provisions operated at the subpolitical level, except as groups formed for or against the new policy or a controversial prospective citizen. When this happened, citizenship was added to those issues already dividing families, factions, classes, and *consorterias*.

THE MATERIALIZATION OF CITIZENSHIP

For all the pressures to remain in one's native civic culture, people did frequently move and create new ties. Hence it is not surprising that questions arose, as in feudal society, over the legitimacy and priority of obligations. Taken together with the fact of mobility itself, the answers of the jurists to these questions illuminate what might be called the demoralization of the medieval city, or, alternatively, the materialization of citizenship.

In the beginning, the emphasis of jurists and moralists had been upon the special identity that birth in a specific city conferred, and upon the almost sacred quality of citizen responsibility. By the fourteenth century, when the needs of government were so great, the new emphasis was upon the financial exchange between city and citizen. No longer was citizenship defined in terms of a unique cultural imprint; now almost anyone might eventually buy or serve his way into the corporation of those benefiting from the advantages of citizenship. This meant that throughout the community of cities there slowly developed the acceptance of multiple citizenship as legist-administrators recognized that the patriotic rhetoric no longer served the state's real needs, which basically were financial.

The institution of multiple citizenship manifests the responsiveness of medieval theories and institutions to changing conditions. The old notion that one cannot shuck off the identity and obligations of paternity and birth had been expressed in the early thirteenth century by Azo, whose focus was upon descent. A child, he says, bears responsibilities imposed by the nationality of the father unless he should be forced by some necessity to live in his mother's city. In that case he must bear a double burden, for necessarily he must continue to aid his father's city. No one, "as it has been said, can reject his fatherland by his own act of will." Azo goes on to say that when two cities make demands upon a person, he must heed those of his birthplace. By the end of the thirteenth century, however, as we have seen, the jurists had developed their emphasis upon the will as a determinant of citizenship, a doctrine which nicely accommodated contemporary realities.[63]

One of these was the developing institution or practice of multiple citizenships, upon which the jurists developed a new position. Poets and moralists continued to speak in traditional exclusivistic terms, but those who shaped institutions had changed their opinion. It may be that Lucas da Penna developed his views out of administrative experience in the Sicilian kingdom; in any event, he is among the earliest writers to place multiple citizenship on a matter-of-fact basis of privilege in return for contribution. One may be a citizen of two cities, he says explicitly, and he then launches into a discussion of priority of obligation that is reminiscent of the discussions of liege homage in feudal law. Faced with presumably exhausting and simultaneous demands upon his resources, what should the individual do? Assist his birthplace first, says Lucas, who goes on to establish a schedule of priorities.[64]

Dual citizenship appears at about the same time in the standard treatise on reprisals of Johannes de Legnano. He believes that citizens may claim the benefit of reprisal wherever they bear burdens, and also that a state may extend jurisdiction over its citizens outside its borders, while they are living abroad. What appears in his discussion is a mobile society in which government retains or attempts to retain control over its people by offering them a benefit or reprisal, or by threatening them with loss of that benefit should their actions hurt, or bring disfavor, on the town. Baldus put the matter nicely apropos the son of a citizen of Bologna adopted by a Modenese. The youth keeps his Bolognese connection and adds the identity of his new parent, for "fatherlands are added not subtracted."[65]

With such a view we are in a new epoch. In citizenship, as in other fields of politics, necessity, which knows no bounds, has prevailed. The state's need for money and services has forced it to cast wide beyond its native-born resident citizens for support. Simultaneously, individuals struggling for success in a very competitive world have come to downplay powerful traditional and exclusive allegiance to one fatherland in an attempt to benefit from relationships with many. The new citizen stands in the world a moral absolute unto himself, willing and choosing out of self-interest now. His rhetoric may be filled with resounding imperatives, but his real motivations often are necessarily self-serving and sometimes, surely, mean, as are the city's.

What may be viewed as an extreme expression of such an attitude is revealed in a *consilium* of Baldus in which the great jurist reproves his city, Perugia. As punishment for his failure to pay a tax, the city has removed a citizen from its rolls and placed him on the tax roll of a dependent town. Baldus forbids the city to do that and denies its assertion that the quality of its citizenship is superior to that of the smaller place. He may argue and opine as he does, but the stance of the city is clear: its governors consider themselves as superior and are willing to use rural status as a kind of prison without bars, for if there were no physical constraints in rural life, there were few legal or social benefits either. The country man found himself in a state of inequality, a condition of lessened legal capacity vis-à-vis the city dweller. Urban citizenship constituted a real benefit, superior in both a legal and cultural sense to that of the village. The Perugian statute is a constitutional analogue to that disgust for the rough, unshaped country boob expressed by Dante.[66]

Contributing to the weakening of the old idealistic citizenship was the growth of princely power, for while citizens were seeking benefit in this kind of financial situation, the prince was extending his power over individuals, making them subjects. The major, or at least most spectacular, part of this story is political and military. In city after city, in Verona, Bologna, Florence, and Milan, for example, some dynast, always with the help of family, friends, and dependents, established his authority at the expense of republican institutions. The administrative and legal side of this transition is more technical and less visible, yet of considerable importance, for it was through the specific acts and judgments of lawyers and bureaucrats that the prince's action took place, and hence that city and country were drawn together by him.

How it happened may be seen in the way Alexander of Imola handled the case of Johannes and Paulus, who have left their little village for Mantua, where the duke granted them citizenship. Included in the privilege was a specific exemption from the taxes they had to that moment paid in their native place, and this is decisive for Alexander. Although he has earlier argued that tax paying was of the very "nature" of citizenship, he concludes that the will, the "motu propio," of the duke is such that the two men, while benefiting from their the new citizen status in Mantua, need not lose "benefits and concessions which they had earlier as citizens . . . and what was given to benefit them should not end up hurting them." In other words, they add new benefits to old, and what determined their ability to do this was princely power. Alexander then argues from analogy that "one may have several residences and be a citizen of several places." His words, however, are not a declaration of financial irresponsibility or a rejection of a civic morality built up over two centuries, for he restates the common-law concept that benefit is given in return for responsible conduct. Nevertheless, citizenship in a specific place is somewhat weakened given the prince's power to affect citizen obligations throughout his entire territory. The pull and claim of a place on the individual is weakened while that of the prince is strengthened. Citizenship is turning into subjectship. And, simultaneously, a larger territorial unit subject to the prince is created as the distinction between the city and its dependent region is partially effaced.[67]

Two developments, then, reinforced each other and militated against the old public citizenship which depended upon the birth or definite act of will of the individual citizen. First, the growing need of the individual citizen for material or legal or political benefit forced him to greater reliance upon the prince. Second, for his part, the prince at that very time was establishing the principle that he, by his act of will alone, could create or destroy any relationship between the citizen and the community, and he was extending this principle of control over wider and wider territories. This is all part of the build-up of the legal omnicompetence of the state, which is to say that Bodin's particular statement of sovereignty must take its place in a long-developing process of princely enhancement sustained by jurists all over Europe, and to assert that this literature was readily available to Hobbes and others in the seventeenth century who were looking for justification of royal absolutism.

6

CITIZENSHIP IN

THE RENAISSANCE

Citizenship survived in the early modern period, but it was quiescent, and for that and other reasons, it is harder for us to grasp. During the Middle Ages cities existed in which citizenship actually flourished as in the ancient Mediterranean world. A portion of the population, invariably male and propertied, made policies and ran the government on the basis of a written constitution and a civic ethic that approved their activity and conferred recognition. However, as we have seen, this self-government existed within a larger political culture that was overwhelmingly princely and hierarchical; in both church and state authority flowed down and was enhanced by religious values. Even where republican government existed, lawyers and other political thinkers frequently tended to assimilate citizen and subject. With the growth of large territorial states, first in Italy and then elsewhere, this melding became more frequent, easier, and more legitimate to make.

So, in the centuries after the Renaissance, citizenship nearly disappeared, crushed by the theories and bureaucracies of the centralizing state. Citizens everywhere became subjects, and the very concept of citizen retreated to the libraries of lawyers and historians, there to survive and eventually revive. However, as we shall see, this long sleep was not without accomplishment. During those years citizenship survived and eventually expanded its meaning and content as European life itself changed and became more complex.

In antiquity and the Middle Ages citizenship was both an abstraction and a reality. The ideas of Aristotle and Cicero were put into practice in Athens and Florence. Since this was not the case in early modern Europe, the focus in these concluding chapters must change and shift largely to a consideration of ideas. It was not until the age of democratic revolutions that citizenship again became a significant Western institution. By then its popularity reflected the great changes that had taken place in the Atlantic world over the previous three centuries, and it had become one of the more important forces for change itself.

One of these changes was the growth of the large territorial state. Political theorists, when they thought of citizenship, now used the term citizen in relation to this kind of monarchy. A second change is related to the first: now a world economy came into being, greatly increasing the wealth of merchants in such places as England, France, and Holland. Science and technology grew apace. The result was a new conception of activism, a new definition of the competent citizen and his responsibilities in the world. Finally, embraced in this new definition, was a tremendous advance in the study of man himself. Shakespeare, Bacon, Montaigne, Harvey, Descartes, Locke, and many others in many fields all participated, and in a sense the end products of all this thinking about man and his environment were Franklin and Rousseau. And if Rousseau rejected the commercial republic of his day, whose perfect specimen was Benjamin Franklin, nevertheless he defined in other ways the new citizen of the modern world—or, if he did not define him, he exhorted him into being.

CIVIC HUMANISM

But, before all this happened, a movement began in Italy that was to influence the three quiet centuries of republicanism and citizenship. Italy produced "civic humanism" in the early fifteenth century, and Machiavelli (1469–1527) gave it force and an edge one hundred years later. What went on in history was not a tepid, scholarly formulation of ancient ideals. Rather, it was the angry cry of the rejected Machiavelli prescribing a citizenship of discipline, soul, austerity, and military might.[1]

Civic humanism came into being at a time when the law of citizenship was being worked out in relation to the territorial state and the power of the prince. It was what we now call, after the interpretation of Hans Baron, that moral theory based on ancient ethical philosophy and historical examples adopted by the Florentine ruling classes about 1400. At that time princely Milan mounted an invasion of republican Florence and might have defeated her but for the sudden death of the duke of Milan, Giangaleazzo Visconti. Faced not only with invasion, but also with the prospect that her republican regime, based on representative principles and institutions and the model of the citizen-soldier fighting for his country, might be replaced by the administrators of a princely state, Florentine businessmen, notaries, lawyers, and other intellectuals recast their history. They reemphasized their links to ancient republican Rome, and in her history found models for heroic resistance, personal valor, and martial virtue. In Latin literature, especially in the works of Cicero, who not only wrote magnificently but also died in defense of his republican ideals, they found the model of the active citizen. Overnight, so to speak, the example of the monk was replaced by that of the citizen. And in the generation following the miracle of 1402, Gregorio Dati (1362–1435), Leonardo Bruni (1361–1444), and other civic publicists advanced, defended, and popularized the twin themes of civic liberty and civic activism.

Obviously, this is too neat an interpretation of events. The kind of history involved here, that of social and political values and realities, is not subject to such sudden cataclysmic change. An event like the Visconti threat is important; it may inspire writers, artists, and musicians; it may make their inspirational creations, their stimuli to action and resistance, more comprehensible and acceptable. But alone, without the existence of objective institutions and situations through which such values and goals may enter history, they do not go far enough to explain the acceptance and success of the active worldly life, which had, in fact, been part of Italian life for centuries. It so often happens in history that rationalization and rhetorization come long after the fact. Such was the case with civic humanism. The reality of the active life *and* its formal defense by lawyers and other apologists came at least a century before the elegant stylists of the Renaissance appeared in the salons of Florence. The job the latter did and their success in doing it are important. But they were not original, not alone, and, in the long run, perhaps not as important as the lawyers whom they served as elegant supplement.

A century later Machiavelli and others had succeeded in developing these early writings into a full-fledged vocabulary for the analysis of proper civic behavior. All argued on the basis of ancient secular history and moral philosophy and ended by providing a new moral theory for a society desperate for some conceptualized endorsement of its worldly achievements. Baron allows that in the world of ideas there were "harbingers and interesting pioneer" efforts, but, he says, "these had never lasted." Only in the struggle against Milan did these "trends" establish themselves on the Florentine scene, eventually to be replicated elsewhere in the city-state world. These were "the civic ethics of the *vita activa-politica*, the new realistic study of history and politics, and the vindication of the *Volgare*," by which he means the acceptance of the vernacular in serious discourse.

This is not the place for an extensive commentary on Baron's thesis, but we must at least distinguish among his conclusions and indicate a position where it matters. To begin with, it should be clear that the interpretation of citizen activity during the Middle Ages given here argues against an interpretation which claims an event, albeit of a few years' duration, to be the principal cause of a great historical shift. For hundreds of years before Milan's invasion, Italy had been changing, becoming a region dominated by a complex social, political, and commercial urban life. Money making and political activity brought honor and power to a person and his family, and if a Christian idealist civilization had not yet found a clear way to justify such actions, serious attempts had been made.

The participation of many classes and professions had been a precondition for the great success of medieval civilization. An entire way of life had come to depend upon the committed activity of many of the best and brightest members of society. There was no alternative to work with one's fellows in the community, to discussion, negotiation, cabal, and compromise. In times of constant danger, friendship and civic love served in the urban world as counterparts to feudal military comradeship and monastic friendship.

To assert this is to emphasize that the active life was out in the open, in the marketplace, which might also serve as the public assembly. One's fellows watched and toted up the marks of his activity, all of which were inscribed in public and private archives. Titles, costumes, banners all testified to political achievement, as did the coats of arms, the *stemme*, stuck on the walls of public buildings. In Arezzo, the arms of Florentine families doing service in the provinces cover the entire fabric of the governor's palace, testifying to meritorious public service over generations.

It was not all for show; politics and government were important to success and survival in the real world. They affected every aspect of a successful life: taxes, perquisites, and the ability to conduct business effectively. In terms of modern social science, the medieval city had a subject-participant political culture, that is, one whose citizens sensed and acted on their identification with the health and function of the whole. They made demands upon the community which were necessary to their well-being and joined others to win common goals. As in ancient Greece, a significant part of the population was involved in this political scene. Once he was part of the governing elite, one could not be apolitical.

It is this long-existing reality that Baron ignores when he stresses the importance of the new civic humanist ideas. They are as important, but perhaps not as novel as he says they are just because the Italian city-states were what they were. If the theoretical justification for business and politics was not entirely in place before the civic humanists, part of it existed in the technical neo-Aristotelianism of the professors at the university or in the Dominican pulpits, and in the subtle political theory of Roman and canon lawyers. Moreover, there were poems, plays, and city histories that extolled civic brotherhood and love of republican liberty.

However, all these did not constitute a sufficient part of the armory of mental comforts carried by the average educated man. The language of the scholastics was too refined, as we have seen, to oppose the powerful exaltation of apostolic poverty and the universal respect for monasticism as an institution. A contempt for the human condition and a ubiquitous Augustinian view of life and man's own powers remained very strong. Ordinary townsmen would not derive any consolatory benefit from schoolmen's distinctions. Their language was not repeatable, created no satisfying heroic image, nor did it stimulate a new popular vocabulary for the discussion of moral values. Legists and theologians frequently spoke to each other in code words and abbreviations and with none of the elegance and persuasiveness that townsmen had come to demand from their leaders and moral guides. For at least 150 years citizens had been used to hearing ever more elegant and effective appeals to their public-spiritedness. As we now know, behind the humanist letter writers of the early fifteenth century lay a deep tradition of patriotic oratory, which depended upon Roman moral language and historical references.

This is to assert that if Baron largely ignored the role that the demanding life of citizens played in the creation of a de facto code of active, as opposed to contemplative, values, he also paid inadequate attention to the literary tradition before 1400, in which there are many kinds of patriotic literature. Much of this harbinger literature was written during crises similar to that experienced by Florence under threat from Milan: some period in which in some city the fragile republican regime faced a threat to its existence mounted by a local family or faction under the leadership of a powerful lord, a would-be dynast, or by a foreign prince. Over the years it provided a code of civic values that was more appropriate for urban Italians than was the aristocratic code of the intrusive rural nobility or the rules of conduct specified in the revered monastic tradition. Manuals of letter writing and speech making form part of this literature from the thirteenth century on, as the content of model letters focuses upon civic problems and the speeches of city leaders are derived from style books provided by professors versed in ancient rhetoric. Ancient history also provided *exempla*, as propagandists reminded citizens of Ancona, Florence, Siena, and other places that as descendants of the ancient Romans they were to fight for the liberty of their native town. They were to be virtuous as the Romans had been. As early as the mid-thirteenth century, in his *On the Government of Cities*, John of Viterbo listed the four cardinal virtues as they were to be taught throughout the Renaissance: prudence, magnanimity, temperance, and justice.[2]

It was this early tradition that the study of ancient literature touched and transformed. From France into Italy came the influence of Aristotle's *Rhetoric* and *Poetics* and study of the classics for the sake of their style. Frenchmen taught in Italy at Bologna and other schools. One very important Italian author who studied Cicero and other ancient authors at Paris and then returned to Florence as an exponent of the new rhetorical studies was Brunetto Latini. He popularized Ciceronian ideas on the importance of literary and rhetorical studies and, in his enormously popular *The Books of Treasure*, lauded republican over monarchical government on the basis of ancient history.

What civic humanism brought into the tradition was an emphasis on style, the employment of those with style in government, and the identification of certain moral questions with the continued well-being of the community: questions of loyalty, activity, military service, and about the reorientation of education for the training of men in virtue and for civic commitment. While lawyers in these very days were treating individuals in terms of their paternity, length of residence, payment of taxes, and investment in real property, for the civic humanists what counted was a person's capacity for love and friendship, his loyalty and compassion, temperance and fortitude. It was in this vocabulary, more and more, that discussions about the nature of the good man, good subject, and good citizen largely were carried on henceforth. Civic humanism, then, united ideals and institutions. Within a continuing Christian framework it accepted the importance of the active life, and of the public life as well, assigning these priority over one dedicated to purely personal or family goals. This meant doing service for the *patria* in public office and on the battlefield. It could also mean putting a talent trained in effective letters and speech at the service of the state. A new curriculum called for the subordination of the central subject of the medieval curriculum, logic, to literature, which was to provide the style and substance with which to shape a virtuous individual. Literature, including ethics and history, was to guide each man as social and political being into constructive human relationships. A vocabulary of love and compassion derived from a study of the ancient pagans and the church fathers would serve to bond men and women together in civic friendship. Such were the high goals of Renaissance citizenship, but, it must be remembered, they rested upon a legal foundation of statute law supported by centuries of discriminating commentary upon the *Corpus Iuris Civilis*.

MACHIAVELLI

What we now call civic humanism was the work of a century and of many minds. In the beginning, perhaps, was Petrarch with his passion for ancient manuscripts, fine style, and recognition of the republican virtue and oratorical skill of Cicero. Boccaccio contributed his defense of literature, Coluccio Salutati his moderate defense of the active life and of literature in its service as embodied in his own career as well as his writing. Leonardo Bruni lauded the city's material state, and its beauty, and wrote a *De militia* in which he extolled a life given over to the public welfare, and especially to service in a citizen army, which, given its spirit, would always be the best defense of a city's liberty. His program joins together an Aristotelian analysis of the social scene which would produce such an army, Livy's discussion of the early Roman constitution, and Cicero's notions of moral obligation. However, the formulation of civic humanism that traveled all over Europe in the sixteenth century was not Bruni's. It was, rather, that of Machiavelli, whose influence and reputation were based not only on the *Prince*, but also on the *Discourses on the First Ten Books of Titus Livius* and other literary as well as political works.

Machiavelli wrote this work over the years 1514 to 1519, by which time it probably had become clear to him that he would never again serve Florence in high public office. The Medici were back; he and his republican friends were now internal exiles destined to talk about politics, but not to rule. For years he had glimpsed the city and its public buildings from San Casciano to the south; now, still excluded from power, he conferred with his fellow republicans in the Oricellari Gardens north of the Arno. Shocked by the absence of order and stability in their times and personal lives, and by the alternation of regimes in the previous generation, he and they examined the nature of successful rule and the forms of government that might have the best chance of success. The *Prince* and the *Discourses* both come out of this search. In Venice, other thoughtful men were examining the reasons for the apparent success of their aristocratic republic.

If it is true that Renaissance humanism was a new educational program seeking to train the entire human personality on the basis of a new curriculum in which literature, as opposed to philosophy and theology, was the central subject of study, then the *Discourses* is an archetypal work of the Renaissance. Machiavelli has a concern for fine style, subjects his own times as well as ancient history to what he meant to be critical, dispassionate analysis, and, like the ancients he studied, he wrote to be read, appreciated, and used.

Machiavelli is so important in the greater history of citizenship because it is his reformulation of the concept and the issues surrounding it that plays a big role in later history, despite the horror attached to his name and the evil reputation of the *Prince*. In effect, what he did was to organize discussions of liberty, citizenship, and republicanism as they had developed over the previous century and pass them on as a corpus of interconnected issues or problems. For a century the humanist Bruni, the Dominican monk, Savonarola, and others had developed theories which he now meant to examine with his professedly new method based on a "proper appreciation of history." Aware of earlier views on the relationship of property and patriotism, military service and liberty, religion and civic virtue, now he was to serve his associates in liberty by determining how it might best be achieved and preserved.[3]

By liberty Machiavelli means two things: first, independence, or self-rule, and second, freedom from the aggression that could destroy that independence. He is interested, therefore, in the nature of a people that would be free and in the political and military arrangements needed to assure that freedom. Actually it is more than static freedom that interests him; he is also after the special conditions that will permit a republic to expand and retain the fruits of its expansion. In other words, he is after the rules and institutions that made Rome great, so that Florence may profit from her example. Necessarily he is concerned as well to discover the faults in Rome's history, so that they may be avoided.[4]

One reason for Rome's success lies in its constitution, and made explicit in the course of Machiavelli's argument is his belief that republics are superior to princely states. He agrees with Aristotle on the ultimate superiority of the judgment of the majority of citizens and, in the debate over the relative superiority of a large or small council as the highest governing body of the state, chooses the large council, what was called *governo largo* in the controversial literature of the day. The participation of citizens from all classes is prerequisite in any republic that wishes to expand, as Florence must want to do.

Expansion raises the question of leadership, which Machiavelli was treating in the *Prince*, written at about the same time, and the question of the army, on which he was to write the *Art of War* a few years later, and which was never out of his mind. In the successful republic, leadership must come from the people, who must exhibit a collective *virtù*, defined as that force or spirit that commands *fortuna* in decisive action, which it knows it must take and then wills to take. But how, he then considers, is that will made virtuous and forceful? And his answer here is very complex.

In part a republic's potential for greatness depends upon the quality of its founder; fortune does play a role in history in providing a founder. If he, ideally, or they are great, giving examples in their own lives of military prowess, observance of the laws, and a commitment to the public good that transcends selfish private interest, then the people will observe and follow, and the republic will flourish. If not, not. Indeed, Machiavelli goes so far as to excuse Romulus's murder of Remus because of the long-range successful outcome of the act: Rome's rise to greatness. Good laws help too, as do institutions of political and social justice that satisfy and pacify the civic body. One activity that is essential in Machiavelli's prescription for political success and greatness is the individual citizen's military service. Physical and moral flabbiness both result from the hiring of mercenaries to replace citizens in the ranks.

It is clear that he does more than accept the theories of the civic humanists of the fifteenth century and pass them on as they were. Indeed, he sharply criticizes their ideas and changes the nature of their program by emphasizing values and activities which the older humanists, with their concern for the exercise of the traditional virtues, would not have countenanced. His republicanism may have been based upon or influenced by that of the medieval Italian communes, for, like medieval political thinkers, he emphasized the need for political independence based upon a rule of law that would guarantee the actual function of republican institutions. His experience and study of history taught him that the bland citizenship of the fifteenth century would no longer serve in the arena of mean politics of his day. Therefore he created a more forceful notion of citizenship by giving greater weight to action and violence. The *Prince*, the *Discourses*, and the *Art of War* are largely about the rational and effective use of violence and the military in the art of government. Machiavelli's foreign service had given him ample opportunity to study this subject.

He also had startling ideas about the relationship of peace to the success of a republic. For hundreds of years the Church had been preaching and organizing peace as a precondition of the good society, and most medieval thinkers had developed theories of society based upon the harmonious function of many parts. Now Machiavelli extols the constructive function of tumult in politics. The success of the Roman Republic over centuries resulted, he claims, from the tension and interplay between political forces organized into senatorial and popular interest blocs in the forum. After the assassination of the Gracchi and the subsequent end of such creative politics, Rome's slide into one-man rule began.

Machiavelli rejects the soft citizenship of the past precisely because it accepted Christianity's emphatic message of peace. He prefers a religion that will not weaken the state by weakening its citizens as Christianity does; he prefers a religion that will stimulate the citizens' appetite for booty and blood. He fumes at the debilitating ethic of Christianity, its weakening effect upon the forceful spirit that brings success in war and politics. Compared to Rome's ritual blood sacrifices, which could excite men to ferocity and victory, Christianity's ceremonial is too delicate, effeminate. Not by passivity, but through the active exercise of *virtù* by the citizen-soldier, as opposed to the mercenary, will a regime survive, expand, and flourish. Since he accepts the importance of religion in the construction of the expansionist state, the precise nature of its religion is necessarily a matter of great concern. Such is the new balance of citizenship elements Machiavelli constructed and passed on.

As well as military service, which will manifest courage and prudence, Machiavelli demands a certain sober goodness from his successful citizens. He therefore takes a stand on the issue of *luxe* that had continually intrigued the humanists. Bruni and Poggio (1380–1459) had endorsed materialist values, and even Savonarola had worried more about the decline in citizen military service than about the corrupting power of superabundant wealth. But Machiavelli thinks differently: "I might indeed discourse at length on the advantages of poverty over riches, and how poverty brings honour to cities, provinces, and religious institutions, whereas the other thing has ruined them; if it had not already been done so often by others." Again the goal of the moral leader is to prevent the victory of the private over the public interest, for however this happens, corruption results. It is this concept of corruption that goes abroad in the dispersion of Machiavelli's works and becomes so influential. In an age in which politics was not by any means separated from religion, corruption was a term easily understood in all its traditional negative associations.[5]

Out of his analysis of ancient and modern history Machiavelli put together a program for public greatness based upon the *vita activa* and *vita civile*. What is more, he did it at a critical moment when the city-state was declining in power throughout Europe—this is even true of Venice and Milan—and when, simultaneously, the dynastic monarchy was becoming the characteristic form of the great influential state. He did it, too, at the time J. G. A. Pocock calls *The Machiavellian Moment*. In his great book, Pocock accords two senses to "moment." In the first, it is the time in which those who are living in and theorizing about their republic see it clearly in terms of past and present history and try to understand it. In the second, it is a time of actual crisis for the republic in which it attempts to maintain its moral character and political independence "in a stream of irrational events conceived as essentially destructive of all systems of secular stability." In defining the paradigm of "the moment," Pocock examines Machiavelli's contemporaries in Venice as well as Florence and then carries the influence of their thinking through to the English and American revolutions.

The Florentines Machiavelli and Guicciardini (1483–1540) and the Venetians Giannotti (1492–1573) and Contarini (1483–1542) wrote as sophisticated observers of, and participants in, a complex Italian scene. Moreover, they were conversant with ancient history and political literature, and with all those authors in the preceding century who had attempted to analyze past and present events and theories. Writers in northern Europe who became familiar with their ideas and the careers of public involvement that influenced the nature of those ideas, knew another, quite different scene. To be sure, cities had been flourishing in the north for centuries. Some, like Paris and Ghent and Bruges, were among the greatest in Europe in terms of size, wealth, and number of specialized workers and intellectuals. Many had developed institutions of self-government roughly similar to the conventionally oligarchical systems of multiple executives and councils of the south. Yet northern cities and their governments were different from those of the Mediterranean world because their freedom to govern themselves, to carry on an external political and military life independent of a king, lord, or bishop who might be their lawful ruler, was limited in law and in fact. Moreover, the political style of the city world did not set the basic, overall style of government throughout the north. This continued to be a region of monarchy where kings or great dukes like that of Burgundy ruled large territorial states in which most of those who exercised authority were aristocratic bluebloods like themselves. It was into this world of courts, as opposed to assemblies, that the ideals of civic humanism eventually penetrated.

They penetrated in the usual ways humanist ideals traveled. Italians went north to the courts of England, France, and the Hapsburg and other princes, where they served as teachers, Latin secretaries, legal advisers, and spies. Northerners went south to see the new look of Italy, to study at Bologna, Rome, and Padua, and to learn how the governments of Venice, Milan, and Florence worked. Famous names are involved in this transmission of techniques and ideas: Erasmus, Pole, Colet, Rabelais, Luther, to say nothing of less famous scholars, technicians, and those English lords who returned home to found humanist colleges at Oxford and Cambridge. And, of course, ideas traveled in manuscripts and, eventually, printed books: classical authors previously unknown or untranslated into a vernacular, new editions of the church fathers, each accompanied by the introduction written by an editor eager to share his discovery and enthusiasm. Not only did the full Platonic corpus enter the Western tradition again at this time, but the fifteenth and sixteenth centuries also saw the recovery of ancient Stoic, Epicurean, and Skeptical works which had been lost or little known during the Middle Ages. By the third decade of the sixteenth century, when Machiavelli's works were being read, a variety of means existed for their transmission. There also existed an appetite for works of political analysis, given the war and intense diplomacy of the age. Finally, the north was ready for the south. Its political, social, and economic circumstances now constituted a society in which the humanist justification of the active civic and political life was needed.[6]

If the word *civis* tied to the concept of a republican city did not make sense in, say, England or France, the justification of the active life tied to efficient, constructive service to the ruler did. This is one way the citizenship tradition survived the Renaissance and Reformation, and, indeed, the entire Age of Absolutism. It did not disappear during this period, which ended more or less with the French Revolution; rather, it masqueraded, assumed protective coloration, by labeling its functions and services to make them compatible with the demands of a courtly political culture.

The survival of a republican vocabulary depended also upon the vitality in a given territory of the Roman law tradition. In England, therefore, the language of the humanist tradition was assimilated to a lesser degree than in France, where, by the sixteenth century, the language of the Romanist tradition was deeply established even in the north, especially at the university in Paris, which was the center of both literary and legal study. It was still easier for English courtiers and royal servants, trained as many of them were in Italy or in the Italian humanist tradition, to avoid the specific concept of republican citizen than it was for, say, Bodin, who served in no less monarchical an ambience.

They could avoid it, too, because there were few, if any, citizenship institutions. During antiquity and the Middle Ages, citizenship was a philosophy of conduct, an educational program, a legal corpus, and a battery of institutions that manifested all these ideas. But during the early modern centuries that situation changed. There were few republics anymore, in the freestanding, self-governing, medieval sense. Now, as we have begun to see, citizen is no longer a term that functions naturally, so to speak, in a direct open association with an institution. It becomes an archaism, a term for literary scholars or historians, a term one reaches for when desiring imprecision, a less than formal statement. Its association with merchants becomes more frequent as they increase in number and importance. Moreover, when the concept of citizen appears in argument during this period it is likely to be in revolutionary or prerevolutionary situations, and those who use it do so purposefully, quite aware of its call, its implicit program. Only in the years before 1789 do the word and its rationale come together and again become part of ordinary political speech, used by mainline theoreticians.

PART III

THE SUBJECT AND THE CITIZEN

7

幻幻幻

AMBIGUITIES OF CITIZENSHIP

UNDER MONARCHY

CITIZENSHIP'S SURVIVAL UNDER ABSOLUTISM

In antiquity citizenship developed within cities that were the creations of warrior-peasants. An active life was approved in this environment, and, indeed, was lauded. During the Christian Middle Ages citizenship flourished in merchant cities in which, although salvation was formally substituted for honor as the goal of life, the individual still needed legal and political recognition and a variety of auspices if he was to succeed socially and economically.

At the beginning of the sixteenth century Europe entered a period of almost three hundred years during which citizenship lost much of the centrality and importance it had had earlier. One reason for this change was the fact that Italy, whose many and important cities had generated the issues surrounding citizenship, no longer counted a great deal. The monarchies of Europe, in which citizenship had not mattered much during the Middle Ages except at the local level, now dominated politics and stimulated the issues which theorists and statesmen had to reckon with. Another reason for the change, related to the first, is that citizenship, with so many of its associations tied to republican Rome, was unwelcome in the courts and universities of England, France, Spain, and the innumerable German and ecclesiastical principalities.

More congenial than "citizen" to the political analyst, his monarch, and courtiers was "subject," if for no other reason than that "subject" lent itself easily to the new scale of politics. Policy now touched people thousands of miles from a European capital as well as those now more effectively controlled only a few miles away from the ruler. Moreover, "subject" had its own associations, those of ancient and medieval monarchy and empire. Late-medieval lawyers had already begun to assimilate citizen to subject as they contemplated the reality of the growing princely territorial states.

"Citizen" survived, nevertheless, because it continued to embrace many subconcepts and traditions. And what proved attractive to the early modern monarchs was not the idea that ultimately all political authority derived from an active people. Rather, it was the state-service side to citizenship, the active-life-in-the-service-of-the-community aspect of the tradition, that allowed for the perpetuation of the currency of the term and its ethos. This activist component appealed to rulers who needed conquistadors, sea dogs, and viceroys abroad, and generals and bureaucrats in Europe. Meanwhile, successful, creative merchants, scientists, engineers, and inventors also began to find a place of honor in early modern society. Moreover, since citizenship had always been compatible with hierarchy, having long served as a principle of differentiation and exclusion, it could continue to function this way in a political atmosphere of grades, titles, and privilege, a variety of inequalities.

It survived too because the tradition of civic friendship and republican virtue related to another of the great accomplishments of modern history: the rise of commercial society. In an age of increasing materialism and of an acquisitive ethic that identified success as private gain, the old-fashioned virtues of civic activism, political participation, and military service found support among those who desired a rationale for human conduct that simultaneously endorsed purposeful activity and directed it toward high public goals. Those in the traditional martial and ministerial orders could identify with the tradition of republican virtue, thus distinguishing themselves from merchants and bankers who claimed office and distinction. In an era of rapid commercial growth and increasing financial speculation, proponents of social responsibility viewed civic humanist values positively. Stalwart, honest yeoman looked good in the age of tulip speculation and the Mississippi Bubble.

Since, generally speaking, citizen now connoted activism and not republicanism, it was able to fit easily into the educational world of the early sixteenth century. Then, as always, education for citizenship was not restricted to the schools, or even to the schools and the churches. It also took place in political activity, whether that meant sitting in a legislative or judicial body, working with relatives or neighbors for a political goal, devising a new constitution for a city or policy for a king, or serving in some royal or municipal office. This public activity constitutes one kind of education and permits the full realization of the individual. Even activity in the streets may be seen as virtuous when done with some view of the public good in mind. So Machiavelli saw dissension's role in Roman history; military service, of course, had its reasons for being in his and other prescriptive curricula.

In early modern Europe all education was suffused by classicism in which citizenship was present as an issue or ideal. It appears in Plato and Aristotle, in Plutarch, Cicero, and all the Roman historians. It appears in the *Corpus Iuris Civilis*, which continues to be the basis for legal education over most of continental Europe and in England in the civilians whose work was known and used well into the seventeenth century.[1] Machiavelli's *Discourses* demonstrate this influence early in the century, Shakespeare's *Coriolanus* at the end. Present in so many texts, citizenship could not be ignored, especially as it was connected to many moral issues associated with public service. Elyot in England and Montaigne across the channel were both concerned with adapting classical moral positions to the demands of career in their own time, each in his own country. Citizenship and service are now discussed in relation to the monarch. The point of departure for a discussion may still be a passage in an ancient author, but the lesson to be drawn is for immediate application in or near the court of one's king.

The influence of the ancient world was everywhere: in formal education and literature, on the walls and ceilings of churches and palaces, in the statues erected in the grand new squares of princely capitals, on the stages of princely theaters. There was not an aspect of aristocratic culture that did not rely on the ancient world for artistic or moral models. The concept and the idealized exercise of citizenship could not be escaped, for Greece had known it, both Sparta and Athens, both Plato and Aristotle, and Rome had known it, both Republic and Empire, both Cicero and Tacitus. If one were a member of Europe's elite during the centuries between Columbus and Rousseau, one would have encountered the *civis* many ways. Moreover, in this age of competing Christian faiths, Catholic and Protestant educators both used the same pagan works to strengthen their positions. The moral insights and persuasive styles of Plato, Cicero, and Seneca were invaluable to both.

The citizen and citizenship thus survive through the Age of Absolutism. The key words still come easily to those writing about politics, law, and administration, for even if they do not have republicanism in mind, the resonances of citizen still serve to encourage the subject to purposeful service of his king. The contrast is with the Middle Ages, when citizen conveyed not so much the full sense of a human being as of a bearer, exploiter of specific rights—or so he appears in the literature, which is overwhelmingly legal and, as such, largely impersonal. Citizen was now sometimes used as a term of historical discourse, linked to the study of a distant civilization's history and literature. Other terms reveal the new range and interests of political and social theorists, words like "man" and "people." Montaigne wrote that he was the first to "communicate" by his "entire being, as Michel de Montaigne, not as grammarian or a poet or a jurist."[2] Scholars have long pointed to the change in the representation of the human body that accompanied the development of a more naturalistic view of man in politics following the reception of Aristotle.[3]

Such a change depends on a new emphasis in thinking about the human being. During the Middle Ages, when a this-worldly existence was not considered paramount, men could think in terms of specific legal benefits and not in terms of the entire personality, or total career, in context. After the Renaissance, when a successful earthly existence was more positively received, the *civis* became more than a holder of a collection of statuses and rights; he became a complex psychological being making complex choices in a complex environment. The extent to which his political activity came to be viewed as inextricably linked to his essential nature can be seen in the works of Hobbes and Locke. Hobbes's psychology comes down to us in part in a work entitled *On the Citizen*, while Locke's politics is based upon his *Essay Concerning Human Understanding* and his *Some Thoughts Concerning Education*, both of which were enormously influential, if not in some sense prescriptive, in the eighteenth century.

This means that Hobbes and Locke were not interested in citizenship in a narrow, traditional, legal sense. Rather, they were, as the ancients were, interested in man as thinking, moral being, embedded in his society and reacting to its demands out of his human nature, whatever that might prove to be, and of his culture. In this they look forward to the modern concept of citizenship as a more generalized and fundamental condition based on some theory of the human personality complete with an epistemology and social needs. During the Middle Ages theologians thought about man in relation to justice and government. Generally the later political philosophers saw him as developing into the modern rational, polytechnical being needed by a changing world for his scientific and administrative skills.[4]

Broadly speaking, citizenship survived in two principal traditions, which this chapter will begin to pursue over three centuries. One developed out of the civic humanist institutions and ideology of the Renaissance, was intensified and formalized by Machiavelli, and then passed through the works of

Harrington and others to the colonies and to the France of Rousseau. The
other tradition came out of the medieval merchants' and lawyers' interest in
the acquisition of property, was given a moral twist and made sober by More,
and then gained greater amplitude as Montaigne, Bacon, Shakespeare,
Hobbes, Locke, Franklin, and many others each added some aspect of human
depth and complexity, psychological, historical, and moral analysis, polytechnic vision, and educational theory. If distinct, these two currents or traditions were not discrete. Theories and influences interacted, spilled over, affected each other. They had, of course, a common basis in antique thought
and institutions; in contrast to medieval sympathy for poverty and idealism,
they both increasingly were committed to success and comfort in this world.
And both traditions understood that the citizen, who in this age was also and
ever more a subject, had to develop now in relation to the monarch of a
national kingdom whose interests were to be served by rational activists.

Still qualifying, we must realize that these later analysts see the citizen/
subject in many more ways than the political: for example, as a learned and
economic man functioning in a society whose changing nature depends upon
science. The concept of the "polytechnic" man needed by society and advanced to leadership because of his ability to envision, plan, and administer
new enterprises is very much an aspect of the new citizen's definition in a
rapidly changing Europe. Such a man is what Hobbes and Locke have in
mind: a figure balancing his commitments to public and private concerns,
religious and secular, now that there really was a significant secular component in European moral life. In this way, for all their differences, they both
look forward to the modern concept of citizenship, which is a more complete,
generalized, and fundamental condition in which the entire human being is
involved. For all of these reasons, we can understand why *civis* did not fade
from the legal or political scene, and why it is such a troublesome word. One
frequently worries what is meant to be understood by its use, especially in
northern Europe, where the great changes are taking place. While in the
south one can assume some familiarity with the full legal and political tradition behind the word, some historical understanding of the ambience in
which the institution flourished, one can not assume the same in every
French or English author. In their works the word may be used, aptly, to
designate those resident in a city, people who do not in any of the full historic
sense of the term participate in the political process. Only slowly during the
Middle Ages did the term acquire the full range of its classical associations,
and then not only because of the revival of Aristotle and the diffusion of

Roman law, but also because of the way artists, sculptors, poets, and historians had come to focus upon the natural man as actor and individual in the real world of nature and politics.[5] We will see what happened to *civis* and citizenship in the *Utopia* of Sir Thomas More.

These confusions in the employment of citizen and subject are reminiscent of an earlier moment in the history of European thought. In the late eleventh century the lawyers "discovered" the *Corpus Iuris Civilis*, and for the next five hundred years they labored to comprehend the ancient vocabulary, product of its own times and issues, and make that ancient vocabulary fit, explain, and clarify contemporary events and institutions. Over the centuries the simple definitions of the earliest school give way to the massive collections of treatises of the late sixteenth century. In between worked the glossators, postglossators, and finally the humanist-historian jurisconsults of the Renaissance. Each school approached the original Justinianic texts on a different intellectual basis, armed with a greater or lesser understanding of history, philosophy, and philology. And each scholar, of course, was influenced by the experiences of his own generation and particular territory.

Between 1500 and 1800 something of this situation may be seen in the various approaches to "citizen" in the era of "subjects." Medieval usage had been confined largely to the inhabitants of cities, if not to the inhabitants of cities given over to commerce. There were few of these, and not all residents in an urban area were necessarily citizens. Now, however, millions might be citizen/subjects—all the (male) inhabitants of a large territorial state such as France, for example. And, under such circumstances, what came to determine citizenship was not the sum of particular legal capabilities inhering in the individual, but the existence of a special personal relationship between the individual and his monarch, repeated millions of times if there were millions of inhabitants.

In the Middle Ages, one had his citizen status as a matter of will and culture. Now residence continued to be important, but what mattered most was not the will or intention of the citizen, but that of the ruler, confirmed by him from above. Such a relationship looks away from the balance of feudal obligations and expectations that obtained between lord and vassal and toward the one-sided, tilted relationship that exists today in the second citizenship between the citizen and the central authority. Indeed, what we are investigating in the sixteenth, seventeenth, and eighteenth centuries may be seen as the prehistory of the second citizenship, or at least as the thinking that eventually helped determine the relationship between the individual and his government after the American and French revolutions.

In the ancient world analyzed by Plato, Aristotle, and the Stoics, citizenship had served as the institution by which the man of substance proved his virtue and received and justified his status thereby. In the opportunity for community service given to him by birth or residence, or both, he differentiated himself from slaves and aliens; one result of his service was an enhanced opportunity to acquire and protect his property. During the Middle Ages, in those areas in which oligarchic and, in Italy, even princely government developed, citizenship again facilitated the domestication, urbanization, civilization of the warrior world. Now bourgeois merchants had their code of morality and virtuous conduct, the pursuit of which eventually might bring land and honor, but which at first brought the exercise of legal, political, and social benefits that conferred economic power. Again, as in antiquity, and in analogous surroundings, performance of civic duties conveyed virtue.

During the Middle Ages, then, citizenship remained as undemocratic and discriminatory as it had been in the ancient world. Compatible with hierarchical feudal and monarchical institutions, it survived in this form into the sixteenth century because it rarely bore a revolutionary threat and continued to promise advantages to those who would fulfill the requirements for success under the new princely politics. This was not difficult. One requirement was the possession of property; another was civil obedience; another, in this age when religious unity was dissolving, was conformity with the beliefs and practices of the established state church. Also persisting was the requirement that one serve the community, now, by 1500 or thereabouts, represented by the prince. It is against this background of continuities that we must understand Thomas More's concept of *civis* in the *Utopia*.

CITIZENSHIP IN RENAISSANCE ENGLAND

More understood the term from his experience on the Continent as well as at the English court. It was meaningful to him also from his study of the ancient texts, including Plato's *Republic*. His imaginary country resembles ancient Athens, as opposed to Renaissance France or modern America. As its territory is small and circumscribed, so is its population. Like Athenians or Spartans, or any small, relatively homogeneous group that has lived under the spell of ancestors for all time, the Utopians have a way of life, a culture, that envelops them, shapes every aspect of their existence. There is a way to handle every situation, including that of social hierarchy, and a variety of political statuses and obligations, which are assumed. Surrounding the Utopians are friendly and hostile neighbors, each of which has its own way of educating its young, going into battle, deciding the value of money in life. In a word, Utopia is a unique community which, like Plato's model, imposes its values and institutions upon its members.

Like Machiavelli, More in many ways is the representative Renaissance author. In the very act of writing a prescriptive educational treatise, he shows his optimism: men may change in a reformed commonwealth inspired by a model from the ancient world. They achieve virtue by working in and for the community, not in actionless, passive solitude. Like contemporary fellow humanists, More accepts a hierarchy in which the Utopian citizen, like the ancient citizen, is a special person, privileged in both his benefits and responsibilities. Almost without exception, *civis* appears in the text in passages describing purposeful activity related to community function and success. The citizen attends "an annual meeting to consider affairs of common interest to the island"; he moves his residence into the country in accordance with public policy on rotation of residence; he performs his stint on the road crew and in other labor obligations in order to have time for contemplation, which, clearly, is not meant to be the Utopian's only occupation.[6]

More has a special concern for the moral education and growth of the citizens. Slaves may slaughter animals, but citizens may not, since their "sense of compassion" may be negatively affected. The sights of citizens are to be elevated, quite literally, as they are made to gaze upon the statues of Utopia's heroes set on high columns in the public spaces. These are to "incite them to virtue." Like many moralists from Plato on, More believes that the welfare or ruin of a commonwealth depends wholly on the character of the officials.[7] Although he does not discuss the issue in conventional terms, More is aware of corruption. He would, therefore, agree with Machiavelli's emphasis on the danger of corruption in the life of any commonwealth. From this follows his extensive treatment of Utopian education, which is meant to instruct all citizens in the ethics of public life lest they become corrupt in office. Education will warn men away from the abuse of power; it will also prevent their falling into the sins of greed and sloth. If More does not offer us a convent, he does prescribe the hard Christian life that goes back to the Apostles and that was making a comeback as an ideal in the days of the glorious Renaissance popes.

In his discussion of warfare, More touches on another of the issues current in the humanist political program; here his view differs from the usual endorsement of either citizen or mercenary troops. Utopians prefer the expenditure of money to that of lives whenever possible and lavishly support the hiring of the best mercenaries available, but when called upon to fight, they fight fiercely and willingly sacrifice their lives, male and female both, for the public weal.[8] His view joins a Christian concern for peace with an admiration for the ancient citizen's willingness to die for his country.

More's moral universe embraces all the great issues of his time and extends far beyond the cloister. In his new world, the *civis* is a participant in the political processes that help define his character by giving him a chance to improve that character. That is to say, a citizen is most a citizen when he is acting within the political framework—we would say constitution in the broadest sense—that makes Utopia work. More does not mention or carefully distinguish among grades of citizens, as would a Roman lawyer, but he does in passing depict a hierarchy in Utopia in which the committed, active citizen is the best man. In More the republican vision survives, albeit in a muted form and linked to a religious vision that puts him in the line of great Christian reformers seeking peace, harmony, and justice. Nor is the "moral physiognomy" of More's citizen spelled out in a single hortatory or prescriptive passage. For a dynamic definition, one must look throughout for a variety of virtuous acts that affect other human beings.[9]

St. Thomas More Christianized activity for the public good, and in the frantically active centuries that followed, which saw the expansion of Europe throughout the world, to say nothing of great commercial, industrial, and, eventually, social developments in Europe itself, Protestant as well as many Catholic thinkers continued to explain away lingering objections to diligent, conscientious activity in the world.

More wrote against the abuses of the Church, state, and society in his own time. He wanted change and reform, and in generally pointing out the failures of medieval society and in his specific duties as lord chancellor to Henry VIII, he acted in a tradition that was assuming a new function or identity in the early sixteenth century, that of royal adviser, "the articulate citizen" of the English Renaissance.[10] What makes the concept of "Tudor citizen" a legitimate usage in the vocabulary of Tudor politics is humanism. In increasing numbers, members of the English ruling class had experienced Italy; that is, in Padua, Rome, Florence, and other cities, they had talked with Italian humanists and had bought, read, and returned with the books recommended by them. These books not only honed rhetorical skills, they also—and here Cicero's *De Oratore* is a good example—praised the use of such skills by the good citizen in the service of his country. Considering what England had gone through in the fifteenth century—war on the Continent, civil war at home, peasant revolt, religious upheaval, and the social dislocation that accompanied these disturbances—it is not surprising that men of moral intelligence trained themselves to offer their best advice to their country.

The tradition of giving advice to one's lord had a long pre-Renaissance history. "Counsel" always had been one of two defining elements in the feudal relationship of vassalage. Now, under the impact of civic humanism, it changed at the very moment royal government's perception changed; slowly conditions, as opposed to events, came to occupy the attention of those who ruled England. Under these circumstances the humanist-trained or humanist-inspired Englishman began to regard it as his responsibility to analyze why some condition should exist, say, a trade imbalance or failure of diplomacy, and then to write a treatise or letter which would commend his thinking to the sovereign. The pen takes the place of the sword, and in a sense citizenship returns to, or reappears in, its original environment, that of an aristocratic society in which responsible, learned, and pacific men establish their position in a government settling down to civilian life. As in the ancient Greek city-state, so now in England and other Renaissance principalities citizenship survives in the code of values of the new courtly, service class. The republican side of the institution gives way to the activist service element, which is essential, and which serves as the basis for privilege in the early modern absolutist state.

The union of contemporary humanist beliefs with those of the traditional feudal past can also be seen in the *Dialogue* of Thomas Starkey, who, like More, served Henry VIII. Backward looking in his espousal of an elective monarchy, Starkey yet sought, as did the best of his friends, and as did More, to make the humanist program benefit his country. If men are to live together in "perfect civility" they must help each other. God gave each man his abilities, which are to be used, for "little availeth virtue that is not published abroad to the profit of others. . . . And this is the end of the civil life, or, me seemeth, rather the true administration of the common weal." Moral action will "bring the whole country to quietness and civility." The civil life is not necessarily the urban life, but rather the community "conspiring together in all virtue and honesty." Thus he would blend the public-spiritedness of Rome with the charity of Christianity: the good man will never miss the opportunity "to apply and endeavour myself to the maintenance and setting forward of the common weal." Starkey never published his *Dialogue*, so it is of use to us only as an example of the kind of "applied humanism" covertly current at Henry's court. Although optimistic, Starkey was not so optimistic as to believe he could survive while openly advocating a return to medieval notions of kingship.[11]

Also paradigmatic was another moralist-educator of the 1530s, Thomas Elyot, whose *The Boke Named the Governour* is usually taken as the classic statement of English Renaissance education. Elyot knew Castiglione's *Courtier* and the tradition of humanist education in Italy over the previous century. He himself translated Plutarch, whose *Lives* was a popular source of information about the ancient world, and which Shakespeare later relied on heavily. He knew More personally, and therefore the tradition of Erasmus. He clearly saw the need for a new kind of education that would prepare gentlemen for state service and, in the preface to his work, called upon parents to follow his educational scheme should they wish their sons to enter the governing class. Elyot saw that the gentry and aristocracy had to prepare themselves for public service with new skills and a new morality.[12] His ideas reappear later in the century in Roger Ascham's *The Schoolmaster*, which similarly advocated the education of a young gentleman "in the interest of his country in which he was born and to which he owes his services."[13] Such ideas came to these Englishmen from Greek and Latin authors as well as from Italian intermediaries. And under the influence of such men the curricula at Oxford and Cambridge changed markedly over the mid-century.[14]

In the works of these humanist educators, the use of *civis* is rare. Yet it is clear that they are writing about citizenship, and with a consciousness both of its historical function and contemporary usefulness. Plato, Solon, Aristotle, Cicero are all in their heads. They are aware of man's need for society as the ancients have described it. They know too how skill with language will bring civil peace—and advance one's career, provided one uses the vocabulary of analysis and recommendation with care. Perhaps this explains in part the use of "gentleman" in contexts in which we might expect "citizen." The terms describe similar persons. Like the citizen, the gentleman is a privileged person, and for many of the same reasons. He is not just like everyone else in the local community; he has legal and social status based on possession of a fair amount of property, usually land. Politically he belongs to the ruling elite, which has none of the negative associations connected with election processes, mercantile occupations, and the tradition of some kind of popular rule as known from ancient literature.

Also, "gentleman" takes the law out of *civis*, somewhat strips away the medieval civilian tradition, which had emphasized specific privileges, and emphasizes rather the patriotic, active individual. It is this broadening of citizenship that the Renaissance as a cultural movement brought to the institution. The entire potential of the human being was seen and challenged, no longer viewed as the bloodless structural element of a hierarchical society.

This circumspection and suspicion with regard to the citizen is evident in Shakespeare's *Coriolanus*, clearly a tale of citizenship and an indication of how the new view of citizenship entered public consciousness through the popular theater. From Plutarch and other writers Shakespeare was familiar with the great men and women of antiquity and the moral significance of their lives. He was aware too of the expectations his country and century had from the new education for civic virtue. In the play he uses all the right words to cue in his audience to significant issues—for example, the need for overpowering leadership in an aggressive state. Shakespeare has little sympathy here for a popular role in government.

For all his stubbornness and arrogance, Coriolanus remains superior to Sicinius and Brutus, the tribunes of the people. He embodies the best of classical virtues: love of country, martial spirit, and a commitment to service. There is no questioning the public side of Coriolanus's character. Shakespeare faults not the prideful hero, but the ignorant, spineless, docile, vacillating citizens who are manipulated by their self-serving tribunes into destroying their natural leader. If, as Shakespeare says, "the people are the city," then he must condemn not only the citizens, but also the entire republican structure of government, which allows the tribunes of the people to exercise such perverted authority. The tragedy of Coriolanus is the failure of more than the man; it lies not only in his humiliation in the "gown of humility" before the masses, but also in the failure of a system which relies on the judgment of people interested only in their bellies and safety. He fails out of greatness, almost an excess of virtue, the overreach of his arrogance and pride; the citizens fail because of an absence of moral vision.[15]

This results from their lack of education. Some of the statesman-writer-reformers viewed the entire range of England's problems—if not Europe's, in the case of More—before making their recommendations; others, like Elyot, wrote for the improvement of a given class. But all these moral critics viewed education as the key instrument of change and betterment. And although they were familiar with the tradition and importance of leisure for contemplation, they all, even More, urged the active life upon their readers. What is more, almost all of them entered public life to serve as living models of their doctrine. Into our own century the descendants of these sixteenth-century moral theorists have continued to view a training in the liberal arts as the best education for public service.[16]

These English writers were all moralists who used "citizen" in a programmatic form. For them, of course, the word had some political significance, but they were really not interested in the legal niceties that differentiated the citizen from others up and down in the community. One contemporary analyst who was both a lawyer and royal servant, and who attempted a mid-century clinical description of how the kingdom worked and where the citizen and every other kind of person and official fit in, was Sir Thomas Smith. Smith perhaps was influenced in his careful formal dissection of English society and government by his training in civil law at Padua; and surely, in northern Italy and in France, which he traveled across on his trip home, he had a chance to see some medieval cities and their citizens in action. Eventually, probably in 1565, he wrote the *De Republica Anglorum*, which appeared six years after his death in 1577, long after he had served as Elizabeth's secretary of state.

Smith meant to lay forth "The manner of Government or policie of the Realme of England," and after an initial sixteen chapters on kingship and attendant institutions he suddenly begins an analysis of the entire hierarchy of English society. (The break is so obvious and the language is so similar that it has been suggested that he borrowed the last eight chapters of the first book from William Harrison's *Description of England*, published in 1577.) He recognizes that one way to distinguish among people is on the basis of place in a hierarchy of political office, while another is according to their status as "private men." Observing that the Greeks, Romans, and the contemporary French so divided their populations, he lists current English classes as "gentlemen, citizens, yeoman artificers, and laborers." These divisions then serve as the structure of his analysis of what we would call the social basis of politics in a commonwealth.

For Smith (and Harrison, whose *Description* was published in successive editions of the popular Holinshed's *Chronicle*), hierarchy or order is assumed, and in his hierarchy, "next to gentlemen, be appointed citizens and burgesses." These are assumed to bear public obligations in proportion to their wealth, but there is nothing in his description of them that recalls the ancient and medieval republican tradition. They are "to serve the commonwealth, in their cities and burrows, or in corporate towns where they dwell." That is all. They have a responsibility for representing their community in Parliament, but "generally in the shyres they be of none accompt." There is no call to virtue through service, though Smith refers to Cato and citizenship in the following chapter, "Of Yeoman." This is only a constitutional lawyer's careful assignment of duty on the basis of place and status.

It is his very distance from the rhetoric of citizenship that gives Smith's text a special usefulness and credibility. If he did, as seems likely, borrow from his friend Harrison, and if this borrowing took place in the last months of his prolonged illness, during which he revised his book, the assumption must be that this was the sense and usage of citizen that he regarded as most accurate, or at least that this was good lawyerly usage that was compatible with the categories of Aristotelian analysis within which he structured his discourse, and that it would be comprehended and found sound by his readers, who would be of his education and class.[17]

Given this brief review of selected English sixteenth-century authors, we may say that several political vocabularies were in use, each serving its practitioners, each employing, consciously or not, some remnant of the republican vocabulary. The question always is: which vocabulary is in the forefront of the writer's mind, that of the Roman law or that of the republican tradition, which embraces so much more? Or must we posit the existence of a contemporary political idiom in which citizenship was always somewhat alien? In the works surveyed it would appear that if the concept of active citizenship developed at all in a late-feudal environment, it did so in the schools and libraries of highborn Englishmen. When that gentleman thought about how England might be improved, or how and with what fervor he ought to serve, he thought in terms derived from the republican ideal. But when that gentleman was in state service, citizenship in the republican tradition counted less than the immediate demands of a modernizing feudal court and a system of local government which depended upon a variety of feudal and financial rewards and expectations to guarantee performance. What he had in his head at that moment probably was the needed concept of loyal subject.

In the interplay between citizen and subject, citizen as an enveloping concept comes to stand for something less than the ancient emphasis on love cum willing sacrifice; it becomes a secondary, reinforcing idea that contributes to the strength of a preexisting, indigenous, feudal aristocratic notion of service that had prevailed all during the Middle Ages. In this era, it could be argued, citizenship survives only as an integral part of classicism. When and where it flourishes, citizenship continues to exert some moral influence. Since northerners still traveled to Italy, and Italians circulated in the north, since Italian books and translations still traveled north, since not even the Reformation kept the Protestant north and the Catholic south completely apart, citizenship values were retained by the early modern monarch, who viewed all men as subjects, whether great nobles or free men.

This fact became the subject for analysis in the early seventeenth century, specifically in the veritable treatise on subjectship of Sir Edward Coke. It is in the tradition of the great civilians of the late Middle Ages, who opined on political matters of great importance in relation to technical points of law. The critical text is *Calvin's Case*, which grew out of a question of inheritance: whether a Scot born after the accession of James to the English throne was to be regarded as an alien or a subject.

In a long and intricate opinion on an issue which he and his fellow jurists recognized as having implications which were "the weightiest for the consequent, both for the present and for all posterity," Coke argued that Calvin was a natural subject of the king. By "natural" he meant a relationship based upon structures of hierarchy and dependency built into the world; the influence of feudal assumptions is clear from the medieval precedents Coke cited. Although Coke argues for a territorial basis to personal subordination to the king, he stressed the element of will in the relationship. It is a quasi-feudal homage, *ligeantia*, and obedience "that make the subject born." And in phrases that are reminiscent of the civilians' demand for commitment, he wrote that "ligeance is a quality of the mind" and, moreover, "is due only to the King."

Simultaneously the will of the prince is emphasized. For example, the king alone may change the legal nature of a man, make an alien a denizen, that is, create for him a new status intermediate between that of the alien and the subject. However, even more fundamental to the king's position than his power based on might and parliamentary association was his function in the divine and natural order. He existed and ruled in order to protect those who existed to work, serve, and obey.[18]

If one asks, therefore, how close citizen and subject were in Tudor thinking, the response must be given very carefully. Legally, constitutionally, there were no citizens of the kingdom, only certain residents of cities or boroughs. In the kingdom all were royal subjects. However, and the qualification is significant, citizen existed as a concept, as a historical influence. Insofar as educated men knew the classics and were susceptible to their influence, citizenship survived and exerted influence every time such a subject chose, consciously, to put the public interest before what he recognized as his own. If history is determined by history, here the example of the heroic, sacrificing ancient citizen, we may say that the ancient model persisted into the age of absolutist monarchs. One explanation for its survival lies in the fact that, as we have seen, the demands upon the citizen for his service, as opposed to the demand for a citizen's active participation in the making of law and government, predominated in this era.

In the city-states of antiquity and the Middle Ages, service was rewarded with privilege. Under the dynastic ruler, the exchange survived; now, however, it was obedience and service that brought from the monarch somewhat new forms of traditional rewards: patents and monopolies, as well as titles, proximity, vast estates, and the exercise of political power through bureaucratic position. Moreover, since the Reformation brought no real change in the Continent's political structure, there was little in the religious picture to alter these relationships, although, as we shall see, some arguments favoring resistance to oppressive tyrants did eventually strengthen the republican side of citizenship. Before that happened in England, it probably took place in France.

CITIZENSHIP IN RENAISSANCE FRANCE

Citizenship in the France of the Old Regime presents its own problems. As in England, a king ruled, and over the years between Francis I and Louis XVI he grew in both regard and power, theory and actuality. As in Italy, the Roman law was known and studied at the major universities, north and south, a body of authoritative doctrine that asserts imperial authority (long claimed by kings) and at the same time that the source of all princely authority is the will of the people. Again, as in Italy, the influence of the ancient world enveloped more than politics; the literature, history, architecture, philosophy, morality, and the heroes of antiquity set the tone of aristocratic French civilization for centuries.

In the late fifteenth and sixteenth centuries, however, France had to be reconstructed after the Hundred Years War. Her kings accomplished this with the help of loyal and able administrators and based their achievement on a theory of royal absolutism largely the work of lawyers who developed the imperialist side of Roman law theory. Charles Du Moulin (1500–1566) and

Petrus Rebuffi (1487–1557) are the best examples of this school, and, of course, Jean Bodin (1530–96) who wrote later in the sixteenth century. Being lawyers, these men knew very well that they were rejecting the republicanism of the ancient Roman law. They were also aware of a traditional medieval constitutionalism such as that formulated by Claude de Seyssel (1450–1520) in his *The Monarchy of France*, first published in 1519. Seyssel was an activist professor of Roman law who served Louis XII in a variety of diplomatic and advisory positions before writing his book as a guide for the young Francis I. He was also the humanist translator of Plutarch, Xenophon, Thucydides, and other historians, all of whom knew and revealed casually the civic assumptions of antiquity.[19]

Yet there is almost no evidence of the current interest in civic virtue in the work of this French articulate citizen of the Renaissance, despite his recognition that it was under the Republic, what he calls a "popular Empire," that "the Romans won the greater part of the world." However, if the Republic brought vast territorial expansion, it also created an ugly new politics and a new governing class which depended upon corruption. Seyssel does not use this word, but what he describes is the rise of demagogues who resort to "pillage, extortion and violence" in their quest for money with which to pay off their plebeian followers. Meanwhile, following the example of their leaders, the troops abandon all discipline and follow their generals into self-seeking civil war. It was just because of this perversion of what might have been that Seyssel ranks popular government at the bottom of the list in his analysis of constitutional forms.

Aristocratic government, of which Venice is his principal example, also fails because its natural division between leading, active citizens and those citizens who are able, aggressive, but excluded from participation in government, generates discord, faction, and unrest among those with "no hope of gaining any important office of which there are not half enough for the lords." By "the gentlemen" he calls "lords" he means those Venetian oligarchs whose families constitute the ruling citizen class of the republic. By "other citizens" and "leading citizens" he means the city people important in commerce, "wise, rich, and spirited men"—in a word, bourgeois. Seyssel's vocabulary does not reveal technical knowledge of the hierarchy of Venetian citizenships but shows that he understands the social and political realities that hundreds of years of successful imperial history have translated into jealousy and ambition.[20]

Admittedly, this is a skewed reading of Seyssel, who is not at all interested in citizens or citizenship, but rather in giving the young new king some specific advice on how to manage his kingdom well. His analysis of French political structure, which relates economic strength to social and political position, shows an awareness of the power of France's merchant class, and of the fact of what we call "social mobility," which allows passage of the bourgeoisie into the aristocracy. In the second part of his book he speaks to the issue of citizen soldiery. But in none of this does one sense the vocabulary of civic humanism, or, indeed, even of the issues raised by Roman law, which Seyssel knew as a professor. What one sees in his scholar's mind is that citizen and subject have easily become one. There is no conflict between the two because there is ideology in neither. Just as there were citizens enjoying their rights as private individuals under the Roman Empire, so under the French monarchy of Louis XII do free Frenchmen, as subjects, enjoy the civil law privileges of their condition as private citizens. The two conditions are complementary, and neither bears with it the obligation of public service except as the king should ask, and except as the private citizen may wish to contribute to the public welfare within bounds of propriety, as Seyssel is doing when he writes for the improvement of the young king and the realm.

Bodin is different. It is not necessary to tease some view of citizenship out of his works. In both the *Six Books of the Commonwealth*, first published in 1576, and the *Method for the Easy Comprehension of History*, written ten years earlier, Bodin carefully examines the concept of citizenship. He writes some fifty years after Seyssel, years of foreign and civil war, of the growing influence of humanist thinking in both law and literature, and of the progressive growth of a consciousness of France among those who count. And, unlike Seyssel, he writes theory qua theory, first in the *Method*, in an attempt to make universal history a basis for legal studies, and later in the *Six Books*, in a promonarchical reaction to the horrible condition of his country in the worst days of the religious wars. Authorities are divided in their estimate of the extent to which Bodin wanted to keep traditional constitutionalist reins on the monarch, but all agree that in its basic thrust the *Six Books* heads in the direction of unlimited monarchy. Certainly his views on citizenship enhance the position of any sovereign.

In the *Method* Bodin discusses citizenship as part of his general investigation of various forms of government; as he often does, he rejects Aristotle—in this instance, his concept of ruling and being ruled—and states simply, "A citizen is one who enjoys the common liberty and the protection of authority." He says nothing about ruling, and nothing anywhere in his long discussion about the participatory ethos that had survived for almost two thousand years. His treatment is contentious and highly selective. Particularly striking is his attempt as a humanist to analyze the hierarchy of citizen statuses that developed in the last century of the Roman Republic, thus to provide a historical basis for his understanding of the law. He sees citizenship as a bundle of political rights and privileges and understands that it is sought precisely for this reason. "Why in order to attain citizenship did they wage wars for so long? The reason is, of course, that they might seek honors and vote in the assemblies. . . . Different rights of different groups are explained by the jurisconsults. It would take too long to explain them here."[21] He allows members of various groups to constitute a citizen body, allows a variety of citizenships in any given republic, and makes them all depend upon the will of the participating individuals; it is the act of commitment that ultimately constitutes the moral basis for membership in the community.

This act of will is not flaccid, but intense, and necessarily has as its object a political entity of a specific culture and historicity. One can not be a citizen of a league or association of independent states bound together by treaties and friendship. One can only be a citizen in a polity with a recognized body of law and a single recognized authority. It is this last demand that becomes so emphatic in the *Six Books* and represents the most significant change in his view of citizenship from that in the *Method*. In the later work he is more interested in integrated policy than before. The pieces of his absolutist state must fit. So, although he may inveigh against Aristotle, he follows his method and uses his vocabulary to get at the essential relationships between a ruler and the ruled. It is not enough to name the stock pieces of any government; one must perceive how they function, how they work together.

Such a perception is his goal in chapter 6 of Book 1 of the *Six Books*. It is not a *consilium* in the familiar form; it rarely, if ever, refers to specific texts in the *Corpus Iuris Civilis*. Rather, it is a treatise based upon ancient pagan and biblical history, Italian civic practices in the Middle Ages and Renaissance, and contemporary practice throughout Europe and its outreaches, ranging from the Ottoman Empire to Portuguese Africa to Spanish America. Bodin was no mean comparative legal historian. He attempts nothing less than a survey of citizenship theory and practice as current in the Europeans' world, and on the basis of this review, he in effect frames a law of citizenship for the new, more sovereign monarchy. He asks the same questions the jurisconsults had been asking for several centuries as they had worked out a common law of citizenship for the city-states of central and northern Italy, but now at the level of the kingdom. With some exasperation he complains that there must be "500 definitions of citizens," which suggests familiarity with the infinite number of possible combinations of privileges and responsibilities, and the discussions thereof.

Citizenship itself entered into the world early, as part of the political system and vocabulary invented when men and their families came together in a higher form of human organization, the state. Thus it is coeval with "lord," "subject," and other basic political institutions and words. Early in his analysis Bodin says that every citizen is a subject, but not every subject is a citizen. He establishes the citizen as a person of political potentiality and action, and, since he is distinguished from the slave, of property upon which to base his service to the commonwealth. The basic relation involved in citizenship is that between a free man and his sovereign. To function in such a contractual situation, a citizen must be free, because only in freedom will he be able to perform proper service to his sovereign. The analogy explicitly is with the feudal tie between lord and vassal. In Bodin's words, he must be "a free subject holding of the sovereignty of another man."

In the manner of the jurist he is, Bodin makes other critical distinctions. The citizen is not necessarily a burgess, that is, town dweller. City walls do not a citizen make, but rather law and culture, and always the action of the prince. Such is the case whether one is born a citizen, naturalized by the sovereign, or freed from some condition of servitude. What counts is personal condition and commitment. And although Bodin may define citizens as those who "enjoy the rights and privileges of a city," he has kingdom in mind as well as city. No matter what the extent of the political unit may be, the key link is personal between the individual and the sovereign. Precisely because of this, the person, the citizen, may not unilaterally abolish his relationship with the sovereign, may not renounce his citizen identity. The bond is too special, too essential to the personality and function of the citizen, to be ruptured by such an act of renunciation. Not the least element of his identity by the time Bodin wrote was the citizen's religious affiliation. That too had become, so to speak, an imposition or determination of the sovereign. A generation had passed between the Peace of Augsburg of 1555, which had enunciated the principle of *cuius regio, eius religio*, and the publication date of the *Six Books*.

There is another long passage in his work, chapter 8 of Book 3, in which Bodin discusses citizenship. Here we have careful social and legal analysis touching on questions of military service, social hierarchy, internal dissension based on guild rivalry, and other matters involving citizens, slaves, and foreigners. But these discussions do not add much to his fundamental accomplishment, which was the creation of a new definition of citizen in an era of subjects. For Bodin, the essence of a citizen is his potentiality for a political life. That activity under a sovereign may be limited, but presumably it will be necessary, having been called into being by the ruler. It will also be based on property, which the citizen is assumed to possess. In something of an extended feudal relationship, the citizen's personal obligation is not to any city or regional lord, but rather to the sovereign king. That sovereign's recognition of him activates and legitimates the subject's will and, in return for the commitment of that will, guarantees protection and certain legal rights, especially that of making a testament and the possibility of rewarding service to the commonwealth. In the revised Latin edition of the *Six Books* which he published in 1586, Bodin emphasizes the power of the king in any contract with a citizen. The position of the foreigner vis-à-vis the sovereign is weakened in terms of what he may expect in the way of protection, and the dependence of the citizen upon the sovereign is intensified. Whereas earlier the text reads: "Privileges make not a citizen, but the mutuall obligation of the soveraigne to the subject, to whome, for the faith and obeisance he receiveth, he oweth justice, counsel, aid, and protection, which is not due unto strangers," the Latin version, written after ten more years of internal turmoil, asserts that "the true citizen either is born [into submission] or else submits himself to the rule and sovereign power of another man."[22] In emphasizing the submission of everyone of the kingdom to the sovereign, making all equally weak in relation to the central authority, Bodin paves the way for Hobbes and Rousseau, both of whom, each in his own way, head in the direction of absolutism.

Apropos service owed the sovereign, Bodin says very little. His view is not enveloped in a mystique created by references to the heroes of ancient Greece and Rome, nor is the language suffused with the hortatory vocabulary of the Italian humanist world. If anything, there are repeated references to various legal and trading privileges, and to office-holding possibilities—just the sort of thing we are familiar with from the interminable calculations of the Italians. But although this is so, true politics does survive, as opposed to slavish self-seeking, mere conniving in the precincts of the royal court. Even in Bodin's proto-absolutist formulation, the subject who is a citizen is to be reckoned with. He has rights, he has property, he has some legitimacy in the political arena, he has skills based on considerable education, which is both moral and legal, and he has supporting him those fundamental laws of France under which, in theory, even the sovereign monarch must govern. Thus Bodin extrapolates the definition of a citizen of a city into that of a citizen of a country. One might ascribe to him a theory of nationality based on law, custom, history, and the will of the sovereign. The forms of feudal aid and counsel have changed somewhat, but they are still oriented toward a suzerain, who is now ever more sovereign.

Certainly Bodin is no republican, and he is no civic humanist in a Florentine sense. Yet he has what might be called a "sense of citizenship." The differentiation between citizen and subject reveals this with its emphasis on, or retention of, some active role in government. Whether the origins of that role lie in the feudal past or the Roman past we may never know; we do know that Bodin chose the Roman term to designate the role. Also, for all his secularist tendencies, Bodin retains for the citizen a traditional obligation to obey the laws of God, in opposition, if necessary, to a tyrannical, un-Christian king. How this position was developed may be seen in the writings of the French Huguenots who wrote in defense of "constitutionalism" during the religious wars.

Bodin's sense of a nascent nationality is also evident in his consideration of the stranger's economic, legal, and political position in a commonwealth. From the time of the Carolingians, if not earlier, there had developed a tradition of royal protection of foreigners. To avoid many limitations on the disposition of his property and possible eventual devolution to serfdom, the alien had to swear allegiance to his local lord. In the case of merchants, all kinds of arrangements were worked out by local authorities, depending on the need of a city or seigneury for their services. Eventually, when every area had its resident aliens, usually merchants, control of these people became an issue between the crown and the great lords. The king began to assert his control over all foreigners in the twelfth century, and two centuries later the foreigner was taking an oath to him alone. Gradually lords' rights over *albani* were limited, and only in a few of the great fiefs did their old powers survive.

In the sixteenth century these matters continued to provoke tension between the king and some of his high lords and entered the law books of Du Moulin and others. If Bodin is taken as representative of current opinion, it is clear that the king has been successful in increasing his control over all men in his kingdom. If aliens still are distinguished, and if they are allowed in theory to maintain their attachment to their natural ruler, they function in many respects, nevertheless, as royal subjects. And what counts in the relationship between them and the king, in their ability to function as legal beings, that is, is their status in the sovereign's eyes.[23] Thus the pull upon all men tends to be exerted from a single sovereign source. Bodin's development of a theory of sovereignty reflects his reaction to the wars of religion and their destructive effect upon France, but it also may be seen as that emphasis upon princely power evidenced at least a century earlier in the Italian jurists.

Taking its inspiration from the same situation is another view of politics that tends in the opposite direction, toward constitutionalism rather than absolutism. In the tracts of the Huguenot constitutionalists, Hotman (1524–90), Beza (1519–1605), and Mornay (1549–1623), "citizen" appears occasionally, but never as the catch-word of a republican revival. It seems to have little, if any, ideological power. Hotman, whose *Francogallia* was a vast exercise meant to establish the elective nature of the monarchy on a historical basis, employs the term in an edgeless way to designate a person of the political class. In every kingdom but that of the Turks, he notes, there has always been a class of persons concerned to preserve "some concept of liberty." These, in effect, are the citizens as they emerge from the more enveloping term, people. His most conceptual use of citizen comes in a discussion of popular participation in Carolingian assemblies. The critical words are, in fact, a quotation from the *Digest*, and Hotman cites them to establish the supremacy of law over the ruler, law that reflects the will of the people.[24]

Theodore Beza also wrote after the St. Bartholomew's Day Massacre of 1572, and like Hotman, whom he knew in Geneva, he sought to develop constitutionalist theories of state, which would establish a basis for religious separatism as well as political opposition to an aggressive and intolerant monarchy. We are not surprised, therefore, to find citizen used in political, indeed, confrontational, contexts: for example, in his discussion of the right of magistrates to resist a tyrannical king. Like other Huguenot writers, Beza is deliberate and legalistic; only the most serious violations by a king against his obligations to his people legitimate opposition against him. And then, like the Romans when they made demands of their early rulers, the people must be "assembled according to their civic ranks," that is, must be legally constituted, be themselves on sound legal ground.

Not surprisingly, in the work of Calvin's successor in Geneva we find extended use of Jewish history to support his theories. Rather than to Rome and its citizens, the reference in Beza's argument is usually to the Israelites, but not to the citizens of Israel. Although they may have acted as politically conscious citizens in their struggles against unjust kings, the conventions of their historical literature made them a people, not a citizen body. What we have in Beza is citizenship in fact, although not in name. He and his associates carefully developed a theory of obstructionism and revolt which, based as it was upon a powerful religious as well as political foundation, was to prove increasingly persuasive over the next two centuries.[25]

More famous than Beza's *Right of Magistrates* is the *Vindiciae contra tyranos*, probably written by Phillipe du Plessis-Mornay in 1574–75, and published in 1579. It was heavily influenced by Beza's work but is based more on law than on history and is more overtly programmatic. In its call for revolt against a tyrant one might expect to find references to citizen action in the ancient world, but this is not the case. Again we face a difficult task in determining what weight Mornay placed on his occasional use of the term citizen when, almost invariably, he used "people" or "subjects" as the counterweights to ruler.

In the one passage that warrants analysis he recommends "force against a prince who commands unholy action or prohibits holy ones." It may be mounted by the people, and analogously "by the leading citizens of the several towns." It would appear that people is a more useful, more embracing term for him and that citizen is restrictive in that it refers primarily to townsmen living within a city within a kingdom. The town context simply limits the force of citizen to burgess. If, however, Mornay makes no use of the long citizen tradition, he does emphasize more vehemently than others a religious obligation to stand for liberty against tyranny.[26]

From these three works it would appear that the force of the citizen tradition subsided, despite the growing importance of the classical world in French education, and the influence of Italian example. Monarchical effectiveness and tradition were strong enough to limit the republican component in classical literature. Moreover, the Roman law, in which many statesmen and bureaucrats were trained, provided imperialist texts to oppose the republican ones. Yet something of a shift took place in that resistance theory came to rest upon a religious foundation, the Bible, especially the history of the people of Israel. In the long run this history was to prove effective, along with secular history, in guiding men and women to resistance.

However, if the source of inspiration changed, the essential nature of citizenship did not. It was not lost; rather, it gained a new source of justification, religion, at a time when religion had acquired a new spirit and power in both old Catholic and new Protestant Europe. Activism once again had a religious impulse. And if Luther joined Catholic theorists in supporting princely authority, other Protestant leaders such as Bucer, Calvin, and the Huguenots tentatively advanced novel republican arguments. These came out of a passion to preserve their religious liberty and identity in a competitive political world in which the principle of *cuius regio, eius religio* now prevailed. Now, there was added to citizenship's conventional burden of fiscal and service responsibilities the obligation to serve the community's faith, if need be, on the battlefield as well as in the church. In return, the benefits to be awarded continued to be spelled out and came to include the promise of salvation as well as the privilege to trade or inherit. Citizenship remained an instrument whereby the community shared its strengths with those supporting it.

One strength was a powerful sense of self-identity, which now became all the more important given the breakdown of the relatively homogeneous Christian culture of the Middle Ages. The religious choice of the community, actually of its ruler or ruling institution, now intensified a distinctive local identity that proclaimed a certainty of salvation as well as temporal protection. That identity might embrace all within a region as large as Spain or as small as Geneva. Within that boundary everyone, no matter what his legal or social status, was now bound by an intense obligation to defend his faith. Although in this age of kings and princes one was less a citizen politically, one was more a citizen religiously. During the Middle Ages religion had been passive in this sense; there was no need to make a big statement. Now religious passion and commitment were necessary as rulers flung their subjects into generations of religious wars. This goes beyond the medieval allegiance to a city's patron saint.

CITIZENSHIP AND THE REFORMATION

Every state saw religion become a political issue; in the Netherlands, Calvinists waged a war for eighty years to gain their religious independence from the pope as well as their political freedom from the Hapsburgs. The history of this region toward the end of the sixteenth century shows how religion acted for a while as perhaps the main propellant for military and political action.

However, religion was not the only dynamic at this time; traditional political and economic needs persisted. The requirements for the new polity established at Dordrecht in July 1572 were set forth by William of Orange, who ordered that the new Estates was to be instructed to establish "a praiseworthy order of government . . . for the protection and defense of the country, and with the least possible burden upon the citizens, and with a view to good union and accord among all classes."27

The use of the word "citizens" should not obscure the fact that in the late sixteenth century the Netherlands was still an advanced feudal society with estates, lords, and semi-independent cities ruled by established oligarchies, all of these living off the peasants of Brueghel's paintings. Basically, the language of protest and revolt was set in the medieval vocabulary of defense of privilege, rights, exclusions and exemptions from taxes and other obligations—in a word, contract, which binds ruler as well as ruled. A maximum of local independence is what the Lowlanders wanted in one form or another, their old ways of doing things. By the 1570s these included Calvinist forms of worship, which fiercely Catholic Philip II would not countenance. All the petitions, remonstrances, supplications, and discourses with which the politics of the period 1565–88 is filled are replete with this kind of language, in which the note of material self-interest is much louder than that of republican idealism. There is little of virtue in this political literature, and much of limitations on royal power confirmed in privileges by previous rulers.28

This is so, apparently, with one exception: "A discourse outlining the best and surest form and frame of government to be established in the Netherlands in these times," which probably was written in 1583 after the failure of the count of Anjou to establish his effective control of the region. After the assassination of William of Orange, the problem of unifying the provinces into some kind of effective political and military force became acute. The Spanish goal was still political submission and the end of heresy. The "Discourse" was one of several proposals circulating at the time that offered a basis for some effective unity. Its opening words strike a new speculative note and introduce us to someone familiar with "Marciovelli," who associates the Florentine with the view "that no more efficient or lasting form of government may be devised or established in these evil times than aristocracy combined with democracy, that is government by the best nobles and the wisest commoners." The language of the citizenship tradition follows, with reference to the Swiss, who established such a government "after shaking off the yoke of the tyrants." Then, correctly introduced, we find the issue of citizen-soldiers versus the employment of mercenaries. However, here the author mistakenly condemns "Marciovelli" for wishing "everything to be done by foreign soldiers," but he correctly relates the issue to "the deliverance and liberty of the country."

Apart from this idiosyncratic "Discourse," the language of the Dutch revolt rarely sounds a literary note, let alone makes references to classical literature. But it is powerful, nevertheless, for it calls upon men to give their best for their country, and for their language and ways; it proposes compromise, even subordination, to a congenial foreigner if he will promise faithfully to preserve local liberties; time and again it bases itself on law and history in an effort to gain legitimacy. In a revolt for freedom and (Calvinist) salvation, the concept of citizen was not deep or natural enough to be widely used. Whenever citizen is used, it designates a townsmen, which usage, although the area was one with a long-established and large urban population, nevertheless would exclude all those of every class living on the land. This suggests that the impact of "classical republicanism" was not strong in this crucial period of Dutch history. Rather, traditional political and fiscal interests played the major role in energizing fighting instincts, along with powerful new religious beliefs, which provided another basis for unity against the lawful, but aggressive and Catholic, foreign ruler.[29]

For all its enthusiasm for Calvinism, the Netherlands never developed the tight link between confession and citizenship that came to characterize other states in early modern Europe, to say nothing of Europe's outposts everywhere. In the heyday of Dutch world importance, Jews, Catholics, and many varieties of Protestants in that country were permitted freedoms not allowed elsewhere. It was in the rest of Europe that religious conformity was demanded, not in the region in which religion had given so much strength to rebellious political forces. And in the rest of Europe, parenthetically, it was the cities that early provided the model for the state church that eventually developed everywhere—in Strasbourg, Geneva, and Zurich, for example. These were small cities with populations under twenty thousand and with citizen bodies much smaller than that. In many ways they were like the Italian cities of an earlier period, and the cities of ancient Greece and Rome.

In Central Europe, as in Italy, towns over the centuries had developed into moral and cultural, as well as territorial and political, entities. By the early sixteenth century, rulers in many cities had regained control of the clergy, integrating them into civic functions and forcing them to take oaths of citizenship and "submit to the jurisdiction of the city and pay taxes." Little distinction was made between the temporal and spiritual fortune of the community, which "stood as a unit before God."[30]

It is not startling that this situation should have continued into the 1520s and 1530s when, in so many little places, a reform party attacked the ruling clergy and proclaimed as truth some variant of Luther's new doctrines and practices. With the help of the elector of Saxony, Luther had instituted a state church in Wittenburg by the end of the 1520s, and a state-enforced system of education to nurture it. Zwingli's organization of Zurich in the same period also retained the close mutual support of church and state. Soon Bucer in Strasbourg, Calvin in Geneva, and Henry VIII in England were doing the same thing. The medieval demand for law and structure founded upon religious orthodoxy was not wiped out when and where the canon law was rejected.

Both because of and despite the Reformation, the city remained throughout northern and central Europe what it had been ever since antiquity, the creator of a total religio-civic existence. If a pastor replaced a bishop, he remained the ultimate leader of a patterned life that wove together religious, political, architectural, festive, and educational elements. New Protestant leaders stepped into a local cultural situation that had been intensified during the long Middle Ages and used it to their advantage. They worked with humanists who understood history and language and with the lawyers who understood men. Calvin himself was trained in both the new humanistic studies and the law at Paris.

What this meant in the history of citizenship may be seen in the statements of a notable of the city of Geneva, Jean Balard, who, after a lifetime of service to his city in high public office, was interrogated by Geneva's prosecuting attorney at Christmas 1539. Balard was fifty-one at the time. He had followed the city through several stages of reform, had changed the obvious forms of his worship as his neighbors did, and had tried to keep his quiet peace. This was not his first interrogation. Now, when asked about his beliefs, he claimed to be "entirely ready to believe all the articles of faith that the whole city believes, and that he wished his body to be united with the body of the city, as a loyal citizen should do." The next day he admitted "he couldn't judge things which he didn't know or understand, but since it pleases the government that he say the Mass is evil, he will say the Mass is evil."[31]

Such confessions were made all over Europe as rulers coerced their subjects into religious conformity. They could not do otherwise in this century of war against the Moslem, Catholic, or Lutheran, as well as the Englishman, Spaniard, or Swede. Late in the previous century Ferdinand and Isabella had made the need for religious homogeneity the basis for politics and war when they expelled the Jews and Moors in the same decade. In an age when the religion of "the other" was viewed as a contagious disease, purity had to be preserved. One could not sleep peacefully at night or leave wife and child when he went to war if his neighbor was not his brother as they knelt together before their god. Such a view is, of course, independent of religious belief. It was held by Catholics and Protestant both. If Calvin's *Institutes* set forth the theoretical basis for one kind of theocracy, Richard Hooker's *The Laws of Ecclesiastical Polity* argued the same position against Calvinists as well as Catholics on behalf of the state church of England.

Although written to defend his own church, Hooker's words explain the theory of every state church that has ever existed; published between 1593 and his death in 1600, they contribute quite clearly to the theory of citizenship of his age. Man needs the association of other human beings; he also needs law, in a variety of senses, to enjoin upon him what is good, to instruct him in his duties as a member of a polity. And he needs religion, for just as he is a member of a polity, he is also a member "of a supernatural society, which society we call the Church." Life in these two communities is a single life and is made easier by our understanding of their relationship. "So natural is the union of religion with justice," Hooker writes, "that we may boldly assert that there is neither where there are not both. For how should they be unfeignedly just, whom religion does not cause to be such; or the religious, who are not proved such by their just actions? . . . Seeing therefore that the safety of all estates appeareth to depend upon religion, that religion sincerely loved perfecteth men's abilities to perform all kinds of virtuous services in the commonwealth . . . we have the reasons why . . . all well ordered commonwealths should love her as their chiefest stay."[32]

In this construction, the good citizen is an activist for God's cause within the laws of his community. Accepting this, Hooker employs Aristotelian definitions of society from Aquinas and, especially, Marsilius of Padua. He also accepts from the pre-Reformation tradition the importance of religious authority in teaching man what it is to do good. The smooth function of a structured society is based upon the ability of religion to persuade men to higher purposes, such as the honest performance of daily and governmental tasks. Without a common morality imprinted upon young minds by a single authoritative church, society can not be safe, by which he means secure in the structure of class and political relationships God meant to prevail. In the early seventeenth century, every Sunday morning, in every one of the sixteen thousand parishes of England, young Englishmen of every class gathered in church, each to learn what befitted him in his station. Whatever that station, the Church taught responsible and loyal work within the royal law, and the attitudes of deference and toward responsibility that one's condition in life entailed.[33]

Reformation theology did more than provide a tough, aggressive theory for the unification of political and religious orthodoxy into a single citizenship. It gave more of an approbation to secular life itself than it had ever received before, thus adding to the dignity conferred on secular existence somewhat earlier by civic humanism and medieval Aristotelianism. It accomplished this by reducing the value accorded the clerical estate; Luther's doctrine of the priesthood of all believers, which was the cutting theory here, was adopted by all the reformers and instantly translated into reality. Across Europe monks and nuns were driven into the world as their vast resources were divided among the laity. This devaluation of the clergy was in effect a massive reordering of traditional society, a leveling that in social theory reduced the clergy to the level of others in the community.

In the key cities of the Reformation, therefore—Geneva and Strasbourg, for example—the clergy became citizens. The dignity derived from their function guaranteed entrance into the citizen body, for which both status and wealth continued to be required. Generally they were accepted into the secular community regardless of any special ability to serve in this or that public office. They accepted an obligation to "pledge allegiance to their cities, pay certain taxes, and become completely subject to the civil law code." What is more, not only did they do this, they praised civic life. After switching to the Reform, Wolfgang Capitio, a leading Hebraist, Catholic theologian, and canon lawyer in Strasbourg, wrote two treaties on clerical citizenship, advocating support of the city that "encloses and protects us," while attacking those clergy who would depend on others in the community to take care of them. He found support for this position in Romans 13 and 1 Peter 2, where Christians are enjoined "to be subject to the governing authorities."[34]

One result of these developments was the introduction of a relatively large number of competent persons into the citizen body, people aware of a formal obligation to support the community. Another was the addition of a new dimension of equality into the body social. Every rank of noble continued to exist, as did hierarchies of burghers in every town, but in Protestant Europe the clergy were no longer regarded as a qualitatively superior caste, protected by a special law. In many areas Protestant clergy ruled behind the scenes, creating de facto theocracies by their moral force and interpretative skill, but that is not the point. The development of equality in Western society is not just a matter of theories, or even laws; it is also the creation in fact of ever larger and more frequently overlapping pools or categories of individuals who are equal to each other in some important respect. One of the long-range influences of Protestantism, for all its fragmentation effect, was to bring clergy to the level of everyman, in this way denying the possibility of inherent distinctiveness based upon occupation, and specifically upon clerical occupation.

In the Middle Ages and the Renaissance we know where we are with the word *civis*. In the Middle Ages the word derived its meaning and usage from Roman law and history and from constant employment in municipal docu-ments, especially in Italy. Its usage might or might not have overtones of republicanism associated with a specific period in Roman history, though frequently it did. It evoked some form of nonprincely government, the activ-ist ethic of Cicero—in general, the kind of government by a responsible elite that was progressively transformed under the Empire.

During the Renaissance, in Italy as well as elsewhere, republican govern-ments were replaced by princely ones, yet the culture of antiquity was such a powerful influence that the theory and exercise of citizenship was perhaps enhanced. Indeed, it received its most brilliant statement by a theorist who himself was pushed to the political sidelines by the return to authority of a princely house. Machiavelli and the Venetians of his generation created pow-erful images that penetrated north, where, if they did not persuade great kings and feudatories to change the system, they at least persuaded their followers that training in civic virtue and skills serviceable to the prince constituted a worthy life. Classical models of action appeared in vernacular versions that invited following; unfortunately, ancient literature provided the example of tyrannicide as well as thoughtful service to the monarch. Thus, in vernacular representations of citizenship in this period there is always a ten-sion, an ambivalence.

Over the sixteenth century the concept of subject tends to drive out the word and concept of citizen. "Citizen" gets lost within the more general "subject," which, after all, had a classical history too, and which had long been confused with, and assimilated to, "citizen," as we have seen. Also, the term "people" pushes forward; like "subject," it was amenable for use with a large population and was unencumbered with the notion of urban dweller, or "burgher," which always was a weight or limitation that "citizen" bore, espe-

cially north of the Alps. And like "citizen," "people" had an intimate association with the Romans as well as with the Hebrews, whose language and
history was a matter of increasing interest even before the Protestant outpouring of theology and biblical scholarship. We are talking now of the words
that come into the mind of a writer as he chooses terms of greater or lesser
association. None of these words had a fixed meaning in this period. We can
never be sure that a writer restricts his use of a word to one meaning in one
context. One must always try to judge meanings by noting the recurring
contexts in which the key words appear. Time and again an author of the
period will upbraid his contemporaries for their imprecision, as did Bodin
with his complaint about five hundred meanings of the word "citizen." But
Bodin's view of the citizen as political person surely would have been meaningful and acceptable to most. This is the sense that was to have the longest
history and provide one basis for the second citizenship.

The Reformation had its own special impact on citizenship. Probably its
greatest contribution to the tradition was the approval most theologians gave
to activism; now entrance into community affairs had divine approval, as,
under certain limited circumstances, did citizen resistance to tyrants. City life
itself gained value as Protestant theologians emphasized history as authority,
pointing to the role of cities in history and the legitimacy of all those offices,
those minor magistracies, that cities depend upon to work. In effect, a whole
political class was dignified. Finally, as a result of the hostility loosed into
Europe and the world by religious warfare, religious conformity became a
new mark of citizen identity and attachment. In Catholic days the city and the
saint were as one in the citizen's prayers. There was no competition for
religious devotion except, perhaps, from a rival saint. Now, in a divided
Europe, religious commitment was a positive assertion, if not of deep belief,
at least of a personal commitment to fight for the faith of one's country or
town.

8

CITIZENSHIP UNDER THE

IMPACT OF REVOLUTION

Not necessarily connected either to monarchy or republicanism, by the seventeenth century citizenship had become an integral concept and institution of European politics. In the sixteenth century Machiavelli and Bodin had contributed important new ideas to the tradition, the former writing out of his Italian culture, experiences, and hopes, the latter out of his reaction to life in France during the religious civil war. Both were influenced by humanist studies and by medieval Roman law analyses which Renaissance jurists continued to read and teach, the doctrines of which had become commonplaces of political thinking—the concept of the public welfare, for example. Now, in the age of Stuarts and Bourbons and countless other dynasties, not only did citizenship survive, it commanded new attention.

Although absolutist in theory and institutional ambition, Europe was often revolutionary in fact. In France, Spain, and, above all, in England, unstable conditions, not for the first or last time in European history, provoked an outpouring of political thought. In that thinking, and with important consequences for the century or so before the American and French revolutions, citizenship was radicalized and amplified. That is, it became associated and identified with a republicanism that was not the constitutional result of historical events in a given city, but rather a program espousing antimonarchical action in the hope of a resulting change of regime. There were also struggles over religious freedom. In all of these clashes, words like rights and liberties, if not liberty, were consciously used. The legacy of Machiavelli and the *Discourses* and of Hotman and the *Vindiciae* was received and understood.

However one defined the issues, there was a place in the argument for heroic individual behavior justifiable in moral terms. There was need too for an extended discussion of human behavior in terms not only of the newly expanded range of Christianity, but also of the wider range of human existence revealed to educated Europeans by the many travelers who had returned from Asia, Africa, and the New World with descriptions of other societies.

This means that the language of citizenship continues to change in the course of the seventeenth and eighteenth centuries. It expands beyond the medieval legalistic interest in status that brought specific privilege. It goes beyond humanist interest in the virtue one achieves in behavior modeled after that of ancient heroes. In a sense, these two traditional concerns or focuses come together in discussions which transcend the citizen or the subject, or even the people, and come down on the nature of man. The natural law writers of the seventeenth century do this, as do both Hobbes and Locke. To determine the nature of society they must return to a state of nature in which the human being is still without social and political characteristics.

At the beginning of the seventeenth century, Europe was organized much as it had been for centuries and was to remain until the early nineteenth century, by which time the French, Industrial, and Scientific revolutions were beginning to show their effects. Almost everyone lived under a king or feudal lord, a prince whose political subject he was, and coreligionist too. Representative bodies continued to exist all over Europe, but with rare exceptions, England being the most notable, their members did not decide policy, let alone run the government. Even in small states, administration increasingly was in the hands of trained bureaucrats, men devoted to raising armies and monies for the central authority. Justice also was in the hands of the state, actually of a class of men trained in the law and its obligation to justice, but, like those of the administrative class, also tied to the executive.

Everywhere city governments were oligarchic. Not everyone who lived in a town was a member of the political community in terms of participating in the law-making process and serving in public office. Sometimes a property qualification, sometimes a social qualification—membership in a group of ancient families or a guild, for example—was prerequisite for full civic activity. Moreover, over the course of time these various groupings had won charters of identity or incorporation from some authority; hence the reality of their dominance was based not only on social and economic fact, but on legal paper as well. Generally these municipal governments acted, if not always in harmony with the ruling authority, at least in general sympathy with the political theory on which both regimes were based. Authority was divinely granted. Only in exceptional circumstances, variously and unclearly defined, might revolt be sanctioned. In Protestant as well as Catholic communities, authority flowed down and life was rigorously ordered. A theory based on religion guaranteed every existing institution.

What has been sketched is, of course, the Old Regime that started tumbling down in France, at least, in 1789. If this structure stood relatively firm for another 175 years or so, it is also the case that it inspired growing criticism. Some criticism came from religionists, some from the new social scientists in the fields of law and human relations. The latter found the methods of the new natural science an invitation to develop similar promising forms of analysis. Moreover, in addition to new arguments for resistance and revolt based on religious obligation, there were traditional medieval theories of contract and legitimate feudal defiance, as well as ancient arguments in support of tyrannicide and popular sovereignty. By the early seventeenth century, thanks to the work of generations of humanist scholars, just about every classical text was available that might support current argumentation and action. In England, France, Holland, and Catalonia, rebellions took place against established governments; each of these spawned justifications in which the rights of people were mentioned, and all these entered the growing armory of such rationales for rebellion available throughout the Continent.

NATURAL LAW THEORY

One of the important and ultimately influential of the new intellectual developments was the revival of a natural law theory, which now was more emancipated from theology than it had been for a millennium. The natural law theorists, still lawyers as many had been in the Middle Ages, sought to discover the keys to human action in terms of temporal and logical priority. Optimistically, they relied on right reason as their basic tool and posited a congruence between the structure of right reason and nature itself. And, although this arrangement was God's work, they managed to edge him out of the picture as not being responsible for the human consequences of his work. As Grotius (1583–1645) wrote in *On the Law of War and Peace*, "The law of nature is a dictate of right reason, which points out that an act, according as it is or is not in conformity with rational nature, has in it a quality of moral baseness or moral necessity; and that, in consequence, such an act is either forbidden or enjoined by the author of nature, God."[1] And in the Prolegomena to the same work, we read: "What we have been saying would have a degree of validity even if we should concede that which cannot be conceded without the utmost wickedness, that there is no God, or that the affairs of men are of no concern to Him."[2]

In brief, natural law tended to subsume the Church (and religion) within itself, subjecting the institution to conventional study in terms of growth and relationships to other institutions. Once emancipated from Roman law and scripture, natural law is "based on pure *ratio*," or at least attempts to be. The province of professors, it nevertheless influenced many writers in the seventeenth and eighteenth centuries whose ideas were eventually to intrude into the salons of the prerevolutionary generations: not just jurists like Grotius and Pufendorf, relatively technical if influential, but Burlamaqui, Vattel, Hobbes, Spinoza, and Locke.[3]

One of the earliest of the natural law jurists was Johannes Althusius (1557–1638), whom some now hail as one of the most important constitutionalist thinkers of the age. His principal contribution to political thought was a theory of associations, which sought to deduce the principles of human aggregation. He saw the "State as the community organized for cooperation toward the attainment of common purposes."[4] Every association within the state—the family, the city—had its place and role in the larger grouping, the study of which was politics itself.

Given the importance of the individual in such a situation, Althusius early faces the issue of the active versus the contemplative life and strongly urges activism. He pictures a community of contributing, caring neighbors who join in many ways to facilitate their own and the community's interests. Social interaction and political maneuvering are part of the process of organized life, if that life is to be successful. The laws and culture of the community shape the individual into a member of the community, and if he contributes to it, it is because earlier it has contributed in an energizing way to his education, his civic identity. One of Althusius's principal interpreters saw him as an early theoretician of the twentieth-century corporatist state. One wonders if this is indeed the case; in any event, he was hardly an original thinker in this vein, for his thought on the relationship of the individual to the community was inspired not only by Aristotelian notions of the power of group life, and the basic theories and realities of the entire medieval period, but also by the nature of the society in which he worked. For more than forty years Althusius served as principal law officer and a statesman in the little north German town of Emden, one of those tightly organized and culturally modeled communities which were then the norm in European urban life.

For Althusius, citizen is essentially a social and political word: social in that the individual becomes a citizen when he moves out of the world of purely family relations into contact with other people with whom he must deal in order to live, and political in that he now must concern himself with superfamilial affairs if both the family and his *collegium*, his unit of more than three persons, are to prosper. In fact, politics presupposes the existence of many *collegia*, all of which are part of the higher symbiosis, the community, called still the *civitas*.

What makes a citizen is his membership in and service to the community. Althusius makes learned reference to citizenship among the Hebrews, Greeks, and Romans; he is aware, given his legal training, of the extensive medieval discussion of the concept, and of the material and legal benefits of the institution. But his interest primarily is structural, philosophical. He distinguishes the citizen from the foreigner, the alien, and the slave, who must "adapt themselves . . . to the customs of the place and city where they live in order that they may not be a scandal to others."[5] The essential mark of the citizen is his full membership in the political order (*politeuma*) and enjoyment of all of the rights and benefits of the city whose laws and government he recognizes. Such people are the ultimate constituents of the state, the true repositories of its sovereignty. They take an oath to support their political order and elect their leader, who rules with their consent. Once the state (*civitas*) has its schedule of corporations, its citizens, leaders, and political forms, what we would call in sum its operating constitution, then, even though it may lose individual members, it survives. "It is said to be immortal."[6]

What Althusius has done, in the name of natural law, is take the long tradition of citizenship, all the elements of which he is aware of at one level or another—and he is very aware of the late medieval literature on benefits and their acquisition—and use it in a defense of ultimate popular sovereignty. Bodin had developed a theory to exalt the monarch as the bearer of sovereignty; Althusius, out of his historical, legal, small-town, and Calvinist backgrounds, makes the consent of the active people, the citizens, in their search for the public welfare, the irreducible element in politics. Yet we must remember, as Gierke does, that for all this analysis out of nature, the world is subject to a "divine order."[7]

Two other natural theorists of the seventeenth century, Grotius and Pufendorf (1632–94), did not allocate the people this much of a stake in government, but they did develop ideals of civic performance that made their citizens perform as Althusius's were supposed to. Long after he discusses "the common duties of Mankind," Pufendorf addresses citizenship in his chapter "On the impelling cause for the establishment of a state" and in his final chapter, "On the duties of citizens."[8]

Like Althusius, Pufendorf is aware of the technical, definitional side of citizenship. But what he is interested in is the moral. Man is able to get most of what he needs in "those little first societies," but when he wants true justice and protection, and a chance to act as "a truly political animal," then he establishes one of those "great societies which go by the names of states." Once in a state, the citizen faces a struggle between the forces within him favoring self-interest and those "general duties . . . of respect, loyalty, and obedience," in deference to which he has "nothing dearer than its welfare and safety," and for which he will "offer his life, property, and fortunes freely." Besides these general obligations, every citizen has particular duties, which in effect define honest performance of his occupation; specifically mentioned are the teacher, jurist, soldier, fiscal official, each of whom contributes in a basic way to the public welfare.

Pufendorf knows that subjects and citizens are frequently confused in the literature of his day, and that not every citizen is a good citizen. His interest is in the latter because it is as a good citizen that one fulfills the demand upon his existence to be a "truly political animal." When a person "promptly obeys . . . strives with all his might for the public good, and willingly subordinates thereto his private good," then he is truly human.[9] Here is the escalation of language that distinguishes political thought from this period on. The social theorist has become interested in behavior, ultimate behavior, which is necessary, definitional, primordial. The interest and depth pass beyond Aristotle's. Two searches proceed together now: one for the first principles of human conduct, the other for the circumstances of the first moment of human organization. Both were carried on largely in the head of the principal investigator, and both started from some original assumption from which all else was deduced.

The new language of politics transcends the old. It is interested in more than the specific rights so central to the jurisconsults of the Middle Ages; its interest extends even to developing the virtues defined in both the classical and Judeo-Christian traditions. Its focus is man qua man, the human being, pure and without culture—now that the multiplicity of cultures known to be in the world frees the theorist from the limitations of a European or Christian myopia. This freedom allows focus on the natural being as he must have been at the dawn of history, man with his basic faculties and wants, at the moment he first saw the need for society, community. This man without history—as yet—will eventually develop nationality, language, religion, law, governing institutions, and all those human qualities, good and bad, that moralists have always discussed.

Theorists eventually will bring all these phenomena under analysis. But they will also, from now on, develop theories of human behavior, psychology, and choice as never before. And it is in this newly expanded literature that the concept of citizenship is developed in the 150 years or so before the French Revolution. The reason for this deepening of thought about man is not just a heightened awareness about him as revealed in the great imaginative literature of the Renaissance, in Shakespeare, for example, which itself is a significant result of deeper and expanded study of the ancients; it is also in the thought of the natural law school, which went beyond considerations of civil and public law to an examination of the human condition. Citizenship in this age before the Revolution may continue, in the old Europe of small cities and city-states, to be concerned with privilege and exclusion in economic and political affairs. But in the new international world of moral science it starts to emphasize the process of individual living in relation to the process of state formation, the development of the individual psyche as well as morality. Citizenship as a subject is now tied to the beginnings of psychology as an area of thought, to questioning about "*tabula rasa*, interest, *amor propre*."[10]

Perhaps this partial shift from politics to something else may help to explain, in part, the survival of citizenship as a concept still to be reckoned with in an aristocratic and monarchical epoch. In this literature, citizenship was not necessarily offered as a real alternative to subjectship, yet it always had to be considered and therefore remembered as linked to one form of political regime, republicanism, that had served great historic states in the past and had received consideration, if not approbation, from some of the greatest political thinkers. Moreover, it called for an active life in the form of service to one's country and thus did not break with either the current view of the aristocracy as a committed service class or that traditional view of man as a social and political animal who reached excellence in action. In all the diplomacy, state growth, and war of the early modern period, rulers continued to need men whose patriotism as well as skill could be depended on.

It survived too—always this problem of survival confronts us—because of its antidemocratic nature, or, if that is too strong, its compatibility with the aristocratic nature of the Old Regime. In this age of nobles and oligarchic minorities, citizenship fit in very well as a mechanism of discrimination. It fit because it possessed tendencies which potentially could work in opposite directions; both were developing in the early modern period: individualism and, for want of a better word, corporatism. Citizenship was compatible with individualism since it was still seen as a specific right or one of a collection of privileges that belonged to this man and not that one. Differentiation was its active quality. It enhanced the corporate body, the city or the community of the realm, because it stressed a love for and dependence upon the community for everything: language, religion, history, every basis for one's identity. Citizenship survived also because men called citizens in local constitutional documents continued to act as citizens everywhere, in little local oligarchies and bureaucracies, in historic regions where estates functioned even if they did not flourish, and even in kingdoms—England, for example, where citizens voted for Parliament during the reigns of James I and Charles I.

THE ENGLISH REVOLUTION

It is clear that under the early Stuarts large numbers of Englishmen were able to satisfy property qualifications and vote in parliamentary elections. The "most widespread" of the urban franchises before 1640 was the freeman franchise; this "included the greater part of a town's adult male inhabitants in some instances, and probably verging on a half of them in many more."[11] On the eve of the civil war at least two hundred thousand participated in parliamentary contests. What may be even more important is that the entire kingdom experienced electoral politics, which even in those days meant discussion of the issues, appeals to voters—in a word, politicking.[12] To be sure, most of these voters were hardly educated and therefore were unaware that their political activity was dignified by a rationale extending back to Plato and Aristotle. But, since the educated class was the propertied class, it is probable that at least a number of the voters were at some level aware of the republican tradition. Spartan or Roman citizens were not necessarily their daily models, but many English political activists in the revolutionary period, men of every political and religious persuasion, were aware of the main currents of republican thought.[13] Education for many of them had included not only Cicero and Plutarch, but also manuals like that of Sir Thomas Elyot, which instructed young and aspiring members of the upper classes on the why as well as the how of advancement in the monarch's service. Moreover, in governing circles, Machiavelli was also known, as was the success of Venice.[14]

It is against this background of mid-century political thinking and activity that we examine the role of civic humanism in a large monarchy. By this time, part of that doctrine, the active life, had been accepted and assimilated into the normal existence of Europeans. Protestantism had assisted in this transformation in those parts of Europe in which an ostensible medieval Catholic passivity had not yet been replaced by Renaissance Catholic acquisitiveness. The other part, however, republicanism, did not receive an immediate and easy reception. Tudor and Stuart theory and monarchy were too strong to allow much development of republican doctrine. It took the union of republicanism with religious inspiration at a time of civil war to loose into the world ideas that had any expectation of acceptance or realization.

Among the most radical ideas that came out of the English Revolution were those of the Levellers, religious dissidents out of the cities, especially London. Though they did not call for social and economic leveling, their social program was radical enough in its insistence on Christian justice in economic dealings to find the movement support. Between 1646 and 1649, in a series of ever more precisely worded demands and petitions addressed to Parliament, the Levellers announced a democratic program. Among other things, they called for popular election of a parliament of three hundred based on a reasonable reapportionment of the entire country, and for the replacement of royal and aristocratic authority with that of Parliament. Citizen is just one of the resonant words they relied on. In addition, they spoke of, and in the name of, "Free-commoners," "the people," and "poor tradesmen," and as this last self-description suggests, a message of social justice was always part of their thrust and appeal. They saw themselves as "part of the whole nation," for whose benefit they constantly risked imprisonment and indifference even as they labored to refine their proposals in a rapidly changing political situation.[15]

Ineffectual in their own time, the Levellers are important in anticipating many of the aspirations that stirred Americans and Frenchmen to action almost 150 years later. They spoke against privilege, especially legal privilege, which would give the nobility or rich city merchants unfair economic advantage. They cried out against any "Tenure, Grant, Charter, Patent, Degree, or

Birth," a sequence of terms that any medieval jurist would easily have dealt with.[16] If they recognized that the economic individualism of the times was pitting man against man, they also recognized that in such a war each man must stand armed against all others.

Finally, they recognized the power of propaganda. Over the few years in which they functioned as something of a political party, they printed many manifestos and distributed them throughout the army and the towns. Thus they, and the other pamphleteers of the revolutionary period who contributed to the publication of literally thousands of works in which religion and politics were interwoven, kept a kind of republicanism alive, a species of antimonarchism that was without the clear advocacy of a republican form of government. Charles I was not yet beheaded. The Levellers were more interested in a reformed and responsive Parliament, a restricted aristocracy, and a responsible, as opposed to tyrannical, king than they were in replacing a regime of kingship with something else. However, one wonders whether the "tens of thousands" who turned out to hear them made these discriminations.[17] Their emphasis on individual rights and the sovereignty of the people, tied to biblically inspired appeals for social and economic justice, was the fundamental basis for their momentary impact.

The period of the English Civil War and Interregnum is too long and complex to be treated in terms of the Levellers alone. For all their vitality and originality in the presentation of republican ideas, they did not last very long or leave a solid heritage. Given their class and education, their treatment of issues was not in conventional terms, which is one reason they did not relate to the grand line of discussion that Machiavelli had put together a century and more earlier. Although they spoke of suffrage and liberty and were themselves soldiers, many of them, and influential in the army, the Levellers did not speak either to the issue of corruption or to the association of "republican liberty and a popular army which we have found as a standard theme in Florentine thought." That was the accomplishment of an officer, Colonel Nathaniel Rich, and later of Marchamount Nedham, the journalist and pamphleteer who, it is said, created "the first sustained English exposition of republican democracy in classical and Machiavellian terms."[18]

Given the facts of revolution and regicide in a country which for almost two hundred years had thrived on a strengthened monarchy, it is not surprising that all sorts of new political programs were advocated, and that some of these necessarily incorporated new human psychologies. We are almost a century beyond Montaigne, half a century and even less beyond Shakespeare and Bacon. As noted, the colonies had been furnishing challenges to the European self-image since 1492, and if Africa be included, long before that. And for almost all of that time, new religious ideas stretching across a great spectrum had forced new appreciations of human potentiality.

No wonder then that a variety of paradigms were at work in England at mid-century through which theorists sought to develop a right constitution for England on the basis of a new view of the individual. The "articulate citizen of the Renaissance" by now had been assimilated to the progenitors of the new social science, and also there were churchmen and public servants in whose books, tracts, and sermons religion, history, formal analysis, and apocalyptic vision all came together in various attempts to find the basis for organized life, and ultimately a solution to the problem of their country's chaos, its instability. What is clear is that the twenty-year period of the constitutional crisis produced several theories in which some version of citizenship appeared. The great figures of English political thought all spoke to the matter and amplified the concept of citizen.

This is true even of Thomas Hobbes (1588–1679), who is almost always seen as the great defender of monarchs, as well as a foe of Aristotle and Cicero, whose political theories and defense of republicanism he thought so misleading to future generations. Hobbes, after all, as we have mentioned, was conscious enough of the history of citizenship to have entitled one of his analyses of the human condition *De Cive*, even if by *cive* he meant a royal subject.

To be sure, Hobbes places the sovereign upon an unassailable foundation, the grant of authority to him by men who desire and need his executive authority. But at the same time he retains for all those men, the subjects of the sovereign, very important rights. They retain the right to life, control over property and over family, in other words, control over areas essential to function as a human being. According to a recent interpreter of Hobbes, these constitute "a sphere of natural law or Fundamental law of mankind outside the public sphere or sphere of positive law."[19] In discussing these areas of legitimate exercise of personal freedom, Hobbes is not interested in the moral development of the person through public service, although he does assume the existence of assemblies and, presumably, accepts the activity of those who vote for them and serve in them. Rather, he is attempting to define spheres of jurisdiction in which behavior proper to ruler and ruled may be carried out. The goal is protection for the individual consistent with the safety of the community, so that his "delightful life" based on the secure enjoyment of his property is maintained. Within this framework, liberty for Hobbes's citizen reminds one of that of the medieval Christian believer. His liberty to live and work within the commonwealth is analogous to the freedom of the good Christian to follow as completely as possible the prescribed rules of the Church.[20] Hobbes, then, does not wipe out the individual. He assures, rather, the existence of the commonwealth as a precondition for individual survival and possible personal success. Within the security provided by the sovereign a "civil Person" now is free to choose and act in his own best interest. What is more, the very existence of an ordered commonwealth results first from the existence, before the commonwealth comes into being, of individuals, each with his senses, needs, will, and mind, and then from the result of a multitude of individual acts of will that generate the commonwealth, call it into being. In his editor's words, "The natural man is the stuff of society," which is to emphasize that for Hobbes the individual human being is the irreducible unit upon which his entire structure of politics is built.

What gives Hobbes such power and importance in later generations is the depth and the seriousness of his analysis, taken together with the energy of his style. We are back, with him, to first principles, to absolute uncomplicated beginnings, unconstrained by empirical data, much as we were with Plato. We are back to the original nature and condition of man, and to the great problems he faces in the world—but without the help of the saints. Hobbes may have been orthodox, but his religion stays outside his system, or, in another sense, is only a part of the entire structure that assures the proper conditions for the enjoyment of family and property. His focus is on individual man reacting to the world and making those decisions that will better his place in the world on the basis of personal judgment. Since Hobbes was widely read, such views became even more influential in the century after his death.

The centering of the individual contributes to the new definition of citizenship shaping up in the mid-seventeenth century. The citizen is more than a bundle of Roman law definitions and specific rights. He is more than a moral agent guided by classical pagan as well as Christian models to the performance of virtue. Now he is defined in physical-psychological terms in a rationally ordered universe in which he must necessarily play certain roles, one of which is participation in public life.

Although both the Levellers and Hobbes were familiar with citizenship and in some way worked it into their plans or theories, neither spent time analyzing the concept, and neither emphasized the purely republican side of citizenship as played out in previous history. One English thinker who did both was George Lawson (d. 1678), a divine whose political thought has recently been linked to that of Marsilius of Padua and, looking in the other direction, John Locke. Lawson's *Politica Sacra et Civilis* was published in 1660, that is, at the end of a generation of civil war and continued civil and religious crisis. Like the *Leviathan*, it can be taken as a response to the problem of order.

It also may be seen as a contrast with Hobbes, whose work Lawson severely criticized. Whereas Hobbes begins with man in some absolute existential sense, Lawson demonstrates his links to the entire medieval Romano-canonical tradition by developing a taxonomy of citizenship in the fashion of medieval lawyers and of Marsilius, with whose own schematization it has been compared.[21] Also, Lawson's ecclesiology reminds us of traditional medieval views in which the secular world is embraced within the religious, there being no essential difference between the forms and goals of government of the two. This must be said, lest in our desire to find modernity and democracy in the seventeenth century we ascribe thoughts to Lawson (or even the Levellers) unthinkable at that time. For Lawson, God is the source of power in and of government, and men are first Christians and then political beings.[22]

These cautions noted, however, we can perceive a strain of republicanism in Lawson. After all, if he relies on Marsilius, he relies on a most outspoken medieval exponent of constitutional and representative government, one whose basic familiarity was with city-states ruled by citizens elected by their fellows to both council membership and executive office. And if he is compared to the lawyers, it is to those familiar not only with the doctrines of Roman law, but also with the assumptions of ancient moral and political life. This suggests that Lawson's republicanism skips over that of the civic humanists more immediately behind him and demonstrates an affinity with the lively citizen governments of medieval Mediterranean society. Citizens are divided the usual ways into many categories; they have a vote if they fulfill property and other qualifications; voting follows status and is not based upon a principle of equality; and the commonwealth is based upon a theoretical harmony among "fellow citizens."[23]

Since his aim in the *Politica* is to bring reason to bear on the relations between church and state at a moment of great trouble, Lawson's tone is quiet and analytical. Before the commonwealth came the community, which was the first form of human organization and was based upon property, personal liberty, and equality. Its members, called citizens, are, so to speak, bare humans, with basic responsibilities toward family and each other. Community exists when human beings first socialize; eventually these form a commonwealth through the adoption of some constitutional device. At this moment the citizen adds subjectship to his being and acknowledges his membership in the new community by the recognition of its laws and institutions. Whether Lawson retains a right of resistance is a matter of some dispute among modern authorities; what is certain is his demand for just cause. Given just cause, the citizens may act; they are the political voice or side of the community.

Lawson's citizenry forms a kind of logical construct: citizens preexist community and bring it into being, and they continue to exist once community has developed into commonwealth. Once this has been established, with a parliament as its law-making body, both the citizens and the monarch are subject to the law. Lawson accepts a constitutional monarch who is not to be "free from the obligations of the natural and positive Lawes of God in force." But his fundamental belief is that "there can be no orderly or lasting Government without consent tacit or express of the people: for men must be governed as natural and free, for such they are as men." Here is a resonance of the natural law thinking of the age, but without the sustained psychological interest of Hobbes.[24]

In sum, he seems to accept the political fact of monarchy and subjects; when he makes the monarchy a community, he makes its citizens something of a higher state, justifying their action on the basis of history and law. Thus, one is a subject, but his activities are those of a citizen, and what he is as a moral being is determined by those citizen activities. When he votes, serves, works in a variety of ways for the public benefit, he is properly a citizen.[25]

For all his medievalism and constitutionalism, which were intellectually fashionable in the mid-seventeenth century, Lawson seems not to have entered the mainstream of English political thought. But James Harrington

(1611–77) did, and from his death in 1677 until the end of the eighteenth century his ideas were well known. James Otis and John Adams praised his thought, and in 1783 the president of Yale College observed with pleasure that the New England states had "realized the capital ideas of Harrington's *Oceana*."[26] He "now emerges as a seminal thinker, transforming a great European tradition of thought and enabling it to contribute to the ideologies of the emergent western world of the eighteenth century. . . . his thought ruralized and anglicized the classical republicanism of late Renaissance Florence and made it available for transmutation into an Atlantic republican tradition in the eighteenth century."[27]

That is one way to read Harrington. Another is to focus upon the institutional emphasis in his work, for, indeed, one struggles hard to find in the *Oceana* and other political writings the case for an Anglicized civic humanism that many have claimed is there.[28] Harrington does advocate the "rotation" of men in office, but more to avoid the perpetuation in power of a man or family, as was commonplace in the constitutions of the medieval Italian city-states, than to distribute among many the opportunity to gain virtue. Likewise, he advocates a citizen army and devotes many pages to its organization, but with an eye to military success rather than the moral enhancement of the citizen. And he establishes a necessary relationship between landowning and military service that would have limited the numbers of active citizens. He certainly did not envision the army as the instrument of a mass popular education for and conversion to virtue.[29]

Indeed, the search for virtue and the active fear of corruption that are so strong in Machiavelli do not figure in Harrington's constitution. His opposition to monarchy and confidence in the possibility of a "republican alternative" lead to an elaborate institutional structure that, rather than guarantee "the release of personal virtue through civil participation," makes it difficult, if not unnecessary, for the citizen to choose and act virtuously. Moreover, the many devices of his government would have handled the problem of corruption so early as to deny the citizen any occasion for the true exercise of his will. If, on the one hand, Harrington extended the limits of his citizenship beyond those proposed by the Levellers and included as citizens even Royalists and recognized opponents of the republic, on the other, he left both dangerous and loyal citizens little freedom to exercise their judgment on behalf of the community. There is no grand Machiavellian vision here, one which would have relied on the individual characters and actions of many thousands, but rather the cautious design of an enormous and well-wrought political edifice by a framer who had real hopes for its eventual construction.[30]

Surely these were the "capital ideas" which Ezra Stiles had in mind in 1783, and which had been assimilated by several generations of constitutionalist reformers in Europe and America during the eighteenth century. If Harrington did not subscribe to late-Renaissance classical republicanism, or at least emphasize and synthesize its components into a mid-seventeenth-century program, he was influenced by the same Polybian uneasiness that had inspired Machiavelli. Both searched for the eternal laws of politics that would assure tranquility and stability in a dynamic world all too prone to systemic failure, in a word, corruption.

"In the air" is an old but still useful concept which probably applies to the currency of republican ideas and models in the eighteenth century. Harrington's schemes were surely influential. That his principles were many allowed followers to pick and choose in the armory of his ideas, which surely contributed to his popularity. And many of his republican sentiments as well as institutions made more and more sense as criticisms of the existing organization of society grew. For all these reasons, although it is less precise, but because it allows us to emphasize his total impact, perhaps we should speak not of Neo-Harringtonian thought, but of a Popular Harringtonianism.

If there are several Harringtons, there are also several John Lockes, and not one of them is in the mainline tradition of republican citizenship. Locke is primarily interested in property and government. Yet, in a work that is not as familiar to us as it was to people all over Europe in the eighteenth century, his *Some Thoughts Concerning Education*, Locke does enter the history of citizenship and influence it enormously. Even if he does not mention as such personal development, virtue, corruption, moral excellence, cooperation with fellow citizens, concepts that tip us off to the presence of the civic humanist tradition, he does write out of a concern for the usefulness of the propertied gentry to their country. Necessarily, therefore, he devises an educational program which will train a youth to achievement in the world of affairs— financial, moral, and political. In this he stands in the tradition of the great moral philosophers from antiquity on down who saw education as the most important force shaping the community. Locke's Englishman had to cultivate his habits and his reason if he was to participate successfully in both politics and business. This is the citizen of the commercial republic of the eighteenth century devoted to wealth as well as virtue.

Locke was interested in the boy who would become a successful man.

Therefore he disagreed with traditional humanist educators over the nature of the curriculum, especially over the place in it of Greek and Latin literature. He is not after knowledge about philology and literature. Greek may be omitted and Latin studied only for what help it may bring to the effective presentation of issues and ideas. Basically there is a sturdy empirical quality to Locke's ideal curriculum, which will enable his pupils to get ahead in the real world. This is to say that his educational ideas are based in his psychology and epistemology; in this book not pure, but applied knowledge was his principal concern, plus the betterment of mankind, which goal could encompass an individual's acquisition of wealth and position. Or so he was understood during the eighteenth century. Both Condillac and Franklin drew from Locke, to say nothing of the generations of gentleman and merchant fathers who purchased the fifteen editions of *Some Thoughts* published between 1693 and 1800.

Locke's is not quite the traditional language of citizenship, yet it merits discussion here because it simultaneously shaped and reflected conduct, and because it carried its values so forcefully into the era of the emergent nation-state. Again and again in Locke we see the patriot determined to advance English purposes. Young men educated his way will contribute to the economic and political power of England in the world. In this Locke stands with the polytechnic thinkers of his age who see applied rationalism as the way to national strength in an ever more predatory international politics. Such a view meshes with so many literary and scientific developments over the previous two centuries; it enhanced the citizen as it enhanced man by seeing him as so complicated a being. Though he may have argued against including in his own curriculum the sophisticated new philosophy and psychology which was examining human knowledge and behavior with an ever closer scrutiny, Locke's writing manifests that modern learning and presents to us the up-to-date, properly trained activist. Born tabula rasa into a world of competitive individuals and institutions, that new man learns quickly that he must enter the political as well as economic world if he is to succeed. Such an attitude was just as compatible with the interests of England or America as it had been with those of Athens or Florence, or in the mid-eighteenth century, still, Geneva.[31]

During the Middle Ages, the citizenship tradition had emphasized the exchange of protection for taxes and service between the citizen and the community. Toward the end of that period, Aristotelian ideas on the need for community involvement as the basis for personal growth gave a new moral side to citizenship. In the Renaissance, Machiavelli and others continued in this emphasis; what mattered was virtue, not the potential for gain that citizen status brought. Now in Locke these two approaches were joined. But this should occasion little surprise given his concern that property be prerequisite for political participation, and that men of property alone should be trained to leadership. What Locke offered was a link between culture, prosperity, and power. In a sense he joins the medieval and modern worlds.

9

THE FINAL CITIZENSHIP

OF THE OLD REGIME

From the era of Louis XIV until the Revolution citizenship was not a major concern of French political theory. Some of the issues with which it had been associated during the Renaissance were no longer provocative or controversial —the legitimacy of the active life, for example. Now the big questions concerned, on the one hand, great public questions like constitutionalism and the relation of monarchs to parliaments and estates, and on the other, policy and technical matters such as questions of taxation and administrative efficiency. Although a few traditional moralists might debate the issue, and although there continued to be debate over the proper relationship between the private and public interest, there was no serious question any longer of Western civilization's dedication to the pursuit of wealth.

In the course of the century Montesquieu, Rousseau, and others did begin to discuss the difficulty of creating institutions and sentiments that would function over large areas. Yet, despite this incipient awareness of the way the world was going, citizenship, when it was discussed, remained tied to the ancient city-state. Only when the Revolution had overthrown the monarchy, thus creating in an instant a republic of some sort, did citizenship become important, and *citoyen* appear on everyone's lips. It might be said that there was very little preparation for the new republican reality other than consideration of citizenship virtues as derived in a traditional sense from the ancient world and mediated through Italian experience, especially as analyzed by Machiavelli and others of his generation.

When, in the early 1750s, Diderot wrote on citizenship in the *Encyclopédie*, he developed the institution in terms of the ancient city-state. Rousseau too, at least in some of his writings, looked backwards and saw in the idealized Alpine community he made of the Geneva of his youth the model of his moral society. For a variety of reasons the greatest social and political thinkers of the Enlightenment continued to think in terms of an intimate geography.[1] They were scarcely aware of what it would take to turn peasants into Frenchmen, or Englishmen, or Americans. If men hardly thought of themselves as Frenchmen until a century after the Revolution, it should not surprise us if even the most conscious political observers found it difficult to think of the implications of citizenship for a people and territory greater than that of the polis. And if it is true that "we shall never understand the *ancien régime*, whether in France or in England, if we do not realize that it believed itself to be modern, and even progressive," then it comes as no surprise to find that it had no need for a new political vocabulary, that is, the substitution of "citizen" for "subject." Moreover, to be up-to-date in that age would be to use the more abstract and all-inclusive "man" or "mankind." This constituted scientific modernity, while "citizen" smacked of the limited horizons of the polis, the ancient moral world that, being so aristocratic and exclusivistic, was not very serviceable to generalizing theories based upon states of nature and social contracts.[2]

Also, we should never forget how immediate the ancient world was to those generations of moderns nurtured on the ancients. Classical texts remained the basis of a proper education, despite the progress of Lockean and other advanced educational thought. Pericles, Lycurgus, Cato, and Cicero were as immediate to eighteenth-century readers as their neighbors and the authors of their own day. Classical geography was probably more familiar than that of distant provinces. We must remember too that most issues of politics were local, indeed, that most life still was local, which meant that the vocabulary of ancient politics, which was also local, still fit and made sense. "Citizen" was a word that Montesquieu and Rousseau could employ comfortably without wrenching themselves into completely new modes of thought.

France in the twenty years or so before the Revolution may be compared in a general way with England in the 1640s and 1650s: in both countries severe dislocations and malfunctions of the system gave rise to profound discussions about its viability. And just as the English Revolution produced an opening toward novel political ideas, so too did the French political, administrative, and economic crises. Indeed, one does not have to wait for the 1760s and 1770s. From the beginning of the century a variety of introspective critics had been busy; Boulainvilliers and Montesquieu gave way to Mably and

Rousseau, and in this passage toward republicanism, the concept of citizenship grew in centrality and importance. Moreover, the visions and the rhetoric became more compelling. The new society was to be based on civism, heroism, sacrifice, and equality.

In announcing this program Rousseau's language was the most powerful and persuasive of all and, moreover, was available in a variety of literary genres, both essays and novels, for example. But there were other art forms, too, that were critical of the Old Regime and at the same time gave a sense of the new world to be. Drama, opera, poetry all expressed new values while criticizing the court and its allied institutions. The plays of Beaumarchais, eventually translated into opera by Mozart, are perhaps the most familiar example of the rampant self-criticism of the cultural and political elite. But more important, perhaps, was the growth of a literate population throughout France as well as Paris, which enjoyed the new antiestablishment culture. After 1750, "readers were consuming as many as 3,500 editions of 150 different periodicals each year." And by 1780, "30 percent of salaried workers and 40 percent of servants possessed at least one book." Most of these were of pocketbook size and were, of course, in French.[3] The appetite for gossip and news grew rapidly during the critical year, 1789. Between January and May some 220 new titles were published, while during the entire year 184 new periodicals were established, and 335 more in 1790. Most of these were ephemeral, but at any given moment during the early months of the Revolution, hundreds were available. Add to this volume the twelve thousand pamphlets circulated between 1789 and 1799, and one gets a sense of the enormous currency of new political ideas.[4]

But already, by mid-century, *citoyen* was becoming one of the fashionable new words in the political vocabulary. It was regaining the fullness of meaning it had had for the civic humanists of the Renaissance and again carried the weight of both activism and republicanism. In citizen, critics found a word that possessed the authority of a classical origin and the inclusiveness of a familiar legal term, one that could again be bent to the needs of both the absolutist and republican traditions. Both Hobbes and Rousseau used citizen in coming to the same conclusion, albeit from different directions: an equality of submissiveness to the sovereign authority.[5]

Montesquieu (1689–1755) first published his *The Spirit of the Laws* in 1748, and again twenty-two times over the next seven years. He was already celebrated and widely read, given the earlier success of the *Persian Letters* and the *Considerations on the Causes of the Grandeur and Decadence of the Romans*.

In many ways Montesquieu reminds one of Machiavelli: both wrote sharp, clear, persuasive prose; both sought the fundamental laws of history, especially as these worked to assure Rome its longevity and great military success; and both believed that an expansionist military policy carried forward by a moral and aggressive people was the basis for such a success. Also, both thought in terms suggested by Plato, Aristotle, Cicero, Polybius, and other ancients and debated with them as well as with their contemporaries in terms of traditional analysis; and both switched back and forth between ancient and recent history to provide evidence for their theories and conclusions. Finally, both very largely determined the immediate future for discussions of republicanism: Machiavelli for the sixteenth and seventeenth centuries, and Montesquieu for the two generations leading up to the Revolution. Citizenship, with its many associations, was very much a part of those discussions.

Reading Montesquieu, one is sometimes startled to find himself in familiar territory, that of the little community, the republic of virtue, the small-scale society whose controlled and enveloping education based on traditional moral literature creates the passionate citizen of Athens or Sparta, or Florence or Venice. In these discussions Montesquieu seems comfortable in the vocabulary and moral atmosphere of the ancient city, the citizen's milieu. Since he was trained in Roman law and history, this should not surprise us. The historic and controversial issues come up accurately and naturally in the course of his extensive survey of world law and civilization: virtue and corruption, luxury and austerity, public versus private good. This is to say that in the forty years before the Revolution, which is also the period of Rousseau's rise to cult prominence, the immense popularity of Montesquieu added to the visibility of the citizen as a worthy political figure. Montesquieu was no republican, anything but, but in his vast work he reiterated the merits, functions, and emotional returns of citizenship and linked them to the achievements of the ancient world, which for many reasons and in many ways were then in vogue.

One such achievement was Rome, whose fall intrigued him. He believed its size and population made it ungovernable, that it was beyond the ability of the state to educate a vast, yet locally oriented, citizenry to patriotic sacrifice. This matter of scale was important for Montesquieu, who is aware of the kingdoms, federative republics, and empires of his Europe, and who attempts to fit them into those categories that had structured political discourse since the days of Aristotle and Polybius. He recognizes that size relates to the effectiveness of the modern state in governing and forces it to choose between despotism and new institutions based on representation. He saw the king-doms of his own day aggrandizing as had ancient Rome and worried about their ability to survive without recourse to despotic institutions. If Rome with its military and civic ethos was no model, then what was? Certainly not a large republic whose citizens would show little moderation in their reach for private, as opposed to public, gain.

The answer was England, as portrayed in the famous Book 11 of *The Spirit of the Laws*. In England he saw a large monarchy whose king was controlled by a constitution, and whose nobility and cities were long established institu-tions under law. Here was a population united by religion, history, and an effective, if limited, mode of participation in politics. Montesquieu is not so much interested in the moral perfection of the English citizen as he is in his liberty. Here, in effect, he approaches the situation of the citizen under the second citizenship, that of the large modern state. The citizen will vote for his representatives in Parliament; he will not necessarily participate in politics other than by voting. He accepts the judgment of his social and intellectual superiors. Moreover, modern England had what Rome had lacked, the theory and practice of representation, and its demands upon the citizen were not as great. It called less for virtue than for obedience to the laws and acceptance of the kingdom's traditions and institutions.

Montesquieu's citizen will thrive in such circumstances of liberty and se-curity, liberty being "a life lived under the rule of law." His citizen is like Locke's in that he contributes to his country's welfare by being law-abiding, by accepting the education that will make him dutiful and productive, a loving subject of his sovereign, by accepting the manners and customs of his national culture, and by contributing with his rationality and strength to the state. There is nothing heroic about this citizen. Trapped in life's obligations, he is virtuous while not living for virtue. Later in the century there will be a chance for that, but not in England.[6]

Of a somewhat later generation, but also a participant in the great self-analysis of France before the Revolution, was the early or proto-socialist, Gabriel de Mably (1709–85), widely read in his late days for his defense of the American Revolution. In Mably we have a French Harrington: an aristo-crat conversant with the long tradition of Continental and English social and political thought. He writes with obvious concern and sophisticated caution, but also with an optimism derived from his self-consciously rationalist ap-proach. In his *Des droits et des devoirs du citoyen*, probably written in 1758, but not published until early in 1789, we find the kind of question that also attracted Rousseau: for example, should his quality as a citizen destroy man's dignity as a man? But we also find a close link to actual politics. Mably writes about a state of nature, and of liberty being "a second attribute of humanity," but he also refers to the recent history of England and France, indeed, to contemporary social conditions and politics. In a modern idiom, he is more involved than Rousseau.

Mably's citizen must be very much a political activist since he lives in a society with rules and magistrates which determine his existence. However, if either or both of these are evil, and Mably is aware of all the difficulties of judgment and legitimation of antigovernmental behavior, then he must act to change both rulers and rules. The obligation to act is absolutely basic, arising from human nature itself. "Should the laws man has created for his own assistance render him a slave?" he asks. Man's rationality, God-given, is his instrument with which to improve laws and the human condition; politics is the proper ambience in which to act. Locke may have seen the right to revolution in legal terms, in terms of the ruler's breach of contract with his subjects. The abbé de Mably sees it rather in moral and political terms, perhaps in a more Catholic tradition.

Mably is, then, less analytical than Montesquieu, more activist than Rousseau. His social vision is different from Rousseau's. There is more of the modern social reformer in Mably; he is more connected with actual issues of taxation and property; he was, we would say, more policy oriented. Rousseau would reform mankind and society out there; Mably would do it down here. One result of this difference was the far greater impact of Rousseau in an age highly susceptible to powerful words and untested visions.[7]

On the eve of the French Revolution, Mably's citizen is faced with the duty to stir up purposeful agitation against the evil ruler of his country. This is a far cry from the view of Ansaldo Ceba, whose *The Citizen of a Republic* was written toward the end of the sixteenth century, and which may be described as a characteristic late-Renaissance summation of the civic humanist code of conduct. Whereas Ceba gives a formal, static catalog of all the attributes that are to be trained into a good, but calculating, citizen, Mably seems to demand action from the very depths of a citizen's heart.[8] If his passion separates him from the likes of Ceba, it very much links him to Rousseau and shows one way in which citizenship had developed over two hundred years.

In the summer of 1789 *citoyen* was on everyone's lips, and the use of this form of address became a proclamation of loyalty to the Revolution and the new French nation. But less than forty years before, as we have seen, Diderot had discussed the citizen completely in terms of the ancient city-state. Now we must ask: why this perpetuation of the traditional view in the age's most up-to-date compendium of scientific knowledge? And why did citizenship emerge so suddenly and completely as one of the central words of the Revolution?

A traditional view of citizenship could be written even in the 1750s because, as the natural philosophers put it, it still "saved the phenomena," since in many respects Western Europe was organized as it had been for thousands of years. Most people accepted citizenship as a feature of the hierarchical world of privilege and gradation of human and physical perfection in which they lived. The social and political lives of most people still were lived on a level of relative familiarity, if not intimacy. Religious life also was overwhelmingly local in both Protestant as well as Catholic territories, despite the existence of central religious authorities. And if the basic structures of European life had remained pretty constant, so had the moral curriculum. To be sure, many Christian books had been written to negate the activist civic values of the polis and *civitas* as formalized by ancient philosophers. But by the mid-to-late eighteenth century those ancient values had long been in the ascendancy and had been made compatible with the real interests of commercial kingdoms and republics. For these reasons Diderot's words made sense to readers whose knowledge of Attica and Latium was probably more specific and vivid than that of the province or kingdom across the nearest frontier, and more value-laden, as well.

Then there was that cultural explosion we know of as Rousseau. He had started to publish before 1750, and by the time of the Revolution was one of the most widely read and controversial writers in France. Scholars have noted that the *Social Contract* was the least read of his works before the Revolution. That may be so, but his books broadly relating to citizenship, moral education, and political and social theory in the widest sense included the extraordinarily popular *Émile*, the several *Discourses*, and the *Nouvelle Héloïse*. A prerevolutionary cult of Rousseau flourished in the 1780s after the publication of the *Confessions*. Between 1781 and 1789 Rousseau was celebrated in plays, on scarves, on canvas, in every possible medium. Among his readers were many of the eventual giants of the Revolution, who referred to his works again and again in speeches and articles in which they glorified the self-proclaimed "Citizen of Geneva" as the ultimate synthesizer of the great revolutionary ideals.[9]

They probably were wrong as well as right. If "the greatest and most constructive single idea of the French Revolution was the idea of citizenship . . . over a wide area . . . of free, rational, and responsible beings, not of mere nationals of a government,"[10] that idea cannot be ascribed to Rousseau. If some of his words were made to serve that vision, other equally characteristic texts reveal a quite traditional model of the citizen, one familiar to us from the time of the Greeks.

Rousseau eventually may have become the theorist of egalitarianism and modern democracy, or modern totalitarian democracy; he may have become, quite quickly, the revered father of the French Revolution. But in his lifetime, Rousseau wrote about, and, indeed, in some works extolled, the ordered and hierarchical society that was destroyed in that and later revolutions. He was in these works closer to, and more comfortable with, the society accepted and assumed by Plato, John of Salisbury, and even Machiavelli than with the new order that was in part, at least, constructed by himself, Robespierre, and the Committee on Public Safety. What is more, he held these ideas throughout a long writing career, from the early *Discourse on Political Economy* of 1755 to *The Government of Poland* of 1772. Rousseau thought about citizenship in the tradition of the old or first citizenship that began with the Greeks and only began to come to an end in the cataclysmic period that followed his death.

Experts argue whether Rousseau was or was not a systematic thinker. His ideas changed and sometimes contradicted each other; even the meaning of certain key words—liberty is one of them—changed. Yet in his notion of citizenship Rousseau was remarkably consistent, and tied to his ideas on the general will, equality, and the proper way to run a country, for example, his view has had an enormous influence over the past two centuries. His Platonism on a grand scale has proved to be one of the basic organizing concepts of modern politics. It is almost no exaggeration to say that, with his style and moral intensity, Rousseau restored the Platonic social and political vision to the foreground of European political thought.

What is that vision? That of the polis, with its small area, small and organically ordered population, single religion, single political culture, and single commonly accepted model of the good citizen. (There are other models for the good slave, the good alien, and the good woman.) It is a society of men who are given their honor and identity by the history of the community, and by personal and family accomplishment. In return for this gift of a cultural and moral persona, those men who are citizens owe obedience, service, devotion, and sacrifice; a moral, honorable life is not possible outside the polis—ideally, not any polis, but the polis of one's ancestors and one's own birth. In this small-scale world, agriculture, not commerce, and comfort, not wealth, are esteemed. The farmer is morally superior to the merchant for the additional reason that his body is strong, fit to serve the polis on the battlefield or at sea. A citizen came to know this value scheme and his place in it because from childhood he was subject to its variety of educational institutions: the knee, the temple, the agora, the ranks, the gymnasium, the streets, the courts. They all provided guidance and mutual reinforcement for this relatively simple man who honestly served his compatriots and trusted and was trusted by his neighbors. Homer was long the dominating, if controversial, work in the literature of this tradition, and Thucydides, Plato, Aristotle, and later Cicero, in a Roman version, passed on its message. Such was the good-press vision of Greek moral life that was still persuasive and somewhat applicable in the Geneva of Rousseau's youth.

In 1755, when he wrote both the *Discourse on Inequality* and the *Political Economy*, Rousseau had not escaped the influence of his childhood and youth in the city-state of Geneva, which, probably more than most small communities, retained the imprint of a powerful founder in the sense of law-giver and moral guide. Indeed, to find elements of his life-long enthusiasm for an emphatic communitarian moral force, one can begin with the preface to the *Inequality*.[11]

The preface itself is a public homage to this city whose statutes, in their approximation to natural law principles, bring order and happiness to its inhabitants. He praises Geneva's smallness, the face-to-face nature of its politics, and the citizens' love of the public good that translated into love of their compatriots, in contrast to mere love of territory. Already he can conceive of a general interest uniting ruler and ruled, one that flourished under democratic rule. He prefers peace to war, law-abidingness to the resolute pursuit of self-interest, and a governmental system in which citizens regularly are elected to serve at a frequency and capacity commensurate with their abilities. It is ironic that Rousseau should have become so important an influence on the development of large national states when, in fact, he was opposed to bigness and delights in the quality of moral relationships usually found only in a small polis like his native Geneva.

Here it is that we get an early picture of Rousseau's ideal man, stripped of the conventions of European civilization. Rousseau's method is like Galileo's or Newton's; it is the methodology of the new science which sees its subject pure, in vacuo, stripped of conditions that might limit its universality. Like the scientists' falling bodies in an ideal environment, Rousseau's man in a state of nature is independent of the limitations of history and geography. His research is "hypothetical," aimed at explaining "the nature of things," not "their true origins, just like those [conclusions] our physicists set forth every day upon the formation of the world."[12] The state of nature in this interpretation is not only a place at an original moment in time, but also a thinker's device with which to construct a society fit for formal analysis.

Once out of the state of nature, man soon found problems, and Rousseau difficulties. If he had praise for the community that formed virtuous citizens, he also saw society itself, whether community or not, as creating conditions of inequality. Like Plato, who determined on an ideal number of citizens, each with an equal amount of property lest envy bring down the community, Rousseau saw dangers in the very existence of society. Yet he recognized that, although these dangers existed, communities did develop over time a sense of self-interest and purpose, which they then transmitted to the young. This communal sense of identity is one aspect of his difficult concept of the general will; it guided the educational scheme of the community and made it the object of the reverence and followership that characterized a good citizen.

Rousseau was aware that "you will have everything if you train citizens," and that "training citizens is not just a day's work." Liberty depends upon the virtue that only a very complex and structured schooling can produce. Not only must the young be instructed in the traditions and goals of the community, for these enter into the general will, they must also be aroused to passion. Emotion is a desideratum of good citizenship because it is the fierce love he bears for his compatriots that constitutes the moral force that makes a citizen's social ambience into a true community.

Such an education must start "the first moment of life." By accepting the high vision of human relationships transmitted by the community's schools, the man becomes the citizen. Only this acceptance, which is translated into active membership in the political community, gives him the opportunity to perform the military and political activities that bring honor and esteem in the community.[13] Obedience to the laws, a sense of the group history, an appetite for service to the community are all the result of a "public education . . . in the bosom of equality." Such education, the "most important business of the state," is to be handled by morally responsible citizens who have proved themselves in a succession of ever more demanding positions of public responsibility. Having been educated and tested by the system, they are ideally suited to inculcate an awareness of the general will. It should be noted that military training is part of Rousseau's curriculum. Like Machiavelli, who resonates throughout these attempts to allocate areas of responsibility to the community and to the individuals who comprise it, Rousseau favors the citizen-soldier to the mercenary.

Years later these still were substantially Rousseau's ideas when he planned the organization of two prospective states, writing as law-giver and founding father, although, as we shall see, he had to compromise some of his most fundamental principles. In 1765, at the request of a Corsican officer in the French army, Battafuoco, Rousseau completed the sketch of a *Project de constitution pour la Corse*, as it is called. This was to be the basis for the establishment of Corsica as an independent state for the first time in its history. And a few years later, in 1772, he advised a Count Wielhorski in *Considerations sur le gouvernement de Pologne*, when that patriotic nobleman sought advice from Rousseau and two other French political theorists on the strengthening of Poland. In both proposals Rousseau's approach is basically the same. He asks for pertinent information on the history, geography, laws, and customs of each region and its people, and for significant facts about the role of religion and the Church, and then makes his specific recommendations. In other words, no doubt following the methodology of Montesquieu, he particularizes his proposal in terms of immediate needs and historic conditions.[14]

In Poland, that need was for a political-military reorganization that might make possible a successful defense against a Russian invasion. In Corsica, which had revolted a generation earlier against Genoese rule, it was for a viable form of self-government that would assure prosperity and independence. Both situations demanded that he accept what, in theory, he abhorred: the persistence of inequality and of the historic Roman Catholic church, established, propertied, and with an enormous influence upon people's lives.

He accepted the church because it was deeply entrenched in Polish and Corsican history. If the national energy is to be revivified and focused quickly, what might be described as the revival of the general will, the role of the church in history must be acknowledged as a necessary precondition for quick development of the nation's potential. And for all his violent language to the contrary, Rousseau accepts inequality because it too is part of the structure of that past upon which he must build. What has matured over centuries cannot be rejected if the people are to recognize and defend their country. The church and inequality are accepted because he saw them as instrumental in preserving a people's identity.

This Old Regime quality of Rousseau's work was one of his important contributions to nineteenth-century political thinking, for it blended easily with romantic notions of nationhood based on a veneration of traditional beliefs, values, and institutions. He is old-fashioned as well in his view of the army, as has been mentioned. The progressive army of his time was a professional, highly trained force, frequently composed of foreign mercenaries as well as native-born troops. Rousseau rejects this as a possibility since Poland and Corsica must depend, he argues, upon a traditional folk militia. This was the army he knew from his native Switzerland, the kind of army whose troops would "always fight better in defense of their own." To such a force no one should be "permitted to send along a substitute," for such service not only would improve the citizen, it would also "effect a change in public attitudes toward soldiers" since the people would then "think of the soldier as a citizen who is serving his fatherland and performing his duty; and not, any longer, as a bandit who sells himself for five sous a day." However, if conservative in recommending a citizen militia, Rousseau is very contemporary in advocating equality of opportunity in that militia. Its officers are to be chosen "without regard to birth, position, wealth or anything else except experience and utility."[15]

Rousseau can allow survivals of the Old Regime not so much because he must be prudent facing the difficult task of "founding," but because his new states are not exactly, or only, real polities. Rather, they are states of mind, moral forces, as they themselves are the products of moral education; as such they reflect the will and mutual love of their constituents. Thus he can write, referring to the Polish military aristocrats who will have to govern the country and lead its defense, that "it is in the knightly order that your republic in fact resides." These nobles, with their distinctive "native Polish qualities," not only will serve the new government, but will do so with effective tactics developed over centuries of historic Polish military accomplishment.[16]

In many ways Rousseau's theory of citizenship must be seen as limited, if not anachronistic. Although he does view patriotism as "the supreme virtue and source of all other virtues," that patriotism still best flourishes, in his view, in the small state, essentially the polis. Although Rousseau recognizes the problem of size in all its difficulties, he never really addresses it. That is, apart from his general words on the importance of a moral, patriotic education in any state of any size, he has no practical ideas on how to translate a highly charged civic emotionalism from the level of the polis to that of the large territorial state as contemporary federalists or proponents of mixed constitutions did. In the last generation of the Old Regime his best vision is of the problem, not the means to its solution—the problem, that is, of creating the new moral man whose sense of responsibility, willingness to participate, and quality of civic/national friendship will transcend, almost literally, the immediate horizon. His best attempt at a guidebook for the making of his "new moral man" was, of course, the *Émile*, published in 1762.

Finally, Rousseau resists and rejects the momentum of his own century in yet another way that ties him to the far past. He insists upon the moral primacy of agriculture and the martial republic at a time when commercial society is booming all around him, and when Locke and Franklin were best-sellers as guides to success in life, not the austere writings of traditional religious thinkers. In this aspect of his thought Rousseau is closer to Thomas More than he is to Adam Smith.

There is a commanding mythic quality to these visions of Rousseau, and perhaps it was just this quality that made him so popular before, during, and after 1789. In a world of confusion and rapid, uncertain change, he presented as serviceable a very ancient, tested, idealized model to be realized in the new age suddenly at hand. However, his dream never appealed to the entire population, and so France never became the great unified moral state he envisaged. Yet, realized or not, Rousseau's idealism and optimism reinforced Hobbes's pessimism and realism, and together they established the theoretical foundations of the modern great state. Both saw the state as necessarily absolute in its potential authority over its citizens and looked forward to the necessary extension of state power over greater and greater numbers of people. In this respect both (but especially Hobbes) went back to Bodin, who had stressed the importance of the sovereign in determining the identity and rights of subjects and citizens, and to Plato (especially Rousseau) in emphasizing the importance of a state-inspired education as the foundation of the citizen's moral attachment to his native land.[17]

The extent to which citizen and citizenship had become part of the accepted or normal vocabulary of politics may be seen in the *cahiers*, which were drafted in anticipation of the meeting of the Estates General in the spring of 1789. "Citizen" appears in many documents, and if it was not the only contemporary catchword, it was used widely throughout France, by nobles and clergy as well as by members of the third estate, in relation to a great variety of grievances and without great precision. Undoubtedly, it had become the word of some weight and general significance that petitioners used to gain the authority of history and universality. Often one finds it in preambles, and in relation to constitutional issues, the availability of justice, and other key matters. The term seems to have been chosen when the issue was of some abstract significance and had some bearing on the way a better France might work, say, with regard to representation in the Estates.

One may also cite the "Declaration of the Rights of Man and Citizen," in which citizen bears the concept of political-legal person. The first five articles of the "Declaration" are general, referring to man, sovereignty, liberty, and the law. But immediately the text becomes specific, and citizen is used with respect to rights under the law, such as that of free expression, and in relation to the police and to taxation. Clearly, citizen is meant to be a solemn, powerful term associated with man in one of his basic human conditions, that of active member of the civil community. The entire "Declaration" may be seen as very much the product of contemporary French society: right-oriented in its catering to the bourgeoisie, and at the same time dependent for its legitimacy upon universal principles rationally derived.[18]

The usefulness of the study of the *cahiers* for our understanding of French public opinion during the revolutionary year has been questioned, although, on the whole, they accurately reflect the contemporary mood, concerns, and thinking. If this is so, then it would appear that the citizenship tradition from Machiavelli to Rousseau had made a significant impression. Tied to demands for equality, the end of privilege, representation, participation, political and, eventually, social justice, as these were expressed by both ancient and contemporary authorities, citizenship had reached a tippy height: it was at the center stage of political thought and action. Into June and July it was still used in apposition to "subject" in an implied acceptance of the Old Regime. After that summer it alone bore the full program of classical republicanism.

CONCLUSION
🗗🗗🗗

By the end of the eighteenth century, republican governments had been established on both sides of the Atlantic in two very different sets of social and political circumstances. One has lasted without interruption from 1783 until the present, for all but a few years of its history under a popularly accepted constitution. The other passed through various kinds of regime until it too, some eighty years after its revolution, emerged from a military defeat and a series of constitutional crises as a republic. Several questions arise in this final chapter: What must be said about the citizenship tradition in relation to the American and French revolutions? What distinguishes the first citizenship, the subject of this book, from the citizenship that has followed over these past two hundred years? And finally, what is the moral, if any, to this story?

An understanding of their Revolution is an imperative for Americans; scholars continue to advance new and frequently startling theories to explain its origins. In recent years, especially since the publication in 1975 of *The Machiavellian Moment*, John Pocock and his followers have emphasized the importance of the Machiavellian republican and idealist tradition for the American Revolution. For the revolutionaries and the Framers, Harrington, not Locke, was the principal political philosopher. Before Pocock, Bernard Bailyn and Caroline Robbins had already suggested the importance of ideas and ideologies in preparing the way for the great act of rebellion. In an age of near universal monarchy, the colonists, we are told, had to have clear and certain thoughts about the justice of their cause. They received these not only from Plutarch and Livy, and more recently from Harrington and Locke, but also from Trenchard and Gordon and other contemporary popularizers of antiestablishment values and institutions.

Leaving aside the question of the relative importance of ideas as opposed to objective conditions and institutions in history, and speaking only to the Harrington-Locke issue, my view is that both sides are in the right, and that it is fruitless to talk in terms of priority and exclusivity of importance. Insofar as ideas, abstractions, influenced the coming of the Revolution as a sustained effort to achieve freedom and create a new government in a republican form, the patriots had a variety of mentors to borrow from, all of them offering the active citizen some role in the new regime. For the entire century before the Revolution—indeed, from the time of the English Revolution—republican, or at least antimonarchical, ideas had been germinating in the English-speaking world. The Levellers, Milton, Sydney, Harrington, Locke, the Commonwealth men all had contributed ideas, slogans, issues, and goals to a broad program of reform and change. As always, the ancients were there to help, studied by every member of the colonial political class, as were, also, contemporary Continental writers like Montesquieu and Voltaire (in his basic antiauthoritarian stance). These critics and their followers read each other, borrowed each other's ideas, advanced a variety of programs, and eventually produced two leaders, a pamphleteer and a political philosopher, both of tremendous popular appeal as well as intellectual power, Tom Paine and J. J. Rousseau.

By the late eighteenth century opposition ideas were numerous, in every possible combination, and, to the eye of this medievalist, of deep historicity, many of them, in the Western tradition. This prevalence should warn us off any exclusivistic approach to the intellectual origins of the American Revolution, as should the availability within this welter of ideas of a spectrum of republicanisms. Once the republic had been established, the very issues of the new American party politics are evidence of the great range of republican commitments. All this constitutes the cultural basis for the politics of the American Revolution. In some respects it did not differ from the situation in France. There too, men entered the revolutionary days with many ideas on if and how a new polity was to be organized.

To have a dream or even a list of specific complaints is not to have the blueprint for a new society. The colonists knew what their grievances were; they also knew what the best societies of the past had created and on what theoretical preconditions, but it took them a long while to establish the exact mechanisms by which to guard against corruption and create the conditions—if they ever did—in which the individual might achieve virtue by participating in the process of his own civil perfection. And if they had to draw upon the Machiavellian idealism preached by the Harringtonians, they also relied on the Lockean tradition, which, with its focus on property and its proper use, went back through Lawson to Marsilius, Thomas, and other medieval philosophers concerned with both civil and political justice.

There were also objective realities that influenced the colonies in their development of a new citizenship. Although their leaders were familiar with the fundamental texts of English law and European politics, they faced physical conditions that made it difficult to lead comfortable and ordered lives. These circumstances demanded an actuality of participatory citizenship and generally required administrative and political service at many levels if small numbers of men were to survive in a still hostile environment. And although social hierarchy certainly existed across the colonies, and the colonists were familiar with ecclesiastical and secular hierarchy in the institutions of the mother countries from which they came, they were relatively free of titles and deference behavior and were accustomed to a large measure of equality in the activities of daily life. Farming decisions, political decisions, and ecclesiastical activities all contributed to a de facto functional equality, much as they had in roughly similar circumstances during the Middle Ages in Europe.

The question remains: what predisposed so many colonists to choose some form of republicanism as the basis for their new country? Though surely not the whole answer, perhaps part of it lies in the fact that in 1776 the overwhelming majority of Americans still lived in the kind of small-scaled community whose life and values we have seen were essentially stable since the Greeks. In terms of law, social theory, and reality, and the relationship of secular and religious authority, Concord, for example, resembled an English village of the late Middle Ages, or, indeed, ancient Sparta. In the size of its population, its acceptance of community values and the community's regulation of public, economic, and personal life, in its constant search for the basis of harmony in the making of corporate decisions, its need for unity and homogeneity in religious affairs, its dependence upon shame to assure conformity, its intolerance of novelty and idiosyncrasy, its dependence upon citizens for the temporary but recurrent exercise of public office—in all these critical ways and matters the similarity of the colonial town to the ancient polis is remarkable.

In Concord, as in early Rome, the good man was a fellow warrior and fellow worshiper who observed his place in the ordered society into which he was born and struggled to suppress his individuality so that community decisions were unanimous, or at least not destructively divisive. The community was not to be imperiled. In these terms, what we call the state was a moral association reflecting Augustine's demand for a "concord concerning loved things held in common." This is to remind us that, strong or weak, at the basis of life in each colony was some religious commitment. Just as

Alexandria followed Arius and Geneva Calvin, so Philadelphia followed William Penn and Boston its Puritan divines. As the new United States attempted to shape and delimit its republicanism, political and social differences were exacerbated by religious ones.

If we see the colonial world in these categories of the *longue durée*, we can better understand why the ideas of Harrington, Locke, and other critics were well received. They made good sense to people concerned with personal and governmental virtue—with salvation and justice, that is—who were suspicious of political power deriving from wealth of a new magnitude and questionable legitimacy, and who, like their not-so-distant medieval ancestors, saw all of society in essentially religious terms.

To put this another way, over the previous 100 to 150 years, within each colony a great number of individualistic little places had been practicing with reasonable success some form of a republican life. In the generation before the Revolution, for a variety of reasons, colonists from these many backgrounds came to see their lives in terms of a common political tradition and rhetoric. Now, under the pressure of rebellion turned into revolution, their leaders faced the problems of creating a new community of great size and establishing that new and virtuous society, which was already seen by some in millenarian terms, on the same foundations of harmony, trust, and common identity that they were familiar with and expected from organized life, given all their previous experience. In effect, they had to create a new citizenship that would incorporate, but not completely eliminate, many of the local allegiances of the past, allow for the entrance of strangers into the new community, decide what few "loved things held in common" were to be revered by all, and then create institutions which would at the same time allow for individual participation and honor and focus the attention of men who now might live a thousand miles apart upon matters of common interest touching a common welfare.

Obviously France differed from America in many ways, yet it faced the same problems of scale and of creating a new national citizenship. How much of what has been said of the American scene holds for France, the nation that came into being after 1789? Village and town life continued along traditional lines, but at the level of the nation there existed only the citizenship theory of Bodin, which subjected the individual to the monarch, and which did not demand "an active participation in the formation of laws." It was this situation that the Revolution was supposed to correct. Sièyes, Robespierre, and other theoreticians saw the need to involve the people in their government, and from the summer of 1789 the creation of some form of meaningful national citizenship was one of their central concerns. That creation was made difficult not only by the long and very significant development in France of regional identities, but also by the fact that by the end of the eighteenth century, and especially after its strident usage by Rousseau and his disciples, *citoyen* was not an ordinary word with a clear, distinct, and universally accepted definition. Long before the Revolution, in its confusion with *sujet* and *bourgeois*, *citoyen* had provoked confusion and complaints about its lack of clear meaning and its penumbra of revolutionary implications. Now, after the fall of the Bastille, it was a call for some kind of action, the exact nature of which was not clear to revolutionary leaders, let alone to those in the streets.

This confusion lasted into the nineteenth century and reflected an early distinction between active and passive citizenship made in 1791 by Sieyes in a commentary on ". . . *des Droits de l'Homme et du citoyen. . . .*" Passive citizenship safeguarded everyone's person, property, and liberty. Active citizenship was reserved for the adult male who would contribute to the welfare of the state with his body and property. Sieyes never worked out the niceties of this basic distinction, but it seems clear that he did not envision France with full male suffrage. His analysis is loaded against the poor and the uneducated, against, that is, the mass of French workingmen in his day. Only the relatively wealthy and well educated, those with the time and intelligence for politics, would function as citizens in postrevolutionary France.

So, although the rhetoric of citizenship flourished, the actuality remained quite limited. Too many structures and beliefs of the Old Regime had survived into the new era for many new men to enter upon the political scene. Politics remained largely in the hands of traditional elites. After 1789 equality was incorporated as an ideal in the new public discourse, but actual participation in politics, although it was slowly and fitfully expanded, was not an immediate result of the Revolution. Men may have thought themselves possessed of a new and greater dignity, but that new worth was not to be exercised in actual citizen activity.

In this interpretation, events followed Sieyes's tepid view of citizenship, which so inadequately fulfilled the dream of true equality that drove the Revolution. In effect, then, the history of France after 1789 was somewhat similar to that of the United States in its early years. In both countries a revolution on republican principles and slogans produced only partial, modest, republican accomplishments. Corruption survived, and possessors of property remained in possession of political power. The eventual principal success of both revolutions was constitutional, a rejection of the institution of monarchy and its replacement by a regime based upon a system in which the executive and an elected representative body now shared power and legitimacy. To be sure, there was, especially in America, some enlargement of the suffrage and of the possibility of office holding open to ordinary men. But neither country witnessed the creation of a truly new order whose demand for political activity and military service would create better human beings.

Neither revolution, then, broke cleanly with the past. The old tradition of citizenship as a limited and discriminatory institution survived for at least another century while nationalist poets, painters, historians, and politicians created images and slogans that portrayed another, more inclusive, reality. Indeed, if one thinks of the elasticity of the suffrage in France as it changed to reflect the nature of the regime, or of the issues of slavery, discrimination, and gerrymandering in the United States, (and of England with its succession of reform acts), and of the long fight for social, legal, and political rights for women everywhere, it becomes clear that the actuality of a truly new and complete citizenship was very long in coming. The Rousseauan citizen model proved an attractive, but illusory, goal throughout modern history. And while the vision grew in acceptance and definition, sociological and technological developments made the life of the armed and independent yeoman impossible for all but a very few. Over the past two centuries most men in the Western world have swapped gun and plow for pen, pencil, and personal computer; it is now very difficult to win republican virtue as some kind of rural or Alpine hero.

Yet an exhortation was buried in the promise of the revolutions, and from the beginnings of postrevolutionary history, citizenship has touched, and has itself been, one of the central defining issues of a nation's history: the ultimate meaning of its revolution, its inclusiveness, the speed with which its promises were to be realized, and the nature of the passion which was to infuse a new national political life.

The final centuries of the first citizenship had prepared the way for the second. As we have seen, from the late Middle Ages on, lawyers and political theorists had diminished the value of civic virtue and stressed that of loyal and obedient subjectship. They continued to assume hierarchies and abhor disorder. At the end of the eighteenth century, after, and because of, their revolutions, most men of education and property tried to keep their world as structured as it had been; the Terror in France and Shays's Rebellion in America gave a glimpse of what mass politics could become. So actual democratic innovations were few and slow in coming; vertical bonds and structures held, and political relationships proved remarkably resistant to change. For many, the second citizenship brought benefits other than virtue through ruling and being ruled.

NOTES

◙◙◙

INTRODUCTION

1. Shklar, *American Citizenship*.
2. Gass, "Exile," p. 94.

CHAPTER 1

1. Throughout I have translated *polis* and *civitas* as "city-state" and have also used that term to designate medieval cities with their surrounding countryside. There are problems with this usage of the word "state," for the polis had little bureaucracy, no standing army, and few of the other appurtenances of the modern state. Surely "polity" and "political community" or "civic community" are better translations. Yet "city-state" has the merit of instant familiarity, and for that reason, despite its shortcomings, I have used it.

2. Cited by Sinclair, *Greek Political Thought*, p. 35.

3. For a short, but incisive, discussion of this issue, see M. Finley's essays in *Economy and Society*, pp. 3–18, 112–30.

4. To say this is to assert that from the very beginning of Greek citizenship, two aspects of the institution coexisted: the first citizenship, describable in essentially Aristotelian terms, which emphasizes self-government, sacrifice for the community, and willing obedience to law; and the second citizenship, simultaneously more passive and more materialistic, interested in the benefits, perhaps more than in the obligations, of citizenship.

5. The text of Tyrtaeus's poems may be found in Edmonds, *Elegy and Iambus*, pp. 50–79, along with translations. They have also been translated by Richmond Lattimore, *Greek Lyrics*, pp. 14–16. The reference to a poem on citizenship comes from the medieval Byzantine source now known as Suda—the text given to Suidas by Edmonds in *Elegy and Iambus*, pp. 50–51. C. M. Bowra has a fine chapter on Tyrtaeus in *Early Greek Elegists*, pp. 39–70. Plutarch's life of Lycurgus may be conveniently found in *Plutarch on Sparta*, pp. 8–46, along with the lives of Agis and Cleomenes and other texts relevant to Sparta, including Xenophon's *Politeia*.

6. On the Spartan constitution, see Talbert's introduction to *Plutarch on Sparta*, pp. 11–19; Forrest, *Emergence*, pp. 123–42; A. Jones, *Sparta*, pp. 13–30; Andrewes, "The Government," pp. 1–20, and *Probouleusis*; and Rahe, *Republics*, chap. 6.

7. See Manville, *Citizenship*, pp. 55–69.

8. Aristotle, *Politics*, 1252b27–30 and 1325b39ff; cited by Manville, *Citizenship*, p. 41.

9. Thucydides, *Peloponnesian War*, 1.126.7; cited by Manville, *Citizenship*, p. 77.

10. Aristotle, *Constitution of Athens*, 5.3, in Loeb edition, pp. 22–23.

11. Manville, *Citizenship*, pp. 93–123.

12. Ehrenberg, *From Solon to Socrates*, pp. 54–66; Sealey, *Greek City States*, chap. 5; Adkins, *Moral Values*, pp. 51–55; M. Finley, *Democracy Ancient and Modern*, p. 30.

13. Ehrenberg, *From Solon to Socrates*, p. 82; Sealey, *Greek City States*, chap. 6.

14. The phrase is Manville's. See his *Citizenship*, pp. 183–84, which goes far beyond any other account or analysis of these events. Here he refers to the speech of Andocides which describes what happened to the tyrants' associates. See, too, Hignett, *Athenian Constitution*, p. 133.

15. Aristotle, *Constitution of Athens*, 21:1–21:4, p. 90; Sealey, *Greek City States*, pp. 150–51.

16. Aristotle, *Constitution of Athens*, 22:2, pp. 62–63.

17. Ehrenberg, *From Solon to Socrates*, p. 89.

18. Aristotle, *Politics*, 1275b3 (1275a3); cited by Hignett, *Athenian Constitution*, pp. 132–33.

19. Manville, *Citizenship*, p. 209.

20. Aristotle, *Constitution of Athens*, 26:3, p. 97.

21. Ibid. 27:4, pp. 94–98.

22. Thucydides, *Peloponnesian War*, 2.35–36.

23. Manville, *Citizenship*, pp. 215–19.

24. See the chapter "On Citizens and Foreigners" in Ehrenberg, *People of Aristophanes*. I am indebted to the late Professor G. Else for this reference.

25. On *metics*, see Whitehead, *Ideology*, p. 70, where he refers to Aristotle, *Politics*, 1278a35–38, and p. 127, for Xenophon's understanding of the real importance of the *metics* to Athenian society. On slaves, see, especially, M. Finley, *Ancient Economy*, pp. 62–94, *Ancient Slavery*, and his *Aspects*, p. 167. On *metics*, slaves, and women, see the appropriate passages in *World of Athens*, and Austin and Vidal-Naquet, *Economic History*, whence I take the references to *Politics*, 1275a1–25, and to Herodotus, *Histories*, 6.137. For a thoughtful examination of the relationship between homosexuality and citizenship, see Halperin, *One Hundred Years*, pp. 88–112, and Dover, *Greek Homosexuality*, pp. 19–31. On the function of homosexuality in Greek military life, see Rahe, *Republics*, chap. 4.

26. On the essentially warlike quality of Greek life, see the monumental *Republics Ancient and Modern* of Paul Rahe and his "Primacy of Politics." Also Adkins, *Merit and Responsibility*, and McIntyre, *After Virtue*, especially pp. 142–53.

27. Marrou, *History*, pp. 77–90; Jaeger, *Paideia*, 1:82–83. For Euripides, see Adkins, *Moral Values*, pp. 117–20. ·

28. Thucydides, *Peloponnesian War*, 6.92.

29. Ehrenberg, *People of Aristophanes*, pp. 209–10; Winkler, *Constraints*, pp. 46–54.

30. Marrou, *History*, pp. 90–94.

31. Jaeger, *Paideia*, 1:83.

32. Manville, *Citizenship*, pp. 215–19.

33. See especially Plato, *Laws*, 634c through 638ab. Also Plato, *Republic*, 546d, 548b. Modern commentary on this issue includes Morrow, *Cretan City*, pp. 40–63, and Pangle's interpretive essay in his translation of the *Laws*, pp. 388–404. Also, Marrou, *History*, pp. 98–118.

34. In addition to the passages cited above, see Plato, *Laws*, 653–54, 708, 718, 737–39, 765–66, 797–99, 801, 804–6.

35. Lord, introduction to his edition of Aristotle's *Politics*, pp. 2–3, 6–8; and Chroust, *Aristotle*, 1:155–76.

36. Aristotle, *Politics*, 1338b1.

37. Lord, *Education*, pp. 200–202.

38. Books 3, 6, and 7 of the *Politics* are fundamental for Aristotle's theory of citizenship. At various times I have used the editions of Barker, Sinclair, and, most recently, Lord.

39. See Lord, *Education*, pp. 181–89; Aristotle, *Ethics*, 1176b13–1178a21.

40. For Aristotle's complicated views on religion, see Chroust, *Aristotle*, 1:221–31.

41. M. Finley, *Democracy Ancient and Modern*, pp. 13–14.

42. On the *ephebia*, see Marrou, *History*, pp. 151–52.

43. Pausanias, *Guide to Greece*, 10.4, p. 410 in Penguin edition.

CHAPTER 2

1. Two fundamental works for the study of Roman citizenship are, for the legal side, Sherwin-White, *Roman Citizenship*, and, for a broader approach as indicated by its title, Nicolet, *The World of the Citizen in Republican Rome*.

2. On the early history of Rome, see Scullard, *History, 753–146 B.C.*, and *Roman Politics, 220–130 B.C.*

3. Livy, *History of Rome*, 1.8. And Scullard, *Etruscan Cities*, pp. 259–60; Grant, *The Etruscans*, p. 98.

4. Nicolet, *World*, p. 17.

5. Raaflaub, *Social Struggles*, p. 198. These paragraphs on the conflict of the orders are based on the collection of essays edited by Raaflaub and on Alfoldy, *Social History*.

6. Nicolet, *World*, pp. 217–315; L. Taylor, *Roman Voting Assemblies*, chaps. 4 and 5.

7. Acts 16:37, 21:37–39, 25:10–12. See, too, Sherwin-White, *Roman Society*, pp. 71–119.

8. On the Gracchi and citizenship, see Stockton, *The Gracchi*, pp. 106–13, 156–59, 185–97; Sherwin-White, *Roman Citizenship*, pp. 134–49; and Nicolet, *World*, pp. 310–15.

9. Wallace-Hadrill, *Patronage*, p. 70.

10. For an excellent introduction to the growing literature on patronage, and not only in antiquity, see the volume edited by Wallace-Hadrill cited above. Generally

insightful is M. Finley's chapter on "Authority and Patronage" in his *Politics in the Ancient World*. A simple but effective definition is given on p. 65 by Wallace-Hadrill: "an objective exchange of goods and services whereby political support is given in exchange for material benefits." A contemporary if inaccurate discussion is that of Dionysius of Halicarnassus, who ascribed the "founding" of patronage to Romulus. See Wallace-Hadrill, *Patronage*, pp. 243–45.

11. Drummond, in Wallace-Hadrill, *Patronage*, p. 93. Also, Syme, *Roman Revolution*, p. 7, and especially chaps. 2 and 25; Badian, *Foreign Clientelae*, pp. 1–15, 154–67.

12. See Earl, *Moral and Political Tradition*; Homo, *Roman Political Institutions*, pp. 133–46; Scullard, *History*, pp. 100–105; Scullard, *From the Gracchi*, pp. 5–8.

13. Bernstein, *Tiberius Gracchus*, p. 101.

14. The *cursus honorum* was a ladder of ascending offices through which an ambitious Roman of a political family worked on his way to the consulship and censorship. One began as a quaestor attached to a Roman legion as financial officer, moved up the judicial magistracy as praetor, and then became eligible for the consulship. The two consuls were the chief magistrates of the Roman Republic; they served as both military and political leaders. Finally, a man might be elected censor. This magistrate supervised public morals and the letting of state contracts, and he not only controlled the rolls of the Senate but also kept lists of citizens and their property. Thus, he determined a citizen's place in the hierarchy of military organizations, which themselves constituted a hierarchy of opportunities for the exercise and acquisition of virtue. There were other honors a Roman could aspire to, such as the analagous competitions in the equestrian order and for municipal magistracies. And, although the ten tribunes rose and fell in importance during the early centuries of the Republic, after the assassination of the Gracchi the tribunate exercised greater political weight. This formal picture gives nothing of the fierce competition and partisanship participation in this race for honors engendered. On Tiberius, see Bernstein, *Tiberius Gracchus*.

15. Hammond, *City-State and World-State*. For Polybius, see Walbank, *Polybius*, and his *Historical Commentary on Polybius*, and Polybius, *Histories*, trans. W. P. Paton.

16. Polybius, *Histories*, 6.4.

17. Ibid. 16.26. Was it that the new Empire was bringing so many *metics* to Athens that the citizen population was increasing too quickly?

18. Ibid. 3.24.

19. Ibid. 6.17.

20. Ibid. 4.20.

21. Ibid. 6.39.

22. Ibid. 38.8, 18.35, 1.59.

23. Ibid. 31.23.

24. Ibid. 31.23–30.

25. Scullard, *From the Gracchi*, pp. 66–67.

26. Cicero, *On the Republic*, 1.32.

27. Diogenes Laertius, *Lives*, 7:117–30, in Barker, *Alexander to Constantine*, pp. 33–36.

28. Cicero, *On the Orator*, 1.7–8; Cicero, *Dream of Scipio*, especially 25–29; Cicero, *On Moral Obligations*, 1.25.

29. Cicero, *On Moral Obligations*, 1.17.

30. Ibid. 2.2; Cicero, *On the Orator*, 1.8.

31. Cicero, *On Moral Obligations*, 2.5.

32. Ibid. 3.15.

33. Ibid. 3.15, 3.24.

34. Nicolet, *World*, p. 38.

35. On voting, see Taylor, *Roman Voting Assemblies*, and the chapter "*Comitia*: The Citizen and Politics" in Nicolet, *World*, pp. 207–315. And on the subject indicated by its title, Earl, *The Moral and Political Tradition of Rome*. Dionysius, 2.14.3, is cited by Nicolet, *World*, p. 213.

36. Mazzolani, *The City in Roman Thought*, pp. 192–93.

37. Epictetus, *Discourses*, 2.10, 3.24, 2.5, in Barker, *Alexander to Constantine*, pp. 313–15.

CHAPTER 3

1. Moore and Myerhoff, *Secular Ritual*, pp. 3, 13.

2. Eph. 2:19.

3. The biblical reference is to Acts 11:26–29. On Chrysostom and Libanius, see Downey, *Antioch in the Age*, pp. 85–133. See Homily 17, sec. 10–12.

4. Heb. 13:14; Ps. 87:3; Ps. 46:4. On the possible inspirations of, and sources for, Augustine, see Mazzolani, *The City in Roman Thought*, chap. 13.

5. Brown, *Augustine*, pp. 323–25.

6. Ibid., p. 338.

7. Patlagean, *Pauvreté economique*, pp. 45–66. I owe this reference to Professor Peter Brown.

8. Gregory, *History of the Franks*, 5:49, p. 321.

9. Pirenne, *Medieval Cities*, first published in English in 1925. Sixty-five years later, given its persuasive style, forceful and attractive thesis, and availability, it remains the first book for nonspecialists, if not the only one.

10. Reynolds, *English Medieval Towns*, pp. 124–25. See, too, her *Kingdoms and Communities*, chap. 6, "Urban Communities."

CHAPTER 4

1. On the strength of religion in Renaissance Italy, see, for example, Weinstein, *Savonarola*, and Bouwsma, *Venice*, chap. 1.

2. P. Jones, "Families," pp. 183, 185–86, 190, 192. The value of family cohesiveness to the city is seen in the usual demand that a new citizen live a certain number of years in town with his family before receiving citizenship.

3. Banfield, *Moral Basis*, p. 10.

4. *Statuti di Pisa*, 1:44. One wonders whether citizens were as "eager" to serve in public office as Lane suggests. Eager out of love of *patria*, or because of the glory and benefits that attached to man and family from service? See his "Roots," p. 411.

5. Raynerius de Perusio, *Ars notariae*, cap. 207.

6. Archivio di Stato, Florence, *Prov.* 48 (11 December 1360), ff. 104–104v, and *Prov.* 49 (21 February 1361), ff. 109v–110. On conditions within Florence at this time, see Brucker, *Politics and Society*, chap. 4.

7. Sherwin-White, *Roman Citizenship*, pp. 451–60, asserts that the attacks of the barbarians upon Rome in the third century sharpened the Romans' sense of cultural distinctiveness and patriotism. Much the same thing happened during the intercity wars in Italy and during the Hundred Years War.

8. Davidsohn, *Tempi di Dante*, pp. 523–25. In her popular *Torregreca*, p. 284, Cornelisen quotes the politician Crispi in 1890 to the effect that the Church still spent some 90 percent of its income on candles, incense, and masses, and only 10 percent on charity.

9. Davidsohn, *Storia*, 2:391. Waley, *Medieval Orvieto*, p. 85, notes that banners were important in creating civic patriotism. See, too, the chapter "The Church and the Faith" in Brucker, *Renaissance Florence*.

10. Fasoli, "Coscienza civica," p. 41.

11. Muir, *Civic Ritual*, p. 5. See, too, his "Images of Power."

12. Morghen, "Vita religiosa," pp. 200–201.

13. Little, *Religious Poverty*, p. 213.

14. C. T. Davis, "Remigio."

15. Trexler, *Public Life*, p. 27.

16. Ibid., p. 95.

17. Ibid., p. 270. On city men and peasants, see p. 106.

18. Weinstein, *Savonarola*, p. 56.

19. Heers, *Fêtes*, pp. 79–83. He also observes that, like the ancient city, medieval and Renaissance cities created public spaces and churches with an eye for their eventual use in the cultivation of a public spirit.

20. Bartolus, *Opera* (1585), to C. 10.39.5: "et no. quod verbum patria et verbum civitas idem important."

21. Cited by Post, "Two Notes," in his *Studies*. Earlier, John of Salisbury, in exile in France, writes of the "sweetness of my native land." See *Letters*, 1:33.

22. Ptolemy of Lucca cites Cicero and Sallust to this effect in his conclusion to Thomas's book of instruction for the young king of Cyprus, now in Thomas Aquinas, *Opera Omnia*, 16:3:4.

23. Lucas, *Commentaria*, to C. 10.32.35 and C. 12.58.5.

24. Riesenberg, "Consilia Literature"; Kisch, *Consilia*; and Rossi, *Consilium Sapientis*.

25. Marianus, *Consilia*, 1:35. Comparable is the situation of N., born in Venice of a Florentine jurist who has lived in Venice for ten years, all the while paying his taxes in Florence. N. claims that he has always maintained a "dulcem amorem patriae." Flor-

ence allows his request for citizenship and grants him ten months in which to meet new responsibilities. See ASF, *Prov.* 116 (27 January 1416), ff. 252v–54.

26. Aretinus, *Consilia*, cons. 163. Students of Renaissance political thought will find here the full range of justification for state action ". . . ad defensionem status communis."

27. Muratori, *Antiquitates*, 4:179–84.

28. Bartolus, *Opera* (1585), to D. 50.1.1, especially sec. 10–14. In effect, this is a short treatise on various legal ramifications of citizenship.

29. A selection of cases on these issues might include Petrus de Ancharano, *Consilia*, cons. 303, on the question of the availability of ecclesiastical income for civic purposes; Johannes Calderinus, *Consilia*, cons. 21, on a city's taxation of a bishop's mill; Franciscus Ripa, *Responsa*, resp. 1, on the Church's responsibility in times of plague; Johannes Riminaldi, *Consilia*, vol. 4, cons. 740, with regard to the maintenance of bridges, dikes, and roads. This list by no means exhausts the subject; the jurists also raised these issues in their commentaries on specific laws. See, for example, Jacobus Rebuffi, *Lectura*, to C. 10.48.3.

30. Baldus, *Opera* (1577), to C. 4.43.1.

31. Davidsohn, *Storia*, 2:576. For a conflict of views on the responsibility of ambassadors, see *Quaestiones dominorum*, 1:500–501. Generally on ambassadors, Martines, *Lawyers and Statecraft*; Queller, *Office of Ambassador*.

32. *Constituto di Siena*, 526–27.

33. Muratori, *Antiquitates*, 3:901–2.

34. According to the late-thirteenth-century Aristotelian Remigio de' Girolami, "The commune must be loved more than one's self because of its similarity to God." See Rubenstein, "Marsilius," p. 54.

35. Romanin, *Storia*, 3:276–81, 289.

36. And it was assumed by at least one jurist that a citizen, old or new, knew what was expected of him. See Johannes Riminaldi, *Consilia*, 3:479.

37. C. 10.40.3. An early opinion is an anonymous twelfth-century gloss that states "incola fit solo animo" (*Vat Lat* 11156, fol. 126). This tradition of discussion that begins in the twelfth century continues into the sixteenth; over this long period the same passages in the Justinianic text serve as the basis for developing political thought.

38. Accursius, *Glossa ordinaria*, to D. 50.1.6 and D. 50.1.17. See, too, Lucas da Penna, *Commentaria*, to C. 10.62.1.

39. Bartolus, *Opera* (1585), to D. 50.1.4; and Baldus, *Opera* (1577), to C. 10.40.7, and (1587), to C. 4.43.1.

40. Marianus Socinus, Jr., *Consilia*, 2:cons. 7.

41. The *Ottimo commento* of about 1333 to the words "tutti colori" in *Paradiso*, 16. These refer to the "little good faith and little love" that characterizes the immigrants into Florence from the towns and farms of Tuscany.

42. Bouwsma, *Venice*, p. 9.

43. Augustine, *City of God*, 19:21–24.

44. Baldus, *Opera* (1586), to prooem, *Digest*; Martines, *Social World*, p. 54.

45. *Liber iurium Janue*, 7:cols. 168–69.

46. *Libri commemoriali*, 1:118. The editor notes that after 1305 the form for all such procedures was standardized by the Great Council.

47. For Volterra, Plesner, *L'émigration*, p. 119 n. 73. On Viterbo, *Cronache*, p. 518. And Baldus (1586), to C. 8.52.2.

48. Santini, *Documenti*, 2:232–36 (1258), and 2:383–84 (1254); *Libri commemoriali*, 1:116 (1311); Manaresi, *Milan*, p. 73 (1167); Santini, *Documenti*, 2:184–87 (1256); *Codice Orvieto*, p. 125 (1230).

49. See his *De represaliis* in *Opera* (1602), especially sec. 1 and 2.

50. Ludovicus Bologninus, *Consilia*, cons. 49.

51. Baldus, *Consilia* (1550), 4:106. In this and cons. 445 of the same volume it is interesting to see the conflict between the private benefit of the citizen who has been hurt and should be helped and the public good that depends in part upon the success of the marketplace, which might be diminished were the right of reprisal invoked. Albericus, *De statutis*, pars. 1, q. 119.

CHAPTER 5

1. For a general picture of the social mix in a medieval/Renaissance city, see Brucker, *Renaissance Florence*.

2. Bartolus, *Opera*, to D. 50.1.1. To give some idea of the difficulty involved in constructing a simple definition, reference might be made to the 1415 redaction of Florence's statutes, which holds that a foreigner is one "who publicly is held to be a foreigner by Florentine citizens . . . even though they may live in Florence and possess the *privilegium civilitatis*." Just to complicate matters, already in late-classical usage *civis* and *municeps* are used interchangeably in the sense of *civis*, specifically in D. 50.23.1, as noted by A. Visconti, "Origo," p. 98.

3. Alexander, *Consilia*, 6:cons. 27. See, too, Paul de Castro, *Consilia*, 2:cons. 89.

4. Bartolus, *Opera* (1585), to D. 50.1.1; Azo, *Summa* (1610), to C. 10.38.

5. On these matters, see the comment of Jacobus Rebuffi (1591) to C. 10.40.7, and of Bartolus to the same law. Bartolus requires that more than half of one's property be in the new location before the *incola* may receive legal benefits. For a late treatise of the sort that is invaluable for all its references to earlier specific texts, see Petrus Antiboli, *De muneribus*. Of special note are the views of Azo, *Summa*, to C. 10.40; Baldus, *Opera*, to C. 10.40; Accursius, *Glossa ordinaria*, to C. 10.40.3.

6. Baldus, *Consilia*, 4:cons. 445.

7. Johannes Riminaldi, *Consilia*, 3:cons. 479.

8. See especially Visconti, "Origo"; Violante, *Società milanese*; and Cortese, *Cittadinanza*.

9. Riesenberg, "Citizenship and Equality."

10. Geertz, *Local Knowledge*, p. 66. Geertz is writing of the people of a town near Fez, Sefron, in which he lived for several years.

11. Riesenberg, "Civism and Roman Law."

12. *Libri commemoriali*, 3:4–5, for Venice; the year is 1322. Almost two hundred

years earlier, in 1149, such a grant was made in Genoa. See *Codice diplomatico*, pp. 250–51.

13. The practice of granting tax concessions was well established by the mid-thirteenth century and was later discussed by Bartolus, *Opera* (1585), C. 10.32.19, and by Petrus de Ubaldis, *De collectis*, f. 97; Petrus opines that the city may make concessions that do not harm the community's well-being.

14. *Statuti Veronesi*, 1:cap. 227. The *podestà* is to inquire into the status and activities of foreigners and to keep a record of all privileges granted to them. On the Florentine Franzesi family's negotiations for Sienese citizenship, see Bowsky, "Medieval Citizenship," pp. 201–2. See, too, Kirshner, "Nature and Culture," pp. 186–87.

15. Among the books and papers found in the study of Ser Cola d'Ascoli upon his death were his naturalization papers. ASF, *Acquisti e Doni*, 302. (I owe this reference to Professor G. Brucker.) Also, see Baldus, *Consilia*, 1:cons. 393.

16. *Statuti di Bologna 1245*, 1:6, rubr. 37, and 2:7, rubr. 9. See Kibre, *Scholarly Privileges*, p. 241, where she notes that from the twelfth century Bolognese professors swore to remain in Bologna in exchange for their tax privileges. Similar arrangements were worked out in other university towns, including Padua and Florence.

17. This issue has recently been discussed by Kirshner, "Civitas sibi," pp. 694–713.

18. Archivio di Stato, di Perugia, *Catasto Catastine*, f. 30. I owe this reference to Professor Roberto Abbondanza.

19. Kirshner, "*Consilium* of Baldus," pp. 301–3, has thoroughly examined Florentine records for the years 1352–79, finds more citizenship grants than I reported in "Civism and Roman Law," yet concludes as I did that the number was relatively low ("in the hundreds and not in the thousands," as he puts it).

20. Herlihy, *Pistoia*, pp. 91–93. On town-countryside relations, see Plesner, *L'émigration*; Fiumi, *Sui rapporti*; Lestocquoy, *Les villes*; and Zarb, *Marseilles*, pp. 140–42, who observes on the extreme reluctance of Marseilles to grant citizenship; in a paragraph that ranges from the thirteenth to the sixteenth century, she asserts that only two to four candidates were accepted each year.

21. *Statuti republica fiorentina*, 5:cap. 120, which in passing remarks, "Cum multi forenses continue habitantes cum eorum familias in civitate Florentie."

22. Jason de Mayno, *Consilia* (1581), 3:cons. 316. Revealing, too, is the case of Magister Nicolaos, a *physicus* who, born in Venice of a Florentine father, applies for Florentine citizenship and asserts that although he has lived in Venice for sixty years, he has always preserved a "dulcem amorem patrie" for Florence. He claims that his father had sustained his Florentine obligations over all those years. Apparently Florence granted his request for citizenship. ASF, *Prov.* 116 (January 1426), ff. 252v–254.

23. Philippus Decius, *Consilia*, 1:cons. 282.

24. Baldus, *Opera*, to C. 8.52.2. For Florence, *Statuti republica fiorentina*, 3:19, 5:41; for Perugia, *Statuti 1342*, 2:27; and *Statuto di Arezzo*, 2:32.

25. Since our inclination is to emphasize the political side of citizenship, we tend to see only two kinds of citizenship, one with political rights, one without. Medieval citizens and lawyers tended to think in terms of combinations of rights, political and

civil, that gave them operational effectiveness. See Paul de Castro, *Consilia*, 1:cons. 21. Here he writes of varieties of citizenships.

26. For this kind of change in Florentine history, see Salvemini, *Dignità cavalleresca*. What makes detection of possible cause and effect relationships difficult is the fact that social and political upheavals or other events did not always produce an immediate and recognizable constitutional change. Laws on citizenship were only a part of any new redactions of statutes. The only scholarly attempts I know of to trace out a city's ongoing citizenship policy are those of Bizzari, "Ricerche," and Bowsky, "Medieval Citizenship."

27. *Statuti del popolo di Bologna*, 1:37. Calestrini, *Popolo di Siena*, pp. 13–15.

28. Every municipal constitution considered citizenship requirements, frequently discriminated between commercial and political rights, and also established prerequisites for city and guild office holding. Requirements varied from city to city and with respect to a city's need for new people. But always a need for loyalty and security is expressed, especially with regard to the city's defenses and survival. See, for example, *Statuti di Imola*, 1:51, a requirement of ten years' residence for eligibility for public office; *Statuti di Bologna 1245*, 10:28, which demands a continuous residence of ten years and a sizable property commitment if one is to be elected to any office of the commune; and *Constituto di Siena*, another ten-year stipulation. Something happened in Como between 1250, when no time requirment was fixed, and 1277, when a thirty-year residence requirement was imposed. See *Liber Cumanorum*, cols. 208–9.

29. *Statuti republica fiorentina*, 5:85.

30. Paul de Castro, *Consilia* (1581), 1:cons. 21. These matters were also discussed in the councils of Florence. See ASF, *Prov.* 39 (21 June 1352), ff. 163–163v, and *Prov.* 40 (3 December 1352), f. 30, which records the grant of citizenship to a Pistoian nobleman, Johannes Panciatiche, whose descendants still live in Florence.

31. Bueno de Mesquita, "Place of Despotism."

32. On the development of equality, Riesenberg, "Citizenship and Equality," and on the Jews, Riesenberg, "Jews in the Structure of Western Institutions." References to Johannes de Legnano and the other medieval jurists mentioned here will be found in these two articles. It was Raphaelus Fulgosius, in his *consilium* 61, who compared lack of citizenship to a human defect or fault.

33. If one remains aware of social and intellectual contexts, one may cautiously generalize from genre to genre and century to century within this period. This is especially true of the legal literature, for the lawyers did not change all that much. Their school texts, teaching methods, and professional experience remained remarkably constant, as did the general structure of the urban and commercial environment in which they taught and practiced.

34. It is in the vast legal literature that we find the best analysis of medieval society, a fact obscured by the nonliterary and technical nature of legal commentary. Only legal historians know that countless short, specialized statements, minitreatises, lie buried in the late-medieval comments on Justinian. Characteristically, these treatises convey not only the author's own view, stated in that succinct, elegant, almost epigrammatic language of the jurists, but also frequently a statement of the pertinent related and

opposing views held by other experts. Baldus, *Opera*, to C. 8.47.7, and Bartolus, *Opera* (1602), to D. 33.9.4. Otto of Freising, two centuries earlier, remarked on the qualities of Italian urban life in *Deeds of the Emperor Frederick*, pp. 127–29.

35. *Glossa ordinaria*, to VI 1.3.11.

36. Jason de Mayno, *Consilia*, 4:cons. 371, sec. 17; Marianus Socinus, *Consilia*, 1:cons. 35, sec. 5; and Marianus Socinus, Jr., *Consilia*, 1:cons. 37, sec. 2.

37. Rubinstein, "Beginnings," p. 223. For Bartolus, see above, n. 34.

38. The crucial verses, lines 46–57 in the translation of the text of the Società Dantesca Italiana by Sinclair, are as follows: "All who were there at the time between Mars and the Baptist able to bear arms were a fifth of the number now living, but the citizenship, which is now mixed with Campi and Certaldo and Figline, was seen pure in the humblest artisan. Ah, how much better would it be to have these people I name for neighbors, with your bounds at Galluzzo and Trespiano, than to have them inside and to endure the stench of the boor from Aguglion and of him from Signa who already has a sharp eye for jobbery! . . . The mixture of peoples was ever the beginning of the city's ills, as food in excess is of the body's."

39. Jacopo della Lana, *Commento di Jacopo*, 3:255–57; *Ottimo commento*, 3:368–72; Petri Allegherii, *Super dantis*, pp. 657–58; *Benvenuti . . . comentum*, 5:163, 167.

40. *Statuti di Bologna 1288*, 5:44.

41. Salvemini, *Magnati*, pp. 340–41.

42. Bartolus's *Tractatus* is included in *Opera* (1602), vol. 10. See sections 6–10.

43. Brunetto Latini, *Tesoro*, p. 282.

44. Vergottini, "Origini," pp. 418–25, and in "I presupposti," p. 52. By the end of the twelfth century, enforced filial devotion had been replaced by a clear subject relationship.

45. Kantorowicz, *Mysteries of State*; Morrison, *Two Kingdoms*; and Gierke, *Political Theories*, n. 75, for John of Salisbury and Aeneas Silvius on the state as *corpus mysticum*. Ptolemy is to be found in Thomas Aquinas, *Opera Omnia*, vol. 16.

46. Grignaschi, "Definition du 'civis,'" pp. 71–180. On John of Paris, see too Ullmann, *Individual and Society*, pp. 130–33.

47. Marsiglio, *Defender*. On Marsilius in the seventeenth century, see Condren, "George Lawson and the *Defensor Pacis*."

48. Lucas, *Commentaria* (1583), Proem, and to C. 10.31.26.

49. Pucci, *Poesie*, 4:210, 264–65.

50. Johannes Viterbiensis, *De regimine civatatum*; Brunetto Latini, *Tesoro*; Guido Fava, *Dictamen*; and the *Occulus pastoralis*.

51. Baldus, *Consilia* (1550), 5:cons. 409. Also his *Opera* (1586), to C. 6.42,31; C. 6.23.9; D. 1.1.2, and *In Decretales . . . commentaria* (1571), to X.1.3.36. In another text Baldus discusses the two treacherous words "fingere" and "fictio" in terms of citizenship. He argues that a city can create a true citizen by legislative act; see his *De statutis*. A very important contribution to Baldus's views on citizenship has recently been made by Canning, *Political Thought*, especially pp. 159–84.

52. Bartolus, *Opera* (1602), to D. 41.3.15, secs. 33, 34, 45. For Florence, see ASF, *Prov.* 40 (17 December 1352), f. 39, and *Prov.* 152 (27 October 1451), ff. 185v–

186v. In both cases immigrants are not required to build a house or be deprived of office-holding responsibilities.

53. Paul de Castro, *Consilia* (1581), 1:cons. 318, sec. 44, and Panormitanus, *Consilia* (1578), 2:cons. 61.

54. A succinct statement of issues may be found in the comment of Jacobus Rebuffi, *Lectura*, to C. 10.62.1; also Bartolus, *Opera* (1602), to D. 3.4.1.

55. Barbadoro, *Finanze*. A useful bibliography is in Sapori, *Le marchand*, and more will be found in Becker, *Florence in Transition*.

56. Ullmann, "Concilium repraesentat," pp. 725–26; and *Responsa*, pp. 226–28.

57. Albericus de Rosate, in his *De statutis*, q. 119, pars. 1, discusses whether a town may break its promise to a citizen poor when granted a tax exemption, but now rich. The jurist says that the pact must stand since the town must observe its obligations to its citizens.

58. Johannes Calderinus, *Consilia*, cons. 21.

59. For example, Raphaelus Cumanus, *Consilia*, cons. 168, and Johannes Crottus, *Consilia*, 1:cons. 171.

60. Pepus, in the Venice (1579) edition of Marianus Socinus, *Consilia*, 1:254v–55.

61. Nicolaus Boerius, *Decisiones*, q. 13.

62. Baldus's observation was cited by Andreas de Barbatia, *Consilia*, 4:cons. 64, while Aretinus's remarks are to be found in his *Consilia*, cons. 27.

63. Azo, *Summa* (1610), to C. 10.39.

64. Lucas, *Commentaria*, to C. 10.31.35.

65. Johannes de Legnano, *De represaliis*, chaps. 129, 134–35; Baldus, *Commentaria*, to C. 8.48.7.

66. Baldus, *Consilia*, 5:cons. 64.

67. Alexander de Imola, *Consilia*, 5:cons. 32.

CHAPTER 6

1. Anyone whose work has touched on the Renaissance in the past thirty-five years has had to confront the thesis of Hans Baron; his *Crisis of the Early Italian Renaissance* appeared first in 1955 and then again, in a revised edition, in 1966. If Baron's work has stimulated sharp negative criticism such as that of Jerrold Seigel, it has also provoked a whole variety of studies that rely on, reshape, and reevaluate Baron's ideas in many ways. Pocock's *Machiavellian Moment* must be seen in this light.

2. Skinner, *Foundations*, 1:23–88, and now his "Prehumanist Origins" in Bock, Skinner, and Viroli, *Machiavelli and Republicanism*.

3. The literature on Machiavelli is infinite. One may start with Gilbert, *Machiavelli*, and Skinner, *Machiavelli* and *Foundations*. More recent contributions include de Grazia, *Machiavelli in Hell*; Mansfield, *Taming the Prince*; and Bock, Skinner, and Viroli, *Machiavelli and Republicanism*, a collection of essays by American, English, and Continental scholars which examines aspects of Machiavelli's career and his influence

into the eighteenth century. Unfortunately, I was able to consult this book only long after this chapter was written.

4. The following discussion is based on the *Discourses*. I refer to the Penguin edition translated by Walker and edited by Crick. Machiavelli introduces his methodology on pp. 93–94 and 97–99. These are the letters to Buondelmonti and Rucellai and the Preface to Book 1, respectively.

5. This interpretation is based especially on the following chapters in the edition cited above: 1:1–12; 2:2, 6–10, 12, 16–18; 3:25.

6. Hay, *Italian Renaissance*, and Mattingly, *Renaissance Diplomacy*.

CHAPTER 7

1. Helmholz, *Roman Canon Law*, chap. 4.

2. Montaigne, "Of Repentance," 3:2, in *Essays*, p. 611.

3. Ullmann, *Individual and Society*, pp. 115–17.

4. Caton, *Politics of Progress*.

5. Ullmann, *Individual and Society*, pp. 120–22.

6. More, *Utopia*, 2:1, 2:4.

7. Ibid. 2:5, 2:7.

8. Ibid. 2:8.

9. Hexter, *Biography of an Idea*, p. 91.

10. Ferguson, *Articulate Citizen*.

11. Starkey, *Dialogue*, pp. 24–27, 39.

12. Elyot, *Governour*, see the Proheme, pp. xxxi–xxxii in the Dent edition.

13. Ascham, *Schoolmaster*, p. 20, and passage cited by Garin, *L'educazione*, p. 177.

14. Besides Garin, *L'educazione*, especially pp. 173–79, which covers the period 1400–1600, also see Hexter, "Education of the Aristocracy."

15. *Coriolanus*, especially 3:1 and 3:3.

16. For a survey of this literature, see Skinner, *Foundations*, vol. 1, chap. 8.

17. Smith, *Discourse*, 1:16 and 1:22. On the controversy surrounding the authorship of this work, see Skinner, *Foundations*, 1:225.

18. The case may be read in its entirety in 7 Co. Rep. 1a (1608); a summary with some commentary is included in Smith, *Development*, pp. 415–18. Kettner devotes pages to its analysis in *Development*, pp. 13–28, as does Holdsworth in *History*, 9:77–86.

19. Hexter, *Vision of Politics*, pp. 213–23.

20. Seyssel, *Monarchy*, 1:2, 1:3.

21. Bodin, *Method*, p. 162.

22. Bodin, *Six Books*, 1:6, 3:8, and McRae's notes on pp. A108–9; Bodin, *De Republica*, the Latin text of 1586. Also, Skinner, *Foundations*, 2:284–301, focused on absolutism, and Mesnard, *Philosophie politique*, pp. 473–546, especially pp. 487–94.

23. Chénon, *Histoire générale*, 2:72–74; Glasson, *Histoire du droit*, 7:62.

24. The passage is found in Hotman, *Francogallia*, p. 347, and his reference is to *Dig.* 1.3.2.

25. Hotman, Beza, and Mornay, *Constitutionalism and Resistance*, pp. 31–39, 101–36.

26. In ibid., pp. 151–54, and Skinner, *Foundations*, 2:323–34.

27. Rowen, *Low Countries*, pp. 42–46.

28. Kossman and Mellink, *Texts*. See now van Gelderen, "Dutch Republicanism."

29. Kossman and Mellink, *Texts*, pp. 243–46.

30. Moeller, *Imperial Cities*, pp. 47–49, 66–67. See, too, Walker's wonderfully textured *German Home Towns*, especially chapters 2 and 4. Although his focus is upon a later period, the quality of community life seems to have remained remarkably stable.

31. Monter, *Calvin's Geneva*, p. 11.

32. Hooker, *Laws*, 1:2, 3, 6, 7, 8, 10, 14, 15.

33. Laslett, *World We Have Lost*, p. 217.

34. Ozment, *Reformation in the Cities*, pp. 84–90; Chrisman, *Strasbourg*, pp. 88–94, and chap. 14.

CHAPTER 8

1. Grotius, *War and Peace*, 1, 1, 10, i. In his commentary on this passage, Sabine asserts that the "command of God . . . added nothing to the definition . . . for the law of nature would enjoin exactly the same if . . . there were no God." *History*, p. 424.

2. Grotius, *War and Peace*, Prol., 11.

3. Sabine, *History*, chap. 21; and Barker in Gierke, *Natural Law*, pp. xli–xliii.

4. Althusius, *Politica*, p. lxv.

5. Althusius, *Politics* (Carney edition), p. 35.

6. For a detailed discussion one must consult *Politica* (Friedrich edition), chap. 5, pp. 39–42.

7. Gierke, *Political Theory*, p. 36. One cannot tell from the English title, but this book is devoted to Althusius and his political thought.

8. Pufendorf, *Duty of Man and Citizen*, 1:8, 2:5, 2:18.

9. Ibid. 2:18, 2:5.

10. See Barker in Gierke, *Natural Law*, pp. 62–63; and Keohane, *Philosophy and the State*.

11. Hirst, *Representative of the People*, p. 96.

12. Ibid., p. 104, and chap. 5, "The Urban Voters."

13. Rawson, *Spartan Tradition*, chap. 13, "The Revolutionary Period in England"; Hirst, *Authority and Conflict*, pp. 84–89; and Worden, "Milton's Republicanism." See, too, Worden's "England: The Republican Tradition," forthcoming in a volume edited by David Wooten in the *Making of Modern Freedom* series to be published by the Stanford University Press.

14. Raab, *English Face*; Donaldson, *Machiavelli*.

15. Wolfe, *Leveller Manifestoes*.

16. "An Agreement of the People," in ibid., p. 300.

17. Hirst, *Authority and Conflict*, p. 273.

18. Pocock, *Machiavellian Moment*, pp. 381–82.

19. Jaume, *Hobbes*, pp. 142–53.

20. Hobbes, *Leviathan*, pp. 129–45.

21. By C. Condren, "Resistance and Sovereignty," pp. 673–81, and most recently in his *George Lawson's Politica*, pp. 50, 96–97.

22. Lawson, *Politica*, pp. 1, 4, and Condren, *George Lawson's Politica*, pp. 43–48.

23. Lawson, *Politica*, p. 15.

24. Ibid., pp. 45, 47.

25. C. Condren has made himself the authority on Lawson. Besides the article cited, see his "George Lawson and the *Defensor Pacis*," "*Sacra* before *Civilis*," and *George Lawson's Politica*. B. Tierney has also written on Lawson in chapter 5 of *Constitutional Thought*.

26. Harrington, *Political Writings*, p. xi.

27. J. Davis, "Pocock's Harrington," p. 683. This article is both a useful summary of Pocock's view of Harrington and an appreciative critique of some aspects of this view.

28. John Pocock in *Machiavellian Moment*, and his many followers. A check of Pocock's statements in his 1975 book and the introduction of his 1977 edition of Harrington on, for example, virtue and military service, reveals that Harrington's words do not support Pocock's assertions. What we have, rather, is a brilliant construction by a great modern historian. The implications of what Pocock has written may be found scattered in Harrington, but the powerful linkage that has so influenced transoceanic scholarship over the past fifteen years is Pocock's. In effect, Pocock did for Harrington what he did over a decade in countless conversations with his colleagues at Washington University: saw implications and meanings in their work of which they themselves were unaware. I am not alone in my fears of Pocock's powers of imagination and persuasion. See the article of Davis cited in note 27 above.

29. On a republican army, see Harrington, *Oceana*, in Pocock's edition, pp. 213, 228, and 303ff. There is substance for Pocock's linkages and interpretations in all this, but Harrington does not make the connections.

30. One may read a recent Pocock article as a partial disavowal of the *Machiavellian Moment*. See his "Between Gog and Magog," published in the *Journal of the History of Ideas* in 1987. Here he wonders why he has been so misunderstood, in effect saying, "Don't blame me; I didn't do it." All he was trying to do, he asserts disarmingly, was to suggest that "republican values were present in the American mixture from the start." And he justifiably complains that his anti-Lockean approach aroused a fierce opposition. If I disagree with Pocock on the percentage of Machiavelli to be found in Harrington, I wholeheartedly agree with his placement of the Framers' thinking in a broad transatlantic context. The reliance of American lawyers and other intellectuals upon Continental as well as English political thought is well documented. And we know too that these activists saw themselves, for whatever influence it may have had

upon their actions, not only in a contemporary Western discussion, but in a tradition that went back to Greeks and Romans.

31. Locke, *Educational Writings* (Axtell edition). See, too, Garin, *L'educazione*, pp. 261–72; Tarcov, *Education for Liberty*; and Caton, *Politics of Progress*.

CHAPTER 9

1. Diderot, *Encyclopédie*, 3:488–89. On Rousseau's romanticizing of the Alpine village, see Miller, *Rousseau*. This is true for Germany as well as France. See Walker, *Moser*, pp. 310–12. In the late eighteenth century this jurist was able to distinguish five categories of citizen, ranging from the very honorable and wealthy down to "common citizens" who were neither. In another passsage he mentions only three, which suggests continuation of the confusion the civilians had complained about four hundred years earlier.

2. The reference is to Weber, *Peasants*; and Pocock, introduction to Burke, *Reflections*, p. xx.

3. Darnton and Roche, *Revolution in Print*, pp. 55–56.

4. Ibid., pp. 128–50, 165.

5. The currency and usefulness of the word were appreciated by, of all people, Catherine the Great. In her "Instruction" of 1767 she used "citizen" in a variety of contexts in which the political side of her subjects is stressed as well as the force and universality of her orders. Dukes, "Instruction," for example, pp. 43, 46, 53. In Catherine the word thus regains the sense it had had under the ancient Roman Empire—and was to have again in many modern states. I owe this reference to Professor Max Okenfuss.

6. Montesquieu, *Considerations*, pp. 24–28, 33–34, 40–46, 85–86, 92–95, and *Spirit*, especially Book 11, but also 9:1, cited by Hamilton in *Federalist*, 9, on the merits of a "confederate republic." See, too, Shklar, *Montesquieu*, pp. 55–66, and her "Montesquieu and the New Republicanism." Also Richter, *Political Theory*, and Pangle, *Philosophy of Liberalism*, especially chap. 5.

7. Mably, *Des droits*, especially pp. 14, 22, 27, 35, 40, 61–65.

8. Ceba, *The Citizen*.

9. See Spurlin, *Rousseau in America*, and Miller, *Rousseau*, chap. 6.

10. Palmer, "Man and Citizen," pp. 150–51.

11. Prefaces are important for Rousseau. As he wrote in the *Political Economy*, p. 65, reason expressed forcefully in a preamble will effectively persuade citizens to obey the law.

12. Rousseau, *Discourse on Inequality* (Ritter edition), pp. 9–10.

13. Ibid., p. 72, and Rahe in "Primacy of Politics," p. 7.

14. The texts are available in Rousseau, *Political Writings* (Vaughan edition). The *Poland* has been translated by Kendall, and new translations of the *Discourses* and the *Social Contract* are available as translated by Bondanella and edited by Ritter.

15. Rousseau, *Poland*, chap. 12, "The Military System."

16. Ibid., p. 85.

17. Jaume, *Hobbes*, pp. 135–76; and Sewell, "Le citoyen/la citoyenne."

18. On the *cahiers*, see Hyslop's *A Guide* and *French Nationalism*. The Declaration may be found in Stewart, *Survey*, pp. 113–15.

BIBLIOGRAPHY

෴

MANUSCRIPT SOURCES

Florence. Archivio di Stato.
  Registri di *Acquisti e Doni*, 302.
  Registri di *Provisioni* 39, 40, 48, 49, 116, 152.
Perugia. Archivio di Stato.
  Catasto Catastine.
Vatican City. Biblioteca Apostolica Vaticana.
  Vat Lat 11156.

PUBLISHED PRIMARY SOURCES

Accursius. *Glossa ordinaria*. Venice, 1591.
Albericus de Rosate. *De statutis*. In *Tractatus universi iuris*, vol. 2. Venice, 1584.
Alexander de Imola. *Liber primus . . . septimus consiliorum*. Lyons, 1549.
Althusius, Johannes. *Politica Methodice Digesta*. Edited by C. J. Friedrich. Cambridge: Harvard University Press, 1932.
———. *The Politics of Johannes Althusius*. Translated with an introduction by F. S. Carney. London: Eyre and Spottiswoode, 1964.
Andreas de Barbatia. *Consiliorum sive responsorum . . . volumen primum . . . quartum*. Venice, 1581.
Angelus de Ubaldis. *Consilia seu responsa*. Lyons, 1532.
Aretinus. *Consilia seu responsa*. Venice, 1572.
Aristotle. *Aristotle's Constitution of Athens and Related Texts*. Edited by K. von Fritz and E. Kapp. New York: Hafner, 1950.
———. *The Athenian Constitution*. Translated by H. Rackham. Cambridge: Harvard University Press, 1935.
———. *Ethics*. Translated by J. A. K. Thomson. Harmondsworth: Penguin, 1955.
———. *Politics*. Translated and edited by Carnes Lord. Chicago: University of Chicago Press, 1984.
Ascham, Roger. *The Schoolmaster*. Edited by L. V. Ryan. Charlottesville: University Press of Virginia, 1974.
Augustine. *City of God*. Translated by G. E. McCracken. 2 vols. Cambridge: Harvard University Press, 1957–60.

Azo. *Summa aurea*. Lyons, 1553.

Baldus de Ubaldis. *In Decretales subtilissima commentaria*. Venice, 1571.

———. *Opera Omnia*. Venice, 1586.

———. *Prima . . . quinta pars consiliorum*. Lyons, 1550.

Bartolus. *Opera Omnia*. Venice, 1602.

Benvenuti de Rambaldis de Imola comentum super Dantis Aldigherii comoediam. Edited by J. Lacaita. 5 vols. Florence, 1887.

Bodin, Jean. *De Republica*. Lyons, 1586.

———. *Method for the Easy Comprehension of History*. New York: Columbia University Press, 1945.

———. *The Six Books of a Commonweale*. Edited by K. D. McRae. Cambridge: Harvard University Press, 1962.

Brunetto Latini. *Il Tesoro*. Edited by P. Chabaille. Bologna, 1883.

Bryskett, Lodowick. *A Discourse of Civill Life*. Edited by Thomas E. Wright. Renaissance Editions #4. Northridge, Calif.: San Fernando Valley State College, 1970.

Burke, Edmund. *Reflections on the Revolution in France*. Edited by J. G. A. Pocock. Indianapolis: Hackett, 1987.

Ceba, Ansaldo. *The Citizen of a Republic*. Edited and translated by C. E. Lester. New York, 1845.

Cicero. *The Dream of Scipio*. Translated with an introduction by Michael Grant. Harmondsworth: Penguin, 1971.

———. *On Moral Obligations*. Translated with an introduction by John Higginbotham. London: Faber, 1967.

———. *On the Orator*. Cambridge: Harvard University Press, 1959.

———. *On the Republic*. Cambridge: Harvard University Press, 1966.

———. *Pro Archia Poeta*. Translated by N. H. Watts. Cambridge: Harvard University Press, 1923.

Codice diplomatico della Città d'Orvieto. Edited by Luigi Fiumi. Florence, 1884.

Codice diplomatico della Repubblica di Genova. Edited by Cesere Imperiale di Sant'Angelo. 2 vols. Rome, 1936–38.

Il Constituto del Comune di Siena dell' Anno 1262. Edited by Ludovico Zdekauer. Milan, 1897.

Le Consulte della Repubblica Fiorentina dall'anno MCCLXXX al MCCXCVIII. Edited by Alessandro Gherardi. 2 vols. Florence: Sansoni, 1896–98.

Il Costituto dei consoli dei placito del commune di Siena. Edited by L. Zdekauer. Siena, 1890.

Cronache e statuti della città di Viterbo. Edited by Ignazio Ciampi. Florence, 1872.

Dante Alighieri. *The Divine Comedy*. Translated by J. D. Sinclair. 3 vols. London: Bodley Head, 1948.

———. *The Divine Comedy*. Translated by C. Singleton. 3 vols. Princeton: Princeton University Press, 1970–75.

Diderot, D., ed. *Encyclopédie, ou Dictionnaire raisonné des sciences, des arts, et des métiers, par une societé des gens de lettres*. Paris: Brisson, 1751–65.

Dukes, Paul, ed. "Catherine the Great's Instruction (Nakaz) to the Legislative Commission, 1767." In *Russia under Catherine the Great*, vol. 2. Newtonville, Mass.: Oriental Research Partners, 1977.

Elyot, Sir Thomas. *The Boke Named the Governour*. London: J. M. Dent & Sons, 1937.

Euripides. *Medea*. New York: Oxford University Press, 1912.

The Federalist Papers. Edited by Isaac Kramnick. Harmondsworth: Penguin, 1987.

Filmer, Robert. *Patriarcha and Other Political Works*. Edited by Peter Laslett. Oxford: Blackwell, 1949.

Franciscus Ripa. *Responsa in quinque libros decretalium*. Venice, 1602.

Gregory of Tours. *The History of the Franks*. Translated with an introduction by Lewis Thorpe. Harmondsworth: Penguin, 1974.

Grotius, Hugo. *De jure belli ac pacis*. Introduction by James B. Scott. 2 vols. Washington: Carnegie Institution, 1913–25.

Guido Fava. *Dictamen rhetorica*. Edited by A. Gaudenzi. *Il Propugnatore*. Nuov. ser. 5 (1892).

Harrington, James. *The Political Works of James Harrington*. Edited by J. G. A. Pocock. Cambridge: University Press, 1977.

———. *The Political Writings: Representative Selections*. Edited by Charles Blitzer. New York: Liberal Arts Press, 1955.

Herodotus. *The Greek Historians*. 2 vols. New York: Random House, 1942.

Hobbes, Thomas. *Leviathan*. Edited with an introduction by Michael Oakeshott. Oxford: Basil Blackwell, 1960.

———. *Leviathan*. Edited by R. Tuck. New York: Cambridge University Press, 1991.

Hooker, Richard. *Of the Laws of Ecclesiastical Polity*. Abridged ed. Edited by A. S. McGrade and Brian Vickers. New York: St. Martin's Press, 1975.

Hotman, François. *Francogallia*. Edited by R. Giesey. Cambridge: University Press, 1972.

Hotman, Beza, and Mornay. *Constitutionalism and Resistance in the Sixteenth Century: Three Treatises*. Translated and edited by Julian H. Franklin. New York: Pegasus, 1969.

Isocrates. Translated by Norlen and Van Hook. 3 vols. London: Heinemann, 1928–45.

Jacobus Rebuffi. *Lectura super tribus ultimis libris Codicis*. Turin, 1591.

Jacopo della Lana. *Commedia di Dante degli Allagherii col commento di Jacopo della Lana*. Edited by L. Scarabelli. 3 vols. Bologna, 1866–67.

Jason de Mayno. *Consiliorum sive responsorum volumen primum . . . quartum*. Venice, 1581.

Johannes Calderinus. *Consilia sive responsa*. Venice, 1582.

Johannes Crottus. *Consiliorum sive responsorum liber primus . . . tertius*. Venice, 1576.

Johannes de Legnano. *De bello, de represaliis, et de duello*. Edited by T. E. Holland. Washington and Oxford: Carnegie Institution, 1917.

Johannes Riminaldi. *Consilia.* 4 vols. Venice, 1576–79.

Johannes Viterbiensis. *Liber de regimine civitatum.* Bibl. iurid. med. aevi. 3. Bologna, 1901.

John of Salisbury. *Letters.* Edited by W. J. Millor and H. E. Butler. 2 vols. London: Nelson, 1955–79.

Kossman, E. H., and A. F. Mellink, eds. *Texts Concerning the Revolt of the Netherlands.* Cambridge: University Press, 1974.

Lattimore, Richmond. *Greek Lyrics.* 2d ed. Chicago: University of Chicago Press, 1960.

Lawson, George. *Politica Sacra et Civilis: or, A Modell of Civil and Ecclesiasticall Government.* . . . London: Starkey, 1660.

Liber iurium Janue. Edited by Ercole Ricotti. Turin, 1854–59.

Liber statutorum consulum Cumanorum iustice et negociatorum (1281). Edited by Antonio Ceruti. Turin, 1876.

I libri commemoriali della Republica di Venezia. Edited by R. Predelli. Venice, 1876.

Livy. *History of Rome.* 14 vols. London: Heinemann, 1922–59.

Locke, John. *The Educational Writings of John Locke.* Edited with an introduction by James L. Axtell. Cambridge: University Press, 1968.

———. *Some Thoughts Concerning Education.* With an introduction and notes by T. H. Quick. Cambridge: University Press, 1902.

———. *Two Treatises of Government.* Edited by Peter Laslett. Cambridge: University Press, 1967.

Lucas da Penna. *In tres codicis . . . posteriores libros commentaria.* Lyons, 1583.

Ludovicus Bologninus. *Consilia.* Lyons, 1556.

Mably, Gabriel Bonnot de. *Des droits et des devoirs du citoyen.* Edited by J. L. Lacercle. Paris: Didier, 1972.

Machiavelli. *The Discourses.* Edited with an introduction by B. Crick. Harmondsworth: Penguin, 1970.

———. *Prince.* Edited by Q. Skinner and R. Price. Cambridge: University Press, 1988.

Manaresi, C. *Gli atti del comune di Milano fino al anno MCCXVI.* Milan, 1919.

Marianus Socinus. *Consiliorum . . . volumen primum . . . quintum.* Venice, 1579–1624.

Marianus Socinus, Jr. *Consiliorum . . . volumen primum . . . quartum.* Venice, 1580.

Marsiglio of Padua. *The Defender of Peace.* Translated with an introduction by Alan Gewirth. New York: Columbia University Press, 1956.

Montaigne. *The Complete Essays.* Translated by Donald M. Frame. Stanford: Stanford University Press, 1958.

Montesquieu. *Considerations on the Causes of the Greatness of the Romans and Their Decline.* Translated with an introduction by David Lowenthal. Ithaca: Cornell University Press, 1965.

———. *The Spirit of the Laws.* With an introduction by Franz Neuman. New York: Hafner, 1949.

More, Sir Thomas. *Utopia*. Translated with an introduction by Robert M. Adams. New York: Norton, 1975.

――――. *Utopia*. Translated with introduction by Paul Turner. Harmondsworth: Penguin, 1961.

Muratori, Ludovico. *Antiquitates italicae medii aevi*. 6 vols. Milan, 1738–42.

Nicolaus Boerius. *Decisionum . . . pars prima . . . et secunda*. Venice, 1551–56.

Occulus pastoralis sive libellus erudiem futurum rectorem populorum. In Muratori, *Antiquitates italicae medii aevi*, vol. 4. Milan, 1741.

Oldradus da Ponte. *Consilia*. Venice, 1571.

L'Ottimo commento della Divina Commedia. Edited by A. Torri. 3 vols. Pisa, 1827–29.

Otto of Freising. *The Deeds of the Emperor Frederick Barbarossa*. Translated with notes by C. Mierow and R. Emery. New York: Columbia University Press, 1953.

Panormitanus. *Consilia*. Venice, 1578.

Paul de Castro. *Commentaria in corpus iuris civilis*. Venice, 1568.

――――. *Consiliorum volumen primum . . . tertium*. Venice, 1580–81.

Pausanias. *Guide to Greece*. Translated and edited by Peter Levi. 2 vols. Harmondsworth: Penguin, 1971.

Petri Allegherii. *Super dantis ipsius genitoris comoediam commentarium*. Edited by V. Nannucci. Florence, 1845.

Petrus Antiboli. *Tractatus munerum*. In *Tractatus universi iuris*, vol. 12. Venice, 1584.

Petrus de Ancharano. *Consilia sive juris responsa*. Venice, 1585.

Petrus de Ubaldis. *De collectis*. In *Tractatus universi iuris*, vol. 12. Venice, 1584.

Petrus Rebuffus. *Feudorum declaratio*. Cologne, 1561.

Philippus Decius. *Consilia sive responsa*. Venice, 1575.

Plato. *Laws*. Translated and edited by Thomas Pangle. New York: Basic Books, 1980.

――――. *Republic*. Translated by B. Jowett. 2 vols. Oxford: University Press, 1921–22.

Plutarch. *Plutarch on Sparta*. Translated with an introduction by R. Talbert. London: Penguin, 1988.

Polybius. *The Histories*. Translated by W. R. Paton. 6 vols. London: Heinemann, 1922–27.

Ptolemy of Lucca. Continuation of Thomas Aquinas, *De regimine principum*. In Thomas Aquinas, *Opera Omnia*, vol. 16. Parma, 1865.

Pucci, Antonio. *Poesie*. Edited by F. Ildefonso di San Luigi. 4 vols. Florence, 1772–75.

Pufendorf, Samuel von. *De officio hominis et civis juxta legem naturalem libri duo*. Translated by F. G. Moore. Washington: Carnegie Institution, 1928.

Quaestiones dominorum Bononiensium. Bibl. iurid. med. aevi. 1. Bologna, 1888.

Raphaelus Cumanus. *Consilia sive responsa*. Venice, 1576.

Raphaelus Fulgosius. *Consilia*. Venice, 1576.

Raynerius de Perusio. *Ars notariae*. Edited by A. Gaudenzi. Bibl. iurid. med. aevi. 2. Bologna, 1892.

Responsa doctorum Tholosanorum. Edited by E. M. Meijers. Haarlem, 1938.

Rousseau, Jean Jacques. *The First and Second Discourses*. Translated and edited by Victor Gourevitch. New York: Harper and Row, 1986.

―――. *The Government of Poland*. Translated with an introduction by William Kendall. Indianapolis: Bobbs Merrill, 1972.

―――. *Political Writings*. Edited by C. E. Vaughan. 2 vols. Cambridge: University Press, 1915.

―――. *Rousseau's Political Writings*. Edited by A. Ritter and J. C. Bondanella. New York: Norton, 1988.

―――. *The Social Contract*. Edited by E. Barker. Oxford: University Press, 1948.

Rowen, H., ed. *The Low Countries in Early Modern Times*. New York: Walker, 1972.

Santini, Pietro. *Documenti dell'antica costituzione del comune di Firenze*. Florence, 1895.

Seyssel, Claude de. *The Monarchy of France*. Edited by Donald R. Kelley. New Haven: Yale University Press, 1981.

Smith, Sir Thomas. *De republica Anglorum*. Edited by L. Alston. Cambridge: University Press, 1906.

―――. *A Discourse of the Commonwealth of This Realm of England Attributed to Sir Thomas Smith*. Edited by Mary Dewar. Charlottesville: University Press of Virginia, 1969.

Starkey, Thomas. *A Dialogue between Reginald Pole and Thomas Lupset*. Edited by K. M. Burton. London: Chatto and Windus, 1948.

Statuta populi et communis Florentiae anno salutis MCCCCXV. 3 vols. Freiburg, 1778–83.

Statuti della republica fiorentina. Edited by Roberto Caggese. 2 vols. Florence, 1910–21.

Statuti della società del popolo di Bologna. Edited by Augusto Gaudenzi. 2 vols. Rome, 1889–96.

Statuti di Bologna del anno 1288. Edited by Gina Fasoli and Petro Sella. Vatican City: 1937–39.

Statuti di Bologna dell'anno 1245 all'anno 1267. Edited by Luigi Frati. 3 vols. Bologna, 1869–80.

Statuti di Imola del secolo XIV. Edited by S. Gaddoni. Milan, 1932.

Statuti di Perugia del' anno MCCCXLII. Edited by G. degli Azzi. 2 vols. Rome, 1913–16.

Statuti inediti della città di Pisa dal XII al XIV secolo. Edited by F. Bonaini. 3 vols. Florence, 1854–70.

Statuti Veronesi del 1276 colle correzioni e le aggiunte fino al 1323. Edited by Gino Sandri. 2 vols. Venice, 1940–59.

Statuto di Arezzo. Edited by G. Camerani Marri. Florence, 1946.

Thucydides. *History of the Peloponnesian War*. 14 vols. Cambridge: Harvard University Press, 1919–56.

Webster, John. *The Complete Works*. Edited by F. L. Lucas. London: Chatto and Windus, 1927.

Wolfe, Don M., ed. *Leveller Manifestoes of the Puritan Revolution*. New York: Humanities Press, 1967.

SECONDARY SOURCES

Adkins, A. W. H. *Merit and Responsibility: A Study in Greek Values*. Oxford: Clarendon Press, 1960.

———. *Moral Values and Political Behavior in Ancient Greece: From Homer to the End of the Fifth Century*. New York: Norton, 1972.

Alfoldy, Geza. *The Social History of Rome*. Translated by David Braund and Frank Pollock. Baltimore: Johns Hopkins University Press, 1988.

Almond, G., and S. Verba. *The Civic Culture: Political Attitudes and Democracy in Five Nations*. Princeton: Princeton University Press, 1963.

———. *The Civic Culture Revisited*. Boston: Little, Brown, 1980.

Andrewes, A. "The Government of Classical Sparta." In *Ancient Society and Institutions: Studies Presented to Victor Ehrenberg on His 75th Birthday*, edited by E. Badian. Oxford: Basil Blackwell, 1966.

———. *Probouleusis: Sparta's Contribution to the Technique of Government*. Oxford: University Press, 1954.

Arendt, Hannah. *The Human Condition*. Chicago: University of Chicago Press, 1958.

Austin, M. M., and P. Vidal-Naquet. *Economic and Social History of Ancient Greece: An Introduction*. 2d ed. Berkeley: University of California Press, 1980.

Badian, E. *Foreign Clientelae (264–70 B.C.)*. Oxford: University Press, 1958.

———, ed. *Ancient Society and Institutions: Studies Presented to Victor Ehrenberg on His 75th Birthday*. Oxford: Basil Blackwell, 1966.

Bailyn, Bernard. *The Ideological Origins of the American Revolution*. Cambridge: Harvard University Press, 1967.

Baker, Keith, ed. *The Political Culture of the Old Regime*. New York: Pergamon Press, 1987.

Banfield, Edward C. *The Moral Basis of a Backward Society*. Chicago: Free Press, 1958.

Barbadoro, Bernadino. *Le Finanze della Republica fiorentina*. Florence: Olschki, 1929.

Barbalet, J. M. *Citizenship*. Minneapolis: University of Minnesota Press, 1988.

Barker, Ernest. *From Alexander to Constantine*. Oxford: University Press, 1956.

———. *Greek Political Theory*. 4th ed. New York: Barnes and Noble, 1951.

Barni, G. "Cives e rustici alla fine del XII secolo e all' inizio del XIII secondo il Liber Consuetudinum Mediolani." *Rivista Storico Italiano* 69 (1957): 5–60.

Baron, Hans. "Calvinist Republicanism and Its Historical Roots." *Church History* 8 (1939): 30–42.

———. *The Crisis of the Early Italian Renaissance*. 2d ed. Princeton: Princeton University Press, 1966.

———. "Franciscan Poverty and Civic Wealth as Factors in the Rise of Humanistic Thought." *Speculum* 13 (1938): 1–37.

Bayley, C. C. *War and Society in Renaissance Florence: The de Militia of Leonardo Bruni*. Toronto: University of Toronto Press, 1961.

Becker, Marvin. *Florence in Transition*. 2 vols. Baltimore: Johns Hopkins University Press, 1968.

Bendix, Reinhard. *Kings or People: Power and the Mandate to Rule*. Berkeley: University of California Press, 1978.

———. *Nation Building and Citizenship*. Berkeley: University of California Press, 1977.

Bernstein, Alvin H. *Tiberius Sempronius Gracchus: Tradition and Apostasy*. Ithaca: Cornell University Press, 1978.

Bickel, Alexander M. *The Morality of Consent*. New Haven: Yale University Press, 1975.

Bizzari, Dina. "Ricerche sul diritto di cittadinanza nella costituzione comunale." *Studi Senesi* 32 (1916): Fasc., 1–2.

Blum, Carol. *Rousseau and the Republic of Virtue: The Language of Politics in the French Revolution*. Ithaca: Cornell University Press, 1986.

Bock, Gisela, Quentin Skinner, Maurizio Viroli, eds. *Machiavelli and Republicanism*. Cambridge: University Press, 1990.

Bolgar, R. R. *The Classical Heritage and Its Beneficiaries*. Cambridge: University Press, 1954.

Bonner, Stanley F. *Education in Ancient Rome from the Elder Cato to the Younger Pliny*. Berkeley: University of California Press, 1977.

Bossenga, Gail. "From Corps to Citizenship: The Bureaux des Finances Before the French Revolution." *Journal of Modern History* 58, no. 3 (September 1986): 610–42.

Boswell, John. *Christianity, Social Tolerance, and Homosexuality*. Chicago: University of Chicago Press, 1980.

Bouwsma, William J. "Lawyers in Early Modern Culture." *American Historical Review* 78 (1973): 303–27.

———. *Venice and the Defense of Republican Liberty*. Berkeley: University of California Press, 1968.

Bowra, C. M. *Early Greek Elegists*. Cambridge: Harvard University Press, 1930.

Bowsky, William M. "*Cives Silvestres*: Sylvan Citizenship and the Sienese Commune, 1287–1355." *Bulletino Senese di Storia Patria* 3.24 (1965): 1–13.

———. *The Finance of the Commune of Siena, 1287–1355*. Oxford: Clarendon Press, 1970.

———. "Medieval Citizenship: The Individual and the State in the Commune of

Siena, 1287–1355." *Studies in Medieval and Renaissance History* 4 (1967): 195–243.

Brady, Thomas A., Jr. "Rites to Autonomy, Rites to Dependence: South German Civil Culture in the Age of Renaissance and Reformation." In *Religion and Culture—The Renaissance*, vol. 11 of *Sixteenth Century Essays and Studies*, edited by Steven Ozment, pp. 9–24. Kirksville, Mo.: Sixteenth Century Journal Publishers, 1989.

———. *Ruling Class, Regime and Reformation in Strasbourg, 1520–1555*. Leiden: Brill, 1978.

Brown, Peter. *Augustine of Hippo*. Berkeley: University of California Press, 1970.

Brucker, G. *Florentine Politics and Society, 1343–1378*. Princeton: Princeton University Press, 1962.

———. *Renaissance Florence*. Berkeley: University of California Press, 1983.

Bueno de Mesquita, D. M. "The Place of Despotism in Italian Politics." In *Europe in the Late Middle Ages*, edited by J. R. Hale, J. R. L. Highfield, and B. Smalley, pp. 301–31. Evanston: Northwestern University Press, 1965.

Burns, J. H., ed. *The Cambridge History of Medieval Political Thought, c. 350–c. 1450*. Cambridge: University Press, 1988.

Calestrini, Giuseppe. "Statuti delle Compagne del popolo di Siena del principio del secolo XIV." *Archivio Storico Italiano* 15 (1851): 13–25.

———. "Statuti delle compagnie del Popolo di Pisa." *Archivio Storico Italiano* 15 (1851): 3–12.

Calimani, Riccardo. *The Ghetto of Venice*. Translated by K. J. Wolfthal. New York: M. Evans, 1987.

Canning, Joseph. *The Political Thought of Baldus de Ubaldis*. Cambridge: University Press, 1987.

Caton, Hiram. *The Politics of Progress: The Origins and Development of the Commercial Republic, 1600–1835*. Gainesville: University of Florida Press, 1988.

Chénon, Émile, *Histoire générale du droit français publique et privé dès origines à 1815*. 2 vols. Paris: Recueil Sirey, 1929.

Chrimes, K. M. T. *Ancient Sparta*. Manchester: Manchester University Press, 1949.

Chrisman, Miriam U. *Strasbourg and the Reform: A Study in the Process of Change*. New Haven: Yale University Press, 1967.

Chroust, Anton-Hermann. *Aristotle: New Light on His Life and on Some of His Lost Works*. 2 vols. South Bend: University of Notre Dame Press, 1973.

Churchill, Henry S. *The City Is the People*. New York: Harcourt, Brace, 1945.

Colorni, V. *Gli ebrei nel sistema del diritto comune fino alla prima emancipazione*. Milan, 1956.

Condren, Conal. "George Lawson and the *Defensor Pacis* on the Use of Marsilius in Seventeenth-Century England." *Medioevo* 6 (1980): 595–617.

———. *George Lawson's Politica and the English Revolution*. Cambridge: University Press, 1989.

———. "Resistance and Sovereignty in Lawson's Politica: An Examination of a

Part of Professor Franklin, His Chimera." *Historical Journal* 24, no. 3 (1981): 673–81.

———. "*Sacra* before *Civilis*: Understanding the Ecclesiastical Politics of George Lawson." *Journal of Religious History* 11 (1981): 524–35.

Cornelisen, Ann. *Torregreca: A World in Southern Italy*. London: Macmillan, 1969.

Cortese, Ennio. "Cittadinanza." *Enciclopedia del Diritto* 7 (Milan, 1960): 132–39.

La coscienza cittadina nei comuni italiani del duecento. Convegni del centro di studi sulla spiritualità medievale, 11. Todi, 1972.

Croiset, Maurice. "The Parabasis of the Frogs." In *Twentieth Century Interpretations of the Frogs*, edited by David J. Littlefield. Englewood Cliffs, N.J.: Prentice-Hall, 1968.

Currie, Harry M., ed. *The Individual and the State*. London: Dent, 1973.

Darnton, Robert, and Daniel Roche, eds. *Revolution in Print: The Press in France, 1775–1800*. Berkeley: University of California Press, 1989.

Davidsohn, Robert. *Firenze ai tempi di Dante*. Florence: R. Bemporad & figlio, 1929.

———. *Storia di Firenze*. 8 vols. Florence: Sansoni, 1956–68.

Davies, J. K. "Athenian Citizenship: The Descent Group and the Alternatives." *Classical Journal* 73 (1977–78): 105–21.

Davis, C. T. "An Early Florentine Political Theorist: Fra Remigio de' Girolami." In *Dante's Italy and Other Essays*, pp. 198–223. Philadelphia: University of Pennsylvania Press, 1984.

Davis, J. C. "Pocock's Harrington: Grace, Nature and Art in the Classical Republicanism of James Harrington." *Historical Journal* 24, no. 3 (1981): 683–97.

Deane, Herbert A. *The Political and Social Ideas of St. Augustine*. New York: Columbia University Press, 1963.

d'Entreves, A. P. *Natural Law*. London: Hutchinson, 1951.

Deutsch, Karl W. *Nationalism and Its Alternatives*. New York: Knopf, 1969.

———. *Nationalism and Social Communication*. Cambridge and New York: M.I.T. Press and Wiley, 1953.

Dewar, Mary. *Sir Thomas Smith*. London: University of London, Athlone Press, 1964.

Diggins, John Patrick. "Comrades and Citizens: New Mythologies in American Historiography." *American Historical Review* 90 (June 1988): 614–49.

———. *The Lost Soul of American Politics: Virtue, Self-Interest and the Foundations of Liberalism*. New York: Basic Books, 1984.

Donaldson, Peter S. *Machiavelli and Mystery of State*. New York: Cambridge University Press, 1988.

Dover, K. J. *Greek Homosexuality*. Cambridge: Harvard University Press, 1978.

———. *Greek Popular Morality in the Time of Plato and Aristotle*. Berkeley: University of California Press, 1974.

Downey, G. *Antioch in the Age of Theodosius the Great*. Norman: University of Oklahoma Press, 1962.

Earl, Donald. *The Moral and Political Tradition of Rome*. Ithaca: Cornell University Press, 1967.

Edmonds, J. M. *Elegy and Iambus*. 2 vols. Cambridge: Harvard University Press, 1968.

Ehrenberg, Victor. *From Solon to Socrates*. 2d ed. London: Methuen, 1973.

———. *The Greek State*. Oxford: Blackwell, 1960.

———. *The People of Aristophanes*. New York: Shocken Books, 1962.

Ennen, Edith. *The Medieval Town*. Amsterdam: North Holland Publishing Company, 1979.

———. *The Medieval Woman*. Oxford: Basil Blackwell, 1989.

Entralgo, Pedro L. *The Therapy of the Word in Classical Antiquity*. New Haven: Yale University Press, 1970.

Fasoli, Gina. "La coscienza civica nelle *Laudes civitatum*." In *La coscienza cittadina nei comuni italiani del duecento*, pp. 11–44. Todi, 1972.

Ferguson, Arthur B. *The Articulate Citizen and the English Renaissance*. Durham: Duke University Press, 1965.

Fine, John V. A. *The Ancient Greeks: A Critical History*. Cambridge: Harvard University Press, 1983.

Finlay, Robert. *Politics in Renaissance Venice*. New Brunswick: Rutgers University Press, 1980.

Finley, M. I. *The Ancient Economy*. 2d ed. Berkeley: University of California Press, 1973.

———. *Ancient Slavery and Modern Ideology*. New York: Viking Press, 1980.

———. *Aspects of Antiquity*. London: Chatto and Windus, 1968.

———. "Athenian Demagogues." In *Studies in Ancient Society*. London: Routledge, Kegan Paul, 1974.

———. *Democracy Ancient and Modern*. New Brunswick: Rutgers University Press, 1973.

———. *Economy and Society in Ancient Greece*. New York: Viking, 1982.

———. "The Freedom of the Citizen in the Greek World." In *Economy and Society in Ancient Greece*. New York: Viking, 1982.

———. *Politics in the Ancient World*. Cambridge: University Press, 1983.

———. *Slavery in Classical Antiquity: Views and Controversies*. Cambridge: W. Heffer and Sons, 1960.

Fisher, N. R. E. *Social Values in Classical Athens*. London: Dent, 1976.

Fiumi, E. "Sui rapporti economici tra città e contado nell'età comunale." *Archivio Storico Italiano* 114 (1955): 18–68.

Forrest, W. G. *The Emergence of Greek Democracy*. London: Weidenfeld and Nicolson, 1966.

———. *A History of Sparta, 950–192 B.C.* New York: Norton, 1969.

Friedrichs, Christopher R. "German Town Revolts and the Seventeenth Century Crisis." *Renaissance and Modern Studies* 26 (1982): 27–51.

———. "Urban Conflicts and the Imperial Constitution in Seventeenth-Century

Germany." *Journal of Modern History* 58, Supplement (December 1986): S98–S123.

Garin, Eugenio. *L'educazione in Europa (1400–1600)*. Bari: Laterza, 1957.

Garnsey, Peter. "Legal Privilege in the Roman Empire." In *Studies in Ancient Society*, edited by M. I. Finley. London: Routledge, Kegan Paul, 1974.

———. *Social Status and Legal Privilege in the Roman Empire*. Oxford: Clarendon Press, 1970.

Gass, William. "Exile." *Salmagundi* 88–89 (Fall 1990–Winter 1991): 89–108.

Gaudemet, Jean. *Institutions de l'Antiquité*. Paris: Sirey, 1967.

Gay, Peter, ed. *John Locke on Education*. New York: Bureau of Publications, Teachers College, Columbia University, 1964.

Geertz, C. *The Interpretation of Cultures*. New York: Basic Books, 1973.

———. *Local Knowledge*. New York: Basic Books, 1983.

Gelderen, Martin van. "The Machiavellian Moment and the Dutch Revolt: The Rise of Neostoicism and Dutch Republicanism." In *Machiavelli and Republicanism*, edited by G. Bock, Q. Skinner, and M. Viroli, pp. 205–24. Cambridge: University Press, 1990.

Gierke, Otto von. *The Development of Political Theory*. New York: Norton, 1939.

———. *Natural Law and the Theory of Society, 1500–1800*. Cambridge: University Press, 1934.

———. *Political Theories of the Middle Age*. Cambridge: Unversity Press, 1900.

Gilbert, Felix. *Machiavelli and Guicciardini*. Princeton: Princeton University Press, 1965.

Glasson, E. *Histoire du droit et des institutions de la France*. 8 vols. Paris: F. Pichon, 1896–1903.

Glotz, Gustav. *The Greek City and Its Institutions*. New York: Knopf, 1930.

Gomme, A. W. *The Population of Athens in the Fifth and Fourth Centuries B.C.* Oxford: Basil Blackwell, 1933.

Graham, A. J. *Colony and Mother City in Ancient Greece*. Manchester: Manchester University Press, 1964.

Grant, Michael. *The Etruscans*. New York: Scribner's, 1980.

Gray, Robert. *A History of London*. London: Hutchinson, 1978.

Grazia, S. de. *Machiavelli in Hell*. Princeton: Princeton University Press, 1989.

Grignaschi, Mario. "La definition du 'civis' dans la scholastique." *Anciens pays et assemblees d'états* 35, *Standen en landen* (1966): 71–180.

Halperin, David M. *One Hundred Years of Homosexuality and Other Essays on Greek Love*. New York: Routledge, 1990.

Hammond, M. *City-State and World-State in Greek and Roman Political Thought until Augustus*. Cambridge: University Press, 1955.

Hanson, Donald. *From Kingdom to Commonwealth: The Development of Civic Consciousness in English Political Thought*. Cambridge: Harvard University Press, 1970.

Harrison, A. R. W. *The Law of Athens*. 2 vols. Oxford: Clarendon Press, 1968–71.

Hay, Denys. *The Italian Renaissance in Its Historical Background*. 2d ed. Cambridge: University Press, 1977.

Heers, Jacques. *Family Clans in the Middle Ages*. Amsterdam: North Holland Publishing Company, 1977.

———. *Fêtes, jeux et joutes dans les sociétés d'Occident à la fin du moyen âge*. Paris: Vrin, 1971.

———. *Gênes au xve siècle. Civilisation méditerranéenne, grand capitalisme, et capitalisme populaire*. Paris: Flammarion, 1971.

Helmholz, Richard. *Roman Canon Law in Reformation England*. Cambridge: University Press, 1990.

Hengel, Martin. *Jews, Greeks, and Barbarians*. Philadelphia: Fortress Press, 1980.

Herlihy, David. *Medieval and Renaissance Pistoia*. New Haven: Yale University Press, 1967.

———. *Pisa in the Early Renaissance*. New Haven: Yale University Press, 1958.

Hexter, J. H. "The Education of the Aristocracy in the Renaissance." In *Reappraisals in History*, pp. 45–70. London: Longmans, 1961.

———. *More's Utopia: The Biography of an Idea*. 2d ed. New York: Harper and Row, 1965.

———. *The Vision of Politics on the Eve of the Reformation: More, Machiavelli, Seyssel*. New York: Basic Books, 1973.

Hignett, C. *A History of the Athenian Constitution to the End of the Fifth Century B.C.* Oxford: Clarendon Press, 1952.

Higonnet, Patrice. *Sister Republics: The Origin of French and American Republicanism*. Cambridge: Harvard University Press, 1988.

Hirst, Derek. *Authority and Conflict: England, 1603–1658*. Cambridge: Harvard University Press, 1986.

———. *The Representative of the People?* Cambridge: University Press, 1975.

Holdsworth, William S. *A History of English Law*. 2d ed. London: Methuen, 1903–72.

Homo, Leon. *Roman Political Institutions from City to State*. London: Routledge and Kegan Paul, 1929.

Huffman, C. C. *Coriolanus in Context*. Lewisburg: Bucknell University Press, 1971.

Hunt, H. A. K. *The Humanism of Cicero*. Melbourne: Melbourne University Press, 1954.

Huxley, G. L. *Early Sparta*. 2d ed. New York: Barnes and Noble, 1970.

Hyde, J. K. *Padua in the Age of Dante*. Manchester: Manchester University Press, 1966.

Hyslop, Beatrice F. *French Nationalism in 1789 According to the General Cahiers*. New York: Columbia University Press, 1967.

———. *A Guide to the General Cahiers of 1789, with the Texts of Unedited Cahiers*. New York: Columbia University Press, 1936.

Jaeger, W. *Paideia: The Ideals of Greek Culture*. 2d ed. 3 vols. New York: Oxford University Press, 1945.

Jaume, Lucien. "Citoyenneté et souveraineté: les poids de l'absolutisme." In *The Political Culture of the Old Regime*, edited by Keith Baker, pp. 515–34. Oxford: Pergamon Press, 1987.

————. *Hobbes et l'Etat representatif moderne*. Paris: Presses Universitaires de France, 1986.

Jebb, Richard C. *The Attic Orators from Antiphon to Isaeos*. 2d ed. 2 vols. London: Macmillan, 1888.

Jones, A. H. M. *Athenian Democracy*. Oxford: Basil Blackwell, 1957.

————. *Sparta*. Oxford: Blackwell and Mott, 1967.

Jones, P. J. "Florentine Families and Florentine Diaries in the Fourteenth Century." *Papers of the British School at Rome* 24, n.s. 11 (1956): 185–205.

Kantorowicz, Ernest. *The King's Two Bodies: A Study in Medieval Political Theology*. Princeton: Princeton University Press, 1957.

————. "Mysteries of State: An Absolutist Concept and Its Late Medieval Origins." *Harvard Theological Review* 47 (1955): 65–99.

Kelley, Donald R. *The Beginning of Ideology*. Cambridge: University Press, 1981.

Keohane, Nannerl O. *Philosophy and the State in France: The Renaissance to the Enlightenment*. Princeton: Princeton University Press, 1980.

Kettner, James H. *The Development of American Citizenship, 1608–1870*. Chapel Hill: University of North Carolina Press, 1978.

Kibre, Pearl. *Scholarly Privileges in the Middle Ages: The Rights, Privileges, and Immunities of Scholars and Universities at Bologna, Padua, Paris, and Oxford*. Cambridge: Medieval Academy of America, 1962.

Kirshner, J. "'Ars imitatur naturam': A *Consilium* of Baldus on Naturalization in Florence." *Viator* 5 (1974): 289–331.

————. "Between Nature and Culture: An Opinion of Baldus of Perugia on Venetian Citizenship as Second Nature." *Journal of Medieval and Renaissance Studies* 9, no. 2 (1979): 179–208.

————. "'Civitas sibi faciat civem': Bartolus of Sassoferrato's Doctrine of the Making of a Citizen." *Speculum* 48 (1973): 694–713.

————. "Messer Francesco di Bici degli Albergotti d'Arezzo, Citizen of Florence (1350–1376)." *Bulletin of Medieval Canon Law*, n.s. 2 (1972): 84–90.

————. "Paolo di Castro on *cives ex privilegio*: A Controversy over the Legal Qualifications for Public Office in Early Fifteenth-Century Florence." In *Renaissance Studies in Honor of Hans Baron*, edited by A. Molho and J. A. Tedeschi. De Kalb, Ill., 1971.

Kisch, Guido. *Consilia: Eine Bibliographie der juristischen Konsiliensammlungen*. Basel: Helbring und Lichtenhahn, 1970.

Knight, Isabel F. *The Geometric Spirit: The Abbé de Condillac and the French Enlightenment*. New Haven: Yale University Press, 1968.

Lacey, W. K. *The Family in Classical Greece*. Ithaca: Cornell University Press, 1968.

Lane, F. C. "At the Roots of Republicanism." *American Historical Review* 71 (January 1966): 403–20.

Laslett, Peter. *The World We Have Lost Further Explored*. 3d ed. New York: Scribner's, 1984.

Leach, Edmund. *Culture and Communication*. Cambridge: University Press, 1976.

Leclercq, Jean. *Jean de Paris et l'écclesiologie du xiiiᵉ siècle*. Paris: Vrin, 1942.

Lestocquoy, Jean. *Les villes de Flandre et d'Italie sous le gouvernement des patriciens.* Paris: Presses Universitaires de France, 1952.

Little, Lester K. *Religious Poverty and the Profit Economy in Medieval Europe.* Ithaca: Cornell University Press, 1978.

L'Orange, H. P. *Art Forms and Civic Life in the Late Roman Empire.* Princeton: Princeton University Press, 1965.

Lord, Carnes. *Education and Culture in the Political Thought of Aristotle.* Ithaca: Cornell University Press, 1982.

Lucas, Colin, ed. *The Political Culture of the French Revolution.* New York: Pergamon Press, 1988.

McIntyre, Alistyre. *After Virtue: A Study in Moral Theory.* Notre Dame: University of Notre Dame Press, 1981.

Maehl, William H. *Germany in Western Civilization.* University: University of Alabama Press, 1979.

Mansfield, H., Jr. *Taming the Prince.* New York: Free Press, 1989.

Manville, Brook. *The Origins of Citizenship in Ancient Athens.* Princeton: Princeton University Press, 1990.

Markus, R. A. *Saeculum: History and Society in the Theology of St. Augustine.* Cambridge: University Press, 1970.

Marrou, H. I. *A History of Education in Antiquity.* New York: Mentor, 1964.

Marshall, T. H. *Sociology at the Crossroads and Other Essays.* London: Heinemann, 1963.

Martines, Lauro. *Lawyers and Statecraft in Renaissance Florence.* Princeton: Princeton University Press, 1968.

―――. *The Social World of the Florentine Humanists.* Princeton: Princeton University Press, 1963.

Masters, Roger D. *The Political Philosophy of Rousseau.* Princeton: Princeton University Press, 1968.

Mattingly, G. *Renaissance Diplomacy.* New York: Houghton Mifflin, 1955.

Mauss, Marcel. *The Gift.* New York: Norton, 1967.

Mayer, Thomas F. *Thomas Starkey and the Commonweal.* Cambridge: University Press, 1989.

Mazzolani, Lidia. *The Idea of the City in Roman Thought.* Bloomington: Indiana University Press, 1970.

Mesnard, Pierre. *L'essor de la philosophie politique au xvie siècle.* Paris: Vrin, 1951.

Miller, James. *Rousseau: Dreamer of Democracy.* New Haven: Yale University Press, 1984.

Moeller, Bernd. *Imperial Cities and the Reformation.* Philadelphia: Fortress Press, 1972.

Momigliano, A. "The Origins of the Roman Republic." In *Interpretation: Theory and Practice,* edited by C. Singleton. Baltimore: Johns Hopkins University Press, 1969.

Monter, William E. *Calvin's Geneva.* New York: Wiley, 1967.

Moore, Sally F., and Barbara G. Myerhoff, eds. *Secular Ritual*. Assen: Van Gorcum, 1977.

Morghen, R. "Vita religiosa e vita cittadina nella Firenze del duecento." In *La coscienza cittadina nei comuni italiani del duecento*, pp. 195–228. Todi, 1972.

Morris, Christopher. *Political Thought in England: Tyndale to Hooker*. Oxford: University Press, 1953.

Morris, Colin. *The Discovery of the Individual, 1050–1200*. New York: Harper and Row, 1972.

Morrison, Karl F. *The Two Kingdoms: Ecclesiology in Carolingian Political Thought*. Princeton: Princeton University Press, 1964.

Morrow, Glenn R. *Plato's Cretan City*. Princeton: Princeton University Press, 1960.

Muir, Edward. *Civic Ritual in Renaissance Venice*. Princeton: Princeton University Press, 1981.

———. "Images of Power: Art and Pageantry in Renaissance Venice." *American Historical Review* 84 (1979): 16–52.

Myres, John L. *The Political Ideas of the Greeks*. New York: Abingdon Press, 1927.

Nicolet, Claude. *The World of the Citizen in Republican Rome*. Berkeley: University of California Press, 1980.

Oliva, Pavel. *Sparta and Her Social Problems*. Prague: Academia, 1971.

Ozment, Steven E. *The Reformation in the Cities: The Appeal of Protestantism to Sixteenth-Century Germany and Switzerland*. New Haven: Yale University Press, 1975.

Palmer, R. R. "Man and Citizen: Applications of Individualism in the French Revolution." In *Essays in Political Theory Presented to George H. Sabine*, edited by M. R. Konvitz and A. E. Murphy, pp. 130–52. Ithaca: Cornell University Press, 1948.

Pangle, Thomas L. *Montesquieu's Philosophy of Liberalism: A Commentary on "The Spirit of the Laws."* Chicago: University of Chicago Press, 1973.

———. *The Spirit of Modern Republicanism: The Moral Vision of the American Founders and the Philosophy of Locke*. Chicago: University of Chicago Press, 1988.

Parry, Geraint. *Participation in Politics*. Manchester: Manchester University Press, 1972.

Pateman, Carole. *Participation and Democratic Theory*. Cambridge: University Press, 1970.

Patlagean, Evelyne. *Pauvreté economique et pauvreté sociale à Byzance 4ᵉ–7ᵉ siècles*. Paris: Mouton, 1977.

Patterson, Cynthia. *Pericles' Citizenship Law of 451–50 B.C.* New York: Arno Press, 1981.

Peters, F. E. *The Harvest of Hellenism*. New York: Simon and Schuster, 1970.

Pirenne, H. *Early Democracy in the Low Countries*. New York: Harper and Row, 1963.

———. *Medieval Cities*. Princeton: Princeton University Press, 1949.

Plamenatz, John P. *Man and Society*. 2 vols. London: Longman, 1963.

Plesner, J. *L'émigration de la campagne à la ville libre de Florence au xiiie siècle.* Copenhagen: Gyldendal, 1934.

Pocock, J. G. A. "Between Gog and Magog: The Republican Thesis and the Ideologica Americana." *Journal of the History of Ideas* 48 (1987): 325–46.

———. *The Machiavellian Moment.* Princeton: Princeton University Press, 1975.

———. *Politics, Language, and Time.* New York: Atheneum, 1973.

Post, Gaines. *Studies in Medieval Legal Thought.* Princeton: Princeton University Press, 1964.

Potter, T. W. *Roman Italy.* Berkeley: University of California Press, 1987.

Queller, Donald. *The Office of Ambassador in the Middle Ages.* Princeton: Princeton University Press, 1967.

Raab, Felix. *The English Face of Machiavelli.* London: Routledge and Kegan Paul, 1964.

Raaflaub, Kurt A. "Democracy, Oligarchy and the Concept of the 'Free Citizen' in Late Fifth Century Athens." *Political Theory* 11 (1983): 517–44.

———, ed. *Social Struggles in Archaic Rome: New Perspectives on the Conflict of the Orders.* Berkeley: University of California Press, 1986.

Rahe, Paul. "The Primacy of Politics in Classical Greece." *American Historical Review* 89 (1984): 265–93.

———. *Republics Ancient and Modern.* Chapel Hill: University of North Carolina Press, 1992.

Randall, J. H., Jr. *Aristotle.* New York: Columbia University Press, 1960.

Rawson, Elizabeth. *The Spartan Tradition in European Thought.* Oxford: Clarendon Press, 1969.

Reynolds, Susan. *An Introduction to the History of English Medieval Towns.* Oxford: Clarendon Press, 1977.

———. *Kingdoms and Communities in Western Europe, 900–1300.* Oxford: Clarendon Press, 1984.

Rice, Eugene. *The Renaissance Idea of Wisdom.* Cambridge: Harvard University Press, 1958.

Richter, M. *The Political Theory of Montesquieu.* Cambridge: University Press, 1977.

Riesenberg, Peter. "Citizenship and Equality in Late Medieval Italy." *Studia Gratiana* 15 (1972): 424–39.

———. "Civism and Roman Law in Fourteenth Century Italian Society." *Explorations in Economic History* 7 (1969): 237–54.

———. "The Consilia Literature: A Prospectus." *Manuscripta* 6 (1962): 3–22.

———. "Jews in the Structure of Western Institutions." *Judaism* 28 (1979): 402–15.

Rist, T. M. *Stoic Philosophy.* Cambridge: University Press, 1969.

Robbins, Caroline. *The Eighteenth-Century Commonwealthman.* Cambridge: Harvard University Press, 1959.

Roelofs, H. Mark. *The Tension of Citizenship: Private and Public Duty.* New York: Rinehart, 1957.

Rokkan, Stein. *Citizens, Elections, Parties.* New York: McKay, 1970.

Romanin, S. *Storia . . . di Venezia*. 2d ed. 10 vols. Venice, 1912.

Ross, W. D. *Aristotle*. 5th ed. London: Methuen, 1953.

Rossi, Guido. *Consilium Sapientis Iudiciale: studi e ricerche per la storia del processo romano-canonico*. Milan: A. Giuffré, 1958.

Rostovtsev, M. *A History of the Ancient World*. 2d ed. 2 vols. Oxford: Oxford University Press, 1930.

———. *The Social and Economic History of the Hellenistic World*. 3 vols. Oxford: University Press, 1941.

Rubinstein, N. "The Beginnings of Political Thought in Florence." *Journal of the Warburg and Courtauld Institutes* 5 (1942): 198–225.

———. "Marsilius and Italian Political Thought." In *Europe in the Late Middle Ages*, edited by J. R. Hale, J. R. L. Highfield, and B. Smalley. Evanston: Northwestern University Press, 1965.

Sabine, George H. *A History of Political Theory*. New York: Henry Holt and Company, 1937.

Salvemini, Gaetano. *La dignità cavalleresca nel Commune di Firenze*. Bari: Einaudi, 1960.

———. *Magnati e popolani in Firenze dal 1280 al 1295*. Florence, 1899.

Sandbach, F. H. *The Stoics*. New York: Norton, 1975.

Sapori, A. *Le marchand italien au moyen âge*. Paris: A. Colin, 1953.

Scaff, Lawrence A. *Participation in the Western Political Tradition: A Study of Theory and Practice*. Tucson: University of Arizona Press, 1975.

Schama, Simon. *Citizens*. New York: Viking Press, 1989.

Schlatter, Richard. *Richard Baxter and Puritan Politics*. New Brunswick: Rutgers University Press, 1957.

Scullard, Howard H. *The Etruscan Cities and Rome*. London: Thames & Hudson, 1967.

———. *From the Gracchi to Nero: A History of Rome from 133 B.C. to A.D. 68*. 3d ed. London: Methuen, 1970.

———. *A History of the Roman World from 753 to 146 B.C.* London: Methuen, 1951.

———. *Roman Politics, 220–130 B.C.* 2d ed. Oxford: Clarendon Press, 1973.

Sealey, Raphael. *A History of the Greek City States, 700–338 B.C.* Berkeley: University of California Press, 1976.

Sennett, Richard. *The Fall of Public Man*. New York: Knopf, 1977.

Sewell, William H., Jr. "Le citoyen/la citoyenne: Activity, Passivity, and the Revolutionary Concept of Citizenship." In *The Political Culture of the French Revolution*, edited by Colin Lucas, pp. 105–23. New York: Pergamon Press, 1988.

Shackleton Bailey, D. R. *Cicero*. London: Duckworth, 1971.

Sherwin-White, A. N. *The Roman Citizenship*. 2d ed. Oxford: Clarendon Press, 1973.

———. *Roman Society and Roman Law in the New Testament*. Oxford: University Press, 1963.

Shklar, Judith. *American Citizenship: The Quest for Inclusion*. Cambridge: Harvard University Press, 1991.

———. *Men and Citizens: A Study of Rousseau's Social Theory*. London: Cambridge University Press, 1969.

———. *Montesquieu*. Oxford: University Press, 1987.

———. "Montesquieu and the New Republicanism." In *Machiavelli and Republicanism*, edited by G. Bock, Q. Skinner, and M. Viroli, pp. 265–79. Cambridge: University Press, 1990.

Sinclair, T. A. *A History of Greek Political Thought*. 2d ed. London: Routledge and Kegan Paul, 1967.

Skinner, Q. *Foundations of Modern Political Thought*. 2 vols. Cambridge: University Press, 1978.

———. *Machiavelli*. New York: Hill and Wang, 1981.

Smith, Joseph H. *Cases and Materials on the Development of Legal Institutions*. St. Paul: West Publishing Company, 1965.

Spurlin, Paul M. *Montesquieu in America, 1760–1801*. University of Louisiana: Louisiana State University Press, 1940.

———. *Rousseau in America, 1760–1809*. University: University of Alabama Press, 1969.

Stewart, John H., ed. *A Documentary Survey of the French Revolution*. New York: Macmillan, 1951.

Stockton, David. *The Gracchi*. Oxford: Clarendon Press, 1979.

Strauss, Gerald. *Law, Resistance, and the State: The Opposition to Roman Law in Reformation Germany*. Princeton: Princeton University Press, 1986.

Struever, Nancy. *The Language of History in the Renaissance*. Princeton: Princeton University Press, 1970.

Syme, Ronald. *The Roman Revolution*. Oxford: Clarendon Press, 1939.

Tarcov, Nathan. *Locke's Education for Liberty*. Chicago: University of Chicago Press, 1984.

Tarn, W. W. *Hellenistic Civilization*. 2d ed. London: E. Arnold, 1930.

Taylor, J. H. "Political Motives in Cicero's Defense of Archias." *American Journal of Philology* 78 (1952): 62–70.

Taylor, Lily Ross. *Roman Voting Assemblies from the Hannibalic War to the Dictatorship of Caesar*. Ann Arbor: University of Michigan Press, 1966.

Thomas, G. M. "Cittadinanza veneta accordata a forestieri." *Archivio Veneto* 8 (1874): 154–56.

Thompson, Dennis F. *The Democratic Citizen*. Cambridge: University Press, 1970.

Tierney, Brian. *Religion, Law, and the Growth of Constitutional Thought, 1150–1650*. Cambridge: University Press, 1982.

Totalitarian Democracy and After. Sermalen: Magness Press, Hebrew University, 1984.

Trexler, Richard C. *Public Life in Renaissance Florence*. New York: Academic Press, 1980.

Ucko, Peter J., Ruth Tringham, and G. W. Dimbley. *Man, Settlement and Urbanism.* Cambridge, Mass.: Schenkman Publishing Company, 1972.

Ullmann, W. *The Individual and Society in the Middle Ages.* Baltimore: Johns Hopkins University Press, 1966.

Vergottini, G. de. "Origini e sviluppo storico della comitatenanza." *Studi Senesi* 43 (1929): 347–481.

———. "Il papato e la comitatinanza nello stato della chiesa (sec. XIII–XV)." In *Scritti in memoria di Luigi Simeoni,* vol. 1. 2 vols. Bologna, 1953.

———. "I presupposti storici del rapporto di comitatinanza e la diplomatica comunale." In *Scritti . . . in onore di Umberto Borsi,* edited by A. Milani, pp. 51–86. Padua: Cedam, 1955.

Vinogradoff, Paul. *Collected Papers.* 2 vols. Oxford: University Press, 1928.

Violante, C. *La società milanese nell' età precomunale.* Bari: Laterza, 1953.

Visconti, A. "Note preliminari sull' 'origo' nelle fonti imperiali romane." In *Studi di storia e diritto in onore di Carlo Calisse,* 1:89–105. Milan, 1940.

Walbank, F. W. *A Historical Commentary on Polybius.* 3 vols. Oxford: Clarendon Press, 1957–79.

———. *Polybius.* Berkeley: University of California Press, 1972.

———. "The Problem of Greek Nationality." *Phoenix* 5 (1951): 41–60.

Waley, Daniel. *Medieval Orvieto.* Cambridge: University Press, 1952.

Walker, Mack. *German Home Towns: Community, State and General Estate, 1648–1871.* Ithaca: Cornell University Press, 1971.

———. *Johann Jakob Moser and the Holy Roman Empire of the German Nation.* Chapel Hill: University of North Carolina Press, 1981.

Wallace-Hadrill, Andrew. *Patronage in Ancient Society.* London: Routledge, 1989.

Walzer, Michael. *Obligations: Essays on Disobedience, War and Citizenship.* Cambridge: Harvard University Press, 1970.

———. *Revolution of the Saints.* Cambridge: Harvard University Press, 1965.

Weber, Eugen. *Peasants into Frenchmen.* Palo Alto: Stanford University Press, 1976.

Weinstein, Donald. *Savonarola and Florence: Prophecy and Patriotism in the Renaissance.* Princeton: Princeton University Press, 1970.

Westlake, H. D. *Individuals in Thucydides.* London: Cambridge University Press, 1968.

Whitehead, David. *The Ideology of the Athenian Metic.* Cambridge: University Press, 1977.

Winkler, John J. *The Constraints of Desire.* London: Routledge, 1990.

Worden, B. "Milton's Republicanism and the Tyranny of Heaven." In *Machiavelli and Republicanism,* edited by G. Bock, Q. Skinner, and M. Viroli. Cambridge: University Press, 1990.

World of Athens: An Introduction to Classical Athenian Culture. Cambridge: University Press, 1984.

Zarb, Mireille. *Les privilèges de la ville de Marseilles du xe siècle à la Revolution.* Paris: J. Picard, 1961.

Zimmern, Alfred. *The Greek Commonwealth.* 5th ed. Oxford: University Press, 1961.

INDEX

𐄁𐄁𐄁

Abelard, Peter, 108
Absolutism, 198
Academics, 110, 130
Accursius, 108, 126, 131–32, 281
 (n. 38), 282 (n. 5), 285 (n. 35)
Achaean League, 57
Active life, 97, 107, 118–19, 141,
 189–93, 197, 253; in medieval Aris-
 totelianism, 168; before civic human-
 ists, 190–93; and republicanism,
 190–94; in Locke, 251
Adams, John, 249
Aeneas Silvius, 285 (n. 45)
Aetolian League, 57
Agape, 90, 93
Agora, 27
Agrippa, 81
Albani, 224
Albericus de Rosate, 137, 282 (n. 51),
 286 (n. 57)
Albertus Magnus, 122
Alcibiades, 31, 33–34, 133–34
Alexander of Imola, 143, 156–57, 171,
 185, 282 (n. 3), 286 (n. 67)
Alexander the Great, 42
Alexandria, 49, 84, 111, 270
Aliens, 109; sense of civic responsibil-
 ity, 119–20
Allegheri, Petrus, 160, 285 (n. 39), 288
 (nn. 4–7)
Althusius, Johannes, 238–40, 288
 (nn. 4–7)
Ambrose, Saint, 90
America, 267–72

Amor, 125, 134
Andreas de Barbatia, 286 (n. 62)
Animus, 125
Antioch, 89 90
Aquinas. *See* Thomas Aquinas, Saint
Archias, 78
Arete, 32–33
Aretinus, 127, 156, 181, 281 (n. 26),
 286 (n. 62)
Arezzo, 137, 190; loss of citizenship in,
 151
Arians, 101
Aristocrats: and Greek civic culture,
 31
Aristophanes, 36
Aristotle, ix, x, xv, xx, xxii, 5, 28, 32–
 33, 38–39, 42–47, 87, 91, 103,
 112, 164–69, 187, 191, 194, 205–6,
 209, 213, 216, 231, 242, 251, 256,
 261, 275 (n. 4), 277 (n. 38); on pol-
 itics, ix, xviii, 28–29, 42, 163; on
 Sparta, 11, 43; on *Constitution of
 Athens*, 12; on Solon, 16; on demes,
 20; on tribes, 20; on *metics*, 21; on
 class and citizenship, 34, 45–46; on
 virtue, 43; on education, 43–44; on
 citizenship, 44–47; influence on stoicism, 75; in Dominican teaching,
 122–23; *Poetics* and *Rhetoric*, 192
Arius, 270
Arnold of Brescia, 128
"Articulate citizen," 211. *See also*
 "Tudor citizen"
Ascham, Roger, 213, 287 (n. 13)

Assimilation, 147–50. *See also* Immigration; Naturalization
Asti, 144
Athens, 12–49, 187; compared to Sparta, 34
Attica, 99
Augsburg, Peace of, 222
Augustine, Saint, 88–92, 133–34, 269, 279 (n. 4), 281 (n. 43)
Augustus, 66, 80–81
Avignon, 127
Azo, 144, 183, 282 (n. 5), 286 (n. 3)

Bacon, Francis, 88, 207, 245
Bailyn, Bernard, 267
Balard, Jean, 230
Baldus, 129, 132, 135–37, 145, 151, 156, 171, 180–82, 184, 281 (nn. 39, 44), 282 (nn. 5–6, 51), 283 (n. 24), 285 (nn. 34, 51), 286 (nn. 62, 65–66)
Baron, Hans, 188–92, 286 (n. 1)
Bartolus, 128, 132, 137, 142, 144, 156, 158, 161–62, 169, 171–72, 175, 180–82, 280 (n. 20), 281 (nn. 28, 39), 282 (nn. 2, 4), 285 (nn. 34, 42, 52), 286 (n. 54)
Battafuoco, 263
Beaumarchais, 255
Benedictine rule, 94
Benefits of citizenship, 135–36; in Polybius, 68; in commercial society, 106; in England, 116
Benvenuto Commento, 285 (n. 39)
Benvenuto da Imola, 160
Beza, Theodore, 225–26, 288 (n. 25)
Birthplace, 106. *See also* Civic identity
Bishops, 97–102
Bloch, Marc, 131
Boccaccio, Giovanni, 193
Bodin, Jean, xi, 186, 199, 219–25, 235, 239, 265, 287 (nn. 21–22)
Boerius, Nicolaus, 180–81, 286 (n. 61)
Bologna, 121, 130, 153, 160, 178,

181, 192. *See also* University of Bologna
Boston, 270
Boulainvilliers, Henri de, 254
Bruges, 112, 114, 197
Brunetto Latini, 161, 170, 192, 285 (nn. 43, 50)
Bruni, Leonardo, 138, 168, 189, 193, 194, 196
Bucer, Martin, 227, 230
Burlamaqui, Jean Jacques, 238

Caesar, 70, 80, 81, 134
Cahiers, 265–66, 291 (n. 18)
Calvin, John, 230–31, 270
Calvinists, 227–29
Calvin's Case, 217. *See also* Coke, Edward
Cambridge University, 198, 213
Campagnia del Popolo (Siena), 153
Campanalismo, 98, 160
Canon law, 104, 126, 230, 247
Capitio, Wolfgang, 232
Caracalla, 82, 91, 180
Caritas, 93
Carthage, 63, 68, 69
Catherine the Great, 290 (n. 5)
Cato, 126, 216, 254
Ceba, Ansaldo, 258, 290 (n. 8)
Charlemagne, 102, 106
Charles I, 242, 244
Christianity: and citizenship, 55, 84
Chrysostom, Saint John, 89–90, 279 (n. 3)
Church: and urban governments, 127–29, 281 (n. 29)
Church fathers, 133
Cicero, 12, 47, 56, 65, 74–79, 81–82, 87, 91, 126, 168, 177, 187, 189, 193, 205, 212–13, 233, 242–43, 254, 256, 261, 280 (n. 22); on civic education, 77–78; on private property, 78
Ciompi, 124

Cité, 142

Citizenship: First, xv, xviii–xix, 272, 275 (n. 4); Second, xviii–xxi; as vassalage, xxi, 135; as principle of discrimination, 3, 107–8; and scarcity of resources, 3–4; effects of war upon, 6; culture of, 30; in Aristotle, 44–47; honorary, 52; monastic, 94–97; in a commercial society, 106; in the revival of Europe, 107–10; common law of, 108–9, 179–82; and exiles, 109–10; and immigrants, 110, 149–51, 153–55; and feudalism, 112–17; in northern Europe, 112–17; motivation for, 134–37, 147–49; and equality, 145–46, 155–57; benefits of, 147–49, 174–77, 182–86; loss of, 151; residence requirements for, 153–54, 284 (nn. 28–30); and princely power, 155–56, 172, 184–86, 203, 208–9, 212, 217, 222–24; in the theologians, 162–68; in law, 179–82; multiple, in the Middle Ages, 182–86; in the large monarchies, 188, 198, 208, 211–12; and the new view of man, 206–8, 240–41; as state service, 213–16, 219–20; and religious conformity, 227–32; in Rousseau, 260–65

Citoyen, 253, 255, 257–58, 271

City: conceptualization of, 157–61; management of, 170; in legal theory, 170–73; homogeneity of urban life, 176–78. See also Urbanism

City of God, 91–93, 97

City of Man, 92, 95

Civic activism, 110

Civic consciousness, 118–20, 125

Civic humanism, 138, 188–93, 199, 243, 249, 255; under a large monarchy, 243–50

Civic identity: conferred by birth, 106

Civic love, 76, 131, 137–39, 161–62

Civil lawyers, 133. See also Roman law

Civis, 143–44, 155, 165, 171, 198, 203–33

Civitas, xviii, xxii, 275 (n. 1); in Althusius, 239

Civitas sine suffragio, 58

Class: and citizenship in Aristotle, 45–46

Classicism, 205

Cleisthenes, 18–22

Coke, Edward, 217. See also *Calvin's Case*

Cola da Rienzo, 128

Cola d'Ascoli, 283 (n. 15)

Colet, John, 198

Comes Gothorum, 100

Comitatensis, 141, 154

Comitia centuriata, 61

Comitia tributa, 61. See also *Concilium plebis*

Commercial society, 106

Committee on Public Safety, 260

Commonwealthmen, 268

Community: as social ideal, xi

Concilium plebis, 60–61. See also *Comitia tributa*

Concord, 269

Condillac, 251

"Conflict of the Orders," 59–60, 277 (n. 5)

Consilia, ix, xii, 126, 143, 145, 150, 154, 156–58, 173–75, 179–82, 184–85; women in, xii

Constantine, 55, 118

Constitutio Antoniniana, 82

Constitution of Athens, 12. See also Aristotle

Contado, 111, 147, 154, 161, 171

Contarini, Gasparo, 197

Contemplative life, 97

Contio, 82

Conventus ante ecclesiam, 102, 104

Coriolanus, 34, 70, 214–15, 287 (n. 15). See also Shakespeare, William

Corporatism, 54, 89; in medieval town, 111

Corpus Iuris Civilis, 56, 108–9, 162, 193, 205, 208, 225
Corsica, 263–64
Cosmopolitanism, 53
Council of Five Hundred, 22; restored, 27
Council of Four Hundred, 22; in Athens, 15; proposed by Peisander, 26
Courts: as education for citizenship, 36
Crassus, 80
Cremona: citizens' benefits, 136
Curiales: under Lombards, 102
Cursus honorum, 66–67, 278 (n. 14)

Dante Alighieri, 133, 159–60, 162, 175, 184, 285 (n. 38)
Dati, Gregorio, 189
Declaration of the Rights of Man, 266
Deme, 20
Demosthenes, 4, 38
Descartes, René, 188
Diapsephesmos, 19
Diderot, Denis, 253, 258–59, 290 (n. 1)
Diogenes Laertius, 75
Dionysius of Halicarnassus, 81
Districtualis, 141, 143–44
Dordrecht, 227
Dual citizenship, 184

Ecclesia, 15–16, 22
Education: in Sparta, 8–11; in Athens, 33, 35–39; in Plato, 40–41; in Aristotle, 42–47; in the *ephebia*, 49; in the gymnasium, 50; in the medieval city, 121–25, 159–61; in Locke, 250–51
Elizabeth I, 215
Elyot, Thomas, 205, 213–14, 243, 287 (n. 12)
Empire, 74, 80
England, 115, 178, 198; in the Renaissance, 209–18; during the Revolution, 242–52, 254, 268

Ephebia, 49–50, 272 (n. 42). *See also* Education
Epictetus, 83
Epicureans, 198
Equality, 145–46, 155–57
Erasmus, Desiderius, 198, 213
Estates General, 265
Etruscans, 57–58, 72
Eunomia, 9, 15
Euripides, 32, 36
Exiles, 109–10

Fathers, church, 133
Federalism, 52, 256
Felinus, 181
Ferdinand (king of Spain), 230
Firma burgis, 115
Florence, 119, 127, 148–49, 153, 156, 175, 177–78, 187–92, 194; patriotism in, 120–21; civic education in, 122–25; benefits of citizenship in, 136–37; loss of citizenship in, 151; cultural requirements for citizenship in, 161; statutes of, 171
Framers, 267
France, 178, 198–99, 218–28, 270–72
Francis I, 218–19
Franciscans, 122
Franciscus Pepus, 180
Franciscus Ripa, 281 (n. 29)
Franklin, Benjamin, xx, 188, 207, 251, 265
Fraternitas, 93
French Revolution, 174, 253, 256, 259, 270–73

Galileo Galilei, 261
Gauls, 57
Gene, 20
Geneva, 229–30, 251, 254, 261, 270
Genoa, 130, 135–36, 147, 174
"Gentleman," 213–14
Germany, 98–99
Gerousia, 11

Ghent, 112, 114, 197
Giannotti, Donato, 197
Gierke, Otto von, 239
Godfrey of Fontaines, 164
Gordon, Thomas, 267
Goths, 100–101
Governo largo, 195
Gracchi, 56, 59, 63–67, 81, 196, 277
   (n. 8)
Gratian, 108
Gregory I (pope), 66
Gregory VII (pope), 104
Gregory IX (pope), 158
Gregory of Tours, 100
Grotius, Hugo, 237–38, 288 (nn. 1–2)
Gubbio, 152, 178
Guelfism, 148, 154. *See also* Parte
   Guelfa
Guicciardini, Francesco, 197
Guido de Baysio, 158
Guido Fava, 170, 285 (n. 50)
Guild, 105, 108, 111, 150, 154; mem-
   bership and citizenship, 116; in Flor-
   entine politics, 123
Gymnasium, 50

Habitator, 145, 156
Hannibal, 62
Harrington, James, 207, 248–50, 267–
   68, 270, 289 (nn. 26–30)
Harrison, William, 215–16
Harvey, William, 188
Hasdrubal, 69
Helot, 8–10, 29
Henry IV, 106
Henry VIII, 211–13, 230
Heretics, 108–9
Hippodamus, 39
Hobbes, Thomas, 186, 206–7, 223,
   236, 238, 240–41, 245–47, 255,
   265, 289 (n. 20)
Holinshed, 215
Homer, 9, 28, 33, 261

Homosexuality, 108, 276 (n. 25). *See
   also* Pederasty
Honor, 65, 77
Hooker, Richard, 231–32, 288
   (n. 32)
Hoplites, 9, 11, 26, 35, 60
Hortensian law, 59
Hotman, François, 225, 235, 288
   (n. 24)
Huguenots, 224–27
Humanists, 119, 168, 213. *See also*
   Civic humanism
Humanitas, 49

Immigration, 16, 19, 21–23, 28, 110–
   11, 141
Imola, 153
Incola, 143–44, 155
Isabella (queen of Spain), 230
Isocrates, 38, 44
Isopolity, 52–53, 78
Israelites, 225. *See also* Jews
Ius commercium, 74
Ius connubii, 74
Ius suffragium, 74

Jacobus de Belvesio, 149
Jacobus della Lana, 160, 258 (n. 39)
Jacobus Rebuffi, 144, 281 (n. 29), 282
   (n. 5), 286 (n. 54)
James I, 242
Jason de Mayno, 150, 159, 283
   (n. 22), 285 (n. 36)
Jerome, Saint, 90
Jews, 54–55, 84, 88, 108–9, 111, 124,
   156–57, 171, 225, 231; as *cives Ro-
   mani*, 156. *See also* Israelites
Johannes Calderinus, 174, 281 (n. 29),
   286 (n. 58)
Johannes Crottus, 156, 286 (n. 59)
Johannes de Legnano, 156, 184, 284
   (n. 32), 286 (n. 65)
Johannes Riminaldi, 145, 281 (nn. 29,
   36), 282 (n. 7)

John of Paris, 163
John of Salisbury, 260, 280 (n. 21), 285 (n. 45)
John of Viterbo, 170, 172, 192, 285 (n. 50)
Julian, 89
Justinian, 108, 140, 284 (n. 34)
Justitia, 93

Katoika, 84
Kimon, 23
Kylon, 13

Lana guild, 121
Latin League, 58–59
Latins, 72
Laudes, 121
Lawson, George, 166–67, 247–48, 268, 289 (nn. 22–25). *See also* Republicanism
Leagues, 52
Legal science, 108
Leo I, 99
Lepidus, 81
Levellers, 243–44, 247, 249, 268
Lex Est verum, 131
Lex Libertus, 132
Lex Sempronia Agraria, 67
Libanius, 82, 87, 89–90, 279 (n. 3)
Libertas: in Florence, 125
Liberties, town, 115
Livy, 58, 113, 267
Locke, John, xix–xx, 163, 188, 206–7, 236, 238, 247, 250–52, 254, 256, 265, 267–68, 270, 290 (n. 31). *See also* Virtue
Lombard cities, 136
Lombards, 101–3
London, 116, 243
Louis XII, 219–20
Louis XIV, 253
Louis XVI, 218
Lucas da Penna, 126, 162, 168–69,

182–83, 281 (n. 38), 288 (n. 48), 286 (n. 64)
Ludovicus Bologninus, 137, 282 (n. 50)
Luther, Martin, 198, 226–27, 230, 232
Lycurgus, 9–11, 254

Mably, Gabriel de, 254, 257–58, 290 (n. 7)
Machiavelli, Niccolò, xx, 8, 188–89, 193–97, 205–6, 210, 233–35, 243, 244, 249, 252–53, 256, 260, 262, 266, 268, 286 (n. 3), 289 (n. 30). *See also* "Marciovelli"
Magnates, 154
Mantua, 132–33, 136, 185
"Marciovelli," 228. *See also* Machiavelli, Niccolò
Marcus Aurelius, 75
Marianus Socinus, 126–27, 159, 180, 280 (n. 25), 285 (n. 36), 286 (n. 60)
Marianus Socinus, Jr., 132, 159, 281 (n. 40), 285 (n. 36)
Marius, 80
Marriage, 23, 26
Marsilius of Padua, 164, 166–68, 175, 231, 247, 268, 285 (n. 47)
Mazzini, Giuseppe, 137
Medici, Giuliano de', 127
Merchants, 106–7, 110, 114–16, 136, 147–48
Merovingians, 102
Metics, 21–22, 27–29, 276 (n. 26)
Milan, 121, 136, 150, 188–90
Milton, John, 268
Mithraism, 84
Mobility, 109–10
Monarchy, 51
Monasticism, 88, 93–97
Montaigne, Michel de, 188, 205–7, 245, 287 (n. 2)
Montesquieu, Charles-Louis de Secondat, 47, 253–57, 263, 268, 290 (n. 6)

Moors, 231
More, Sir Thomas, 207–13, 215, 265, 287 (nn. 6–8)
Mornay, Philippe de, 225, 288 (n. 25)
Moslems, 111
Moulin, Charles du, 218, 224
Mozart, Wolfgang Amadeus, 255
Municeps, 143–44
Municipiu, 74
Mussolini, Benito, 138

National character, 69
Naturalization, ix, 21–22, 141, 153–54, 177, 181
Natural law theory, 237–42
Nedham, Marchamount, 244
Neoplatonism, 91
Netherlands, 227–29
Newton, Sir Isaac, 261
Novi cives, 149

Oath: of citizenship, 129
Occulus pastoralis, 170, 285 (n. 50)
Oldradus, 182
Opizo of Piacenza, 136
Opus Dei, 95
Oresme, Nicholas, 164
Orthodoxy: as basis for citizenship, 229–32
Orvieto, 137
Otis, James, 249
Ottimo Commento, 160, 285 (n. 39)
Otto of Freising, 285 (n. 34)
Oxford University, 198, 213

Padua, 136, 166, 171, 178, 215
Pageantry: as civic education, 120–21
Paine, Tom, 268
Panaetius, 53, 75
Panathenea, 17
Panormitanus, 171–72, 181, 286 (n. 53)
Paris, 197. *See also* University of Paris
Parlasium, 104

Parliament, 243–44, 257
Parte Guelfa, 154. *See also* Guelfism
Patria, 125–26
Patricians, 57, 59
Patronage, 64–66, 277 (n. 10)
Paul, Saint, 63, 74, 89, 91
Paul de Castro, 154, 156, 171, 180, 182, 282 (n. 3), 284 (nn. 25, 30), 286 (n. 53)
Pausanius, 50
Pazzi conspiracy, 127
Pederasty, 29, 35, 108. *See also* Homosexuality
Peisander, 26
Peisistratids, 19
Peisistratus, 17–18
Peloponnesian War, 22–23, 26, 37, 39, 57
Penn, William, 270
Peregrini, 52. *See also* Pilgrim
Pericles, xxiii, 9, 23–26, 33, 39, 56, 254
Perioikoi, 9–10
Persia, 22, 31
Perugia, 134, 145, 149, 151–52, 171–72, 177, 184
Peter Lombard, 108
Peter of Auvergne, 164
Petrarch, 175, 193
Petrus Antiboli, 282 (n. 5)
Petrus de Ancharano, 182, 281 (n. 29)
Petrus de Ubaldis, 283 (n. 13)
Petrus Rebuffi, 219
Pheiditia, 10
Philadelphia, 270
Philip II, 228
Philip of Macedon, 42, 52
Philippus Decius, 151, 156, 283 (n. 23)
Philo, 91
Phratriae, 19
Phylai, 19
Pietro Alighieri, 160, 285 (n. 39), 288 (nn. 4–7)
Pilgrim, 92. See also *Peregrini*

Pirenne, Henri, 107

Plato, xxii, 5, 8, 11–12, 32–33, 38–41, 44, 69, 205, 208–10, 213, 242, 256, 260–62, 265; on women, 29; on education of the citizen, 40–41, 44

Plebiscita, 60, 65

Plebs, 57, 59–60

Plutarch, 8, 56, 114, 205, 213, 219, 243, 267, 275 (n. 5)

Pocock, J. G. A., 197, 267, 286 (n. 1), 289 (n. 18)

Podestà, 136

Poggio Bracciolini, 196

Poland, 263–64

Pole, Reginald, 198

Polis, 5, 275 (n. 1)

Politeuma, 30, 54, 84, 96; in Althusius, 239

Polybius, 67–71, 81, 168, 256

Pompey, 64, 80

Popolares, popolari, 154, 156

Posidonius, 75

Principate, 74, 80

Privatism, 55

Property: and citizenship, 109

Prostitution, male, 29–30

Proxeny, 52–54

Prytany, 22

Psychology: the new, 240–47. *See also* Citizenship; Hobbes, Thomas

Ptolemy of Lucca, 162, 280 (nn. 19, 22)

Pucci, Antonio, 169, 285 (n. 49), 288 (nn. 8–9)

Pufendorf, Samuel von, 238, 240, 288 (nn. 8–9)

Punic Wars, 62, 69

Puritans, 270

Rabelais, 198

Raphaelus Cumanus, 180, 286 (n. 59)

Raphaelus Fulgosius, 284 (n. 32)

Raynerius de Perusio, 280 (n. 5)

Religion: and citizenship, 53–54; in Renaissance Italy, 279 (n. 1)

Remigio de' Girolami, 281 (n. 34)

Remus, 195

Reprisals, 137

Republicanism, 113, 243, 250; classical, 229; in Althusius, 239; in Levellers, 243–44; in Lawson, 247–48; in Harrington, 249–50; growth of, 267–68; variety of, 268; in America, 270

Residence, 103; requirements for citizenship, 136

Rhetoric, patriotic, 125

Rich, Nathaniel, 244

Robbins, Caroline, 267

Robespierre, 260, 270

Roman law, xxii, 83, 114, 126, 131, 133–34, 140, 142, 156, 161–62, 166, 177, 179–82, 198–99, 208, 215–16, 218, 220, 226, 230, 235, 247, 256; influence on medieval citizenship, 108–9; in England, 117; on the active life, 119. *See also* Civil lawyers

Rome, 56, 122; and Greek ideas on citizenship, 47; citizenship policy of, 57; meaning of citizenship, 63; benefits of citizenship, 73–74, 79–80; civic education of, 80

Romulus, 195

Rousseau, Jean-Jacques, 46, 47, 188, 207, 223, 253–55, 258–66, 268, 271–72, 290 (nn. 14–16)

Sabine War, 57

Saintly power, 99

Sallust, 280 (n. 22)

Salutati, Coluccio, 175, 193

Samnites, 72

Samnite War, 58, 65

San Marco (Venice's saint), 122

Savonarola, Girolamo, 125, 194

Science, the new: and citizenship, 240–41

Scipio, 69–70
Seleucids, 49
Servius Tullius, 57, 61
Seyssel, Claude de, 219–20, 287
    (n. 20)
Shakespeare, William, 34, 70, 188,
    205, 207, 213–15, 245. See also
    Coriolanus
Shays's Rebellion, 273
Siena, 129, 134, 148, 153, 171–72
Sièyes, Emmanuel, 270–71
Sixtus IV, 127
Size: and citizenship in Montesquieu,
    256–57; in Rousseau, 264–65
Skepticism, 198
Slavery, 28–29, 276 (n. 26)
Smith, Adam, 265
Smith, Thomas, 215–16, 287 (n. 17)
Social War, 71–73
Società del Popolo (Bologna), 153
Society: small scale, xv
Socrates, 23, 37, 133
Solon, xxiii, 10, 12–17, 19–20, 33,
    213
Sophists, 37–38
Sparta, 6–12, 33–34, 68, 269, 275
    (nn. 5–6); citizenship model of, 7; in
    Plato, 40; in Aristotle, 43
Spinoza, Baruch, 238
Starkey, Thomas, 212–13, 287 (n. 11)
Statuti, 135, 153, 177, 182
Stiles, Ezra, 250
Stoics, 50, 53–55, 57, 70, 74–79, 91,
    198, 208
Strasbourg, 229, 230, 232
Subditus. See Subject
Subject, xx, 138, 144–45, 203–33, 254
Sulla, 72, 80
Switzerland, 264
Sydney, Sir Philip, 268
Symmachus, 75, 82, 87
Syssitia, 10

Terror, 273

Theater: as education for citizenship, 36
Theodosius I, 84
Theseus, 12
Thetes, 15, 26
Thomas Aquinas, Saint, xix, 47, 163,
    165, 169, 172, 175, 231, 268, 280
    (n. 22), 285 (n. 45)
Thucydides, 8, 24–26, 33, 56, 219,
    261
Timai, 28
Tithe, 104
Tower association, 123
Trenchard, John, 267
Tribes, 20, 22, 61–62, 72
Tribunate of the people, 57, 60
"Tudor citizen," 211–18
Tusculum, 57
Twelve tables, 60
Tyrtaeus, 8–9, 16, 275 (n. 5)

Umbrians, 72
University of Bologna, ix, 108
University of Paris, 199
Urban conflicts, 105
Urbanism: as education, 50–51; under
    the Germans, 99–104; revival of,
    106; social complexity of, 111; fac-
    tionalism in, 161; in Roman lawyers,
    168–69; in medieval poets, 169–70;
    and feudalism, 178–79. *See also* City

Vassalage, 113, 212; and citizenship,
    135–36
Vattel, E., 238
Venice, 111, 126–27, 130, 135–36,
    147–48, 150, 159, 171, 175, 219,
    243; civic history and pageantry of,
    121–22; under San Marco, 122;
    benefits of citizenship of, 135–36
Verona, 122, 148
Virtue, xviii–xxi, 9, 195–96, 250, 278
    (n. 14); in Aristotle, 43; in Cicero,
    78; in monasticism, 95–97; in Mon-
    tesquieu, 257; in Rousseau, 264; in
    revolutionary America, 268

Visconti, Giangaleazzo, 188
Viterbo, 136
Volgare, 190
Volterra, 136, 268

War: defines Greek society, 276 (n. 26);
    defines personal identity, 280 (n. 7)
Wealth: derived from citizenship, 109
Weber, Max, 5
Wielhorski, [Count], 263
Will: determines citizenship, 131–34,
    137

William of Orange, 227–28
Women: as citizens during Middle
    Ages, xi, 108; in Greek political life,
    29

Xenophon, 11, 219, 275 (n. 5), 276
    (n. 25)

Zeno, 75
Zurich, 229–30
Zwingli, Ulrich, 230